Paul Verhoeven

Paul Verhoeven

Rob van Scheers

translated by Aletta Stevens

faber and faber
LONDON · BOSTON

First published in the Netherlands in 1996
by Erven J. Bijleveld Press B.V.
Janskerkhof 7
3512 BK Utrecht
The Netherlands

First published in Great Britain in 1997
by Faber and Faber Limited
3 Queen Square London WC1N 3AU

Typeset by Faber and Faber Ltd
Printed in England by Clays Ltd, St Ives plc

A CIP record for this book
is available from the British Library

ISBN 0-571-17479-5

10 9 8 7 6 5 4 3 2 1

Contents

The Sardonic Pleasure:
Starship Troopers

'And the winner is . . .'

On 25 March 1996 in the Blossom Room of Hollywood's Roosevelt Hotel, the same room in which the first Academy Awards were presented in 1929, an ironic celebration has been organized, costing exactly $752, paid for by the 175 members of an organization of professionals, critics and self-declared film-buffs. This time no congratulations will be offered, because the Golden Raspberry Awards are designed to single out the worst films of the year; in California every yin must have its yang.

The members of the Golden Raspberry Award Foundation announce their choices on the afternoon before the Oscars are awarded. Paul Verhoeven's *Showgirls* has been nominated in eleven of the thirteen categories, ranging from worst production to worst director. Verhoeven's view of the dark side of the American Dream, as expressed in the journey through the Las Vegas show world made by the main character, Nomi (Elizabeth Berkley), has had, to put it mildly, an effect far different from what he had intended. Verhoeven had envisaged *Showgirls* as an ultra-realistic moral tale about an environment where people are bought and sold, but the critics exhausted themselves in the autumn of 1995 with devastating doses of sarcasm: '*Showgirls:* All about Sleaze'; 'Nudity sells, *Showgirls* smells'; 'A high-priced peep-show'; 'Un-bare-able'; 'Cynical *Showgirls* falls on its face'; 'Tasteless: *Showgirls* takes sleaze to a new low'; '*Showgirls* confuses deep with cheap'. That the film went on to live a second life in late-night screenings in New York and Los Angeles as a camp event must have reinforced this equally camp jury of the Razzies in their verdict.

'And the winner is . . .'

Paul Verhoeven has not experienced such an overt attack from the film critics since 1980, when *Spetters* seemed to anger the entire Dutch nation.

Nevertheless, it is precisely this oscillation between admiration and unconcealed hate that has accompanied him throughout his career and has made him one of the most talked-about film-makers of our time. Much to the surprise of the room filled with drag queens, he has turned up at the Roosevelt Hotel – the first director in history to collect the Raspberry Award in person.

'. . . a one-time Dutch master whose work here got him in Dutch with critics everywhere and for his efforts he was labelled everything from an "insane fourteen-year-old" to "Hollywood's most annoying dirty old man" . . . Paul Verhoeven!'

The director mounts the platform with the same sardonic pleasure he seemed to possess in the making of *Showgirls*. With the knowledge that his film has broken all the previous Raspberry records with seven prizes (including 'worst script' and 'worst leading character'), Paul Verhoeven casts a quick glance at the audience before starting his acceptance speech. Prophets, he explains, quoting 'a very wise Jewish peasant from about 2000 years ago', are never appreciated in their *own* country.

'When I was making movies in Holland my films were judged by the critics as decadent, perverted and sleazy . . . [huge applause] . . . so I moved to the United States. This was ten years ago. In the meantime, my movies are criticized as being decadent, perverted and sleazy in *this* country . . .' [more laughs and applause from the audience].

The only explanation that Paul Verhoeven can find for receiving his awards, he continues, is 'that this dishonour can only be gathered by me in my own country, which has apparently become the United States. And so . . . I am very glad that I got all these awards, because it certainly means that I am accepted here and that I am a part of this great American society. I thank you very, very much!' Pleased with himself, he waves his awards at the slightly baffled audience and hurriedly leaves to get back to preparing *Starship Troopers*. He is, in his own words, working on his next 'decadent, perverted and sleazy' film. Despite the ample budget of $100 million (of which around $40 million has been reserved for special effects) and with the flop of *Showgirls* still fresh in his mind, he has promised that *Starship Troopers* will definitely not be any less daring than his earlier work.

If past history has taught the cinema viewer one thing, it is that whatever Paul Verhoeven makes is guaranteed to have an *edge*, a distinctive idea. Otherwise, he says, he wouldn't even dare to undertake such an unpleasant journey as the making of a film.

The speech at the Raspberry Awards was a typical Paul Verhoeven turn ('It was, in fact, turning the other cheek'), and worthy of his reputation as the 'Sultan of Shock' – as *Time Magazine* once called him. He doesn't know where his villainous behaviour comes from, but he recalls that when he was a schoolboy, he used to snatch the ball away from his class-mates and throw it immediately over the playground fence. Even at fifty-eight he still enjoys playing with fire, as Joe Eszterhas, the writer of *Basic Instinct* and *Showgirls*, observes: 'The guy is like his movies: brilliant, mercurial, very daring, perverse, a wonderful series of paradoxes and con-tradictions. He is one of the most complex people I've ever met.'

In the past, Paul Verhoeven has often described himself as a director who examines the discrepancy between reality and the way reality is nor-mally depicted. His motto is: to tell is to show. He has linked this princi-ple to the realism characteristic of the Dutch school of painting of the fifteenth, sixteenth and seventeenth centuries – in his younger years he envisaged a career as a painter. Hieronymus Bosch portrayed a vagabond pissing against a brothel. Jan Steen and Pieter Brueghel were not in the least prudish – nor was Rembrandt. In 1631 Rembrandt painted his wife squatting next to a tree urinating in *The Peeing Woman*; in 1640 he immortalized himself and his wife making love in *The Bed in French Style*, or *The Happy Position*. These artists were not hampered by puritanism; their works of art were meant to be seen as 'polaroids' of our prosaic exis-tence. The same is true of a Paul Verhoeven film.

Even without such a rationalization of his work, it is clear that his love for controversy 'greases his machine'. Even a film-maker has to have a reason to get out of bed in the morning, he once explained, and although the French director Jean-Luc Godard once said teasingly that his real rea-son for making films is to flirt with the script-girl, for Paul Verhoeven it is the search for that one moment, that one scene that will carry the film.

RoboCop's journey into his past (when he visits the house which he used to occupy as agent Murphy) is one such scene. Or the moment during *Total Recall* in which Dr Edgemar appears in Arnold Schwarzenegger's hotel room and, with his cryptic dialogue, gives the story a new twist. Or Sharon Stone's interrogation in *Basic Instinct*, with the famous shot in which the actress lets the audience take a peek between her legs. Or Rutger Hauer and Derek de Lint dancing a tango in *Soldaat van Oranje* (*Soldier of Orange*) or the dialogue in the hospi-tal between Rutger Hauer and the dying Monique Van de Ven in *Turks Fruit* (*Turkish Delight*). For Verhoeven, it was at these rare moments that being a director meant euphoria: '*To wake up in the morning and think, today, let's film something that people will be talking about for years to come.*'

In addition to his sense of what the audience wants, Verhoeven knows what the audience doesn't want. They usually get both in his films, as Peter Weller, who played *RoboCop*, knows: 'There is a lot that you can say about Paul, but not that he's a neutralist. His is a very aggressive kind of movie making; he's in your face. Some of the greatest directors of the past would let the story do the work, like François Truffaut, for instance, who would tell a story with a very neutral camera. But working with Paul Verhoeven, you feel it's not just a movie that you are making, you feel that this guy has a vision and it is going to happen his way or else he is going to die.'

Michael Douglas, star of *Basic Instinct*, had a similar experience: 'The most difficult aspect of being an actor with him is that Paul hears the rhythm and the melody of the movie in his head. All he wants to do is to replicate this pace in the picture. Anything different from that doesn't interest him. Your job as an actor is not so much to interpret, but to try to fulfill the director's vision. He would say: "Just trust me, ja?"'

Jan de Bont, now famous as the director of *Speed* and *Twister*, often worked with Verhoeven as his Director of Photography: 'Paul's films are so sharply contrasted that the audience can never sit back and relax. In fact you can only be *for* or *against* them.'

Verhoeven's lack of compromise has left deep traces behind him. When he left Holland in 1985, he was not only cited as a brilliant crafts-man but also as a confused, moralistic, provocative and pessimistic critic of society, evoking resistance and fierce debate. On the other hand, long after his departure from his home country, his films are still among the highest-attended Dutch productions: the love story *Turks Fruit (Turk-ish Delight)* is at number one with a total audience of 3.3 million; the comedy *Wat Zien Ik (Business is Business)* is in fourth place; the cos-tume drama *Keetje Tippel (Cathy Tippel)* ranks seventh and *Soldaat van Oranje (Soldier of Orange)* is tenth. It is undoubtedly true that now that he has gone the domestic film industry is at an all time low: in 1994 less than 1 per cent of the total cinema audience went to see a Dutch film.

Meanwhile, in the Netherlands, Paul Verhoeven's American career is being followed with a mixture of astonishment and admiration. Apart from bringing his talent to America, he has also brought his ability to cre-ate controversy – witness the reaction by the gay movement against *Basic Instinct* which brought back memories of the Dutch reaction to *Turks Fruit* and *Spetters*. The fact that Paul Verhoeven antagonized the entire American continent with *Showgirls*'s unflattering portrait of Las Vegas, makes him, in some ways, a true ambassador of an 'enlightened' Holland.

Although *Showgirls* (world-wide takings $80 million) proved to be more controversial than successful – hence the seven Raspberry Awards – his acceptance speech is valid: he definitely has established himself in the United States. The success of *RoboCop* (1987, world-wide revenue $120 million), *Total Recall* (1990, revenue $250 million) and *Basic Instinct* (1992, world-wide revenue $370 million) has guaranteed that. This impressive track record is the reason why he is called the most successful 'film-immigrant' since Fritz Lang and Alfred Hitchcock.

For the past four years he has taken a comfortable place on the Hollywood powerlist – the pecking order of the film industry published by film magazine *Première* – where he is characterized as: 'Not a puritanical molecule in him. Intense.' During a visit to the set of *Showgirls*, the *New York Times* noted: 'Mr Verhoeven is an odd fish, a European intellectual with an untamed appetite for the cinematic equivalent of red meat. The Verhoeven approach: technical finesse, earthly tastes, a lurid imagination and a zest for putting the "big" back in the "big screen".' It's an adequate translation for: *to wake up in the morning and think, today let's film something that people will be talking about for years to come.*

Putting the 'big' back in the 'big' screen certainly applies to *Starship Troopers*. It's October 1996, on a terrace in Santa Monica. Having just returned from a 125-day shoot in the tough Badlands of South Dakota and Casper, Wyoming – plagued by freezing cold, mud streams and blistering heat – Paul Verhoeven talks about his latest film. In line with recent Hollywood fashion, it is a science-fiction film written by Ed Neumeier, author of *RoboCop*. Neumeier's script for *Starship Troopers* is based on the book of the same name by Robert Heinlein, the science-fiction writer who died in 1988.

Published in 1959, *Starship Troopers* won Heinlein the prestigious *Hugo Award* for the best science-fiction novel of the year. However, the book did his reputation no good. The former marine officer was accused of 'militarism', 'glorifying violence' and promoting a 'fascist ideology'. In the film, school children are taught: 'Here in History and Moral Philosophy we've explored the decline of Democracy when social scientists brought the world to the brink of chaos, and how the veterans took control and imposed a stability that has lasted for generations since . . . You know these facts, but have I taught you anything of value? Why are only citizens allowed to vote?'

The correct answer is that citizens work for the Federal Service, in other words, for the military system. Only they have a right to vote or to start a family; the government doesn't grant this right to normal civilians. Although he understands that the big attraction for the audience will probably be the intergalactic war between the Federation and the terrifying bugs of planet Klendathu, Verhoeven draws parallels with Ancient Greece and Nazi Germany. His fascination with the dilemma of choosing between good and evil, which he expressed previously in a documentary on the Dutch National Socialist leader Anton Mussert, as well as in films such as *Soldier of Orange* and *Flesh + Blood*, can also be found in *Starship Troopers*.

It is clear that in *Starship Troopers* he is poking fun at contemporary

America – a country in which the population see themselves as 'God's own people', where burning the flag has been declared a capital offence, where race is still a divisive issue, where private gun ownership is a sensitive subject, where school uniforms are again becoming customary and where television is *reality*.

Although the film is science fiction, the way Verhoeven sketches this puritanical society is, although exaggerated, reminiscent of the innocent America of the 1950s. Drugs no longer exist. There is no crime. The pseudo-fascist state has 'solved' all of that. Someone arrested for a crime in the morning will be convicted in the afternoon and electrocuted that same evening. These executions are broadcast live on television. Under the alien threat, the regime has to tighten the reins even more; the *Brave New World* is more and more grim-faced.

Paul Verhoeven explains the subtext of *Starship Troopers*: 'The United States thinks itself very liberal, but whether that is true remains to be seen. In my opinion, the world of *Starship Troopers* and recent America are not so far apart. I recently heard somebody on the news say that the free speech we are experiencing here would not be possible in Japan – but how can you say that after Watergate, Irangate, Whitewatergate and all the other gates? The belief in spiritual freedom is the most powerful myth in this country.' A myth he experienced at first hand with the reception to *Showgirls*.

Naturally, his disappointment with the reaction to *Showgirls* has been great, but he didn't have much time to mourn. Before the release of *Showgirls*, he had already signed with Columbia Tri-Star to make *Starship Troopers*. '*Showgirls* has been the victim of the moral standards, or better, the immoral standards, of its characters,' he explains. 'I still stand behind the content of the story, since it was based on exhaustive interviews with dancers. Again, it's the difference between reality and the way reality is usually depicted in films.'

He never really gave much thought to the possibility that the relative failure of *Showgirls* could seriously damage his career; after all, the film amply retrieved its cost of $38 million. Even Steven Spielberg doesn't always strike gold; with *1941* and *Always* he has faced the other side of success. 'You try something. You think this is fun. And then the public says: no thank you very much. Nobody, of course, could undergo such a crisis without pause, but it helps if afterwards you can see it as part of your own personal development.' He has detected hardly any films in Hollywood during these past few years that have a social issue as their basis. In his opinion it is all action, science-fiction or oversentimental love stories. In Europe, films occasionally have something to say, but then he finds these films exceedingly boring. 'Now that I work in America myself, you could say that my films are part of this increasing trend towards *easy* entertainment as well. With *Showgirls* I tried to change that, because I find that films have virtually degenerated into decadence.'

So now there is *Starship Troopers* – and the possibility of reaching a bigger audience with a film about alien monsters than he did with his harsh portrait of Las Vegas. A survey published by *Newsweek* revealed that 48 per cent of Americans believe in the existence of UFOs (towards the end of the seventies it was 11 per cent) and 29 per cent are convinced that we have made contact with alien civilizations. An astonishing 48 per cent of the American public are convinced that the government has covered up the real facts – numbers that will have only increased after the enormous success of *Independence Day* and the *X-Files*.

This UFO-mania has not dropped from the skies. American parents grew up with the Apollo flights, Stanley Kubrick's *2001: A Space Odyssey*, the books of Kurt Vonnegut and the adventures of Captain Kirk; their children with *Star Wars, Close Encounters of the Third Kind* and *E.T.*; their grandchildren are now growing up with futuristic computer games, *Star Trek: the Next Generation* and the *X-Files*. Popular culture has thus succeeded in creating a parallel universe for all ages where it is satisfying to linger when things are going wrong in the real world.

However, the most important reason for this phenomenon is not purely escapism: the lack of suitable enemies is equally decisive. 'The US is desperate to find a new enemy,' Paul Verhoeven explained in *Time Magazine*, when in July 1996 they dedicated their cover story to the success of SF movies. 'The communists were the enemy, and the Nazis before them, but now that wonderful enemy everyone can fight has been lost. Alien sci-fi gives us a terrifying enemy that's politically correct. They're bad. They're evil. And they are not even human.'

Therefore, you can shoot them without compunction, just like John Wayne used to do with the indians. That's exactly what happens with the bugs in *Starship Troopers*. Watching some of the scenes on the editing machine, we see them crawling towards certain death. The men of the Mobile Infantry Roughnecks shoot anything that moves – and they shoot to kill. Page 81 of the script describes it as follows:

EXT. TANGO URILLA – DAY

Bug Warriors stand sentry on earthworks that tower above the entrance to their colony, where an endless line of Workers enter, bearing foodstuffs appropriate to this exotic jungle planet.

A distant sound. A warrior looks up, curious. Suddenly, a formation of Tac Fighters screams down from high orbit and a white-hot nuclear firestorm consumes the landscape.

Bugs scream as they twist and kick in the wall of flame. Heat melts the dirt into dark glass. Ash turns the sky red. Then, out of the smoke, come Lieutenant Jean Rasczak and his Roughnecks.

Rasczak: Spread out, teams of three. When you locate a bug hole, secure it, gas it, and close it.

As a matter of fact, the bugs come in all different types: there are hopper bugs, worker bugs, tanker bugs, plasma-shooting bugs, queen bugs and – the spiritual leaders – the brain bugs. When mutually co-ordinating, they prove to be dangerous enemies for humans – and in more ways than just shooting meteorites at the Earth.

Suddenly during a patrol on Planet P ('Planet P? What kind of name is that?' 'They ran out of names a long time ago in this part of the Galaxy') a number of hopper bugs appear, described in the script as 'airborne arachnid warriors with powerful rear legs and pop-out wings for gliding'. They look like pterodactyls and they rule the air. In the film they capture a sergeant called Gillespie. He screams in pain as he is being thrown against a rock, to be devoured by the bugs. Lieutenant Rasczak (a role played by Verhoeven-veteran Michael Ironside) yells for a gun. He aims. He shoots. Not the bugs, but Gillespie. 'I expect anyone in this unit to do the same for me,' he tells the shocked troopers and, without doubt, the equally shocked audience. *To wake up in the morning and think . . .*

The way in which an alien biosphere of bugs is presented in *Starship Troopers* is an idea that Paul Verhoeven had played with before. Directly after *Total Recall* he conceived the idea of making a film about dinosaurs. There was already a script by Walon Green and, together with Industrial Light & Magic's Phil Tippett (the special effects wizard who, among other things, worked on the *Star Wars* saga and gave the film *RoboCop* its clumsy robot ED 209), they intended to create a complete prehistorical world, which would serve as a background for a fable on evolution. The main character would be a small mammal, surrounded by both friendly and dangerous dinosaurs. The dinosaurs would all eventually die out through the collision of a meteor with earth and its effect on the atmosphere. Modern science roughly supports this theory that the lack of food made the dinosaurs disappear as if by magic – while the mammals survived.

Paul Verhoeven presented the project, estimated at $30 million, to the Disney Studios. The then Chairman, Jeffrey Katzenberg, rejected the project, exactly three years before Steven Spielberg's *Jurassic Park* earned $900 million.

What remained with the director was the desire to work with Phil Tippett once more, which he has now been able to do with *Starship*

Troopers. Led by Tippett's work with computer-animation, the bugs have now become a much bigger part in the film than in the original Heinlein novel. 'We looked at a number of documentaries about insects,' Verhoeven explains, 'and it is remarkable how indestructible they are. Unlike the book we have tried to make their appearance and behaviour as close to biological reality as possible.' In addition to this, *Starship Troopers* incorporates references to fifties films about terrifying monsters and insects such as *War of the Worlds* and Jack Arnold's *Tarantula.*

Of course, other military solutions to the problem of the bugs are possible. (Verhoeven: 'Yes, I have pointed that out as well – why send people to those planets? You could just say let's out-nuke them. But anyhow, in sci-fi films illogicality comes with the genre.') But the main character, Johnny Rico, and his friends, go to war against the monsters because they have been incited by the propaganda campaign: 'Join the Mobile Infantry and save the world! Service guarantees citizenship. Would you like to know more?'

Johnny Rico (played by Casper Van Dien) is only interested in the army because he wants to impress his high-school sweetheart Carmen Ibanez (Denise Richards), who, in turn, has applied for a place as pilot in the Star Fleet. Johnny wanted to become a pilot as well, but didn't pass the exams. Out of fear of losing Carmen to his rival Zander (who has been accepted as a trainee for the starship fleet) he decides, against the wishes of his parents, to go with the Infantry. There he has to learn things the hard way. In fact, he is about to give up when the bugs, out of the blue, destroy his home town with a meteor, killing his parents. Johnny vows to take revenge and, with the help of Dizzy Flores (Dina Meyer), who has secretly been in love with him for some time, his battle against the bugs commences.

It is, as Verhoeven point out, a soap opera turning grim. 'They go to school. They play football. They fall in love. The threat of a possible war seems far away, just like they are not too aware of the rigid state system. It's *Happy Days.* Then, inevitably, we get the prom, the "Farewell Dance" with his fellow students. Carmen chooses a career instead of Johnny, which will change his life for ever.'

The intergalactic hostilities have grown worse because, despite the warnings of the Federation, a group of 300 'extremist Mormons' have founded a colony on Tango Urilla, just within the territory of the bugs, the Arachnid Quarantine Zone. The bugs are not pleased. On the news there are images of bugs eating the colonists. Soon after, they send a meteor towards the Earth. In the wake of this devastating event, reporters sound out the feelings of those in the military training camps:

Net Correspondent: Some say the bugs were provoked by human attempts to colonize within the AQZ, that a 'live and let live' policy is preferable to war with the bugs . . .

Johnny: Yeah well, I say kill 'em all!

With the battle in the second half of the film, *Starship Troopers* is transformed from a high-school drama into a war film. With this idea in mind, script-writer Ed Neumeier gave Paul Verhoeven the standard work on military strategy by Karl von Clausewitz (1780–1831) entitled *On War*. This Prussian general, who became known as the 'prophet of total war', defines military conflict as an extension of diplomacy. Although he preferred defensive military forces, his book is one long plea for the destruction of every enemy – both morally and economically. *Starship Troopers* predicts the future in much the same way. Verhoeven: 'The film is a kind of Battle of the Bulge, with the bugs playing the Nazis.'

Another reference to World War II is found in the very propagandist tone of the newscasts, in which the 'Would you like to know more?' works like a recurring cliff-hanger. It is also a reminder of the Frank Capra documentary series *Why We Fight*, as well as the World War II Fox Movietone newsreels – the 'information films' that Paul Verhoeven knows so well. They were shown in Europe directly after D-Day to aid the process of denazification: 'Is it their world or ours? Freedom against slavery; civilization against barbarism; good against evil.' From a filmic point of view, these newsreel flashes have another function. They explain what is happening back on Earth and serve as a background for Johnny's actions. Verhoeven explains: 'Ed Neumeier tried this technique before in *RoboCop*, although the messages are less ironic this time. I am very interested in this style, because in this way you can put across a lot of information to the audience without interrupting the story. It reminds me of the structure in the work of Dutch painter Piet Mondriaan. The different story elements can be compared with Mondriaan's white, blue, yellow or red squares. My news flashes correspond with his black lines: they keep the whole together.'

In the spirit of Heinlein's novel, *Starship Troopers* often uses a fascist idiom. The young heroes of the story are all extremely handsome, like old photographs of the Hitler Youth. When, after the meteor, Sky Marshall Dienes (the man in charge) declares war against the bugs in the presence of the Federal Council, we can see eagles on the big banners next to him. When the Sky Marshall addresses the cheering masses, the camera films him from underneath. Suddenly we seem to be in a Leni Riefenstahl production.

Sky Marshall Dienes: We are a generation commanded by fate to defend humankind! We must meet the threat with our valour, our blood, with our very lives, xvii The Sardonic Pleasure

to ensure that human civilization, not insect, dominates this galaxy now and always.

According to Verhoeven, the most important difference between this and other recently released science fiction films is that *Starship Troopers* does not intend to reassure the audience. Whether you look at *Star Trek* or *Independence Day*, even as they keep you in suspense, you know that the forces of good will triumph in the end. 'You feel safe, because you know that they won't let the main characters die,' says Verhoeven. 'With me you can't be sure. And rightly so, because three of the main characters kick the bucket in the end. In my film, the viewer undergoes some really distressing situations.' In retrospect he sometimes wonders how the studio could ever have given it the green light with such a budget. 'It is a story on many different levels. I think it is quite a daring project, but then again, I thought that of *Showgirls* as well.'

Paul Verhoeven's overall theme in *Starship Troopers* concerns a species in danger of extinction – in this case, human beings (which is similar to his earlier idea of the film about the dinosaurs). 'The issue raised in the film is the following: is a temporary dictatorship allowable when such an outside threat presents itself? The film goes a step further and asks the audience: do you want this? Could you accept this? It is not all fiction, of course. During World War II the same dilemma faced Britain when Churchill acted as an enlightened despot. Strong leadership – in the end, society will always return to such a situation because there is simply not enough time to debate endlessly in Congress. So for me, yes, this temporary dictatorship is allowed in *Starship Troopers*, with the proviso *only then*.'

This display of force is interlayered with jokes on militarism. In one particular *Catch-22*-like scene we find old General Owen (Marshall Bell) hiding from the bugs, petrified with terror, in a freezer at the headquarters of the 4th Brigade on Planet P. 'My military advisors on the set were not too pleased with this,' jokes Verhoeven. A real general, they said, would never do such a thing. A real general is a man of honour. *To get up in the morning and think* . . .

The work of Paul Verhoeven is not, in everybody's opinion, synonymous with having a good time; the images might be too gruesome and the themes too grim. Involvement is further hampered by the fact that his main characters often display nasty behaviour (*Showgirls*) or have a nihilistic, Nietzschean attitude towards life. However, it is beyond dispute that Paul Verhoeven has made this particular use of imagery and mythology his own.

The connections in his body of work are clearly visible. Just like *Basic*

Instinct could be interpreted as a sequel to *De Vierde Man* (*The Fourth Man*), *Showgirls* does the same for *Keetje Tippel (Cathy Tippel)* and *Spetters*. Even in *Starship Troopers* we can distinguish references to earlier work. The way Paul Verhoeven has shot the high school scenes with the film's two eighteen-year-olds, Johnny Rico and Carmen Ibanez, recalls his early film *Feest*; it is done in an endearing, almost naïve way. The warfare in the second part of *Starship Troopers* similarly recalls the scenes he shot in 1965 for the documentary *Korps Mariniers*, which bordered on being a propaganda film (at the time it was described by critics as a 'mini-Leni Riefenstahl production.') Instead of twelve amphibious vehicles, three spaceships come ashore, but that is about the only difference.

Verhoeven also borrows from other people's work. *Basic Instinct*, for example, is clearly a homage to Alfred Hitchcock. For *Starship Troopers* he watched old Dutch documentaries about the battle against the sea, and the difficulties involved in herring fishing, then set about shooting the interior scenes in the spaceships as if they were boats in the open sea – a speciality of the Dutch school of cinema. Exactly as in the documentaries by Herman van der Horst – *'t Schot is te boord* (winner of the Grand Prix Cannes, 1952) or *Vieren Maar!*, both of which were about fishing – the camera and the horizon stay static on screen, while the fishing-boat, or in this case, the spaceship, shakes about violently. The mechanism is based on a tripod with a ball, called a Dutch head, which allows the camera to move smoothly on three axes.

The almost archaic images from Dutch documentaries have been etched into the consciousness of the director. Likewise, his ability to effortlessly sketch whole scenes from David Lean, Orson Welles, Fritz Lang or Sergei Eisenstein proves his deep passion for the cinema, as well as the talent to picture the film in his mind's eye. Every time he starts a new production he draws the film almost frame by frame on a storyboard; the scripts adapted in this manner bear a strong resemblance to the much loved comic strips of his youth. This visual skill is an especially welcome bonus when whole fight scenes are being shot without a bug in sight – they will be added later with computer animation. In this state of chaos, as Paul Verhoeven calls it – between the rain, the mud, the heat, the fainting extras in their full battle dress, the broken limbs and the thumping spaceships (filmed by sliding cameras on sloping rocks) – when all that the actors can see of an explosion is a few flashing lamps, Verhoeven's ability to visualize gives him complete control. It is not without reason that he once said: 'To me an actor is someone who walks from A to B, and when *I* snap my fingers *they* turn.'

This was when he was still working in Holland and his remark was meant teasingly, to contradict his fellow film-makers, who were struggling artistically with actors who saw themselves as '*auteurs*'. Verhoeven has no truck with this. The first thing he demands from a film is tension, within a very clear story.

Paul Verhoeven had always imagined that his explicit and rapid-cut images would find a place in Hollywood. He was more anxious to see whether his view of humanity would coincide with American film morals. Some of this anxiety was confirmed by the seven Raspberry awards, but he felt this dubious honour was no reason for surrender. With *Starship Troopers* he is trying to move away from the schematic representation of reality of the average American film, by using elements like dying heroes, sensitive issues and a bit of nudity – all of which is inherent to his motto as a film-maker: *to wake up in the morning and think, today let's film something that people will be talking about for years to come.*

When asked about the net result of his cinema career, Paul Verhoeven likes to refer to the defining moment of his life, when graduating from the University of Leiden with a degree in maths and physics in 1964, he had to make the decision whether to become an artist, a teacher or a film-maker. Analogous to the most bizarre understatement in world history – '*Ich aber beschloss, Politiker zu werden*' from Adolf Hitler's *Mein Kampf* – he says with a sardonic smile: 'I, however, I decided to become a film-maker.' More than thirty years later the smoke still hasn't cleared.

Starship Troopers: Paul Verhoeven with Michael Ironside, the tough Lieutenant Jean Rasczak.

Man confronts bug: the battle to end all battles.

Starship Troopers: Casper Van Dien as Johnny Rico leads the 'Roughnecks Patrol' on Planet P.

I The Formative Years

The student film-maker.

Paul with his father in 1940.

Paul with his mother in 1938.

Paul Verhoeven's first special effect.

After the bombardment.

Chapter 1

War on the Retina

The Hague, 3 March 1945, just before nine o'clock in the morning. On the Schenkweg a six-year-old boy holds an older man's hand and looks worriedly into the distance. The boy's name is Paul Verhoeven and his parents are missing. Before him is a sheet of flames – a hellish red glow as far as the eye can see. The entire world seems to be burning.

His parents, Wim and Nel Verhoeven, have left an hour previously with a handcart in the direction of 7 Gerard Reynststraat to fetch the most important possessions from their home. Because of the German V2 rocket installations, the area has been the target of bombing several times before, albeit 'friendly fire' from the British. Nevertheless, the family thought it wise to look for temporary accommodation with friends. As Mr Verhoeven pushes the handcart packed with household effects, he suddenly hears a whirring noise. The planes are not visible, but the shrill whistling which follows is all too familiar. A shower of high-explosive bombs pours out over the area, the Bezuidenhout district. The bombardment lasts barely ten minutes. A stiff wind whips up the blaze.

'Where have they got to?' the boy asks, pointing at the disaster area. His father's friend replies, his voice deliberately upbeat, 'Oh, they'll be back soon. Your parents know the way.' For a moment the boy is reassured. However, the sight of such devastation and the smell of burning soon fill his head with other ideas.

Owing to thick cloud, visibility had been rather poor when the fifty-six twin-engined Mitchell and Boston medium bombers appeared over the city. The planes – Wing number 137 and Wing number 139 – were part of the British Second Tactical Air Force, whose mission was to eliminate the V2 launch sites near the Marlot residential district, the Duindigt racecourse and in the Haagse Bos. Since 3 September 1944, rockets had been fired from moveable platforms there in the direction of England, in a last attempt to set London ablaze and thus turn the tide of the war.

Large parts of Europe, including the southern Netherlands, had already been liberated, but for The Hague the end of the occupation was not yet in sight. The suffering of the civilian population was at its worst because of food shortages, and hostilities had never seemed so fierce. The V2s were launched with ruthless regularity. In return, the Allies continued to bomb the German positions.

However, because the effectiveness of the attacks had been unsatisfactory, London had decided at the beginning of 1945 to use heavier equipment – although they realized this would present a greater danger to the civilian population. Their concern turned out to be justified when, on the morning of 3 March, the British squadron made a tragic mistake. The cause, it would later emerge, was a mix-up of the horizontal and vertical co-ordinates on the maps before departure. The bombs landed a mere 1250 metres from the targets, but the consequences for the residential district were catastrophic. In addition to the 520 dead, there were many wounded, and at least 12,000 of the residents were made homeless. Later, looting broke out in the area.

'My parents found themselves in the middle of that inferno, but miraculously survived by taking cover under a viaduct,' Paul Verhoeven explains fifty years later. This happy ending determined his view of the war years once and for all. 'I think I would have experienced that whole period, my whole life, differently if my parents had been killed in that bombardment.'

Verhoeven has stored away in his subconscious what he calls a 'childlike vision', which he expressed in his film *Soldaat van Oranje* (*Soldier of Orange*, 1977) through the character played by Rutger Hauer: 'A bit of war might be exciting.' Rationally speaking, Verhoeven understands the falseness of this statement, but his imagination will not accept it. In his war dreams, which he still has, he is completely untouchable.

'It's always bombs, fire, broken glass, bodies and chaos, but everything goes all right. I see myself running around with a short carbine, hopefully on the side of the good guys, and firing at the enemy. Streets collapse behind me and houses explode, but I effortlessly jump on and off a train. Nothing can touch me. I realize, of course, that it's all because my parents returned unscathed from those smoke clouds.'

At 1.30 a.m. on 18 July 1938, at the Juliana Hospital in Amsterdam, Paul Verhoeven was delivered by forceps by Doctor Van Wely – the same gynaecologist who on 31 January that year had been involved in bringing Crown Princess Beatrix into the world, as Mr Verhoeven would proudly (but erroneously) say at all his son's birthday parties. Paul weighed 3.5 kilograms, and since his head was somewhat rumpled owing to the force with which the forceps had been handled, the new-born baby appeared, to the onlookers in Amsterdam, rather Chinese.

However, this did not in any way reduce his parents' joy. It had been a difficult labour, and at one point it looked as if they would have to choose between mother and child. It did not come to that, although the doctor told Mrs Verhoeven that any subsequent childbearing – especially in view of her age, thirty-six – could be fatal.

That is why the Verhoeven family, living at the Amsterdam Tuyll van Serooskerkeweg, had no further children. Doctor Wely was a man of authority. He had managed to solve Mrs Verhoeven's infertility problem with a small operation. The parents had been trying to have a baby since their marriage in 1927, but without success. First there was a miscarriage, and after that came Paul, who was named after his grandfather on his mother's side. He was the son of an exemplary Dutch couple.

Wim Verhoeven (1901–86) was appointed headmaster at the age of twenty-seven. He was a typical primary school teacher: straight-backed and dressed in a grey pin-striped suit, he would walk, bicycle at his side, across the school playground. His father owned a plastering firm in Dordrecht, and the young Wim, one of four sons, would have preferred to have become a doctor. Such studies, however, were only for the élite, and in those days a clever boy with little in his pocket had to choose a career in education.

Paul's mother Nel (1902–93) was one of the four daughters of the painter and decorator Paul van Schaardenburg, who also owned a company in Dordrecht. In her youth she had trained as a hatter. Although she was expert with needle and thread, there was little she could do with this skill after her wedding. It was considered inappropriate for the wife of a headmaster to work, as she was supposed to support her husband in his career. So she was limited to domestic duties – the fate of many a wife who married a local dignitary, whether headmaster, doctor or mayor. In later years, this subordinate role brought out her depressive side. The woman who had appeared in old photographs as the the life and soul of the dance or the skating party was increasingly given to sombre reflections and worry.

But this was not the case after Paul was born. She noted with satisfaction that her baby was developing well. According to the maternity care record, he started crawling on Saturday 22 April 1939, sitting on Friday 28 April 1939 and standing on Saturday 29 April 1939. By now he was 70 cm long. Both parents had great hopes for their only child, the apple of their eye.

Then on 10 May 1940 the Germans invaded the Netherlands, the same day that Winston Churchill became prime minister of Great Britain. After more than a century of peace, and neutrality in politics, world history took the Netherlands by surprise. The Verhoeven family had just moved from Amsterdam to Slikkerveer, a small village within easy reach of Rotterdam where Wim had been offered a new position as headmaster. The new family residence was built next to the state school. From their attic window the family saw the heavy bombing of Rotterdam, after which the Netherlands capitulated to Germany on 14 May 1940.

'Of the first years of the war,' Paul Verhoeven recalls, 'I remember that my parents were often roused out of bed by the British planes heading for Germany. You could see the enormous beams of the searchlights above Rotterdam and hear the noise of anti-aircraft guns. Sometimes a plane would be hit and disappear behind the horizon, burning. And yet these images did not fill me with fear; instead, they were exciting – the ultimate special effect. You couldn't wish for anything better really.'

In Slikkerveer, evidence of the German occupation was limited to having to wear itchy woollen underwear and take the compulsory daily dose of cod-liver oil. The only real disruption was the fact that the school where Wim Verhoeven taught was requisitioned to accommodate German cavalry. This quiet life changed when the Verhoevens moved to The Hague in 1943. Father went to teach at the state primary school in the Van Heutszstraat, and the family came to live in a spacious house at 7 Gerard Reynststraat. At that time The Hague had half a million inhabitants and had been the centre of government in the Netherlands since the sixteenth century. This is why the German plan of attack in May 1940 had been to take The Hague by surprise, with the aim of capturing the royal family, the government and the supreme command of the Dutch armed forces in a single operation. Queen Wilhelmina and her entourage took the gold stocks and escaped from Paleis Noordeinde via the Hook of Holland to England, just before the army waved the white flag after four days of unequal fighting.

Daily life in The Hague soon returned to normal, although unlike in Slikkerveer the presence of the Germans was tangible. The city was crawling with German military. The German-Austrian Reich Commissioner Dr Arthur Seyss-Inquart had his headquarters in the royal capital, and in the Lange Voorhout there were daily parades organized both by the German occupiers and by the collaborating NSB party (Nationaal-Socialistische Beweging).

The cinemas in The Hague were now showing mostly German-made anti-Semitic propaganda films: *Der Ewige Jude* (*The Eternal Jew*) by 'Reichsfilmintendant' Dr Fritz Hippler, and *Jud Süss* by Veit Harlan. There were also the regular German UFA-newsreel complications (with triumphant titles such as *Sieg im Westen* [*Victory in the West*]). Already on 8 January 1941, it was officially forbidden for Jews to visit all cinemas. Growing up in wartime meant that if young Paul climbed up on to the roof he could see the bombers, and later the V1s and V2s, flying life-size

6

overhead. This spying had to be done quite carefully, since the flying bombs were often defective – if the droning stopped, the inhabitants of The Hague knew that the 'reprisal weapon' would explode somewhere in the city. Occasionally, the danger came very close. One day, a British bomb fell into their neighbours' garden and the Verhoevens had the windows of their house blown in. Sometimes Paul's father hid under the floorboards when there were round-ups for the *Arbeitseinsatz*, the forced labour organization.

Towards the end of the war, German intimidation increased. Paul Verhoeven remembers how, on 15 December 1944, he and his father were forced to walk past the bodies of twelve recently executed prisoners in the Laan van Nieuw-Oost-Indië. At home, his mother suffered from hunger oedema because her portion of the little food they had – mainly sugar-beet cooked on an iron stove – she saved for her son.

These images are burnt into Paul Verhoeven's memory. 'And yet the war did not really have a traumatic effect on me,' he says today. The most threatening incident was when a jeep filled with Germans stopped while he was playing with a friend. 'They put us against a wall and said they were going to shoot us. Click went the gun, but it turned out not to be loaded. Just a little joke. But I did wet my pants.'

Verhoeven knows it often causes misunderstandings when he says that it's a gift for an artist to live through a war – meaning that it gives you the chance to see a different world, one in stark contrast with the peacetime that follows. He also says he feels great sympathy with the conclusion reached by the Dutch writer W. F. Hermans – also obsessed by the years 1940–45 – that 'war is man's natural state' and that the outbreak of peace is in fact the real exception. What concerns Verhoeven is that through children's eyes war looks very different, as shown in John Boorman's *Hope and Glory* (1987). As the boys who are the main characters are fishing, a bomb suddenly falls into the water. But far from being afraid, they jump for joy as the surface of the stream fills with dead fish. They had never had such a catch! Nor was the bombing of their school cause for concern, since it meant extra holiday. 'It's the type of film I would have liked to have made about my own memories.'

In 1945, after the chaos of the closing years of the war, the strict routine of home began once again. At around six o'clock, dinner time, the vase of flowers was lifted and the wooden table was pulled out. A cosy lamp hung above it. Sometimes mother played the piano in the afternoon; not Mozart, but the songs of Mario Lanza. She also had a great liking for Edith Piaf. Religion did not play an important part in the family's life, although they were originally Dutch Reformed Protestants. Their political preference was for the Conservative-Liberal Volkspartij voor

Vrÿheid en Democratie (VVD). In the summer the family often went to Scheveningen beach. Mother would arrive an hour or so later with the sandwiches and wait at the agreed time under the big clock, since she would not have been able to find Paul and his friends on the crowded beach. If it became too busy for her, she would mumble: 'I'm seeing stars.' And on Saturdays she baked pancakes.

Robert Haverschmidt, one of Paul Verhoeven's childhood friends, says, 'His parents were rather strict people. If you arrived at Paul's home you always ran the risk of his father saying, "Spell 'immediately' for me – I M M E D I A T E L Y!"' But he was not without a sense of humour. 'The school inspector would come round and Paul's father would say, "You know, this is a really nice school. I always give the children the day off on my birthday." The inspector would look shocked – until he realized that his birthday was on 30 April, the Queen's birthday and a public holiday.'

Wim Verhoeven was a teacher twenty-four hours a day and no respecter of persons. In 1946 Paul, now eight years old, was sent to his father's school, where he entered the fourth form – a very young pupil for his year. This was not because the boy was exceptionally advanced. On their arrival in The Hague, his parents had sent him to school a year early so that he could meet other children in his new city through the Haagsche School Vereniging (School Association of The Hague). Later the family decided it was more practical for Paul to travel with his father to Van Heutszstraat. Inevitably, he was forced into the son-of-the-head-master role.

'I was always punished or praised to extremes,' Paul Verhoeven vividly remembers. 'Punished if I got out of step when the children were walking in line, and boxed on the ears in front of the class. Praised for my intelligence, because my father would not let a moment pass without showing off how clever I was. When I was still in the fourth form and he was teaching the sixth form, he would sometimes have someone send for me. When I arrived, there would be a maths problem on the blackboard which I would have to solve in front of the group, because they could not manage it themselves. Then I would hear my father say "Thanks" behind me, and he would continue, "So if that boy can do it already, why are you lot so dumb," and so on.'

It made Paul terribly ambitious as a boy. If there was a poem to be recited, he would always choose the longest one. Not that he knew what it was about, 'but I thought that its sheer length would make an impression.' Little Paul, he remembers, always wanted to get top marks. And it has always remained that way – up to and including his film work.

As the youngest and smallest in the class, he had to reassert his position almost daily. 'This is why at secondary school my Dutch language teacher once said, "It would be a blessing for that boy if he could retake a year, then he would be among pupils of his own age." My father was furious. In his opinion you could not let the son of a head-master retake a year. That would be a disgrace. That is why, at his insistence, I always had extra lessons. Especially in Latin and Greek.'

Robert Haverschmidt says, 'At secondary school Paul was younger than the average pupil. I am two years older than him. We often teased him about this. On Friday night we always went to play table tennis. Sometimes we would put his bike on the roof of the bicycle shed for a joke. We would all laugh, of course. But Paul was very straightforward. He would climb on to the shed and throw his bike down without batting an eyelid. And then ride off on it.' As his beloved Dick Bos would have done.

Dick Bos, the intrepid creation of Alfred Mazure (1915–74), was Paul Verhoeven's childhood hero, the Dutch equivalent of Dick Tracy, only cleverer. The first fifteen now-classic episodes of the comic strip appeared in 1940–43, and describe Dick Bos's skirmishes with crime in a variety of adventures. A check-suited, sturdily built gentleman in a world of riff-raff, private eye Bos resorted to ju-jitsu only as a last resort, accompanied by exclamations such as *Hela!* ('I say!'), *Verdorie!* ('Darn!') and *Allemachtig!* ('Good heavens!').

Mazure had copied these masterly ju-jitsu throws from Maurice van Nieuwenhuizen, the Netherlands' first ju-jitsu champion. In the presence of the illustrator, van Nieuwenhuizen had, with infinite patience, demonstrated his range of ju-jitsu techniques, while Mazure tried to record them as quickly as possible in his sketchbook.

After Dick Bos made a tentative start as 'a detective serial in drawings' in the family magazine *Weekrevue de Prins* in May 1940, collected editions of the serials soon became very popular with young people. The strip was banned by the Germans in 1943 because Mazure refused to make Dick Bos into an SS officer – which only increased his stature. In the post-war years, Bos was a role model for growing boys – a forbidden role model, for comic strips were still taboo.

'The first Dick Bos books I got hold of were enormous treasures. I couldn't keep my hands off them. In primary school I was constantly flicking through them under my desk.' It was the expressionistic drawings, with long, flamboyant lines, which appealed to Verhoeven. 'A very visual comic strip; you feel that Mazure drew it with love and pleasure. Such a perfect full moon above the Lange Voorhout in The Hague. Dick Bos heading for adventure. The stories are not all equally good, but the drawings still stand the test of time. They are much better drawn than, say, the original Dick Tracy. They have more atmosphere, because there is always

Dick Bos.

that intriguing, shadowy light.' If it came to it, he could also put into practice what he had learned from Dick Bos. 'My great triumph was when I had to do some shopping for my mother and a group of overgrown youths blocked my way. The biggest boy, who knew of course that I was the son of the headmaster, threw me to the ground. Then he tried to kick me, but I knew this situation only too well from the Dick Bos stories – which we had practised more than once. I grabbed his legs, pushed against them with my shoulders, and he went down with a crash. Completely dazed, of course. The others were dumbfounded. After that I got away quickly. I thought, "Don't try and see whether it works a second time." But I also thought, "This one was for you, Dick!" – a hero for life!'

Not only can this kind of action be seen in many a Verhoeven film, but he brought up his two daughters, Claudia and Heleen, with it. At bedtime he would tell them the stories from memory. 'And if it became very dangerous, with villains coming at him from all directions, there was always that ultimate comment: "But Dick Bos knew jiu-jitsu!"'

The Killer.

As a boy, inspired by Dick Bos, he had also begun to draw comic-strip stories – something he still does for his films, even though they are now called storyboards. His favourite creation is *The Killer*, the story of a villainous cowboy who terrorizes a town in the Wild West. This strip – 'a dark comedy really' – can still be found in Verhoeven's files. The drawings he made as a thirteen-year-old tell how The Killer, a sort of vengeful angel from the Old Testament, comes to teach a lesson to the people who have stood in his way in the past. The horrific details are drawn with great care. A quack is forced to drink his own potion, after which The Killer simply throws a match down the man's throat. A gigantic explosion follows. *Robocop* (1987) before the fact.

Being the son of the headmaster may have been awkward for a young boy, but when Verhoeven talks about his childhood, it is the good memories that prevail. His father was particularly good at telling stories. 'It was often at the end of the afternoon. It would be getting dark outside – there was nearly always thunder. In the classroom my father would start his history lesson by first lighting a cigar. I would stare at the burning end and let myself be carried off on a stream of images. It was all about knights, crusades, the East India Company. He spoke with great attention to detail. And very graphically – he told the stories as if he were a reporter, an eyewitness in the thick of the fight.'

On festive occasions, Paul's father sometimes brought home the film projector from school, in a huge heavy suitcase on the back of a big black bicycle. First they would have their meal, then they showed films. These would be about things like peat-cutters, and there was always the family portrait an uncle had once shot, where the Verhoeven family goes to the beach at Scheveningen for the day. Young Paul quickly learned how to feed a film into the projector.

This was even better than the time at the end of the war when he had walked past the Puchri studios in The Hague just after the building had been hit by a bomb. The force of the explosion had hurled many cans of film into the street, and Paul and his friends found tangled 35mm strips. 'We took them away with us and watched them for whole afternoons with great fascination.' It was his very first contact with film. His father showing movies at home was the next stage – though it was a pity that he could not show Errol Flynn as *Captain Blood* (1935) or *Tarzan's New York Adventure* (1942), the films to which he regularly treated Paul in the centre of The Hague.

There was plenty of choice. Now the war was over, Western Europe was flooded with American films, and there was a huge backlog to catch up on. It was a time the Dutch author K. Schippers, a contemporary of Paul Verhoeven, described in his novella *Het Witte Schoolbord* (*The White Blackboard*):

I sat in a cinema for the first time and saw the most beautiful erotic misdemeanours in the films of Ernst Lubitsch, the quicksilver romances of Fred Astaire and Ginger Rogers, the ingenious misunderstandings of Buster Keaton . . . I was extremely lucky to be able to make my acquaintance very quickly with all the phenomena, concepts and emotions which make up life. Colour, time, space, love, emotion, tragedy, humour: the crash course I received in these made me older than I was. Adults did not even notice that in the cinema, a child could get a head start on subjects such as eroticism, fear and deceit which were still taboo at home.

These, the first moving images Paul Verhoeven ever saw, made an overwhelming impression on him. Totally obsessed, he absorbed them all. 'They were always films classified for fourteen-year-olds and older. But because I was with my father, they turned a blind eye at the ticket window, looking at him as if to say, "I suppose he's fourteen, isn't he?"' Later, they must have seen *The War of the Worlds* (1953) ten times – 'we both thought it was fantastic'.

It is, Verhoeven says, the same spiritual process that Luis Buñuel describes in his autobiography *My Last Breath* (1983): a 'hidden continuity', an almost secret agreement between film-makers from different generations. In the same way that Buñuel was struck by the early films of Fritz Lang, which had an 'instrumental role in determining the course of my life', Verhoeven became intoxicated with the adventure genre that swept through Dutch cinemas in the post-war years. 'In the trams in The Hague they used to hang leaflets from the cord with which the conductor pulled the bell. These listed the latest films – generally the B-movies which were shown in our neighbourhood cinema, because at the Thaliatheater in the Boekhorststraat they really did not show first-run pictures. But I should add that quite a few of the films I saw there were acclaimed as masterpieces years later, as happened with *The Crimson Pirate* starring Burt Lancaster.

'If Buñuel is right,' says Verhoeven, 'and there's a good chance that he is, then the films you see as a child, roughly between the ages of eight and sixteen, determine your creative taste later on. You will even quote from them as a director without specifically or consciously searching for them. These images are in your head – after all, they are the images that stirred you to direct in the first place, aren't they?'

Verhoeven also pored over the pages of *Wie-Wat-Waar* (*Who-What-Where*) magazine, which included articles about Hollywood and the film industry, about special effects – for example, showing galloping horses on a conveyor belt against a moving background. 'When I saw that, I thought, "Gosh, is that how they do it?"' Verhoeven also collected pictures of film stars, particularly male ones – whenever possible, he leapt off the trams in The Hague just like Johnny Weismuller. In this way he managed to impress his friends, as well as the host of children who came to the family house for extra lessons with Mr Verhoeven, or to stay there for a while. The Verhoeven house became a 'foster home', offering accommodation to the children of ambassadors, or pupils whose parents lived temporarily in the Dutch East Indies, as well as to boys with learning difficulties and children who had lost their parents in the war.

All this was part of his father's idealistic view of the world, which in those days was quite common among primary school teachers. 'It started with just one boy, but by the time I was halfway through secondary school, in the 1950s, we had five children staying with us. When more children came for extra lessons at half past four, the living-room was full. I thought it was great fun, because I did not have any brothers. It was also nice because they were generally rowdier types than me – the "*gymnasium*" type of secondary school is of course fairly élitist. At the weekend we often went to the cinema together. After that, we would surreptitiously walk through the red-light district and then quickly home.'

*

In August 1949, eleven-year-old Paul Verhoeven was registered as a pupil at the *Gymnasium* Haganum at 57 Laan van Meerdervoort, The Hague. The *gymnasium* was the highest level of secondary education, where Latin and Greek were part of the curriculum. Although the Haganum was a state school, it had a reputation for élitism. To this day, former pupils recognize each other by whistling the first line of the school anthem. It was also very Haganum to look down on all the Lycea or Hogere Burger Scholen types of secondary schools which taught Greek and Latin only as an option or not at all.

Once inside, the first thing that struck the new pupil was the classical Greek statues in the school hall. These titillated Verhoeven; he was still very young, and knew hardly anything about the bodily functions which serve to facilitate procreation. His mother had always referred to his private parts as his *mucky-mucky* – in the sense that they were not to be fiddled with! At these moments, his father would keep quiet.

Secondary school gave Paul Verhoeven a wider view of the world. He learnt algebra and geometry, physics, chemistry and biology, as well as four modern languages – French, German, English and Dutch – and two classical languages, Latin and Greek. His cultural heritage was vigorously drilled into him by Miss Van der Toolen: 'You could tell her mood just by the colour of her dress. And if she stood in the doorway rubbing her hands, we immediately knew we would be getting a test. She was so strict that she once gave me 2 minus minus in a test.'

Verhoeven's school reports reveal that Latin and Greek were not his favourite subjects. Thanks to extra lessons, he finally managed 6 minus for classics in the sixth form. Paul's marks for maths (almost never under 7.5), physics, Dutch, French and biology were much better; for these subjects he consistently scored above the class average.

The classes were small – sixteen pupils on average – and because of the war there were considerable differences in age. Verhoeven's group included boys who were seven years older than him, and under whose tutelage he became more street-wise. They explained to him, for example, the purpose of that curious piece of equipment on the toilet at his family home. 'A glass cylinder with all kinds of protruding metal rings and tubes, about which my parents always said, "Oh, that's for rinsing out."' His classmates explained to him in whispers exactly what it was that needed rinsing out.

With the beginning of his adolescence the relationship between the son and the parents changed. When the house was full of 'foster' children, Paul would more and more often retreat to his own room. There he drew his comic-strip stories and read the kind of books his parents had little taste for: not only Dutch authors such as Simon Vestdijk and Louis

Couperus, but German writers like Heinrich Böll and, albeit with difficulty, the French existentialists. His Dutch language teacher Mr Bras did much to inspire his passion for reading. The world that emerged from these books was a far cry from the one he was familiar with from discussions at home.

'From the age of thirteen or fourteen I cut myself off from my parents,' Verhoeven remembers. 'Not so much emotionally as intellectually. I felt they could no longer share my interests.' Another schoolfriend, Andrew van Nouhuys, who had grown up in the more artistic and élitist milieu of a doctor's household, introduced him to the world of modern composers – in particular Stravinsky, Ravel and Debussy. Fascinated, they analysed this music, sometimes encouraged by Andrew's mother, who had previously been married to the Dutch composer Alexander Voormolen (1895–1980), a follower of Debussy. 'It was as if a door to a secret room had been opened for me.'

Paul too was sometimes allowed by his parents to buy a recording of modern music – but when he played Stravinsky at home, his mother was not amused. In addition, the boy turned out to have a great talent for the abstract world of mathematics; but although his father shared this interest in maths, they inevitably drifted apart as far as schoolwork was concerned – despite the fact that Wim Verhoeven contacted his son's maths teacher to update his own knowledge.

Mrs Verhoeven sensed the estrangement, but was unable to do anything about it. To shield her only child from the evils of the outside world, she became more and more protective. Andrew van Nouhuys says, 'Because in Mrs Verhoeven's eyes I was well brought-up, she often phoned my parents to get advice on child-rearing. In the later years of secondary school we often went to a pub in the Zoutmanstraat, and his mother would invariably worry and shout at him, 'You're always looking at the wrong people and at the wrong girls!"

For his part, Paul sometimes felt remorse at this loss of contact with his parents, but he was equally unable to bridge the gap. To spare his mother, who often worried about him, he would take the Dutch Crisbakes with milk she faithfully left out for him every night and dutifully eat them, though he disliked having to do so. He dared not tell her so, 'otherwise she would have thought that I did not love her any more.' Nor would he discuss with her the length of his hair, the suits and ties he wore, or what the outside world would think of the family. At home, there was the *status quo*; outside, there was adventure – with his friends or in the cinema. Andrew van Nouhuys says, 'Paul's parents were really fond of him, but extremely fearful he would go down the wrong path. He was warned against it nearly every day.'

*

This difficult relationship has not improved over the years, and the gap between their perceptions of the world has never been bridged. Although Paul Verhoeven followed his parents' wishes until the later years of his university studies in Leiden, where he obtained his doctorate in mathematics and physics, he decided to draw the line there. He wanted to become a film-maker – ironically, the seeds of this passion had been sown by his father and the school projector. The man who, because of his origins, had never been able to achieve his own ambition of becoming a doctor would never really understand that choice. He and his wife had dreamed of a career for their son as a teacher or preferably a professor of mathematics – especially the degree ceremony, complete with mortarboard. They hoped Paul, a social climber, would enhance the family's standing and be a boy to be proud of – although as good Dutch Calvinists, pride was not a word in their vocabulary. To them, film was a circus – and it made for an uncertain future.

'With pain in their hearts,' Verhoeven recalls, 'they tried to accept my choice. My father must have gone to see my first full-length feature film *Wat zien ik* [*Business is Business*, 1971] about ten times. He quit after the second film. It was because I let Rutger Hauer, as the artist Erik in *Turks Fruit* [*Turkish Delight*, 1973], say: "I fuck better than God!" He was certainly not religious, but he found such explicit language absolutely unacceptable. He said, "I would love to see the film, son, but if it includes that kind of language I cannot go."' Verhoeven's mother did go, however, together with her sister. For years his parents continued to buy all the newspapers on the day following every new Verhoeven première and put the reviews in a scrapbook. Robert Haverschmidt says, 'At night you could see them in the distance walking past the cinemas in The Hague because they wanted to see with their own eyes how long the queues were.' Often, though, Wim Verhoeven openly criticized Gerard Soeteman, the scriptwriter who in his eyes was primarily responsible for the nudity, the violence and the human aberrations so frankly shown in his son's films. Verhoeven's parents did, however, go to the premières of *Soldaat van Oranje* (1977). On this occasion they were introduced to Queen Juliana and Prince Bernhard. Standing on the stairs of the Tuschinski Theatre after the show, the Queen spoke: 'Well, we're off then.' Paul's mother answered, 'We are too, I guess.' Not even the royal interest in their son's work could dispel his parents' ambivalent feelings.

The day he departed in September 1985 for the United States to continue his career as a film-maker with *RoboCop*, Paul Verhoeven was a very successful director. His *Turks Fruit* was the best-attended Dutch film of all time and received an Academy Award nomination in 1973; in addition he had won the LA Film Critics' Award for Best Foreign Film in 1979, as well as the Golden Globe for *Soldaat van Oranje*; his *De Vierde Man* (*The Fourth Man*, 1982) had received the LA Critics' Award for Best Foreign Film. Nevertheless, his elderly father sent him a letter, which Verhoeven received on the morning he left. Enclosed was an advertisement, which his father had cut out of a newspaper: 'Required: mathematics teacher'.

1957: Paul's year club
at the University of
Leiden; the mathemat-
ics and physics student
is in the back row,
fourth from right.

Eén Hagedis Teveel.

La femme assise: Paul Verhoeven's contribution to the
'Surrealist Encounters' exhibition.

Chapter 2

Among Artistic Types

In 1956 Paul Verhoeven began his studies at Leiden, the oldest university in the country. To his parent's delight, he chose mathematics and physics. He was not alone in this since 80 per cent of his classmates chose to study a science subject. In the wake of all the destruction of the Second World War, the youthful élite had a strong feeling that they were going to rebuild Europe.

The choice of subjects to study in those days included law, medicine, mathematics and physics, chemistry and biology – humanities and arts courses were not taken very seriously. Moreover, at secondary school Paul had shown himself good at subjects that required precision, so his choice was obvious. 'But I followed the course without much commitment for the first couple of years. It was nice if I got a good grade for an exam, but that was all.'

Much more exciting was the fact that his studies enabled him to break his ties with home – although his mother came round with her cleaning things more often than he would have liked. There was also a lot to entertain him in Leiden, where life had traditionally been dominated by the presence of the university (which dates from 1575, when King William donated it to the city in gratitude for its resistance to the Spanish occupation). It was at the university here that the Pilgrim Fathers spent some time before their departure for America. Around the Rapenburg, the university quarter in the old town centre, there was a distinct student atmosphere; there were canals and narrow streets with student cafés and cheap eating-places. This area left impressions that Verhoeven would later incorporate in his film *Soldaat van Oranje*.

He came to live in student lodgings at 69 Langebrug, in the very heart of the city, where he shared accommodation with his old school-friend Robert Haverschmidt. The floor beneath was rented by two contemporaries of Princess Beatrix, who was studying Dutch law at the university.

Verhoeven applied for membership of the Leiden Studenten Corps Minerva, a student association with an extremely conservative reputation.

It was based on seniority, and the initiation rituals the freshmen had to put up with – shaving one's head was only the beginning – were severe and humiliating. Inside the association's premises at the Breestraat – the heart of which was a rectangular room with chandeliers and red velvet curtains next to a billiards room – what mattered was not so much having brains and talent as coming from a good family and being able to speak, or after the consumption of alcohol, shout in an affected manner, as a sign of self-confidence.

On joining the association, Verhoeven was told not to have any big ideas. 'My father did not have a university education, and in the eyes of the Minerva members this was a slur on my own reputation. They would ask me, "What does your dad do? Headmaster? Oh well, that's no good. Got an uncle with a degree? An aunt? No? So you're the first in the family to go to university? Oh well, you may as well piss off then, we only want people of the right calibre here."'

Nevertheless, it was traditional – certainly in the 1950s, long before the democratization of university life – for first-year students to want to join the association. Whether the members were considered arrogant or not, the friendships formed here could be beneficial for the rest of one's professional life – the first step into an Old Boys' Network.

Minerva was also powerful throughout Leiden. When the 'first-years' with their shaven heads sat down on the tram-rails, thus disturbing the whole of city life, not a single policeman dared to act. Paul Verhoeven particularly remembers, as part of the Minerva initiation rite, being thrown into a dark room where there were ten whores sitting on a table. 'That's to say, they were men dressed in women's clothing who started to push you about and flirt with you. There was a lot of closet homosexuality in the association, but of course this was not openly admitted. Yet it comes as no surprise to me that a number of boys I knew from those days came out of the closet after their marriage.'

The association had strict codes of behaviour, so it was easy to be conspicuous. In the eyes of other Minerva members, Paul Verhoeven had something suspiciously 'arty-farty' about him. Always dressed in a black donkey jacket and fashionable clogs, he was not exactly the model Leiden student. Moreover, he was rarely seen at the association, which was probably the main reason for the suspicion he aroused.

'I didn't really feel at home there. I've never liked boozing and bullshitting about women the way they did. Actually, I've never been very macho. I would rather have a cup of coffee with a woman than a glass of beer with a man. In their eyes that made me rather hard to fathom.'

When not attending lectures or reading at the university library, Verhoeven was drawing illustrations for the *Leidse Studenten Almanak*, the student year-book. He also painted sets for the association's annual Sempre ball, which was always based on a theme such as the Arabian Nights; culturally inclined Minerva members were each given a room to decorate. Verhoeven soon joined *KAF-T*, a small avant-garde magazine in Leiden that was a hybrid collection of budding talent and what were then called 'modernist frogs'. Under the chief editorship of John Leefmans, *KAF-T* regularly caused a stir with its erotically tinged poetry. The subsequent director of Amsterdam's Stedelijk Museum, Rudi Fuchs, also contributed to the magazine, as did the poet Jan van Mastrigt, who was to become a good friend of Verhoeven. Here, he was among artistic types for the first time.

'There was a rather existentialist atmosphere in the editorial room. They always started the evening by playing Brecht songs on the record-player. After that, it was Juliette Gréco. They recited their own work. The conversations were about poetry and philosophy.' Verhoeven, with his experience of comic strips, drew the magazine's covers and illustrations. And as a result of a stay in France, he knew more about Paris than the rest of the editors put together.

In 1955 Verhoeven had been sent abroad by his parents because they thought him too young to start his studies in Leiden. He had been invited by friends of the family to St Quentin in northern France, where he attended the Lycée Henri Martin to retake the sixth year of the *gymnasium*, but this time in French and without examinations. Mr Verhoeven, himself a Francophile, had judged this visit to be good for his son's education. For his own enjoyment, Paul attended evening classes and at the weekend went to the art school, the Ecole de la Tour, where he was free to indulge his love of drawing. There were trips to Paris, where he had made a penfriend, Yvette. Meanwhile, he was also doing a course in Russian – but more significant was the stimulus he received from his Latin and French teacher, Monsieur Collet.

'He thought it was quite amusing that a Dutch boy should come to France to get acquainted with culture.' Monsieur Collet had set up a film club in St Quentin, to which Paul was invited every week. The films shown included *Le Corbeau* (1943) and *Les Diaboliques* (1955), thrillers by Henri-Georges Clouzot, the director later recognized as the French Hitchcock. There were other films in which the action and dialogue seemed extremely erotic to the young Dutchman. And he saw the documentaries by Alain Resnais about Van Gogh (1948) and Gauguin (1951), as well as the recently released meditation on the horrors of the concentration camps, *Nuit et Brouillard* (*Night and Fog*, 1956).

French cinema made a profound impression on Verhoeven – a counterpoint to his earlier passion for American-produced spectacles. 'This is when I had the idea of studying at the French film academy, the Institut des Hautes Etudes Cinématographiques (IDHEC) in Paris. But I was too late to apply. Moreover, my parents wanted me to go back to the Netherlands.'

His familiarity with the French culture that was then so influential made Verhoeven a welcome addition to the editorial staff of *KAF-T*, although he remained a somewhat eccentric figure with his black horn-rimmed glasses. Koosje Berkhout, his girlfriend at the time, says, 'Paul was a bit of an absent-minded professor; he was always working on something in his head. Sometimes I would meet him in the street, walking to the university with an open book in his hands and Crisbakes on it. That was his breakfast.'

His friends found it difficult to understand Verhoeven's curious pact between art and science. But he himself had discovered unsuspected parallels. 'It was not until Einstein's theory of relativity was introduced into my course that I became really gripped by the subject matter. It still interests me that a mathematical formula can serve as a blueprint for the entire universe. Einstein's theory is a miracle of elegance, like a Mozart symphony. I spent months in the library trying to get to the bottom of it. When you are finally able to do so, you feel incredibly satisfied. You could say that Einstein's formulae offer you the theoretical possibility of breaking through time – this means that your childhood is still there, even though in practice you cannot reach it any more.' He explains that there is a dialectic tension in that idea. 'The hope that, theoretically, it will one day be possible to break through time versus what the Dutch poet J. C. Bloem says about the past and its irreversibility.'

As Verhoeven later discovered, it is possible to capture this tension on celluloid. 'In retrospect, I'm glad I studied mathematics and physics, especially for my film work; not only because you can abstract those leaps in time, but because you can justify them logically. *Basic Instinct*, for example, fits together like a set of mathematical cogs. My university course taught me to think in big curves, not scene by scene as most directors do.'

Verhoeven's love of film, encouraged by Monsieur Collet, next found an outlet in a camera, a Kodak Cine Special, that he was given in 1955 by an uncle named Arie de Groot, who was repatriated from the former Dutch East Indies (now Indonesia). This was a very special camera for its time, as it was suitable for 16mm film rather than the standard amateur 8mm format. Verhoeven set to work at once. Initially, he gave the main role to his father. 'He would light a cigar and with the camera I would follow the smoke spiralling up to the ceiling. When I played it back, I thought it looked very impressive. So I thought, "Hang on a minute – if *this* is possible, then *that* is too."'

Then it was his friends' turn to be filmed, including Marja Habraken, who later became an actress. Robert Haverschmidt remembers, 'He was always doing three-minute films. One of our house-mates, Wim

Hulscher, who later became a professor of physics, usually played the male lead. I remember a short film we shot on a platform at Leiden station. It was about suicide because of unrequited love. A girl was going to throw herself in front of the train, and we had to catch her outside the frame. How Paul was ever going to film that in a believable way was something we were happy to leave to him.'

They also shot some short films on the Waalsdorper Plain and Scheveningen beach. For the indoor scenes, Mrs Verhoeven's sunlamp served as a spotlight. Koosje Berkhout soon found herself sitting under that lamp as an 'actress': 'It was quite funny how Paul began to behave more and more like a director. He would, for example, imitate the viewfinder with his hands, as though he was always looking through a camera. And he would tell you exactly how to walk through a door. He was very involved, and that enthusiasm rubbed off on us.'

Where film was concerned, the usually timid Verhoeven was sure of himself. Robert Haverschmidt: 'Paul had an argument with another student about Hitchcock's *Vertigo* [1958], a film he had seen about twenty times. "That is such a good film," Paul began, but the other boy corrected him, "No, you can't say that. You should say, '*I* think it's a good film.'" "Oh, should I now?" Paul continued, "Well, I have seen that film so many times now that I *can* say that it *is* a good film." His ability to get under his opponent's skin during discussions was evident even then.'

After settling arguments like this, Robert Haverschmidt and Paul Verhoeven would often leave Leiden on their Vespa scooter to go to the Film Club in The Hague, where film journalists and other enthusiasts would earnestly discuss the latest films.

With such a passion for the medium, it was inevitable that, despite his parents' concern, Verhoeven should register with the newly founded Nederlandse Filmacademie in Amsterdam. His parents allowed him to register for the academic year 1959–60 on condition that he did not give up his mathematics and physics studies. This was possible, since the academy, which had opened in October 1958, then offered a two-year course involving only twelve hours of tuition per week.

The tuition, intended as the Dutch counterpart to that provided by the IDHEC in Paris and the Centro Sperimentale in Rome, was still at a rudimentary stage; lectures consisted primarily of theoretical discussions about the Tenth Muse. But it should be explained that the school then had a budget of only 30,000 guilders (about £12,000 or US$ 19,000) at its disposal, from which it was just about able to pay the salaries of the teaching staff. The school was subsidized by the Bioscoopbond (Cinema Association) and the Ministerie van Onderwijs, Kunst en Wetenschappen (Ministry of Education, Art and Sciences); lectures were given in rooms at the Oostindisch Huis in Amsterdam's Kloveniersburgwal, or at the showroom of a film-hire company so that it would be occasionally possible to show films.

Cameras for the students' own work had to be borrowed – although it was more usual for them to use empty toilet-roll tubes as imaginary camera lenses. After finding a nicely framed image, the student would keep his hand as still as possible and call the lecturer, who would say, 'You could go in a *bit* closer.'

Nevertheless, the founding of the Nederlandse Filmacademie was a sign of cautious optimism about the possibilities of a national film industry. Two years earlier the government had set up a fund to stimulate Dutch feature films, the Productiefonds, in which the Bioscoopbond had a 20 per cent stake. This fund was part of the long Dutch tradition of government patronage (which as early as the seventeenth century had also benefited Rembrandt). For approved film projects, the Productiefonds would advance 30 to 60 per cent of the budget in the form of a loan. If the film was successful, the loan was paid back from its revenue. But if the film was not successful, the producer would not be liable for the debt. It was hoped that this form of guaranteed funding would generate a flow of home-grown productions.

Up to that time there had been no feature-film industry to speak of in the Netherlands. Film in the Netherlands meant documentaries, the genre with which Joris Ivens, Herman van der Horst, Max de Haas and Bert Haanstra had received international acclaim as the *Hollandse School*.

During the post-war reconstruction period there had been no interest in feature films, but now at the Filmacademie it was possible to study direction and scriptwriting in Department A, technical subjects (camera, sound, editing) in Department B, and aspects of production in Department C.

Despite its good intentions, the academy fell short of Verhoeven's expectations. He enjoyed the lectures by Professor Peters, the first film academic in the Netherlands: 'Apart from Truffaut and Godard, he thought David Lean was excellent.' But he was less fond of the teaching of the well-known man of letters and film-maker Anton Koolhaas (director of *De Dijk is Dicht*, 1950), who was in charge of scriptwriting. 'It was a bit strange, because I had attended some lectures of his in Leiden, where he gave an expert analysis of *Metropolis* [Fritz Lang, 1926]. But now Koolhaas was only talking about typically Dutch films such as *Dorp aan de Rivier* [Doctor in the Village, 1958] by Fons Rademakers. Not that it isn't a nice film, but I wanted something different. We all had to make Dutch realism: windmills, clay, potatoes, lots of dykes and so on. I quit the course early in the second year. I had the feeling I wasn't learning anything.'

Paul Verhoeven's exam results for Christmas 1959 give a good idea of his cinematographic interests:

Artistic and social development of film art 7+
Aesthetic analyses of film 6½
Psychology of film 8
Sociology of film and cinema 5½
Editing technique 7
Sound technique 7½
Lighting theory/modern techniques   10 –
Expressive possibilities of film medium and special effects 8
Dramaturgy of the feature film 7½
Developments in contemporary literature 7
Structure and development of a film script 7
Visualization for film 7 –
Commentary and dialogue 5

After he left, Paul was not missed by the academy board; they thought him rather a strange specimen. Not without a touch of megalomania, he confessed that in future he wanted to make films on an epic scale: about Alexander the Great, the Crusades, or at least his own *Ben-Hur*. To the academy board, this seemed slightly premature, particularly for someone who had shot only a few home movies. But this was soon to change.

In 1959, the same year that Verhoeven made his appearance at the Filmacademie, the Minerva student association organized a competition to film an anniversary celebration. It was obvious to Paul's circle of friends that he would want to take part in this. His main competitor was fellow association member Frits Boersma.

They both had to show their work to the anniversary committee, which had brought in some expertise in the form of Emile Brumsteede, film critic on the newspaper *Het Vaderland*. 'It was a very strange evening,' Boersma remembers, 'I showed a part of my thriller, and then it was Paul's turn. What we saw was an incomprehensible story with continuous interaction between a cup of coffee and two people. The heads looked at each other and at the cup of coffee, and it seemed as if the cup of coffee looked back each time too – and in doing so, made the teaspoon jump. Nobody understood it, but it was clear to everybody that this was art. In our film we had performed a play and put a camera in front of it, but Paul had used an original visual language. In filmic terms he was light years ahead.'

Verhoeven remembers his 'hypnotic little film' well. It lasted three or four minutes, the leading role was played by Marja Habraken, who puts two cups on the table, after which she stares into her own cup with great concentration. In the reflection of her coffee, she sees a ghostly appearance, which she has invoked, materialize behind the second cup. When Habraken looks up, the ghostly appearance has vanished, but the teaspoon which had been on the second saucer is now on the table. 'So, something has definitely happened! Though exactly what, nobody knows.'

The anniversary committee acknowledged his talent, though they found the film confusing. However, thanks to the intercession of Emile Brumsteede, they decided to let Verhoeven direct the film. Frits Boersma was to do the camerawork. Jan van Mastrigt, an acquaintance from *KAFT* – who as a result of this collaboration was to become one of his best friends – was to write the story. The title was *Eén Hagedis Teveel* (*One Lizard Too Many*, 1959).

In October 1959 the new collective started its task of 'writing a script suitable for filming over a short time-scale and within a budget of 2000 guilders,' according to a press release issued at the time by the Nederlandse Studenten Filmindustrie. They soon decided that the screenplay was to be a love story about a complicated triangular relationship, a theme which appealed to the rather timid young men.

In more than one respect the story is reminiscent of Hitchcock's game of double identity in *Vertigo*. In *Eén Hagedis Teveel* the unhappily married wife of a visual and make-up artist starts a relationship with a student. She explains to him how her husband has tried time and time again to sculpt her face in clay. He is able to render any woman except her. This is why the artist forces her to take on a different identity while posing, in the hope of creating a true-to-life sculpture. She realizes that he is more in love with what he wants to see in her than with who she really is.

The situation becomes even more complicated when it turns out that the student also has a girlfriend. (The first lizard crawls ominously through the image.) For a moment the wife and the girl teeter on the edge of a confrontation, but eventually agree to a bold plan: the artist's wife asks the girl to take her place as her husband's model, to assume a different identity by wearing a wig and make-up.

After a time, the husband discovers the deception. But he is not perturbed; on the contrary, he is extremely enthusiastic. His problem is solved, but that of his wife is not. When she seeks solace with her student, she encounters a second lizard (one lizard too many) crawling ominously down the corridor – a surreal symbol for a not very happy ending, although we are left only with vague notions.

The director shot two and a half hours of 16mm Kodakfilm for *Eén Hagedis Teveel*, which was reduced to thirty-five minutes during editing. The shooting took place in their own student rooms, in the attic above Tom Westen's hairdressing salon, in the Leidsche Schouwburg (the local theatre), the Minerva student association, the Academiege-bouw and the streets of Leiden – not always easy filming. At the Minerva student association, for example, the director was refused entry, although it was the association itself that had commissioned him to make the film. 'Put a tie on first,' muttered the porter. 'Yes, but . . . I am the director.' 'Nothing to do with me.'

The main roles were for Hans Schneider, the brother of the future actor Eric Schneider, who had gained some experience in the student cabaret where the future cabaret artist Paul van Vliet also appeared; Erik Bree – a typical association boy – the main reason for letting him take part being that he was the source of the financing, because, according to cameraman Boersma, he couldn't 'string two sentences together, and in view of his enormous height was difficult to spotlight'; Marijke Jones, a typical student, and Hermine Menalda, a real femme fatale, who was mistaken at the association for 'the whore of Leiden', but in any case brought some personality to the proceedings.

Verhoeven had known Hermine since their schooldays at the *gymnasium*. They were in the same class, and at that time the director had looked up to her enormously because she had such an unapproachable aura about her: 'If it was time for the school play, she always landed the leading role – which is why I asked her to be in my film.' In *Eén Hagedis Teveel* she plays the role of the make-up artist's wife in an unemotional but convincing way. Her blond hair is reminiscent of that of Kim Novak or Eva Marie Saint. Or, as the director enthusiastically points out when he sees the photographs of *Eén Hagedis Teveel* after so many years: 'She is exactly like Sharon Stone!' The lizard of the title was borrowed from the terrarium of Verhoeven's friend Andrew van Nouhuys.

'We worked on the shots until the early hours of the morning,' Frits Boersma remembers. 'As it was a rather muddled story, it turned out to be difficult to film. The key to it was a wig which caused a case of mistaken identity. Anyway, I can recall a shot in which the wig was put down on the floor and I had to stand on top of it with my camera. Paul sat next to me with a hair-drier. He blew hot air through the wig because he thought it had such a nice surrealist effect. The rest of the crew rebelled, they really thought it was crazy. As far as I was concerned, Paul's genius was way beyond us.'

The rebellion was caused not so much by the experimental wig shot, Verhoeven remembers, 'but more because, at my request, Hermine Menalda had lain down on the floor half-naked. Her boyfriend was there at the time, and he thought this was quite enough.' Little did the young lover know that a *Nouvelle Vague hollandaise* was being born.

Jean-Luc Godard had just made *A Bout de Souffle* (*Breathless*, 1959), and Verhoeven had decided that his own début film had to be something similar. A wheelchair had been borrowed for the camera work in the street. In the attic room they had laid heavy wooden rails so that the camera could be moved on a dolly. 'The visual style of *Eén Hagedis Teveel*', Verhoeven recalls, 'was based particularly on the serene, artistic dolly shots of Alain Resnais's *Hiroshima mon Amour* – whereas Godard did all that in a much jumpier way.'

The film-crazy students were assisted by an old hand, Ernst Winar, a Dutch film-maker who before the war had spent a long period in the German feature-film industry. For Verhoeven, Winar was more or less the only valuable contact which he had made during his short stay at the Film-academie. He was introduced to him by his lecturer, Willem de Vogel. 'When I met him, Ernst Winar was almost seventy, and he told us the most wonderful stories about his years at the Berlin UFA studios; about the total decadence of that time, the cocaine and the bisexuality. Soon Jan van Mastrigt and I went out to dine with him almost every week.'

Ernst Winar was entered in the registry of births in 1894 under his original name Wilhelm Eichhoff, but when he became an actor he had chosen a pseudonym so as not to upset his family. In 1920 he went to Berlin, where he managed to secure a total of thirty-five roles in UFA silent films, including one as the co-star of Lilian Harvey in *Die kleine von Bummel* (1925). Later, Winar also became skilled in the techniques needed behind the camera, but the rise of the Nazis to power in Germany in 1932 made him decide to return home to Leiden.

In 1935 he directed the Dutch comedy *Op Stap*, and in the same year shared the directorial credit for the film *De Kribbebijter* with Hermann Kösterlitz, a German director who later gained fame in Hollywood as Henry Koster. After the war, in 1947, Winar directed the Dutch children's film *Dik Trom en Zijn Dorpsgenoten*, as well as *Kees de zoon van de stroper* in 1950.

Meanwhile, Winar was working as a technician at the Stichting Film en Wetenschap van de universiteit van Utrecht (Film and Research Foundation of the University of Utrecht) where, at the instigation of Willem de Vogel, Verhoeven was allowed to edit his film. 'I thought it a great miracle that there was someone walking around in the Netherlands with so much film experience. Ernst Winar became a friend to me, a real mentor – I consider him a bit like my film father. I learnt a lot from him, not only about technical matters, but about how to deal with producers and how to establish your autonomy as a film-maker.'

Under Winar's benevolent gaze, the rough material was distilled into a real feature film, which had its première on 15 June 1960 at the Luxor cinema theatre in Leiden, in the presence of Crown Princess Beatrix.

The reviews were surprisingly good. '*Eén Hagedis Teveel* is a film in which the role of the moving camera and the necessity for visual design have been brilliantly understood,' wrote the *Nieuwe Rotterdamse Courant*. The magazine *Film* reviewed it as follows: 'After only one credit the story begins immediately, in the streets of Leiden at night, and when it has got going, the other credits follow. A neat imitation of Mr Hitchcock and company, but in a way which we are very happy to accept.' A favourable notice in the *Haagse Post* was followed by a short interview: 'Both the leading actress Hermine Menalda and the director Paul Verhoeven are considering the possibility of giving up their university courses to pursue a career in the film industry. "But," says Verhoeven, "I am experiencing a fair amount of resistance from my parents. They have a different way of looking at things – they think it's crazy to give up four years of studying for an uncertain future in film. But those are problems experienced by many artists."'

For Verhoeven, the surrealist slant of *Eén Hagedis Teveel* was more than just a case of Buñuel *à la néerlandaise*, since alienation and mysticism were themes that had preoccupied him greatly in his student days. It was no coincidence that he often muttered to his friends about UFOs and other occult phenomena – and he had also started to paint in a surrealist style.

Through Jak van der Meulen and Marianne van Ophuijsen, an energetic, art-loving Leiden couple whom Verhoeven knew from *KAF-T*, he came into contact with a group of artists who embodied the Dutch surrealist movement, among them the now famous Jopie Moesman and Emile van Moerkerken. They met in Leiden under the aegis of Her de Vries, an art connoisseur and collector, who was the founder of the Dutch Bureau de Recherches Surréalistes and knew André Breton personally.

The members of the surrealist circle around Her de Vries were then mostly unknown, which prompted them to organize their own exhibition at LAK, the Leids Academisch Kunstcentrum (Leiden Academic Art Centre). The exhibition covered almost the entire surrealist universe, in which visions partly sexual and partly cruel were presented to the visitor within the framework of a dream world. Paul Verhoeven was represented by one work, a 40 x 50cm oil painting entitled *La Femme Assise* (*Woman Sitting*). Briefly seen in his film *Eén Hagedis Teveel,* it depicts a girl with blond, Gretchen-like pigtails seen from behind. She is sitting on a velvet rock and looks out over a sombre, desolate landscape.

His modest contribution did not prevent him from being very much present in the group photo taken on the occasion of the exhibition. The youngest member, he stands in the midst of the surrealist company in his black donkey jacket, his head down. The setting is a demolished building at the Gelderse Kade in Amsterdam, and this posing on the rubble gives the photograph an apocalyptic feel.

Reactions to the exhibition itself were not enthusiastic. A reviewer from the *Nieuwe Leidse Krant* talked of 'intellectual yobbishness' and the poet and reviewer Gerrit Kouwenaar wrote in *Het Vrije Volk*: 'They still exist, the real surrealists, the common folk of the subconscious, the Freud-worshippers from the orthodox little Magritte and Dalí school, who with their tongues hanging out of their mouths, daub fine-grained canvases full of black cartoons.'

This was meant as a devastating critique, but since then appreciation of the work of the Dutch surrealists has grown, as is evident from the prices their work now fetches. Thus *Het Gerucht*, a large canvas by the now-dead Utrecht painter Jopie Moesman owned by the Amsterdam brewer Freddie Heineken, is worth around 1 million guilders.

Her de Vries does not know how much the real Verhoeven, since then hanging on the wall of his house, is worth: 'I think I bought it from Paul at the exhibition for 90 guilders. The painting has something of Magritte, although it is not mere imitation. It is not devoid of talent.'

Verhoeven remembers the sale, particularly because his father, who had put the painting in a beautiful wooden frame, was very sad that it now had to leave the house. 'I felt extremely flattered. In those days I was a great admirer of Salvador Dalí and Yves Tanguy, so I wanted to paint in a surrealist manner too. Just as *Eén Hagedis* was my attempt at Buñuel.'

For a long time he had contemplated a career as a painter. 'I was not entirely happy with my mathematics course, so I did drawing, painting, filming.' But his friend Andrew van Nouhuys beat him to it. Three weeks before he was to sit his intermediate examinations in mathematics and physics, he decided to quit his course and become a painter. 'That was a very radical step of his. I had so much respect for his decision that I thought "Now *I* won't go and paint as well."' From then on, he would also give the surrealist evenings in Leiden a miss.

'Thank God', said Frits Boersma later, 'Paul has a complicated personality in which his well-developed powers of reasoning and his strong intuitive side fight for precedence. In those days there was a big gap between his emotions and his rational thinking.' He doesn't think you have to be a great psychologist to recognize Paul's parents in this duality. His father was balanced and sensible: Paul's mathematical side. His mother was much more irrational: 'She was reflective, she had something mystical about her.' This was the boy who sat obediently in the lecture theatre by day, and at night occupied himself with experiments in hypnosis in his student's room (whose walls he had papered with old newspapers). Sometimes he seriously wondered whether his thoughts were determining reality, whether what he saw was merely a projection of his own mind. To prove it, he claimed that with extreme concentration he could immediately summon a tram.

'At that time,' Verhoeven recalls, 'I bought a well-known manual of hypnotism, a hefty tome. With the knowledge I gained from this, I used to put my friends into a trance and then take them back to a previous life – I remember that with one of them, Dirk Smink, I actually went to the municipal archives in Delft to find out whether the results were correct. It appears that he was a blacksmith one or two centuries ago, but unfortunately we could find no evidence for it.'

As a student, Verhoeven for years attended the lectures of Professor W. H. C. Tenhaeff of Utrecht, who held the chair of parapsychology and conducted experiments with the nationally famous psychic Gerard Croiset. 'At one point, Professor Tenhaeff asked me, "Are you searching, Mr Verhoeven?" I immediately said, "Yes, I am!" He invited me to become a member of the Lodge of Freemasons, but nothing came of it.'

Meanwhile, his parents were becoming concerned about Paul's obsession and the experiments that accompanied it; they noticed that he was far too thin for a growing boy. And they were not the only ones who looked on anxiously.

'Painting like a surrealist and experimenting with black magic brought out his irrational side,' Frits Boersma says. 'If he had pursued that, I think he would have ended up in an asylum.' Filming saved him. Only when he was behind the camera did Verhoeven's rational and intuitive sides completely merge. The technical aspects of filming were, of course, the equivalent of mathematics. The artistic aspect was the intuitive, emotional side. 'As early as the shooting of *Eén Hagedis Teveel* you could see that he was entirely in his element, mentally balanced, all his concentration on a single track. Paul never played at being an artist. Filming comes from within him. It is a psychological necessity. This is how he has so far managed to retain the balance between the two very opposite sides of himself. That is why he is a genius and not a psychiatric patient.'

Apart from not wanting to compete with his friend Andrew van Nouhuys, Verhoeven's choice between painting and filming was made easier by the success of *Eén Hagedis Teveel*. At the international student film festival, Cinestud, held in Amsterdam in September/October 1960, the film won first prize out of eighty-one entries from twelve countries. His talent had been recognized. 'And yet,' says Verhoeven, 'I have never been entirely sure I took the right decision at that time. I have always regretted giving up painting.'

He made his decision in a rather rigorous way. The early work *Femme Assise* is the only remaining evidence of Verhoeven's aspirations as a painter. As if to underline his emotional choice, he destroyed the rest of his work, putting his foot right through the canvases.

Jan van Mastrigt.

Feest: the young director
at work.

Martine Tours (at the front) in the
Haganum school orchestra.

Chapter 3

Crossroads

Early on the morning of Saturday 13 June 1964 an ambulance stops outside the house in the Leidse Kloksteeg occupied by Jan van Mastrigt, law student, film critic, poet and Paul Verhoeven's artistic partner. They had met at *KAF-T* in 1959, and immediately recognized each other's talent. Van Mastrigt is the writer who commits the ideas to paper; Verhoeven is the driving force, the enthusing element in every project. Together they had devised and shot some short student films as well as *Eén Hagedis Teveel* (1960), *De Lifters* (*The Hitchhikers*, 1962), *Niets Bijzonders* (*Nothing Special*, 1962) and *Feest* (*Let's Have a Party*, 1963). It now appears that, completely unexpectedly, Jan van Mastrigt has ended his life. The previous night at three o'clock he had gassed himself.

Jan van Mastrigt died at the age of twenty-four. His friends in the Leiden film circle – alongside Paul Verhoeven there were the veterans Frits Boersma, Dirk Wiersma, Robert Haverschmidt and Koosje Berkhout, and the newcomer Martine Tours – could only speculate about his motives. It might have been fear of failure; that very Saturday, van Mastrigt was to resit an important law examination. Unlike his friends, he was not doing well in his course.

Just the week before, for example, Paul Verhoeven had passed his doctoral examinations in mathematics and physics (main subject: theory of relativity), to the great admiration of Jan van Mastrigt. 'When I came out of the examination hall, Jan was standing there, very emotional. He embraced me and kissed me. I remember it so well, because such strong reactions were certainly not common in those days.'

Van Mastrigt's own detours from his studies were often the subject of conversation at his parents' house. These usually ended in rows, especially when his father caught Jan at home in bed with a girl, the model Evelein de Ruyter. Without further ado she was branded a slut, and Jan was forbidden to see her again. But even though the years of post-war reconstruction were undoubtedly stifling for young people, was this a reason for committing suicide?

Paul Verhoeven says, 'We were completely taken by surprise. I had hardly known there was such a thing as suicide, that it could come so close. I must have been incredibly attached to that guy, because I have been having dreams about Jan for thirty years now. I dream that he has been in hiding all these years, that he has been slogging away to catch up with the backlog of his course, and that he has just passed the exam. After that he reappears, alive and kicking. That is the dream, in a lot of variations.'

Naturally, Verhoeven felt guilty that, despite their seemingly close friendship, they had lived separate lives. Their relationship had been based purely on film. During the following months, the mere sight of a cinema made Verhoeven feel nauseous. 'In our film club Jan van Mastrigt was the person who impressed me the most, because he moved in artistic circles with such ease. I thought he was a man of the world, a real artist. To my mind, he was much further along than the rest of us. He not only wrote scripts, but poetry and articles about film, and he went to the Cannes and Venice film festivals – all very sophisticated.'

A Leiden student with an Amsterdam attitude, that is how Verhoeven remembers him. The son of a Rotterdam lawyer, Jan van Mastrigt had a flair for wearing suits and just the right shirt, accompanied by a snazzy black umbrella. *Un beau garçon*. Successful with women – 'He would say, "The girls think I'm a little too fat, I'd better go and run round the block," and we would run round the block together' – as well as men. Someone to envy.

In Verhoeven's short film *Niets Bijzonders* (*Nothing Special*, 1962), Jan van Mastrigt plays the leading role, a part he wrote for himself. The script is loosely based on a quotation from William Faulkner, who at that time was an inspiration to many young Dutch writers. The quotation recurs several times in the film, as when van Mastrigt mumbles, 'In a book I once read, somebody says that the population would decrease if each man were twins and had to go and watch himself being intimate with a woman. He would laugh so much that he would never do it again.'

Jan van Mastrigt appears in the film as a neatly turned-out young man with piercing eyes and a slightly affected accent. His delivery of the lines is not without irony. In a café, behind a glass of beer, he carries on an interior monologue about the pros and cons of love, then suddenly sees in a corner of the same café his girlfriend Marina – with another man. 'Who is that? Oh, that's me. Who did you think it was? Have a look while I get another lager.' There is bebop music in the background, the room is smoky, people dance – black polo-necks are in fashion. 'That man in the book is mad. The four of us should all go out some time,' the main character concludes.

Niets Bijzonders is a nine-minute story with a light touch. In the continuously circling camera and the 'meaningful' silences the influence of French cinema is clearly visible, although the film also reveals much about Dutch student life in those days. The notions about love are exemplary: a girlfriend was still called a fiancée – although not without a touch of irony. Probably the most mischievous aspect of the film is the fact that it was shot in the Het Achterom café in The Hague, then frequented by the 'almost world-famous' young writer and painter Jan Cremer, who was working on his scabrous *I, Jan Cremer* – a novel that was to cause a literary earthquake in the Netherlands in 1964. His paintings are clearly visible in the background. 'We all looked up enormously to Jan Cremer,' Verhoeven remembers. 'Naturally we tried to persuade him to take part in our film, but he refused point-blank. But if you look carefully you can see Cremer moving very briefly through the frame.'

Jan Cremer, who had just dared to put one of his artworks up for sale at one million guilders, had the flair that the members of the Leiden film club completely lacked at that time – although in their eyes the well-groomed Jan van Mastrigt came very close. His status is evident from the fact that many of those who later worked with Paul Verhoeven have memories of van Mastrigt, precisely because he moved so much in artistic circles. Scriptwriter Gerard Soeteman, who from 1968 was to take Jan van Mastrigt's place as permanent writer to Paul Verhoeven, knew him from Rotterdam, where they had spent their youth. As did Hans Kemna, who some ten years later became actor, casting director and assistant director for Verhoeven. 'I admired Jan van Mastrigt. He had a classiness about him. He always surrounded himself with the most beautiful women. I secretly had a thing with him too, a bit of kissing – I don't think that Jan was really homosexual, although it would not have surprised me. He was the "both men and women desire me" kind of guy.'

Now, a young but sombre group of people waited at his graveside. They did not know each other, but some of these friends of Jan were about to become the young Turks of Dutch culture. Silently they stared at the coffin: Paul Verhoeven, the budding poets Armando, Hans Sleutelaar, Hans Verhagen and Bastiaan Cornelis Vaandrager, then Hans Kemna, the future museum director Rudi Fuchs, and the poet Simon Vinkenoog – who had taught Jan to smoke marijuana.

In addition to writing for *KAF-T*, Jan van Mastrigt did film reviews for the weekly magazine *Haagse Post*. He had his poetry published in *Gard Sivik*, the avant-garde magazine originally based in Antwerp, with which Armando, Hans Sleutelaar, Hans Verhagen and Cornelis Bastiaan Vaandrager were involved, and which later became well known in the Netherlands when it moved offices to 127b Essenburgsingel in Rotterdam, the home of Sleutelaar.

The latter remembers: 'I had known Jan since secondary school, the Erasmiaans *Gymnasium* in Rotterdam. He was a few years below me, but he belonged to the small club of poetry enthusiasts whose work was published in the school magazine.' A few years later, when van Mastrigt was seventeen, they used to bump into each other on evenings out in Rotterdam, particularly at the Pardoel café in the Oude Binnenweg – a meeting place for Angry Young Men. This led to more frequent contacts. They went to parties together, then to Paris and the south of France. Sometimes they hitchhiked on meat lorries from the Rotterdam abattoir. It was possible to get a lift for ten guilders and arrive early in the morning at Les Halles in Paris with a hangover. The driver would have given them too much brandy with their coffee out of gratitude for keeping him awake. Sometimes, however, the journey was made in a car borrowed from van Mastrigt's parents.

'His father was an old warhorse who forbade him everything. Jan must have suffered enormously under him. One summer, the four of us went to the south of France. Jan was using his father's car, but when his father discovered that Jan had taken his friends with him, he phoned the police at the Côte d'Azur to intercept the lot of us. There was always trouble.'

This classic father–son conflict must have been the reason for his suicide, thinks Hans Sleutelaar. Jan van Mastrigt had everything going for him: he was clever, he could write, he made films, he looked good, and his father had money. 'Those were wild years for that boy; he wanted to explore his limits, he took a bite at both sexes – *à contre-coeur*, of course, and he did feel guilty about it. Especially as regards his mother, because she was a very sweet, warm person.'

The three poems by Jan van Mastrigt printed by Hans Sleutelaar in the January 1958 issue of *Gard Sivik* certainly have something pure about them, though the style is undeniably adolescent:

> . . . and everything I did:
> striking fire from the horizon
> or singing against the wind
> had a dry reflection
> a slow death upon its heels.

Elsewhere, the death-wish is plain:

> . . . go away and name me no more
> A fearful and skittish one I am.

Or about his parents:

Your body (so many thoughts already tunnelling under the skin)
is a pale youth who hides with his parents
his mother, love,
his father, a distant vision.

Jan van Mastrigt was careful about mixing the different worlds in which he moved. If he was with Hans Sleutelaar, he would only discuss literature; if he was working with Paul Verhoeven, he would only talk about film.

Hans Sleutelaar: 'Sometimes Jan gave a little away about what they had filmed, and he did mention Paul's name occasionally; he always spoke of him as his friend, but that was all. He never invited his literary acquaintances to the premières of any of his films. And he never told me he had won a prize for *Eén Hagedis Teveel.*'

Paul Verhoeven now feels he never really got to the bottom of Jan van Mastrigt's character – and not just because he did not anticipate his suicide. For example, he had never been aware of Jan's struggle with his sexual identity because he had so often seen him with girls. 'If he concealed it, I do understand; in the Leiden Student Association, to be openly homosexual was totally unacceptable.' The members thought Jan van Mastrigt a slightly strange figure, but this did not prevent him from regularly appearing at the Minerva club-house.

The obituary published on Tuesday 30 June 1964 by *Virtus Concordia Fides*, the organ of the Leiden Student Association, was not so far from the truth as it must have seemed to Jan's friends in other circles at the time. It said, 'We got to know Jan van Mastrigt as someone who was very interested in the most diverse facets of life. In this he was aided by a great intelligence, which enabled him to assess a situation quickly. This, however, meant that he soon lost the excitement of the new, and his playful mind and imagination would force him to start something else . . . To many he was someone who was not completely understood in his rapidly changing life.'

Since that time, Verhoeven says, he has never worked so intensively with anyone else. For his part, Jan van Mastrigt must have seen Verhoeven as the person who made it possible for his stories to be realized on the screen. It was a relationship of mutual benefit.

However, not everyone was convinced of Jan van Mastrigt's capabilities, or those of Paul Verhoeven. In 1962, to their surprise, the two students managed to enrage one of the Netherlands' most prominent film critics, who devoted a whole page to their film *De Lifters*, which was only seventeen minutes long. It was Verhoeven's second film, a story about a Studebaker, three boys and a girl, and about how they all compete for her favour. The film had a modest première, as the short before the main film in the Amsterdam art cinema Kriterion; on this occasion, as happened so often, there were problems with the sound owing to poor equipment.

The review appeared on 16 June in the respectable newspaper *Algemeen Handelsblad*. The author was the critic Jan Blokker, who had also co-scripted Bert Haanstra's film *Fanfare* (1958) and Fons Rademakers's *Makkers Staakt uw Wild Geraas* (*The Joyous Eve*, 1960). In 1950 he had received a literary prize for his début novella *Séjour*, but since then he had concentrated on journalism and scriptwriting. He was known as an advocate of the new French cinema; he often referred favourably to 'the *Nouvelle Vague* mentality' which could 'convey' a certain attitude to life, a certain 'tone'. Apparently Verhoeven had not managed to convey this in the seventeen minutes of *De Lifters*. Blokker wrote in his page-long tirade:

Leaving aside the shortcomings caused by technical limitations, there is something wrong with the attitude behind this work. *De Lifters* is based on an anecdotal script (Jan van Mastrigt) which is an incoherent mess of inanity and vulgarity. This is all well and good; it is possible to make an interesting film out of even the most obvious anecdotes. But Paul Verhoeven is *not* capable of that. His images reveal nothing – they are hard, unpoetic, utterly lacking in even the slightest expressiveness, and arranged according to the tedious ABC that his so-called 'film language' has revealed to him.

In short, here we have an uninspired, harebrained scheme retold in pictures with a convulsiveness completely devoid of inspiration. We are dealing with the zenith of creative impotence.

Does such an 'unpretentious' film justify such an extensive criticism? Yes, for someone who is looking beyond the efforts of a group of amateurs – who apparently want to leave this amateur phase behind them one day – for the talent, culture and mentality that will one day turn a film craftsman into a film *auteur*. Yes, however sad this may be, it has to be said that the makers of *De Lifters* completely lack the potential for such an evolution; they have used their 'artistic freedom' for little more than fooling around with outmoded accoutrements. And finally, yes, because it is not a criticism about a failed film by a group of industrious students, but about an utterly repulsive attitude within the Dutch film world.

Thus a feud was born. Paul Verhoeven and Jan Blokker were often to meet each other again in the small world of Dutch film-making, and seldom pleasantly.

Verhoeven was dismayed at the unequal conflict with this established critic. Frits Boersma clearly remembers it: 'Paul came to see me with the article. He was completely devastated by it. I was merely angry, but to Paul it was as if his being, his whole existence, had been denied.'

The only reason they could think of for the attack was the fact that their first film, *Eén Hagedis Teveel*, had won first prize in 1960 at the Cinestud Festival, a competition for students that received many entries from the newly founded Nederlandse Filmacademie. The award for *Eén Hagedis Teveel* had been pushed through at the intercession of Emile Brumsteede, film reviewer for the newspaper *Het Vaderland* and member of the festival jury.

'Our victory', Verhoeven remembers, 'was especially at the expense of *Het Moreelse Park*, a film by Frans Weisz and Rob du Mée, who *were* students at the Filmacademie at that time. This was something that Jan Blokker, as a member of the jury, could not swallow. He just took his revenge.'

With his first prize, Verhoeven had publicly defeated the academy he had abandoned after a year because he felt he wasn't learning anything. At the award ceremony he had said something like, 'We've got the prize – so you see you don't need that school after all.' This was regarded as typical behaviour for a Leiden Student Association member. Frits Boersma thinks it must have been this which Blokker was referring to when he mentioned the 'utterly repulsive mentality'. Verhoeven is able to endorse this: 'I suppose we had the affected air of right-wing students from Leiden.'

However small the Dutch film world was at the time, such controversies were a frequent occurrence, as Bob Bertina (born 1915), one of the 'fathers' of Dutch film criticism, remembers. Immediately after the war he started his reviews for the newspaper *De Volkskrant*, and as a leading voice he too was a member of the Cinestud jury in 1960. 'You could compare it with the squabbling surrounding the documentary group of the Hollandse School. Film history books always describe the group as a unit, but I was witness to their pretty nasty *jalousie de métier*.'

The controversial voting of the jury at the Cinestud Festival appears to have been a more prosaic affair than all the commotion would lead us to believe. Chairman A. van Domburg first called out the title of the film and then asked the members to vote aloud. The first may have said: 'A six.' The next person then called out a higher mark, which may have been merely to be one up on the previous member of the jury.

The Leiden club, which released Verhoeven's films under the banner of the *Nederlandse Studenten Film Industrie* and scraped together the money for the productions by issuing 'shares' for each project, had not been too disturbed by the criticism. In 1963 they were given a new project entitled *Feest* (*Let's Have a Party*) – again with a script by Jan van Mastrigt, loosely based on the character Anton Wachter, protaganist of an eight-volume series of novels by Simon Vestdijk. This time the inspiration came from his book *Terug tot Ina Damman. De geschiedenis van een jeugdliefde*. As a lover of Vestdijk's work, Verhoeven looked forward to making the film, since this writer's work encapsulated the quintessential elements of life for Verhoeven at that time.

The film was to be shot at *Haganum Gymnasium*, Verhoeven's own secondary school. The Ministry for Education, Art and Sciences gave a subsidy of 18,000 guilders, which was a new experience for the young director. The camera work was done by Ferenc Kálmán Gáll, a Hungarian refugee and above all a professional with a reputation in the industry. Ernst Winar took care of the editing. As mentor to the enthusiastic students, he played his part with verve, and he had developed a blossoming friendship with Verhoeven.

Set in a *gymnasium* school, *Feest* is the story of awakening love between a fifteen-year-old boy in the fourth year and a girl in the second year. The idyll, which is characterized by authentic secondary-school gaucheness ('Could I walk with you a little way?'), has an abrupt ending at a party, when the school bully forces the couple into a kissing game where the girl is blindfolded. Furious, she hurries away from the party, abandoning her boyfriend in a state of bewilderment.

During the shooting in the spring of 1963, the *Eindhovens Dagblad* newspaper paid a visit. Jan van Mastrigt was quoted as saying with some pride, 'We've got a beautiful *dolly*. A wheelchair, just like Godard used in *A Bout de Souffle*.' This youthful enthusiasm can also be seen on the screen. As a tribute to the *Nouvelle Vague*, we hear the pupils during their break chanting not only the usual Latin declensions *rosa, rosae, rosae, rosam . . .* but, unmistakably, *Godard, Truffaut, Chabrol, Rohmer . . .* Verhoeven feared that no one would understand this, but van Mastrigt insisted it should be included.

Since the script was inspired by Vestdijk, its structure was considerably better than those of previous films. Moreover, Verhoeven knew the milieu of the *gymnasium* school in The Hague very well; he was more or less filming his own schooldays. It shows in the friendships between the boys and their shyness towards the girls. It feels very authentic, and is filmed with an affection rare in Verhoeven's subsequent work. The history teacher portrayed in the film is the spitting image of his father. The male lead, the character of Peter, was played by a blond boy, a genuine squire named Dick (Diek) de Brauw. The girl Anja was played by Yvonne Blei Weissmann, and the school bully by the future radio broadcaster Wim Noorhoek.

Feest is still very dear to Verhoeven; he calls it his best film from his student days, 'my first professional product'.

It was the first of Verhoeven's films to transcend the student milieu. The

Nieuwe Rotterdamse Courant wrote on 8 November 1963: '*Feest*, the short feature film by the Leiden student Paul Verhoeven, gives evidence that this film-maker, whose début *Eén Hagedis Teveel* had promise that he did not fulfil with his second film *De Lifters*, has found his niche as a director.' In the intellectually aspiring weekly magazine *De Groene Amsterdammer*, the renowned film reviewer Charles Boost spoke of 'a film-maker of class, who conducts the camera with great virtuosity' and 'a sublime preliminary study for larger work.'

The Dutch critics were not alone in their praise. *Feest* won the first prize at the Cork Film Festival as well as commendations at film festivals in Oberhausen, Locarno, Melbourne and Paris. Verhoeven's fond memories of the film are perhaps coloured by the fact that the twenty-four-year-old director met his future wife Martine Tours during the shooting. At that time she was seventeen years old and a pupil at the Haganum school, as well as secretary of the pupils' council. The director had to negotiate with her the times when the extras, who were also pupils at the school, would be available for filming. The school orchestra, in which Martine Tours played the violin, was also involved.

'The first time I saw Paul was during a rehearsal with the orchestra. He was leaning nonchalantly against a pillar in his unfashionable shirt and caramel-coloured jacket. He was twenty-four years old and, compared with the boys in my class, a grown man. What I found attractive about him was that inward gaze, the feeling that he had more to offer than was apparent on the surface. After that, we were always bumping into each other 'deliberately by accident' in the corridor, and our excuse for talking was an exchange of mathematical brain-teasers.' Soon, they also went to the cinema together.

Not until years later did they discover that Martine was born almost in Paul's back garden. She came into the world on 7 December 1944 at a maternity clinic in The Hague that bordered on the fence of Verhoeven's parental home. Martine's childhood in a family of three children was not without its problems. Originally, the Tours had been a family of high-ranking civil servants in The Hague, but succeeding generations had not managed to maintain this social position. Her father was head clerk at the Post Office. Her mother had had to leave secondary school early. They pinned their hopes of regaining the social eminence they had lost on their children; they were determined they should go to the *gymnasium* secondary school.

After some time, the parents split up; one of her mother's younger cousins had conceived a child by Martine's father. After the divorce, her mother started teaching at a secretarial college and pulled the family through the lean years under her own steam. Despite this adversity, Martine radiated a social and cultural expertise that Paul had not acquired in his own home. In addition to becoming Verhoeven's wife, she was to develop into his guide and philosopher.

As well as Verhoeven, Jan van Mastrigt was rather impressed by Martine Tours; during the shooting of *Feest* there was tension between the two men and a suppressed rivalry. The feelings were not mutual. She recalls that 'Jan always managed to give you the feeling that everything you did was inferior.' When the school year finished she went to Leiden to study psychology. There she became better acquainted with the film club, and her friendship with Verhoeven developed into a love affair.

On the morning of 13 June she saw the ambulance. 'I had just come out of the Academiegebouw where I had done an exam. I saw Jan being taken away on a stretcher.'

Only the previous afternoon, Jan van Mastrigt, Dirk Wiersma and Verhoeven had enjoyed lunch at the popular student restaurant Peter Leenen, and all had seemed well. They had made plans for new films, then Jan had gone to the hairdressers – after all, he was going to take an examination. 'I stood looking at him from the bridge,' Verhoeven remembers, 'and I said to Dirk, "Look at him walking there. What a strange guy he really is." I don't know why I said that – I must have sensed something. When I see photos from those days, the photos from the shooting of *Feest*, I notice time and time again that he has a penetrating expression as if he is looking straight through things, very absent-minded. His suicide must have been the end of a long process, but it was not something I had consciously seen coming.'

The tragedy symbolized the end of Verhoeven's youth. The Leiden film club, which gathered in sadness and drunkenness that night, would never make another film. Their student days were over, and from now on Jan van Mastrigt's death would cast a permanent shadow over all their memories. They knew this was a crossroads from which they would go in different directions. Verhoeven had to do military service. The future was unknown, but there was the certainty that nothing would ever be the same again.

II Film-making: The Netherlands

The Dutch film-maker.

1964: Paul Verhoeven is promoted to lieutenant-commander in the Navy.

During the shooting of *Het Korps Mariniers*: the storming of Texel Island.

Chapter 4

Between Heaven and Earth

Paul Verhoeven had just turned twenty-six when he was ordered to report to the military barracks in Frederikstraat, The Hague. He planned to use his military service to put some distance between himself and his student years, which had so abruptly ended with the death of his friend Jan van Mastrigt. First he was to receive six weeks of combat training, and then he would be promoted to lieutenant-commander. He quite liked the idea of the soldier's life, partly because the army command welcomed recruits with Verhoeven's level of education – the officer training was, in fact, a piece of cake.

What promised to make military service interesting for Verhoeven was the fact that, soon after being conscripted, he would be assigned to the Marine Filmdienst (Marine Film Service). He had deliberately lobbied for this posting at the Ministry of Defence, having initially been called up by the Air Force. Because of his mathematics background, the civil servants at Defence had thought Verhoeven particularly suited to calculating rocket trajectories from Germany to the Kremlin. Pointing to his curriculum vitae, in which he had carefully listed his prizes for *Eén Hagedis Teveel* and *Feest*, he managed to convince the career committee of his abilities as a film-maker. Three weeks before he was to be billeted with the Air Force, his transfer to the Navy was approved. A lucky coincidence had supported Verhoeven's appeal. The Marine Corps was about to celebrate its tercentenary, and this occasion was to be marked by a film – which, to his delight, the young director was asked to make.

It was to be an ambitious project, for which he submitted a list of requirements soon after his arrival at the Marine Filmdienst. To give a good impression of the activities of the marines, Verhoeven felt it necessary to ask the army command for rubber speedboats, amphibious vehicles, divers, helicopters and even the aircraft carrier *Karel Doorman*, as well as a number of marine divisions. And although General Van Nass, who was responsible for the project, more than once appeared to have doubts about this young intellectual – one of those 'typical students' they had brought into the service – he rarely refused Verhoeven's ambitious proposals.

The film's budget was 100,000 guilders, but Paul Verhoeven had already decided to use this money for a visual spectacle along the lines of the by now so popular James Bond films *Dr No* and *Goldfinger*. 'The marines were going on exercise anyway. It didn't cost them any more if they were doing it for me.'

In accepting the commission, Verhoeven realized that *Het Korps Mariniers* (*The Marine Corps*) had to fulfil its intended function: a cele-bratory film which could be used for recruitment purposes long afterwards. This is why he chose to make it into a real action film – a film which, because of its scale, he would never have been able to shoot as a civilian. 'I saw it as a practical lesson for the future.' To reinforce the James Bond effect, he commissioned the resident conductor and com-poser of the Royal Marines Band, H. C. van Lijnschoten, to write dynamic film music in the style of John Barry, including electric guitars which would be played by the 'hipper' section of the band. To familiar-ize van Lijnschoten with this type of music, Verhoeven gave him the James Bond soundtracks as a present.

For this, his first colour film, Verhoeven was able to call on a profes-sional crew from Cinecentrum, a Hilversum company that worked for the Dutch broadcasting companies. After viewing some of their produc-tions, Verhoeven chose the experienced Peter Alsemgeest as his director of photography, with two assistants at his disposal for the large-scale action scenes. The editing was again entrusted to Verhoeven's mentor and friend Ernst Winar, the man who had taught him the dynamic edit-ing style that was to dominate the director's later feature films.

On completion of his combat training, the young lieutenant-commander in Special Services moved into a room in a guest house in Scheveningen, the harbour and seaside resort of The Hague. He was not often there, since his film required lengthy research, beginning at the Rijksmuseum (the National Gallery of the Netherlands) in Amster-dam, where Verhoeven studied seventeenth-century paintings of Dutch naval scenes. After that he went abroad. He made a trip to Toulon to visit the marine frogmen training there, and then went to England to watch a joint exercise of British and Dutch marines. After a few months of research, he was able to divide his shooting schedule for the film into four parts. First, he would take his camera crew to the barracks in Doorn to shoot film of the Royal Marines, as well as a troop inspection by General Van Nass. By granting the commander-in-chief this moment of glory, the director ensured his unconditional agreement to his plans for the film. After that, he would go to De Harskamp, a training centre in the Veluwe region, to show how the hard-working soldiers took the assault course with bullets flying around their ears.

The second part of the film showed the visit of the troopship *Hare Majesteit De Poolster* to the West Indies, where the Netherlands still had the colonies of Aruba, Bonaire and Curaçao. The highlight of this section was to be an event planned in the spring of 1965: the storming of the Dutch island of Texel by hundreds of marines using heavy equipment. Undeterred by the knowledge that the entire film would last only twenty-three minutes, Verhoeven threw himself into the project with the fanaticism for which he would later become famous. 'Even then,' the director remembers, 'I could be incredibly opportunistic. It didn't interest me one bit whether my film would cause more people to join the marines or not. What mattered was the quality of the film.'

Since as a lieutenant-commander he was not sufficiently high ranking to give orders to his superiors, Majors Eikenboom and De Jonge Oudraat acted as intermediaries. The cry 'And . . . action!' was translated into 'ATTACK!' – which in this case came to the same thing. The latter turned out to be a competent producer: through the informal military circuit, he managed to persuade the commander of the Dutch naval base in Curaçao to telephone his American colleague in Panama.

Verhoeven had been looking forward to showing troops hacking their way through the jungle in the style of David Lean's *The Bridge on the River Kwai* (1957), but to his disappointment there were no forests in Curaçao. They considered going to Surinam instead, but the Dutch marines did not have a good reputation there. That is why the commander of Fort Clayton, the training centre for US marines in Panama, was contacted. Within two days a Douglas DC7 arrived to take the entire film crew plus 'actors' to the jungles of Central America. As was done later in *Apocalypse Now* (Francis Coppola, 1979), they were carried upriver in a boat to take the required shots deep in the interior. As cameraman Peter Alsemgeest later remembered, all the shooting abroad was done by himself and Verhoeven without a sound or lighting crew. 'Paul didn't want to have people around him. We simply had to record the image and finish the rest with music and effects in the studio. It was quicker and more mobile that way. He didn't know anything about cameras and lenses then, but he always looked through the viewfinder with me.'

Their efforts were not in vain. In *Het Korps Mariniers,* after a short historical introduction, Verhoeven shows with military precision how the manoeuvres are done on the assault course. The loud roar of the guns and the action scenes as the troops storm the sandy beaches of Texel are reminiscent of the film *The Longest Day* (Ken Annakin, Andrew Marton, Bernhard Wicki, Darryl F. Zanuck, 1962). The underwater camera shows frogmen planting plastic explosives on the sand barricades; just before these are detonated, we see the divers being dragged out of the water by their colleagues in speedboats. By now, the camera is also turning at full speed above the water. The marines jump out of the landing craft with their machine-guns rattling. A load of TNT explosive is thrown into a bunker, after which a flame thrower is passed over it. In these almost euphorically filmed acts of violence, all that was needed was for the sergeant to shout, 'I love the smell of napalm in the morning.' In Paul Verhoeven's film, the Dutch army shows a readiness for battle which it was never credited with in real life. 'Rather than a realistic documentary, it became my enlarged childhood fantasy.'

What makes the film so remarkable is that, in the midst of the clash of arms, the director, with so little experience, filmed in such a dynamic and disciplined fashion. The camera, whether in a helicopter or on the beach, always seems to be in exactly the right place. 'The trick is to go and stand with the camera where you most like to be as a spectator – assuming for the moment that you are untouchable,' Verhoeven explains. In imagining a scene, he looks for this vantage point first. 'It is a kind of virtual reality game in my head. I choose a point, then I rotate around it in my mind until I have found the right position for the camera. Then I think, "The scene is moving that way, then that way" – so the next viewpoint logically flows from it. Thinking in images is something I have always been able to do.'

The hard editing of wide shots to close-ups – combined with the complete lack of stabilizing medium shots – gives the long visual sequences in *Het Korps Mariniers* an inescapable drive. Much of the visual technique Verhoeven tried for the first time in this film can later be found in the complicated action scenes of *Soldaat van Oranje* (*Soldier of Orange*, 1977), *RoboCop* (1987) and *Total Recall* (1990): in *Soldaat van Oranje*, for example, Rutger Hauer is dragged out of the water in the same way as the frogmen in the marine film.

'It's all a matter of jump cuts and matching. Ernst Winar taught me how to make a car overturn – with no more than three or four shots – in a way you would never be able to do in reality. The images are building-blocks. The viewer fills in the missing actions, and his mind accepts the incident as credible.'

Verhoeven believes that *Het Korps Mariniers* has been crucial to his career. It was precisely because he was able to work without restrictions in making his first colour film that he became so inspired by the medium, that he finally made the decision to become a film director. The festive moment was celebrated in the autumn of 1965 at the film's première in the Rotterdamse Schouwburg theatre by consuming the delicacies displayed with a rare eagerness. Shortly afterwards, he heard that *Het Korps Mariniers* had won the first prize at an international festival for propaganda films in France; Verhoeven took this as added encouragement. The fact that the film had been shown as the supporting programme at the Amsterdam Cineac for several weeks was another stimulus in determining his future career. When in the spring of 1966 Verhoeven's twenty-four months of military service were completed, it was with some reluctance that he said goodbye to the Marine Film-dienst. 'I felt I had had the time of my life.'

The enthusiasm with which Paul Verhoeven had embraced the possibilities of military service meant that he was now rather far removed from the spirit of the times. Especially in Amsterdam, the Dutch student world had fallen under the spell of the counter-culture of the 1960s. Now that the post-war economy was healthy and wealth was steadily increasing, 'mental well-being and personal development' became part of the social debate. Young people no longer wanted to do military service, they wanted rock 'n' roll. They claimed a hedonistic right to happiness, and expressed a longing for everlasting adolescence that was in conflict with the strict values of their parents, the generation of post-war reconstruction. Revolutionary visions of emancipation, participation and democratization replaced the traditional political points of view, which had been dominated by the Calvinist virtues of industry, thrift and sobriety. Typical of this social turbulence was the Amsterdam PROVO movement, short for *provocatie* ('provocation'); ideologically it was inspired by anarchism, and it was also anti-monarchy and anti-military. 'Better long-haired than short-sighted.'

This change in the cultural climate of the Netherlands was perhaps most clearly seen on 10 March 1966, the day Princess Beatrix, heir to the throne of her mother Queen Juliana, married the German diplomat Claus von Amsberg. Owing to the setback to German–Dutch relations caused by the Second World War, this was a sensitive issue, although a survey revealed that three-quarters of the Dutch population did not object to the match. The problem, however, was 'that the marriage ceremony was to take place in ever-turbulent Amsterdam. And Paul Verhoeven, who was still doing his military service at the time, was there to shoot a documentary about the event for the Marine Filmdienst.

On the morning of 10 March he had set out early with a camera crew of five to gather material about the part being played by the Royal Navy in the festivities. Shortly afterwards, the 1960s broke out before his very eyes. Near the Raadhuisstraat, and exactly opposite the national monument to the victims of war, a smoke bomb was thrown from the crowd into the midst of the royal procession. 'This marriage is a chance to declare war on society,' the PROVOs had declared. And although at the critical moment all the leaders of the movement were out of town or had stayed at home, they *had* managed to inspire a student to throw the home-made smoke bomb.

The incident was seen live on television and caused a great commotion. The battle-lines between the establishment and the critical new generation had been drawn. The incident was described in the press and at the universities for years as 'the watershed of the minds'. In left-wing intellectual circles, the smoke bomb grew into a litmus test for a new definition of right and wrong. Needless to say, in this situation Verhoeven, with his officer's uniform, was seen to be on the wrong side. Long afterwards, he was still being reproached for being a 'right-wing' film-maker, and his 'mini-Leni Riefenstahl' documentary, *Het Korps Mariniers*, was put forward as incriminating evidence.

Although in the eyes of many of his generation he was a 'square', who preferred Stravinsky to the Rolling Stones and had studied mathematics at Leiden when humanities at the University of Amsterdam was now state-of-the-art, Paul Verhoeven had worries of an entirely different kind. Making the decision to become a film-maker was one thing – to accept its consequences was another. 'Thinking that you could go through life as a feature-film director in the Netherlands was at that time a vain hope, of course – I agreed with my father on that.' Before Bert Haanstra's comedy *Fanfare* was released in 1958, nobody believed in a Dutch film industry. The first, only and (for the time being) last flourishing period for the Dutch sound cinema had been during the economic crisis of the 1930s, when the feature film was seen as the ideal form of escapism.

Thus, between 1934 and 1940 a total of thirty-one full-length Dutch feature films were premièred in approximately 365 theatres, as well as six foreign productions dubbed for the Netherlands – all of them were 'light entertainment'. This was a breakthrough compared with the period 1930–33, when only one Dutch film was made, the silent *Zeemansvrouwen* (*Sailors' Wives*, Henk Kleinman, 1930). The main reason for this modest output was that the Dutch government regarded film as strictly a private enterprise. While other European countries were beginning to protect their national market against foreign productions, particularly by stimulating their own film industry, there were no import restrictions in the Netherlands, and the production or sale of Dutch films was not subsidized.

The situation changed as a result of political developments in neighbouring Germany. Film-makers, many of them Jewish, fled to Amsterdam, and this meant that an unprecedented amount of experience and talent entered the Dutch film world. Thanks particularly to these exiled directors, standards of camera work, editing and sound reached maturity. Famous names of those days were Ludwig Berger (*Pygmalion*, 1937) Max Ophüls (*Komedie om Geld*, 1936) and Kurt Gerron (*Het Mysterie van de Mondscheinsonate*, 1935). Director Hermann Kosterlitz made *De Kribbebijter* (1935) in Amsterdam, assisted by Ernst Winar. Kosterlitz departed for Hollywood to make a name for himself as Henry Koster, and Ernst Winar shot *Op Stap* in the same year. This parade of songs, comedians and popular, sentimental stories with characters such as *Bleke Bet* and *De Jantjes* came to an abrupt end when Germany invaded the Netherlands on 10 May 1940.

Five years of occupation followed, and after liberation, reconstruction was given top priority. It was not the feature film but the documentary which reached maturity in this post-war period, a form of cinema perhaps better suited to the unfrivolous, Calvinist character of the Dutch people. The Hollandsche School of film-makers such as Herman van der Horst, Bert Haanstra, Joris Ivens and Max de Haas showed how the country was being rebuilt after the destruction of war and celebrated the Netherlands' age-old struggle against the sea. A relationship with reality was always central to these films; in that sense, they are the counterpoint to the fictitious world of the 'entertainment film', a genre that in the Netherlands had always been regarded in the same light as a funfair attraction.

Nevertheless, in 1966 Verhoeven decided to try to make a living as a feature-film director, knowing that there was no existing infrastructure in the Netherlands. There were no scriptwriters, producers, stars or technicians. There were neither traditions nor standards, and the founding of the Dutch Filmacademie in 1958 brought little change. The two Dutch film-makers who were seen as models – Bert Haanstra (born 1916) and Fons Rademakers (born 1920) – were atypical: before Haanstra made *Fanfare*, he had already had a career as a documentary film-maker, and in 1958 he had just received an Oscar for his short documentary *Glas* (*Glass*). Fons Rademakers was a respectable man of the theatre who in the mid-1950s had been sent by the government on a placement to the Cinecittà studios near Rome. Yet when in 1958 he wanted to shoot his own film, *Dorp aan de Rivier*, Rademakers was told to seek the advice of a foreign film-maker. Rademakers chose Ingmar Bergman, who officially agreed to co-operate and then 'reported sick' – thus allowing Rademakers to work in his own way. After the shoot he took his material to Sweden, where Bergman and his crew helped him with the final editing – successfully, because *Dorp aan de Rivier* was nominated for an Oscar.

These were the modest exploits of the Dutch feature-film industry; even the government's well-meaning subsidy scheme, the Productiefonds

(Production Fund), bore little fruit in these years. The figures speak volumes. In the period 1957–65 the following number of feature films were made with the support of the Productiefonds:

1957: 2
1958: 3
1959: 1
1960: 2
1961: 1
1962: 3
1963: 3
1964: 2
1965: 0

Nor did the business community regard the feature film as a serious industry in those days. The involvement of Freddie Heineken, beer magnate and founder of the production company Cineurop, was to be limited to 'one and a half' feature films, although he appeared in his white yacht off Cannes to add lustre to the film festival. When Rademakers' film *Als Twee Druppels Water* (1963) did not receive an award, he soon lost interest.

A second film-loving captain of industry, the wealthy Rotterdam ship-owner Anton Veder, in an outburst of cultural solidarity had set up the Nederlandse Filmproductie Maatschappij NV (Dutch Film Production Company), or NFM, in 1959. The funding was 400,000 guilders, and the staff consisted of one director and one secretary. This director was Joop Landré, who later gained broadcasting fame on the popular TROS television channel. As an executive producer he was less of a success. As the actors still vividly remember, whenever Landré arrived on the set of one of the few productions, he immediately started to look worriedly at his watch. Apart from Rademakers, Johnny Korporaal, a Dutch director who worked mostly in Mexico, was given the chance to shoot two films for the NFM. Neither his thriller *Rififi in Amsterdam* (1962) starring Rijk de Gooyer, nor the more artistic *De Vergeten Medeminnaar* caused a stir. It was not surprising that sour jokes were made about Dutch films. For example, a man calls the ticket-office to ask what time the Dutch film starts – and the answer comes back, 'What time would suit you?'

This lack of success made even established directors turn away from feature films. Bert Haanstra soon returned to documentaries after the flop of his second feature film *De Zaak MP*, a comedy about the theft of the famous Brussels statue Manneken Pis. In 1962 the Dutch war film *De Overval* had to be directed by the English documentary film-maker Paul Rotha.

Verhoeven attempted to start his career with a script based on a novel by

Simon Vestdijk, at that time the Netherlands' most prominent writer. The young director wanted to film the parts of Vestdijk's Anton Wachter cycle dealing with the character's student years, material Verhoeven had worked with before in his short film *Feest*. To write the script he called on Kees Holierhoek, who had recently won the literary Reina Prinsen Geerligs Prize with his first book *Hanen in de Kloostertuin*. Verhoeven wanted to film the Wachter series not just because Vestdijk was his cultural hero, but because the character Wim Mesquita resembled his dead friend Jan van Mastrigt. As Vestdijk wrote: 'He was so brilliant that they did not notice he was burning out to the last drops.' In the Vestdijk story Mesquita, like van Mastrigt, commits suicide.

The script is still in Verhoeven's archive. 'Although Wim Mesquita is peripheral in the Vestdijk novels, in our version we deliberately tried to bring him to the fore.' All Verhoeven's memories of Jan van Mastrigt have been incorporated in the script; this is especially evident if we read Verhoeven himself into the main character Anton Wachter. 'At the time I strongly identified with Anton. Just like me, he was a boy from a bourgeois milieu who had had problems adapting during his student days.' In addition to his shyness with women, Anton is overcome by uncertainty when he has to enter a smarter milieu. When he goes with Wim to visit the Mesquita family, he does not know, for example, that it is 'cocktail time' – as happened to Verhoeven when he visited the home of the van Mastrigt family. And just as Verhoeven sometimes helped his friend Jan with his studies, so too does Wim ask the same of Anton. As the script says: 'Anton looks up to Wim. Wim has a car, a Corvette. Wim is successful with the girls. Wim has rich parents. Anton would like to be Wim.'

In a scene starting on page 37 of the script, the clash between Anton and the upper-middle-class milieu of Wim is described in detail. The scene also hints at the later suicide of Mesquita who, just like Jan van Mastrigt, had a troubled relationship with his father:

Seen from above: Wim and Anton side by side in a car driving through an avenue with high trees on either side.

Pastoral atmosphere. Country house of Wim's parents. Exterior. Afternoon. A large house, white and light. On the enormous lawn in front, light and dark spots alternate as clouds pass in front of the sun.

Wim and Anton drive into the long drive. Wim honks. On the terrace in front, Wim's father and mother are drinking tea: white garden chairs, parasols, a shining tea trolley, an elderly servant with a white bonnet on her head. The car stops near the garage. Anton and Wim get out and walk across the lawn to the tea party. A dog, barking loudly, comes running to Wim and jumps up at him. Wim plays with him.

They have a drink, then the telephone rings. It is Joan. Father says angrily: 'Are you still seeing that girl? I thought we had agreed otherwise!'

Wim's room in his parents' house. Interior. Early evening.

   Anton and Wim are putting on their tailcoats (they are going to a student party). A breeze blows through the open doors: the curtains flap wildly on a stream of air. The room is still very much a boy's room. On the wall is a painting, a landscape. There are model airplanes on shelves. On the wall are also photographs of film stars, school posters, childhood photographs. On a bookshelf, some old school-books, neatly jacketed, school diaries and copies of the school magazine. In the corner is a painter's easel.

Anton is fiddling with his bow tie in front of the mirror. He tries to get it into the right shape.

   Anton: 'What has your father got against Joan?'

   Wim: 'Oh, he's being a bit silly.'

   Anton wants to know more about it, and persists: 'Doesn't he like her?'

   Wim: 'We went to bed here once. He found out. And now he thinks she's a slut.'

   Wim notices that Anton cannot get his bow tie right, and with the air of someone who has been in this situation before says: 'That's not the way to do it. Come here a minute.' And he ties it properly: 'There, at least you look like a gentleman now.'

A little later in the script, the main characters attend a party which breathes the atmosphere of the Leidsche Studenten Corps. There is much drinking and a lot of silly jokes about homosexuality. Things become more serious when Anton and Wim see the girl Joan dancing intimately with another boy. Anton thought that Joan was Wim's girl-friend – surely he didn't have a row with his father over her for nothing? Anton wants to warn his friend. He says that Joan seems to be a kind of vampire. 'Can't you see she's playing with you?' Anton asks him directly. 'You talk just like my father. I don't need that,' ripostes Wim, and turns angrily away.

   The matter gets out of hand when Anton walks up to the boy, Boss-cher, who is dancing with Joan and tells him he's not the only one who is sleeping with her. Bosscher immediately takes the girl outside and slaps her hard across the face. Wim notices this and says to Bosscher, 'I advise you not to hit that girl again, or you will have me to deal with.' Bosscher looks at Wim and hits Joan again so that her make-up things are scattered all around. Bosscher says, 'Right, and now you.' He talks so loudly that everyone hears him. He makes a few boxing gestures from which Wim recoils. Bosscher stops, but when Wim has recovered and approaches again, he repeats the gestures. Mocking laughter is heard. Wim feels humiliated, but is unable to do anything about it.

   Meanwhile, Joan has gathered up her possessions, and Bosscher pulls her, still pale with fright, along with him. He turns round to Wim once more and loudly says, 'Now everyone knows how brave you are.' Anton's face is sombre. He feels guilty about Wim's humiliation.

The next morning. Wim's student lodgings. Exterior.

An ambulance stands in front of the house. Someone is carried out on a stretcher, under a blanket, unrecognizable. Someone says: 'Suicide.' Someone else: 'Probably another student.'

A friend quickly walks into a pub to telephone Anton. The latter goes to the hospital as quickly as possible.

Hospital. Interior. Morning.

Anton walks down the hospital corridor. A couple of male students come through a door. When they see Anton, they shrug their shoulders, and say: 'Finished.'

The group walks on with grave faces.

Anton asks a nurse whether he can go inside for a moment. She nods and leads him into the ward. In the centre, on a stretcher, a body lies under a white sheet. The nurse walks up to it and pulls the sheet away from the face.

Anton looks into Wim's face.

He is dead.

Hospital. Exterior. Morning.

From above, filmed from very high: Anton comes out of the hospital, a small figure. He crosses the hospital square, lit up by bright sunlight. All the shadows are sharply drawn.

Verhoeven and Holierhoek completed the script for the feature film *Anton Wachter* in October 1966. In the *Algemeen Dagblad* newspaper, Simon Vestdijk spoke encouragingly about the projected filming of his novel-cycle: 'Why do I welcome it? Firstly, vanity, and secondly, vanity.' But it soon transpired that the intended producers, Cor Koppies and Gied Jaspars, could not get the project off the ground financially. Although VARA Television showed an interest, Verhoeven soon realized that Guus Rekers, VARA's Head of Drama, wanted to take on the role of director himself. The realization of this project, so dear to Verhoeven, suddenly seemed further away than ever. It was a rude awakening: with his student films and *Het Korps Mariniers* he had been able to do things his own way, but now, when he was trying at the age of twenty-seven to get his foot in the door of the profession, the possibilities seemed much more limited than he had hoped. On top of everything else, his girlfriend Martine became unexpectedly pregnant as the result of a torn condom. This news was the prelude to a major personal crisis. 'From one day to the next, my future as a film-maker had suddenly become impossible, because I was going to have to take responsibility for a child. The bourgeois fuss about extramarital pregnancy probably made it worse. I became totally confused.'

The unappealing idea of giving up filming and looking for a job – they obviously could not live on Martine's grant alone – bored into Verhoeven's consciousness: 'The next day I was talking to Martine at a tram-stop in The Hague. We were not talking about the child, but about religion, and we had let three trams go past when a woman walked up to me, a member of what later turned out to be a Pentecostal-type church group called Stromen van Kracht ('Streams of Power'). She pushed into my hand a leaflet which said, 'If you are looking for God' – and somehow this pierced me to the heart, because I was very preoccupied with the Bible at that time anyway. The magic of religion was something that flowed naturally from what had fascinated me so much in my adolescence: UFOs, occultism, hypnosis, things like that. Anyway, I followed up the woman's advice because I thought it could be the solution to my problems.'

That same week Verhoeven went to the Pentecostal church in The Hague. 'It was all "inspired Christianity" there. They spoke in *tongues*, and because I was new, there was a special message for me. It was a very emotional experience, although naturally I could not understand a word of it. The weird thing was that you could physically feel – because that was what it was all about – the Holy Ghost descending, as if a laser beam was cutting through my head and my heart was on fire. The preacher said, "Thank you, Lord Jesus, for being with us here tonight" – and it was clear that yes, He was there, I could feel it.

'Because of my schizophrenic relationship with Christianity, at the same time as I was being moved to tears listening to that message, I knew that there was a logical explanation for the whole thing. For example, when you are so emotional, the organ music can really stir up your feelings. I heard the man speaking in tongues – it sounded like "MAGAAAJI-BURUGAJJJ-NISH!" – and, as was the custom, someone translated these cries to the community. I immediately realized that the woman who was translating the message for me (she had positioned herself behind me) was the one at the tram-stop. Before the meeting I had told her how worried I was about my future. Of course, she immediately told me what she thought should happen. I was not to become a film director after all – that was such a decadent profession – no, it emerged from her undoubtedly precooked translation of the divine message that God wanted me to go to faraway countries to preach the gospel. He had chosen me for a mission to Africa.'

After the meeting, the mentally tormented Verhoeven went to see his girlfriend Martine. That night they were going to tell their parents that they had to get married. First they went to the Verhoeven family. Paul advised Martine to stay in the car, after which he was covered in disgrace at his parental home. Then they paid a visit to Martine's mother; they found her, together with some colleagues from work, making surprise packages for the feast of St Nicholas. The real surprise of that evening was only briefly discussed. Then they went to see Andrew van Nouhuys,

Verhoeven's childhood friend. He offered to help. 'He said, "Why don't you come upstairs for a minute?" We went to his father's study – he was an anaesthetist at a large hospital in The Hague – and Doctor van Nouhuys said, "Do you want a child, then?" The answer was "Well, no, not now."'

An appointment was made for an operation within a week. It was a solution Paul and Martine had not thought of. They were once again masters of their own situation; the crisis was averted. The following day, Paul, Martine and Andrew decided to go to the cinema. Merian C. Cooper and Ernest B. Schoedsack's *King Kong* (1933), a film that had always been a favourite of Verhoeven, was showing at the Cinetol theatre in Amsterdam. But what should have been a relaxed evening out turned into a nightmare. 'Before the film they showed some advertisements, and one of them said, "IN THE SCRIPT OF YOUR LIFE, GOD PLAYS THE MAIN ROLE" – this in the middle of us organizing an abortion. I thought this could not be a coincidence. Then King Kong appeared and turned into an avenging angel from the Old Testament. He had come to demand satisfaction from me, of course – it all fitted together quite well, I must say. King Kong trampled people, cars, an entire city – bang, bang, bang – and I could no longer distinguish between film and reality. I had deliberately to turn aside, to look at Martine and Andrew, to know that there was a reality. I only just made it through that evening, thanks to Martine's help. But it was quite a close thing. I mean, with Nietzsche a psychosis like that blew his whole mind away, didn't it?'

Helped by her studies in psychology, Martine was able to rationalize the crisis – although she now says that, with such a desolated person, there is little you can do except take him firmly into your arms. To give some idea of the chaos raging in Paul's head, she draws a comparison with a mosaic that represents the human personality. 'When our mind experiences something that does not quite fit into the mosaic, the trick is to take a couple of pieces out, clean them and carefully put them back. This is how the pattern of the mosaic is restored, how the event is mentally absorbed. But with Paul the whole mosaic blew up in one go. To get everything back in its proper place is a process which takes years, and you can only hope that you have correctly labelled the pieces as they were before the explosion.'

Above all, Verhoeven's crisis had shown his inner need to be an artist. Inevitably, the event had an enormous effect on his work. Fifteen years later, he shared this religious episode in his life with his cinema audience. In the film *Spetters* (1980), Maja, the main character's girlfriend, has a similar experience when her love for him is no longer returned. Verhoeven says, 'She tries to get a grip on her life by becoming part of that curious Pentecostal church community. In that sense, she is a kind of off-shoot of myself – although in my case it was more of an economic and artistic rejection.' Rien is a motocross rider who becomes an invalid after an accident. Maja takes him, more or less against his will, to a meeting of the Pentecostal church and asks the preacher to heal him.

The emotive way in which Verhoeven visualizes the moment of faith healing in *Spetters* reveals the impression his own visit to the Pentecostal church had made on him. A bit of light flaring in the camera lens creates a halo above Rien's head. In the background the canvas of the church tent flaps violently in the wind and there is thunder and lightning, as if the Holy Ghost really has descended to the believers. Like Verhoeven, Rien finally refuses to accept the idea and mentally rebels. Halfway through, his state of ecstasy is abruptly broken, and he falls back distraught into his wheelchair. 'The effect this whole episode had on me was that, as an antidote, I started to film in a hyper-realistic way. My work became my anchor in reality. Hence the need to show everything so explicitly: the fucking and the pricks and the shit and the drugs and the violence. In the Netherlands people always got enormously worked up about that, and of course there was an element of provocation in it – but the background to it was my always wanting to have both feet firmly on the ground. Fear, it was fear that I might slip away mentally. This is why my films have always been firmly anchored in reality instead of ideas.'

That element, he says, has always been underestimated.

Rutger Hauer as the medieval knight Floris.

Floris and Sindala watch Verhoeven demonstrate an
attack with a sword.

Chapter 5

In the Saddle at Last

The rack, pestilence, the gallows, sword fights and a masked executioner – the first example of Verhoeven's new taste for realism was a children's television series set in the Middle Ages and named after its main character Floris, the Ivanhoe of the Low Countries. There were twelve episodes of his adventures, and *Floris* became a phenomenon for anyone growing up in the Netherlands in the 1960s.

The leading role was given to the unknown twenty-four-year-old actor Rutger Hauer. Although his Floris acted clumsily in the presence of ladies, his photograph was pinned to the wall of every Dutch child's bedroom by the autumn of 1969. Every Sunday evening, the opening credits would show Floris and his mystical sidekick Sindala galloping across the sand-dunes of the Veluwe region, driven on by the clarion call of the title music by Julius Steffaro and the Metropole Orchestra; in every Dutch living room, expectations rose with equal speed. 'Let's go!' Floris would call heroically, on his way to another half-hour adventure. And while in the British television series *Ivanhoe* (1957–8) the sword fights had made the walls of the cardboard castle tremble, the locations in *Floris* were real fortresses; unlike Roger Moore's knight in the TV series, Rutger Hauer did all the stunts himself, including diving from a turret into a moat. At that time, the Netherlands had only two television channels, colour television was fairly new, and a Dutch hero of the calibre of Floris had never been seen. So it is not surprising that his adventures were acted out in the playground by a whole generation.

For Paul Verhoeven, the series offered an excellent opportunity for making himself known to a larger public as an action-oriented director. The commission came from the Nederlandse Televisie Stichting (Dutch Television Foundation) or NTS, whose Head of Children's Programming, Ben Klokman, had liked Verhoeven's film about the marines, recognizing in it the dynamism indispensable for directing an adventure series. By now, Verhoeven was thirty years old and the commission came as a relief. Although his own plans were not getting off the ground, the television series gave him the chance to work with a professional crew on a story that reminded him of one of the comic-strip heroes of his youth, Eric de Noorman (Eric the Viking). Thus he was able to break out of the rut of the 'attic years' during which, according to his wife Martine, he 'regularly buried his head in the carpet.'

After the crisis of the unplanned pregnancy – prelude to Verhoeven's psychotic episode – he and Martine Tours were married on 7 April 1967. As their economic prospects were not particularly bright, the couple went to live at 12 Douzastraat in Leiden, where Martine had a student room on a floor belonging to the delicatessen next door. A black iron stove heated the sparsely furnished space; there was a bed, a cooker and a television. Their income was 380 guilders per month, Martine's grant as a psychology student. For his graduation, Verhoeven's parents had given him a Morris Minor, in which he and Martine went to the beach at Scheveningen or to the cinema. These outings usually concluded with a shared shish kebab or a portion of satay, since restaurants were not an option on their tight budget.

The fee of 2300 guilders per month that Paul Verhoeven was to receive for shooting *Floris* was the key to unheard-of luxury, and at the same time confirmed his talent. Although he had had no success in finding backers for his completed script of Simon Vestdijk's *Anton Wachter*, Verhoeven remained convinced of his vocation as a director, and would not consider earning a living as a cameraman or by making commercials. This would have been an obvious solution to his meagre finances. Instead, he preferred to spend his time planning new film projects. His wife supported him in this uncompromising stance. She was six years younger, but with her analytical mind and strong constitution she gave Paul his day-to-day grip on reality – a sobering role she was to continue to play in their relationship.

So it must have been with some relief that on the morning of 15 July 1968 she saw him leave for the set of *Floris* for the first time. He was to film the story of the nobleman Floris van Rosemond, who returns to the Low Countries in 1500 after a long sea journey. He finds his castle besieged and used as a toll house by Maarten van Rossum, stooge of the villainous Duke Karel van Gelre. Together with Sindala, the Oriental magician he had met on his journey around the world, Floris sides with the Burgundians in support of Lord Oldenstein, and from the latter's castle they make impromptu attacks on van Rossum and his well-equipped army throughout the series.

The creator of Floris and Sindala was Gerard Soeteman (born 1936), who after studying Dutch at the University of Leiden had become a translator of foreign television productions at the NTS. Following the example of the Belgian television channel BRT, the NTS director Carel

Enkelaar had decided to commission a spectacular children's series along the lines of *Johan en de Alvenman* or the French *Thierry la Fronde*, romantic and popular stories of knights he had always watched with envy. The proposed writers were the children's authors Miep Diekmann and An Rutgers Van der Loeff – both very well known but with little television experience. When that collaboration came to grief, Gerard Soeteman was given a chance. Because he had translated children's series from abroad, he had been able to make a close study of the scripts.

For his début as a scriptwriter Soeteman chose the late medieval period from around 1500. This turbulent time – with its fear of the plague, invention of gunpowder, magic, mystery and courtly love – was a perfect setting for the picaresque adventures of the main characters Floris and Sindala. To ensure that the background was historically correct, Soeteman often consulted *Herfsttij der Middeleeuwen* (*The Autumn of the Middle Ages*), the *magnum opus* of the renowned historian Johan Huizinga. Putting the story on paper was one thing, but who was going to put the story on film? Ben Klokman and the proposed producer Max Appelboom made a suggestion after three episodes of the script had been completed. Gerard Soeteman says, 'The name Paul Verhoeven didn't mean anything to me until I was introduced to him. He turned out to be that slight boy with small glasses who always sat opposite me in the library when I was studying at Leiden from 1955 to 1962. We never said a word to each other in all that time. Actually, he always irritated me – I thought he was a bit of a twit.'

Nevertheless, they started to work together. Soeteman submitted a script, Verhoeven put some scribbles on it and together with Kees Holierhoek (the scriptwriter he had worked with on *Anton Wachter)* made some changes to the dialogue – after which the script was double the length and had to be sent back to Soeteman. But since the concept of the series was strong, it was not difficult to reduce the story to a manageable length. The archetypal characters of Floris and Sindala seemed to complement each other well; the way in which their roles were distinguished was reminiscent of the Lone Ranger and Tonto. Where the bony knight Floris would say boldly, 'You'll pay for that. Say your last prayer!', Sindala limited himself to quasi-philosophical utterances such as 'The will of a master is sharper than a spur, my friend, and more castigating than a whip.' Gerard Soeteman: 'The series was organized according to the iron laws of drama. After a specified number of minutes, the tension had to be raised almost mechanically, and a scene was usually rounded off with a joke.'

The character of Sindala as the clever Oriental – his name is an anagram of Saladin, the legendary Arab strategist – was, in fact, a nod towards the hippy culture of the time. 'Sindala was a mystic, though for the most part he delivered himself of traditional proverbs. He was a good counterpoint to Floris, the dumb Teuton who would first give someone a good beating and then think about it.' Sindala was to be played by Jos Bergman, an actor whose previous experience was in musicals; he had grown a mysterious goatee for his performance. The dumb Teuton was assigned to Rutger Hauer, although this charismatic actor had not been Verhoeven's first choice. Initially, he had cast Carol van Herwijnen as Floris, but the offer of a stage role had taken priority. Through the mediation of Gerard Soeteman, he asked Rutger Hauer at the last minute. A friend of Soeteman, Wiebe Hogendoorn, a teacher at the Amsterdam theatre school, had suggested his ex-student Hauer on hearing the profile of the character: 'A big blond hunk who dares to do anything.' At the time, Hauer was doing theatre for farmers and country people in the province of Frisia. His company, the Noorder Compagnie, aimed to bring culture to the countryside. By now, Soeteman had been promoted from translator to editor of the NTS arts programme *Open Oog* (*Open Eye*), and he decided to shoot a programme about the theatre group in order to meet the twenty-four-year-old Rutger Hauer in passing. 'The first thing he said was, "Have you got any money on you? I'm starving." In the Frisian countryside everything was closed at night, but Rutger knew someone who was doing a little catering, where you could get a hot meal in the living room.'

Because Hauer's big old Harley Davidson wouldn't start, he was given a lift by the film crew. 'When we arrived at the establishment, a woman whose accent we could hardly understand opened a tin of peas from the cupboard and served them with an enormous steak. Rutger shouted that he was a vegetarian but if it came to it, he could forget that he was. Open-mouthed, we watched those great square paws of his as he wolfed down that steak in no time. I immediately thought, "He could be it, this Hauer."'

Since Rutger Hauer seemed better at jumping off horses than speaking, 85 per cent of his lines were scrapped. This was not a problem, as he had other qualities. Of the twelve swords specially made in Italy, he single-handedly broke eleven. Producer Max Appelboom remembers: 'Of course, Rutger was little more than a stunt man then. Early in the morning he would exercise to keep his body in good condition. He would come back with his nose dripping with sweat and enter the make-up tent. We would say, "Good morning, Rutger," and he would merely mumble, "Huh?" But even though Rutger was not a Big Actor, he did have the charisma of a star, someone like John Wayne. As the king of the B-movie he just used to mutter his lines – but with a very beautiful, tough, steel face.'

Verhoeven had also noticed Rutger Hauer's toughness, but for a long time he doubted his abilities as an actor. 'There are a lot of scenes in *Floris* that make you think "Oh oh, well well, dear dear", but during the six months of shooting you could see Rutger getting better and better, and becoming more aware of the camera.' Eventually Verhoeven had so much fun directing Hauer that it became at the expense of the other protagonist Sindala. 'The series was originally called *Floris en de Fakir* [Floris and the Fakir] and in the beginning I maintained that balance visually, but I gradually noticed that the camera was shifting more towards Rutger Hauer. As a director I was led by his appearance.'

Verhoeven's admiration for Hauer would become evident in later feature films. As Fellini had done with Marcello Mastroianni and Truffaut with Jean-Pierre Léaud, Hauer became a vehicle for the director's self-expression. 'Not in an autobiographical sense, but as an alter ego. A fantasy of a person I could have been – or rather, would have liked to have been.' This evolution began with the adolescent-like Hauer playing Floris, through his more complex role as an artist in *Turks Fruit* (*Turkish Delight*, 1973), to his convincing performance in *Soldaat van Oranje* (*Soldier of Orange*, 1977), the role which was the springboard for his international career. Their collaboration came to an abrupt end in 1985 with *Flesh + Blood* – a kind of *Floris* for adults – but by that point both actor and director had achieved recognition. Until that time they had needed each other; a love born of necessity.

It was promising to be a sunny day when Paul Verhoeven appeared on location on 15 July 1968. They were going to do the shoot in the lake district of Loosdrecht and the sight of a complete film crew put him in good spirits. Everything was there: light, sound, camera. He had waited for this for a very long time. With cameraman Ton Buné and assistant producer Joop Visch, Verhoeven ran through the script, and then sent Floris and Sindala to the waterside. Scene One of the shooting schedule showed the heroes in a boat. It was with feigned self-confidence that the director called 'And . . . Action!'

Verhoeven had been given fourteen weeks' shooting time, but as early as the first day producer Appelboom realized that the schedule might be too tight for the director. 'Paul shot 1:32 that day.' This meant that of every 32 metres he filmed, he would use only one metre in the episode. 'I immediately sent my assistant to the chemist to get a tube of indigestion tablets because I was getting acute stomach pains. Paul asked, "What *is* allowed then?" I said, "1:6." He didn't want to know about that. Eventually we agreed on 1:12.'

Now that Verhoeven finally had the opportunity to realize his ambition, he seized it with both hands. It was only television, but it was shot on film and on location. The call sheet listed eighty actors, two thousand extras, seven horses, a monkey, goats, chickens and pigs. Verhoeven remembers the cutters sighing at the editing table. 'They said, "My God, it's a feature film!" Of course they all thought I was going to shoot it like a simple children's series, such as *Pipo the Clown*, on the moors behind the studios in Hilversum.' Verhoeven decided that in order to capture the medieval atmosphere, it was necessary to travel to the historic Belgian towns of Ghent and Bruges. The stunt men and special effects were a first for Dutch television. For the last episode, a big joust was organized.

Max Appelboom felt that the inexperienced Verhoeven had everything under control. 'He rarely hesitated. Paul is a rambler on the set. He walks around a lot, things going round and round in his head until he is clear: "That's how we'll do this shot."' And then there is that fanaticism. There is a very revealing photograph of Verhoeven taken during the shooting of *Floris*. He is holding a sword in his hand and triumphantly thrusting it into the sky. He seems to be shouting, 'No mercy.' It is addressed directly to his troops. And he means it. Max Appelboom continues, 'I was talking to one of the actors outside Oldenstein Castle when I suddenly heard terrible screams. Actor Tim Beekman, who plays one of van Rossum's sergeants, comes running out in full regalia. Paul Verhoeven is running after him. "He wants to murder me! That man wants to murder me!" screeches Beekman. It turns out that in the story the sergeant has fallen into the hands of the Floris camp, where he is given a good beating. Paul was going to show Rutger Hauer how to kick someone's face in with his foot. He did it with such abandon that the sergeant thought it was his final hour. But it had to be realistic, didn't it?'

Everyone involved in the making of *Floris* has his own anecdotes about the series, which became legendary in the world of broadcasting. This was not only because of its later success, but because of the unprecedented number of calamities that occurred during the shooting. Firstly, the budget was exceeded by nearly 1 million guilders, a fortune in those days. The series – which to the producer's regret was shot in black and white because of the small budget (this later hampered foreign sales, as Europe had just changed to colour television) – had been allocated 355,000 guilders, but eventually cost 1.2 million. This was not so much the fault of the director as of the small print in the old-fashioned, broadcasting statutes, which resulted in an unexpected and merciless increase in overheads. In practice, it meant that the sets and facilities that would normally be obtained from a joint department serving all television broadcasting companies, and which the makers of *Floris* had counted on during their calculations, now had to be paid for. The statutes said that if one did not work in the television studios, but on film and on location, one was not eligible to use that joint department. Appelboom: 'That's when the big figures started to hit me.'

Every week the NTS accountant Jan Herselman appeared on the set to count the receipts. Shooting time was extended from fourteen weeks to eight months, since no one in the Netherlands had experience of making a series of twelve episodes in such a large-scale setting – not even Appelboom, the most experienced. In 1948 he had produced the first Dutch feature film after the war: *Nederlands in 7 Lessen* (*Dutch in 7 Lessons*) about the post-war reconstruction, with a very young Audrey Hepburn as a KLM stewardess. In 1953 Appelboom left to pursue a career in Hollywood. He built up a modest existence as a scriptwriter for radio and television shows, and in the mid-sixties returned to the Netherlands to work as a freelance producer.

But Appelboom's experience counted for nothing when the production was confronted with unforeseen circumstances. They had to work with 'direct sound' on the set, but when the wind blew in the wrong direction, they could hear the boats hooting on the nearby Rhine and shooting had to be abandoned for the day. During a crowd scene on the Ginkelse moors near Arnhem they suddenly found themselves in the midst of a military exercise. A flu epidemic followed, then a mutiny over the bad food. Hans Culeman, who played the role of Maarten van Rossum, main opponent of Floris and Sindala, was struck by a bad attack of stage fright; stunt man Hammy de Beukelaer had to remove him from a very tall wardrobe at home, and he was transported to the set by ambulance. Jos Bergman disappeared in mid-December for a serious operation: during a mental crisis he had cut his wrists. Continuity was threatened by the changing weather conditions. The contracts of actors who had been expected back in the theatre long since had to be bought off. This chaos was symptomatic of inexperience in film-making.

But the shooting of *Floris* continued, as it had long since passed the point of no return. 'It was, in fact, four feature films,' says Verhoeven. 'I did have a shock at the beginning – it was so difficult. I thought, "Jesus, is *this* the choice I have made for my life?" As I remember it, the first months were fraught with crisis. I did not have that much experience. I looked up to the actors quite a lot. For me, as a student from Leiden, the whole environment had something of Sodom and Gomorrah – dangerous women and homosexuals. Welcome to the perverse, decadent world of film.' In addition to the refined acting techniques of established actors, the director became acquainted with the sharp guys in the Hammy de Beukelaer stunt team. 'Hammy was a revelation to me. One of those hard-boiled guys from Amsterdam. He would hold out his hand when the horses were shitting, then he would come up to me and say, "There's a little cake for you, Paul. Pure nature – oats and grass, no rotting meat or stinking fish – the purest you can get."'

De Beukelaer, a square-shouldered kind of guy, was not only the leader of the stunt team, but in charge of the horses. He partly blames the shooting delays on the fact that, although it was a series about knights, most of the actors, with the exception of Rutger Hauer, didn't know how to ride a horse at all – despite the fact that they had said that they could on their application forms. 'Jos Bergman, who played Sindala, had a chronic fear of those animals. He would come out in a cold sweat if he came anywhere near them. He should have had a big nag, a strong cart horse, just like Floris, but we managed to get Jos a very small horse: Wampie, the little fjord horse.' The animal often escaped. One night during shooting Wampie made off and landed in a nearby army camp, where it stood in the lieutenant-colonel's pea soup. The medieval soldiers had to do a fair amount of negotiating to appease their twentieth-century colleagues.

However difficult the shooting may have been, the reception the series was given more than compensated. On Monday 6 October 1969, immediately after *Floris*'s first appearance on Dutch television, the influential television journalist Nico Scheepmaker wrote: 'Just like you, I have seen only the first episode. But I thought it was excellent. Well filmed, very reasonably acted (certainly by comparison with what we are used to in that department in the Netherlands), most skilfully edited (Jan Bosdriesz) and very well directed by Paul Verhoeven. Of course, they have not gone off the beaten track of *Robin Hood* and *Ivanhoe*, but the quality of this first episode was no less than that of the aforementioned foreign examples.'

Although the staccato narrative pace was sometimes marred by the camera suddenly zooming in – a much-used sixties technique and intended for dynamic close-ups in moments of danger – as a whole, *Floris* was surprisingly well constructed. Highlights included the episodes about the magic realist painter and historical figure, Jeroen Bosch; the eerie doctors with their pestilence hoods in 'De Vrijbrief' ('The Permit'), and the final episode's double bill, 'De Byzantijnse Beker' ('The Byzantine Cup'), in which two knights, Roland and Govert, go to the sickbed of Maid Isabella, who is coveted by both of them. They attack each other after whispered tones: 'How is she, Doctor?'

'Bad.'

'Can we do anything?'

'Get a priest.'

The dialogue usually sounded as if it had been written in bubbles for a comic strip, as did the many 'oohhhs' and 'aahhs' from the villains as

Floris violently taught *them* another lesson. This was precisely the right tongue-in-cheek tone for the series, since the main characters not only walked around in doublets, but demonstrated a level of civilization that was 'medieval'. But the series was not to everyone's satisfaction, as the following letters from viewers demonstrate:

Dear Sirs, surrounded by my three children of eleven, nine and five years old, I have just watched *Floris*. I am very tolerant and I understand that not all programmes are intended for children, but it filled me with such horror that I could not control my emotions and, in the scene where an old man is tortured, I switched off the TV.
 E. Engelbert, Aalst.

If the odd person is hit, if artifice is used, if people fall through a table or are thrown into the water (shallow), that's as may be, but what we saw yesterday was too terrible.
 D. Schermer, Enkhuizen.

Worried parents were in the minority, although an entire national radio programme was devoted to the violence in *Floris* – the sort of fate that none of Verhoeven's later productions were to escape. Scoring an average of 7.4 out of 10, *Floris* became the most highly appreciated and widely viewed Dutch television series of 1969. The first episode drew 2.8 million viewers, and the third 3.6 million people of fifteen years and over. Since this was first and foremost a children's series, the number of people tuning in must have been considerably higher, but children were not included in the ratings.

Looking back, Paul Verhoeven says, 'The series had a warmth which my later films never had. For me, that's what makes it so sympathetic. Years later, I saw some of it again, and when at the end of the last episode Floris and Sindala ride off together, I still found it very moving.' The last shot of the series shows Floris triumphantly holding the Byzantine Cup. He lets his horse rear once more, waves and turns away from the camera. Then he spurs his horse and, together with Sindala, heads off for new adventures. As is often the case with television series of an individual character, *Floris* achieved cult status in the 1990s. The series was repeated a number of times on television, and was shown again in its entirety at the Nederlandse Filmdagen of Utrecht in 1994, the annual Dutch Film Days festival in Utrecht. The thirty-something members of the audience had difficulty in keeping dry eyes on this occasion, as they saw not merely Floris the knight but the lost innocence of their childhood.

It was a pity, therefore, that the heroes themselves did not want to be reminded of the series. Jos Bergman made an unsuccessful suicide attempt not long after shooting was completed, losing the sight of one eye. After a period of drug rehabilitation, he decided to turn his back on the acting profession to work as a nurse in Amsterdam. Rutger Hauer, who during the Dutch Film Days festival was honoured with a retro-spective on the occasion of his fiftieth birthday, said that he 'had always been surprised at the success of *Floris*. There was really quite a lot of humour in it.' Now that he had made numerous films in Hollywood, the memory of *Floris* seemed more insignificant to him than his earliest admirers could ever have suspected. And yet his downbeat remark sounded a little absurd. It was as if Clint Eastwood had just denounced his role as Rowdy Yates in *Rawhide*, Diana Rigg had not wanted to be reminded of Emma Peel, or William Shatner no longer wished to be rec-ognized as *Star Trek*'s Captain Kirk. To the youngsters of the 1960s, Rutger Hauer's appearance as Floris had been of that order of magni-tude. He was nothing less than the first Dutch television hero, and was regarded as not so much an actor as the daring but much admired boy next door.

For Paul Verhoeven, the success of *Floris* had been cleansing. Although his fear of social failure had played tricks on him before, he now thought it possible to make a living as a film-maker in the Netherlands. The series even brought a modest improvement in his living standards, since it enabled him and Martine to exchange the attic room in the Douzastraat in Leiden for a flat (price 31,000 guilders) in a suburb of the same city. Four floors up, no lift, but with a balcony. At the same time as studying, Martine was now working as a freelance psychologist – so that the lean 'attic years' were a thing of the past. This was not immediately apparent from the way the flat was furnished; in between the wicker chairs and the do-it-yourself cupboards, the prize item was a new red leather sofa. On the wall were paintings by Andrew van Nouhuys, and underneath an aquarium full of guppies.

While making *Floris*, Verhoeven had found a partner in crime in the shape of scriptwriter Gerard Soeteman, with whom he could realize his future film ideas. Unlike Kees Holierhoek, the writer with whom Verhoeven had tried to get *Anton Wachter* off the ground and who was specializing more and more in small-scale television dramas, Gerard Soeteman thought in terms of the big screen. For Verhoeven, who since his earliest collaboration with Jan van Mastrigt had realized that devis-ing stories was not his strength, an association with a like-minded scriptwriter was indispensable. A script was the necessary basis for his work.

This is how the collaboration with Gerard Soeteman operated until 1985. For every new film, Soeteman gave Verhoeven a first version writ-ten with a fountain pen in an exercise book, after which the director sat down in front of his typewriter to work on a second draft. In doing so, he concentrated especially on the dialogues, and added filmic, visual elements. This revised script was usually too long, so Gerard would go through it again with a felt-tip pen. 'Like a game of ping-pong, we kept hitting it backwards and forwards until the script was finished to our mutual satisfaction.'

It was a method that had worked successfully with *Floris*, but it did have a down side, however. The knight's adventures may have had excellent viewing figures, but a 1 million-guilder overrun on the budget (highlighted in the press) was disastrous for Verhoeven and Soeteman's reputations. Soeteman remembers, 'Wherever we knocked on the door with new projects, they cringed. You could see them thinking, "There are those expensive idiots again."'

They were never short of plans. There was a proposal for a six-part television drama with Rembrandt paintings as its starting point – the stories would be transposed to the present. The episode about the painting *De Man met de Gouden Helm* (*The Man with the Golden Helmet*), for example, would be about a dishonest marines officer whom Verhoeven had come across during his military service. 'That's what we went on the road with,' Soeteman continues, 'but they all thought our plans would mean the end of the drama budget for the next few years.'

They also explored feature-film subjects. There was an idea for a medieval drama, a *Floris* for adults, to be called *De Landsknechten* (*The Lansquenets*). Fifteen years later, this would form the basis for *Flesh + Blood*. And there was also a plan to make a film about Hans van Z. and Ouwe Nol, a Dutch criminal twosome whose trial in 1969 was the most notorious since the Second World War. It dominated public consciousness because it revealed the most shocking details about the duo's three robberies with murder. As well as a serial killer, the twenty-six-year-old Hans van Z. also turned out to be a necrophile. The fact that they had killed their victims – an eighty-year-old man from Utrecht, a forty-seven-year-old man from Heeswijk, and a thirty-seven-year-old woman from Amsterdam – with a lead pipe made the court reports even more gruesome. Verhoeven and Soeteman began to go through the articles about the case in the *Haagsche Courant* newspaper in the hope of distilling an exciting script. 'We went three times,' Paul Verhoeven remembers, 'but every time we came out after an hour or two feeling sick.'

One of the scenes they reconstructed showed the transvestite Hans van Z. on his bed, reading a book about the Holocaust and painting his nails bright red with the utmost concentration. He is disturbed in these activities by a girl, whom he murders without hesitation. Afterwards, he lights a cigarette and makes love to the dead body. 'Based on real life,' Verhoeven stresses. 'We thought, what do we do with this? Can we change this to make it a bit more positive?' Perhaps Ouwe Nol offered more potential. 'But we couldn't find anything positive in Ouwe Nol either. He was a crook of the first order. So we said, forget it. It's simply too sad, not a soul would go and see it. It was so depressing I couldn't work on it any more, which I must say is very unusual for me.'

So the director who later in his film career would be given the title of 'Sultan of Shock' by *Time* magazine discovered that for him there were limits to the realistic content of his work.

Since he couldn't get a new film project off the ground, Verhoeven decided at the end of 1970 to occupy himself with a project he had previously started with Kees Holierhoek: *De Worstelaar (The Wrestler)*, a twenty-minute burlesque specially devised for Hammy de Beukelaer, chief stunt man on *Floris*. It was a story about a young man (Wim Zomer) who has an affair with the sexy wife (Mariëlle Fiolet) of a sturdy publican who is also a feared wrestler. The young man is playing a dangerous game. His father (Bernhard Droog) warns him, but then nearly brings disaster upon himself when the wrestler–publican thinks that the father has his eye on his sweetheart.

The film was to be shot by cameraman Jan de Bont. He was a member of the '1,2,3-groep' ('1,2,3 Group'), a gathering of puppies from the Nederlandse Filmacademie that included Frans Bromet and René Daalder; he was building up a reputation as an inspired cinematographer, which was why Paul Verhoeven asked for him. The subsidy for the film came from the Ministry for Culture, Recreation and Social Work (CRM), but before a single metre was shot Paul Verhoeven saw his leading actor, Hammy de Beukelaer, incapacitated. His character is introduced inside a wrestling ring, but as he bent over to step through the ropes into the ring, his back suddenly seized up. Hammy de Beukelaer remembers: 'Totally locked! "Paul," I said, "I've got lumbago." "What?" he answered furiously. "You can't have! The film!" and he stomped off. After that, I never saw Paul again.'

De Beukelaer was replaced by Jon Bluming, a he-man of the same build. When *De Worstelaar* went into circulation as part of a package of five short feature films made by up-and-coming Dutch directors, the critic Bob Bertina wrote in *De Volkskrant* newspaper for 4 June 1971: 'The only carefree film-maker without a message was Paul Verhoeven, who made Kees Holierhoek's light and enjoyable script into an amusing film which can go straight into the cinemas (with success). Verhoeven proves that even in a provincial Dutch city you can make a burlesque with stock Dutch figures. The humour, in word and image, of the Verhoeven/Holierhoek duo constantly approaches the banal. Its strength lies in the details.'

For Verhoeven, *De Worstelaar* was a good exercise in genre. The light

71

touch he used for that short film he would also use for the project which, as if by magic, was presented to him on a plate in the summer of 1970. He received a telephone call from a woman who introduced herself as Ineke van Weezel, assistant to the Munich-based Dutch film producer Rob Houwer. They were looking for a director for a new feature film and they had rather liked *Floris*. Would Verhoeven like to come and talk to Rob Houwer, accompanied by Gerard Soeteman? They made an appointment to meet in Bergen, in the province of North Holland, at the producer's holiday home.

What Paul Verhoeven knew about Rob Houwer was mostly based on the news items and interviews he had read about the thirty-two-year-old producer. A former student of theatre and advertising, he was portrayed as someone who had made a name for himself by setting up a medium-sized film production company in West Germany. Initially, Houwer's ambition had been to make a career as a director (he was one of the signatories of the Manifesto of the Oberhausener Gruppe in 1962, the inspiration for the *Neue Deutsche Film*) and in that capacity he had made his début with the short film *Hondsdagen* in 1959. He decided however that his talents were more suited to the financial side of the film industry, partly because there were few top people in that field in Germany or the Netherlands. As he told *Elseviers Weekblad* in April 1968, he was hoping to become a 'creative producer with a background in directing and an eye for the business and artistic opportunities of a project – a kind of Sam Spiegel.'

The magazine presented Houwer as a shrewd and sometimes petty businessman. Tough, bold and with a nose for what the 'mainstream Dutch public' wanted to see – this was how he liked to display himself in the press, unhampered by modesty. Paul Verhoeven was to collaborate with Houwer on five feature films, but after their first meeting, at Houwer's holiday home in Bergen, he had his doubts.

Rob Houwer appeared to have bought the rights to a very successful book, *Wat Zien Ik . . . Gesprekken met Blonde Greet (What's That I See? . . . Conversations with Blonde Greet)*, containing 'outpourings on Amsterdam life by a woman' – in this case, 'life' meant prostitution in Amsterdam's famous red-light district. The author of the book was Albert Mol, a dancer, actor, cabaret artiste and television personality who achieved national fame in the 1950s as the leader of the orchestra in the Dutch feature film *Fanfare* (Bert Haanstra, 1958). His book, a collection of newspaper articles, had been published in 1965, and within a year it had been reprinted twenty-two times and had sold 360,000 copies. It was written in a broad Amsterdam vernacular and was not without humour – but it was on a totally different level from the novels of Vestdijk that Verhoeven had for so long wanted to film.

The book mainly consists of spicy stories about the peculiar preferences of Blonde Greet's clientele: for instance, the man who wanted to play doctors, or the male prostitute who preferred to dress up in a sailor suit. Much later, Mol would explain that Blonde Greet was an amalgam of characters he got to know when living in Amsterdam's red-light district; the prostitutes who indulged these games usually turned out to be transvestites who were unable to provide the usual hetero-sexual services.

An important source for *Wat Zien Ik* was a gay prostitute who called herself Leidse Willy, described by the author as a 'gigantic woman' – Mol claimed she told anecdotes that would make the Marquis de Sade blush. 'So vulgar that they couldn't be included in the book. For example, the one about the man who let a prostitute eat marzipan for two weeks and then served up the excrement to her on a dinner plate. With candlelight and romantic music.' Rob Houwer's idea to film *Wat Zien Ik* scared Soeteman and Verhoeven. Initially they had thought it a good idea to make a feature film in 35mm and in colour. Gerard Soeteman: 'Rob Houwer said, "You know what! We'll make it a porno film. We'll use all the has-been actors from abroad, who don't mind dropping their pants for two days for $5,000. We'll ask Orson Welles!" But we didn't think that was a good idea at all.'

Although pornography had always existed in the Netherlands, the sexual revolution which had hit the country meant these titles could now be seen above ground; 8mm and 16mm films containing nudity no longer had to be classified as naturist films.

Against this background, Houwer had conceived of *Wat Zien Ik* as a 'popular' sex comedy, but the proposal put Verhoeven in a real dilemma. He discussed it with Gerard Soeteman on the drive back from Bergen. Was Albert Mol's book the kind of thing to make your long dreamed-of feature-film début with? No, of course not – not if you'd always secretly wanted to film Vestdijk, or Louis Couperus's novel *Iskander* about Alexander the Great, for a wider public. On the other hand, what *was* the alternative? The current fashion was for navel-gazing, low-budget art films, the Dutch *Nouvelle Vague* productions that usually sent him to sleep. This imposed artiness in films increasingly irritated him. Whenever he felt that the Director's Vision was being rammed down the audience's throat, he preferred to leave the cinema. His realistic conclusion was what he was often to repeat in later interviews: 'As a film-maker in the Netherlands you have two chances: your first and your last.'

With Verhoeven torn between the pros and cons of *Wat Zien Ik*, it was Gerard Soeteman who finally made the decision, remarking that he could 'probably do something with the stories'. Verhoeven had to accept

Wat Zien Ik for what it was: work. He wondered whether as a director he would still dare to walk the streets without dark glasses after *Wat Zien Ik*. His wife Martine said that she thought he would – her remark was meant to sound encouraging.

There was one plus, however: Houwer had agreed to let Paul Verhoeven and Gerard Soeteman write the script in their own way – the porno idea was abandoned. But they still had to solve the problem of the fragmentary stories that made up *Wat Zien Ik*. While Verhoeven ventured out on to the Amsterdam quaysides to talk to street women, Soeteman looked for clues in the scientific study *De Arbeidsstructuur van de Prostitutie (The Labour Structure of Prostitution)* by J. W. Groothuyse, a physician with extensive experience in this area.

In late summer 1970, Verhoeven and Soeteman presented a forty-page outline for *Wat Zien Ik (Business Is Business*, 1971) at the Munich offices of Rob Houwer. The budget was no more than 600,000 guilders, of which the director received 10,000 guilders. 'The comedy genre is not one of creative chemistry,' Gerard Soeteman now says. 'It is about placing your effects. In my student days I did a lot of theatre, and we used to race through an entire Molière in three-quarters of an hour. That's when you see how humour works – you notice, for example, that people are always prepared to laugh at an anti-doctor joke. We put all those tricks into *Wat Zien Ik*. In the end, the skill in the writing and filming is carefully concealing those effects, otherwise they are not funny.'

The film was put together in the spring of 1971. The main location was the upstairs rooms of Blonde Greet. Again the cameraman was Jan de Bont. 'While filming,' the director remembers, 'I made very sure the acting didn't go over the top. That could easily have happened – it was that sort of material.'

Henk Molenberg, one of the many popular Dutch TV stars in this feature film, played a type who gets his kicks from dressing up as a maid and tidying up other people's mess in the brothel: 'What's that I see – dust?' Blonde Greet would snarl, and then give the maid a good beating. Molenberg remembers, 'Paul knew exactly what he wanted even then. He said, "You realize your head will be life-size on the screen – don't use theatre gestures, play with your eyes." We, the actors, thought Paul was rather a tough customer, certainly compared with what we were used to when we acted in the theatre. He could be unrelenting, but we did realize there was a lot at stake for him.'

Although most of *Wat Zien Ik* is what would now be called 'camp', in 1971 what it had to offer was an entertaining and fast-moving story. The film was edited to increase the pace, scenes following each other so quickly that the viewer had no chance to escape, let alone think about what was being offered. If the director and his team were overcome by depression during the editing – a recurring experience – there was at least the one moment they all thought hysterically funny. Blonde Greet is being courted by a cheerful fellow named Piet; she falls in love with him and he takes her to a smart chamber music recital at the Amsterdam Concertgebouw. A clash of cultures: the songs are rudely interrupted by Blonde Greet eating a large bar of chocolate. After many angry looks in her direction and a row with Piet, she leaves, insulted, scrambling out over the heads of the concertgoers. 'Very funny, but in the cinema this scene does not work at all. We overdid the editing.' But you never know for certain with comedy, Verhoeven says, and before the release of *Wat Zien Ik* he was plagued by sleepless nights.

To his amazement, after the première on 10 September 1971 there were long queues of people in front of the cinemas. He was even more astounded when during several showings he attended he saw the audience with tears streaming down their faces. Laughing. By the autumn of 1971 the attendance figures reached 2,358,946, which makes *Wat Zien Ik* the fourth most popular Dutch film ever.

The reviews were generally benevolent. 'At least it did not turn into horseplay,' Bob Bertina wrote in *De Volkskrant*. And *Het Parool* recorded, 'The director has managed to keep up the tempo, hardly skipping one detail from the book by Albert Mol, who also appears on screen . . . Verhoeven films fast but very effectively.'

However, Verhoeven knew that what he had made was on the slender side. In the *Algemeen Dagblad* of 10 November 1971 he expressed his anxiety that 'after the bewildering success of *Wat Zien Ik*, we may only be allowed to make films that are sex romps.' He was alluding to a film that had been premièred a few weeks after *Wat Zien Ik,* and which marked the real sexual liberation of the cinema: *Blue Movie*. Inspired by German 'sexploitation' films, director Wim Verstappen and producer Pim de la Parra claimed that the main reason for making *Blue Movie* was to blow apart the Dutch film censorship board (the Dutch MPAA). This work by the two PROVOs was interlaced with nude scenes to end all nude scenes. The action takes place in the Amsterdam suburb of Bijlmermeer, designed as the ultimate homage to the Dutch ideal of the sleepy, middle-class town. *Blue Movie* showed an entire tower block of residents who have casual sex in each other's apartments – the password for the participants was 'Have you got a cup of sugar?'

In May 1971 the film was denied public release. But on 28 July of the same year it was given the green light after an extensive report by the interested parties. The advertisements promptly said, '*Blue Movie* shows what *Wat Zien Ik* does not.' The film attracted 2.3 million people into the cinemas, making it the fifth most popular Dutch film of all time, immediately after *Wat Zien Ik*. The filmgoing public's craving for sex was obvious, and revenues were up into the millions. Producer Rob Houwer immediately suggested *Wat Zien Ik 2*, but Verhoeven was not interested. This time he wanted to tell a real story. He wanted to film the Jan Wolkers book *Turks Fruit*.

Wedding day, 7 April 1967.

Wat Zien Ik, 1971: Verhoeven observes Jan de Bont shooting the 'chicken client' of Blonde Greet.

Long queues in front of the cinema for *Wat Zien Ik*.

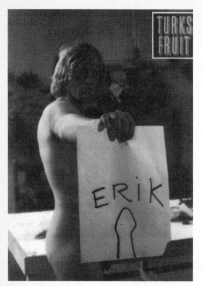

Turks Fruit: the 'angry young man' (Rutger Hauer) handing out a souvenir.

Turks Fruit: Paul Verhoeven with Jan de Bont, Monique van de Ven and Rob Houwer.

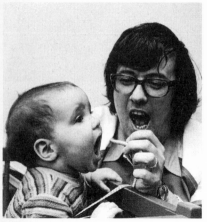

Paul Verhoeven with daughter Claudia at nine months, 1973.

Turks Fruit: the high pitch of romance.

Turks Fruit: Olga fears death, Erik comforts her.

Chapter 6

The Dutch Romeo and Juliet: *Turks Fruit*

The bohemian Jan Wolkers was everything the bourgeois Paul Verhoeven was not. This was obvious to the director when he met the writer and visual artist for the first time in Amsterdam in 1967. Wolkers was twelve years his senior, an author whose seemingly autobiographical prose was written in a plain, almost non-literary style, containing words that Verhoeven, as a former student from Leiden, would not normally use.

The main theme of Wolkers's work is the human desire to survive in an indifferent universe. His characters realize they are fighting a losing battle in the long term, and are motivated by this realization towards sexual vitality and a euphoric zest for life. They know it is essential to resist death while living, although Death constantly shows itself in apocalyptic visions and images of decay. In Wolkers's books, this fear of death is warded off with macabre jokes – which is why at least one critic wrote that 'because of the stench from it, his work should in future be sold in a fish shop.'

Admirers of Wolkers, whose numbers were increasing in literary circles in the 1960s, realized that his earthy prose had to be read as a reaction to the strict Calvinist beliefs of his parents, with their promise of a better life after death. The fact that this concept was of no consolation to the writer was obvious from the vigour with which he rejected every religious idea. Wolkers had a unique position in Dutch literature, because he demonstrated on every page of his work that he was living life to the full. Verhoeven had noticed that Wolkers's literary contemporaries, such as Harry Mulisch and W. F. Hermans, usually looked at the world from behind their desks, hiding themselves behind an academic approach. In this sense Wolkers had more in common with Henry Miller or Charles Bukowski, and because of his elemental qualities – and ferocious appearance – he had become Verhoeven's personal favourite. Thus Wolkers succeeded Simon Vestdijk, the refined and slightly esoteric writer Verhoeven had admired for so long. 'A robust man with style,' was Verhoeven's memory of his first meeting with Jan Wolkers.

'He completely knocked me out. For years I worried whether my work could ever reach his level. Street dancing instead of classical ballet.'

The purpose of Verhoeven's visit to Wolkers in 1967 was to propose the filming of his first prose work *Serpentina's Petticoat* (1961). In this book the writer had recorded his sometimes horrific war memories, illustrated with drawings he had made in the 'winter of hunger' in 1944. On publication of *Serpentina's Petticoat*, the critics had called it 'stories with the sparks flying', but also 'stories which radiate a pervasive sadism'. For Verhoeven, the Dionysian attitude Wolkers had to life fitted in with his own decision after his religious crisis to film in a starkly realistic way. This was why he proposed to Jan Wolkers that he adapt *Serpentina's Petticoat* for the big screen. As so often during the 'attic years', this turned out to be a doomed project. It was not until 1973 that Verhoeven managed to get a Wolkers adaptation into the cinemas.

What went wrong in 1967? During his visit to Wolkers's studio in Amsterdam, Verhoeven showed him the outline he had written of the *Serpentina's Petticoat* script. Wolkers, who liked Verhoeven's films *Eén Hagedis Teveel* and *Feest*, concluded that it was not so much his childhood memories that the director had put to paper but those of Verhoeven himself. They mentioned the German horses Verhoeven had seen in the playground of his father's school in Slikkerveer during the war; one of the animals, a grey horse, was to feature in an important scene. 'There is already one white horse in film history,' Jan Wolkers muttered, referring to Eisenstein's *October* (1928), and in a friendly but firm way showed Verhoeven the door.

Three years later Verhoeven showed up at the studio again. This time he had under his arm a copy of *Turks Fruit*, the passionate novel that Wolkers had published in November 1969. It had been a big hit: in four years it was reprinted thirty times and sold 300,000 copies. The story of the young sculptor's euphoric relationship with his girlfriend, and the pain of its collapse, was a firm favourite on student reading lists. It was producer Gijs Versluys who had asked whether *Turks Fruit* would work as a film.

Remembering his previous experience with Jan Wolkers, Verhoeven decided this time to ask the author himself to write the script. There was only one problem. Gijs Versluys had already asked for an appointment with the Productiefonds, and would have to come up with a script within three days. Did he have any objections? Inspired, Jan Wolkers set to work. But after bashing at his typewriter for twenty-four hours non-stop, he became disheartened, deciding that his efforts were pointless.

'Listen, guys, this really can't be done,' he said sombrely to the duo. Gijs Versluys said, 'Well, just give us these sheets then. At least I'll be able to show that we are working on it.' This remark infuriated the author.

'No, this is rubbish!' he thundered, and began to tear up the script while Verhoeven and Versluys were trying to pull the pages from his hands. The shreds whirled around the room. It was clear that the film of *Turks Fruit* would not materialize.

Shortly afterwards Verhoeven set to work on *Wat Zien Ik*, and the idea for *Turks Fruit* was pushed into the background. But his desire to film Wolkers's work received a new impulse in the autumn of 1971 when Gerard Soeteman, in a meeting with Houwer and Verhoeven, again brought up the subject of *Turks Fruit*. Now that *Wat Zien Ik* was a success, the scriptwriter and director felt they had earned the right to make a more daring production, a film in which Verhoeven would be able to develop himself as a film-maker. Verhoeven got his way. The third time he knocked on Jan Wolkers's door, everything clicked. Producer Houwer and Verhoeven took the writer out for a wintry walk. Within five minutes the deal was done. Jan Wolkers received 35,000 guilders for the rights. Gerard Soeteman was to write the script. Paul Verhoeven would be able to shoot the Wolkers film he had wanted to. Openmouthed, he had watched the bold way in which his producer had operated. 'Rob Houwer knows no equal for shrewdness. For a tiny sum he had persuaded Jan Wolkers to hand over the rights to *Turks Fruit*, and he had never even mentioned video exploitation, foreign distribution, television showings, soundtrack or any other spin-off of the film. A complete sell-out, of course.'

The others became aware of the consequences of this transaction only when the enormous success of *Turks Fruit* confirmed Verhoeven's long-held conviction that he was the director best equipped to handle Wolkers's work. In addition to being nominated for an Oscar in 1974, this explosive love story became the most successful Dutch film ever, a position it still holds today. *Turks Fruit* attracted an audience of 3,334,044 – which meant that one in three Dutch people over fourteen years of age went to see it. At that point, the recognition that he was a successful film-maker meant more to Verhoeven than the money. He liked to read the reviews, as he had never had such a reception before. After the Dutch première on 22 February 1973, Dr H. S. Visscher wrote in the *Trouw* newspaper, 'You come out having experienced the same emotional charge as when you close the book. I can think of no greater compliment.'

'The best Dutch film production so far,' was *Elsevier*'s opinion. *De Volkskrant* said of Paul Verhoeven, 'His talent, so clearly visible to insiders in *Wat Zien Ik*, has obviously been confirmed. He could be very significant for Dutch feature films.'

And after the American première in September 1973, the *Los Angeles Times* wrote: '*Turkish Delight* makes such an all-out assault on our bourgeois sensibilities that a second viewing may be essential to appreciate the full magnitude of its achievement . . . *Turkish Delight* stacks up as an imported Dutch treat that can be cited for its liberating impact in the same breath with *Last Tango in Paris* and *La Grande Bouffe*.' After his long march through the institutions which had begun with *Eén Hagedis Teveel*, Paul Verhoeven had at last been able to show himself as a film-maker of an international standard. In this, Jan Wolkers had showed him the way: 'street dancing instead of classical ballet'.

As well as being an accurate portrayal of Amsterdam in the 1970s, *Turks Fruit* also showed the director's ability to empathize, to put himself into the shoes of the main characters. Although Verhoeven had had a brief spell as a painter, his daily life was quite unlike that of the sculptor in the book, with its 'artistic' milieu and exceptionally turbulent love-life. These elements were Wolkers's, but the vitality with which his world is portrayed by the director is what gave *Turks Fruit* its infectious charm.

Unlike the rebellious Erik (played by Rutger Hauer) – who has all the time in the world to find his own way in the private universe of his workshop – home life was getting more complicated for the thirty-four-year-old Verhoeven. On 13 June 1972, a month before shooting began, his daughter Claudia was born, and he knew that he now had to assume the mantle of responsibility. Yet he had at least one thing in common with Jan Wolkers: Verhoeven moved with his family from Leiden to Oegstgeest, the author's birthplace. There, Verhoeven worked on the shooting script, with a photograph of the female lead Monique van de Ven – who plays Erik's beloved Olga – always on his desk. Verhoeven had decided that *Turks Fruit* would be his statement of cinematic freedom; a fiercely realistic story that would suit the tone of Jan Wolkers, about whom the *New York Times* once said that he 'wrote without sparing our morality or senses'. Now that Verhoeven's colleague Wim Verstappen had already exploded Dutch film censorship with his *Blue Movie*, self-censorship was no longer necessary.

As was usual in their collaboration, Gerard Soeteman wrote the first version of the script. He searched the novel for themes other than the zest for life so passionately displayed by the lovers Olga and Erik. Thinking it would be good for the film to have a specifically 'Dutch' scene, he shows the unveiling of a sculpture made by the main character, an event which even the Queen attends. Soeteman juxtaposes this scene of bureaucratic panic with one in which Olga dies of a brain tumour – at that time, his own father was dying an extremely unpleasant death from lung cancer. 'The comic and the tragic scene form a mirror-image within the script. To me, *Turks Fruit* was not so much about eroticism as coming to terms with the loss of someone very dear to you.'

The film-makers were further helped in their understanding of Jan Wolkers by the book *Werkkleding* (*Work Clothes*) which the writer had published in 1971. This contained newspaper cuttings, posters, letters from admirers and critics, diary notes and lectures, but also offered a new perspective on Wolkers's career through the many photographs from his private collection. Much of the detail given in *Werkkleding* has been accurately transferred to the film, including the religious images Wolkers had made as a student in the caves at Valkenburg, as well as his later sculptures. Wolkers had also included photographs of his former lovers; in *Turks Fruit* he has the main character snip off locks of his girlfriend's pubic hair as a souvenir.

During the pre-production period it seemed far from easy to write a script based on *Turks Fruit*. The very first sentence of the book was in the first person.

I was in a pretty awful mess after she left me. I lay between my dirty sheets all day and stuck up nude pictures of her by my face so I could imagine her long eyelashes moving as I jacked off.

The novel derived much of its strength from this first-person form, but it was an unreliable perspective for a film adaptation. 'We suspected', Verhoeven explains, 'that Jan portrayed the almost autobiographical main character in *Turks Fruit* more positively than he is in reality. He was a rascal underneath, and that was the sort of person we wanted the narrator to be, because it would be much more interesting for the film. Not a lily-white hero but someone with a shadowy side.'

In addition to this ambiguity about the moral qualities of the main character, there was another problem with the adaptation of the novel. Wolkers's book has a collage-like style; it is a collection of flashbacks and flash forwards, with continuous jumps in time. Only at the end of the book do all the strands come together. After seeing the film *Slaughterhouse Five* (1972), Verhoeven and Soeteman decided not to tamper with the non-linear story line. In the same way as Kurt Vonnegut had done in his novel, the director of the film version, George Roy Hill, has the main character Billy Pilgrim travel through time at any given moment, even landing him on the fictitious planet Tralfamadore. Verhoeven and Soeteman felt that if a Hollywood film could afford to do this, they could certainly do it in the Netherlands.

In the end, the story line of the film more or less follows that of the novel. The action begins in the present. This is followed by a very long flashback. After that loop is closed, the story is concluded in the present. At the beginning the audience sees the young artist Erik, played by Rutger Hauer, lying in his completely neglected workshop. He has been abandoned by Olga, and has malicious fantasies about how he will kill her and her new lover. Because of his great passion for Olga, he intersperses these moments of despair with lustful recollections of her physical appearance. In the first ten minutes of the story he tries to rid himself of the pain of losing Olga by making love to a variety of women – a hopeless quest, since none can match up to Olga.

To flesh out her character, there follows a long flashback which explains how Erik first met Olga in the south of the country, near the tourist village of Valkenburg. After completing a dubious sculpture commission, Erik is hitchhiking along the motorway and she picks him up. Soon they are making love in the car. In the heat of the moment Erik's member is caught in the zip of his jeans. It is a small accident compared with what happens moments later, when the car shoots off the road: a total write-off. Olga's mother, a typical Dutch shopkeeper with a domestic appliance store, sees Erik as a trouble-maker and forbids him to see her daughter. Their love is unstoppable, however. They get married, and then follow months of lust and sexual hysteria – albeit poetically portrayed. The mother continues to put pressure on the relationship, and eventually Olga leaves Erik for a respectable bourgeois accountant her mother wants her to have. Olga justifies her behaviour by saying that Erik's wild life-style is driving her mad, but perhaps she abandons Erik because the brain tumour is already doing its destructive work. Gradually the tumour changes her personality.

The third part of the film takes place eight months later. Erik bumps into Olga in a smart department store in Amsterdam. Mentally, she has deteriorated. She collapses in the store; she has an operation, for which her head is shaved. During his hospital visit it is clear how much Erik's lust has transformed into unselfish love. He reads her twee stories from women's magazines, brings her Turkish delight, and buys a wig for her bald head. Nevertheless, the inevitable happens: Olga dies. Erik leaves, throwing the wig into a refuse bin. The viewer knows that though his life is starting again, the wound will never heal. Fade out.

Verhoeven knew that by structuring the action of *Turks Fruit* in this way, he was adopting a typically European way of story-telling. 'An American film always has a central question: Does he get her back or not? Is she going to murder him or not? Do they catch *The Fugitive* or does he slip through the net? From beginning to end the entire film is subservient to that one question. In many European films, such as *Turks Fruit*, the incidents are not so deterministic. The events are anecdotal, though not without logic. Real life is more of a collage and much more chaotic than the average American script. But in the absence of a driving dramaturgy, you have to use other narrative techniques.'

Verhoeven had chosen to tell the story at the greatest possible speed.

Turks Fruit contains about 1190 shots, which means an average length of six seconds, the kind of sharp cutting from one image to the next which was not used until the music videos of the 1980s. This may be compared with his later, highly stylized film, *De Vierde Man* (*The Fourth Man*), which consisted of 600 shots with an average length of twelve seconds. By orchestrating *Turks Fruit* in this compact way, the director found a filmic equivalent of Wolkers's staccato narrative style. To improve the 'street cred' of the film, cameraman Jan de Bont suggested shooting all the scenes with a hand-held camera.

With this semi-documentary style, the torrid tempo of the image changes. Verhoeven managed to make his second full-length Dutch feature film into his first American-style production, despite the fact that the story line was in the European 'collage' tradition. With this approach to directing, he showed his hand as a popular film-maker – within the Dutch film-making world, he would be totally on his own for a long time.

Although during the shooting of *Wat Zien Ik* Paul Verhoeven still looked like a mathematics professor, *Turks Fruit* aroused very different emotions in him. The process of identifying with his main characters led him to dress in a much more bohemian way, with long hair and eye-catching orange jeans. For the moment, Paul Verhoeven too had turned into a Wolkers-type artist.

This metamorphosis was not an isolated instance, nor was it inspired only by changing fashions. During the shooting of his biker movie *Spetters*, he suddenly appeared dressed completely in leather. For his magic-realist thriller *De Vierde Man*, he revealed a tendency towards superstitious rituals. The remark 'Paul is living his movie' was one that would often be made by his American actors in his subsequent Hollywood existence.

The shooting of *Turks Fruit* began on 11 July 1972 in Amsterdam West and continued until the end of August. The budget of 1 million guilders was considerable for Dutch standards. The leading roles had been given to two newcomers: Olga was played by Monique van de Ven, a nineteen-year-old first-year student at the theatre school in Maastricht. Erik was the twenty-eight-year-old Rutger Hauer – a choice for which Jan Wolkers demonstrated his approval in typical fashion: 'At least Rutger showed in *Floris* that he was good at piercing with his lance.'

But it was not clear-cut that a relatively expensive film should be carried by two faces with so little experience. Initially Rob Houwer had wanted to give the female lead to Willeke van Ammelrooy, who at the time was the leading lady of Dutch cinema. In 1971 she had starred in *Mira* by Fons Rademakers and was the embodiment of sensuality in the Low Countries. This was precisely Verhoeven's objection. He sensed that the actress was too old to play a girl who still slept with her thumb in her mouth. He preferred Monique van de Ven, a 'bouncy girl' presented to him by casting director Hans Kemna. He remembers that when she was face to face with the director 'the vibrations went through the roof'. Monique van de Ven remembers the meeting because of one perhaps unintentional but certainly crafty manoeuvre. 'After we had talked a little I went to the window to see whether the taxi had arrived yet. I was on tip-toe, and because I had to hang out of the window, I was leaning forward slightly. This must have been very sensual in Paul's eyes. In those days I was one of those girls whose skirt blows like the wind.' To Verhoeven she seemed exactly the kind of half-grown woman he needed for the film. She even had that beautifully endearing puppy fat, but whether it would be Rutger Hauer who would be allowed to nibble at it was still an unanswered question for the director.

Initially Verhoeven thought that Hauer, whom he had got to know so well as the churlish nobleman Floris, was light years away from what he had in mind for the artist Erik. A parade of candidates followed: from the Flemish actor Hugo Metsers, who had caused a sensation in Wim Verstappen's *Blue Movie*, to the up-and-coming actor Hidde Maas. At Rob Houwer's insistence, Rutger Hauer was also invited for a test. At that moment Verhoeven was converted. 'We filmed the scene in which Erik visits Olga in hospital. He takes sweets for her, Turkish delight, and because her disease is in an advanced stage, she thinks that her teeth are loose. "Feel them," she says. Rutger pulls at her teeth. They are still firmly in place. A dramatic moment, but Rutger and Monique played it so fantastically together that I forgot all my doubts.'

The decision to shoot *Turks Fruit* in a realistic way resolved one last objection. Because of the technique of the shooting, the film had to be dubbed in its entirety afterwards, as direct sound was not feasible. 'Rutger, who always has such difficulty with his voice, was able to concentrate totally on his acting. It gave him exactly the freedom he needed.'

Many of the scenes were devised for Hauer on the set. Jan de Bont remembers that they did not ponder about things for too long, but kept on shooting. It was not until the morning, in the car on the way to the set, that Verhoeven gave Monique van de Ven her lines, which he had often worked on until the last minute. To enliven the long days of shooting, they played cheerful pop records in the background during the workshop scenes. At night the film crew went out to eat together. It was a group solidarity that Jan de Bont never again experienced with any other film. He describes the atmosphere as a 'continuous natural high . . . We stuck together so much; we were working twenty-four hours a day for six weeks. When the shooting was over, it seemed as if something very dear had been taken from us.'

The momentum of *Turks Fruit* had, he says, everything to do with the fact that crew and cast were still very inexperienced, which meant that not everything was done professionally. But nobody became frustrated or cynical: 'Especially not Rutger and Monique. They did not worry about showing their bodies, or about their roles, their egos or their future.'

Though Verhoeven had second thoughts about Rutger Hauer, from the very beginning the actor seemed perfectly suited to the role of the wild young Erik. 'On the basis of the Wolkers book, I had a crystal-clear image of Erik in my mind,' says Hauer. 'It was a character I really wanted to play. And not without justification, it now seems. After that, Paul always let me play figures who do not have too many problems, who trust in their luck and have absolute confidence in coincidence. A nice kind of opportunist. Even more than Floris, Erik is a textbook example of that.'

In the same way as Monique van de Ven had much in common with the Olga figure, Rutger to a large degree played Rutger, says van de Ven. 'Although there is not a mean bone in his body, Rutger is thick-skinned, of course, like Erik in the film.' She tells of shooting a scene near Rotterdam when Rutger suddenly whispered, 'Come on . . . we're going.' With his pay packet, which cannot have been much more than her own 6,000 guilders, he wanted to buy a motorbike and Monique had to come with him. They left in his jeep – which she had to drive back, although she did not have a driving licence. 'Then he gets on that big Harley and I drive behind him. Back to Amsterdam for the next scene. In the middle of the Rokin, in the heart of the city, Rutger parks his motorbike. Without locking it. Uninsured. When we had finished shooting, he rushed outside. His bike was gone of course. He had no more money. Typical of Rutger!'

And yet there was more to this tough, perhaps slightly naïve actor than just bravura. After he had seen the full-length version of *Turks Fruit* for the first time during a press showing, he dashed out of the viewing room at full speed before the credits rolled and without waiting for compliments. 'What is Rutger doing now?' the director, co-star and cameraman wondered. He later admitted that the film had made such an impression on him that he had fled outside to absorb the impact of his own performance – under Verhoeven's direction he had surpassed himself.

What Hauer still likes about *Turks Fruit* is its earthiness. 'The acting is not posing. Paul's images are far from whitewashed. Flesh and rubbish are mixed together. Abroad, *Turks Fruit* was compared with *Love Story*, but I think that's inappropriate. In that film everything was much smoother, the images had been spotlit to perfection. In film, I like to work with my hands, which fitted well with the character of the sculptor Erik. But after

I went to the States, they kept going on about my dirty fingernails, even if I was playing an android or a serial killer. To my surprise, clean hands are compulsory in Hollywood, even for the worst villains. One of the things you can never accuse Paul of is stretching the truth about life, as he clearly showed in *Turks Fruit*.'

In a free improvisation on Wolkers, the film begins by showing Erik's tormented and promiscuous behaviour point-blank. The moment where a dog licks up the waters of a very pregnant bride during the marriage ceremony was thought up by Verhoeven on the set, and looks like a quotation from the Rembrandt painting *De Doop van de Kamerling*. The dog represents a creature that does not understand sacred events; in this instance, it drinks from the life-giving waters. When Olga is lying in bed in the workshop, Erik throws her a bunch of flowers; worms suddenly creep out, a reference to her impending death. Olga's fear of cancer, which haunts her family, becomes intense when she thinks she has found blood in her stools. Very practically, Erik examines them; it turns out she had eaten a typical Dutch dish with red beetroot the previous evening.

Verhoeven also shows Olga in a mirror, lying on a bed. In the candlelight, she has the virgin purity of a Madonna. The image returns later in the film – but this time she is upside down in the oncologist's chair while he takes pictures of her shaven skull. These were all counterpoints to the idyllic love story. In addition to the fact that it expresses Wolkers's theme that death is always at the centre of life, *Turks Fruit* showed Soeteman and Verhoeven's taste for brusquely tilting a scene. For example: In his workshop Erik sells a drawing to a visitor – whom we recognize as the man who became panic-stricken during the festivities surrounding the royal unveiling of Erik's sculpture.

Meanwhile, Olga cheerfully comes in with her shopping. Erik enthusiastically tells her that he has sold a drawing. It turns out to be a sketch of him and Olga making love. The customer's remark – 'Is that you, madam?' – sends her into a rage.

The man leaves with the drawing. Erik is angry with Olga. She says, 'You shouldn't do that' – meaning that the drawing is an intimate moment between the two of them. 'Oh, shouldn't I?' Erik replies. 'When you're dead, I'll even sell your body to the hospital.'

Outside it begins to thunder. Olga runs out through the front door. Erik goes after her. He sees her from the back, standing in the downpour. Then he goes up to her; her gaze is distant. Only when he kisses her does she recognize him.

The rain is now pouring from the sky. Olga is splashing in a puddle. Erik fetches some glasses and red wine. In the rain they drink to their eternal love; this high pitch of romance is also expressed in the music.

Their happiness is short-lived. At the height of their tenderness a car comes into view. It is Olga's woman friend, who asks her to come to a party in Alkmaar. Erik is left behind in the rain. Although he does not know it yet, this is the last time he and Olga will share such a euphoric moment.

Verhoeven gives his actors no more than three minutes to express this chaos of moods. While the viewer is gasping for breath, happy that the lovers are reconciled in the rain – a scene deliberately filmed in a beautiful way – there comes Verhoeven's inevitable 'knock on the door'. The plot takes a new turn, with an abrupt shift of perspective. It shows that the change in Olga's mental state owing to the tumour in her brain has already begun, and therefore the scene had to express both tenderness and threat.

Jan de Bont puts it into a wider perspective. 'Paul *always* lures the viewers with beautiful pictures first. Their expectations are led in a certain direction – then he says, Cut! Back to harsh reality. Thus you are forced to go with him when the story shoots off in another direction. It is his way of focusing on the subject. The audience can only say Yes or No to that.'

In the book, the main characters make love for some time after the romantic rain ballet. In Verhoeven's universe, where the rain had to be delivered by three men from the fire brigade holding hoses – the Dutch Hollywood did not have rain machines then – too much tenderness would have held up the story. This is why sincere emotion is immediately followed by something unsavoury. Olga goes to the party, where she is chatted up by the bourgeois man. 'Sometimes,' says Monique van de Ven, 'Paul is just like a child kicking at his most precious toy: "Let's not get sentimental now!" At the same time, that's also his strength. After such a tender moment, the audience still hopes that things will be all right. You do not blame Erik because their relationship fails, nor Olga. No, you're sitting on the edge of your seat and your anger is directed at the woman friend, that twit in her car, who disturbs the moment. You start to hate the mother because she is obstructive. And of course that asshole of a civil servant, because he cannot take his hands off Olga. It is all intended to strengthen the bond between Erik and Olga for the audience.'

The only time in the film where Verhoeven refuses to let the tone of a scene shift halfway through is at the end, when Erik is beside Olga's deathbed. He reads her a fairytale about love and gives her sweets. This is the most fragile moment in the film, and it is shot without irony or cynicism. 'The film could easily have gone over the top, but the acting of Rutger and Monique was so natural that it just steers away from being kitsch,' the director says. A great relief. Although throughout most of the film the weapon of fast-cutting a sequence of flashing images could be used, this would not have been suitable at the end. Had the ending of *Turks Fruit* disappointed the viewer, the entire film would have been sunk.

Together with the prelude in the department store, where Erik meets Olga again after eight months and she collapses after a brief conversation and a cup of tea, Verhoeven considers the final sequence of the film the most interesting from the point of view of acting technique. 'You can coach them as much as you like, but in the end they have to play it.' He describes the director's influence on the actors as *latah*, an old Malay medical word meaning the tendency of people to imitate behaviour so that their own will is subjugated; it's also called 'echokinesis'. 'You can't get what's not there. So you have to explain to the actors what sort of feeling they have to conjure up. Delving into these emotions is some-thing you do by constantly talking to them, by acting it out yourself – until *they* feel what *you* mean.' If it is right, that emotion then becomes a part of the actor's personality. 'A talented actor can then produce those feelings at any given moment and in the right proportion – although he does have to believe in them. With *Turks Fruit* I was lucky in that respect. Because of the carefree way in which both Monique and Rutger lived at the time, I as the director was able to colour them in completely.' This was partly the reason why Verhoeven would always, even in Holly-wood, prefer to work with actors who are not yet established.

'Seventy-five per cent masterpiece,' was Jan Wolkers's judgement after seeing *Turks Fruit*. On Thursday 22 February 1973 the film had its Dutch première in twenty-four cities. The extensive advance publicity, fol-lowed by the mostly positive reviews, meant that, as with *Wat Zien Ik*, there were long queues at the cinemas. This time Verhoeven enjoyed it all much more. With *Turks Fruit* he had really been able to present his credentials as a director. The author's approval, which he had worried about for so long, especially pleased him. Wolkers had called *Turks Fruit* much better than *Last Tango in Paris* (Bernardo Bertolucci, 1972), if only because he thought Marlon Brando was cowardly in his long under-pants. Rutger had a 'nice, fleshy bottom which is worth looking at'. The news that cameraman Jan de Bont and leading actress Monique van de Ven had fallen in love had not surprised him, since de Bont had so lov-ingly captured her on camera.

'What was so good', Jan Wolkers still believes twenty years later, 'is that Jan de Bont also made a hero out of Rutger. Rutger looks a bit like an egg sometimes, a bit soft. Do you know why? Because of his chin. If you film him in a particular way from below, the audience is suddenly faced with an empty shell. But in *Turks Fruit* he is always charismatic.' Wolkers's only criticism was that Hauer hit Monique van de Ven so hard on her bottom. 'I would have hit her on the bottom in such a way that it kept its shape and got nice and red. Then I would certainly have put my mouth to it to make up. Rutger sticks a rose in it!'

In the Netherlands of the early 1970s, there was little resistance to the sexual frankness of *Turks Fruit*. Clearly, whoever filmed Wolkers could not avoid an ode to carnality without reducing the force of the story. One Christian newspaper had its doubts, but was corrected by a Protestant weekly. 'A vital film about death,' wrote *Hervormd Nederland*, not hitherto known for its progressive views. But Verhoeven's journey to becoming director of the most popular Dutch film ever was not entirely smooth. In Amsterdam, some cinemagoers were handed pamphlets by campaigners from the recently formed Vrouwen Bevrijdings Front ('Women's Liberation Front') – predecessors of the wave of feminism soon to hit the Netherlands.

The pamphlets read: 'ERIK THE GREAT, a children's story for grown-ups. The women and girls in this great film are all thumb-suckers and bitches. That is why Erik is allowed to pester and humiliate them all. Erik is also allowed to fuck them all. "Erik *can* be nice, but first you have to be very sick and die." This is the umpteenth film confirming existing ideas about women. Passive, powerless, thumb-sucking things with no will of their own, who can be used for anything.'

Verhoeven was undoubtedly reminded of this outburst in 1992 when there was a similar commotion in the United States about *Basic Instinct*. 'There has always been trouble surrounding my films – usually sheer nonsense.' As far as he is concerned, the love-making scenes in *Turks Fruit* are all indications of something else; at the beginning of the film, when Erik drags so many women into his workshop, he does it purely to forget Olga. The earlier amorous encounters with Olga are a celebration of life. When he tries to take her by surprise in the third part of the film, it is a sign of despair. Erik tries to regain with violence what he lost a long time ago: her love for him.

'If you merely have people lie on top of each other and pant, it doesn't express anything. It is even boring: "Oh, I suppose we're getting a biology lesson now." I don't believe you can find gratuitous sex scenes in my work. In all my films the narrative simply continues during the act of love-making. That is the case in *Turks Fruit*, but equally in *De Vierde Man* and *Basic Instinct* – which has the longest love-making scene I have ever made. Why some people emphasize these sex scenes so much is because I have always managed to avoid those ridiculous soft dissolves you see so often in American films. That's why it sometimes seems as if I have neglected the erotic or emotional impact of the act of love. But I think the public should be able to see through the fucking in a love-making scene.'

Turks Fruit was also criticized from an unexpected quarter. The Cannes Film Festival refused to admit the film to the competition. In March 1973 the selection committee decided that 'the artistic qualities of *Turks Fruit* were out of proportion to the amount of nudity shown'. This remarkable action arose from the fact that the French government had just issued new guidelines for the Cannes Festival to minimize sex and violence on the screen. Verhoeven was later told by the top civil servant for cultural affairs, J. G. van der Molen, that the Ministry for CRM (Culture, Recreation and Social Work) had even received a furious telegram 'which wondered how the Dutch government could send such a perverse, decadent film' to Cannes. The complaint caused amazement, because up to then the French cinema had not exactly been known for its puritan values.

But this rejection had already been forgotten when in February 1974 came the news that *Turks Fruit* had been admitted to the competition for the Academy Award – despite the fact that the annual Oscar ceremony was not usually the home of liberal, libertarian views. It was nominated Best Foreign Film. It seems that after the first wild ten minutes of the film there were just about enough Academy members left to vote for *Turks Fruit*; the rest had walked out in shock. The other candidates for Best Foreign Film were *La Nuit Américaine* (*Day for Night*) by François Truffaut; the Israeli film *The House on Chelouche Street* by Moshe Mizrahi; Claude Goretta's *L'Invitation* from Switzerland; and *Der Fussgänger* (*The Pedestrian*) from the Austrian director Maximilian Schell.

Although producer Rob Houwer was flattered by the nomination, he let the opportunity slip through his fingers. Now was the time to campaign intensively, to shower the Hollywood community with dinner parties, presents, posters, stickers and other kinds of lobbying, all of which costs money. For the Oscar night itself, the director and the leading actors had been invited by the Academy – they only had to pay for a ticket. The producer did not want to do this either. In his defence, Houwer said that he had not received the travel subsidy for which he had applied to the Ministry of CRM. After the film's major success in the Netherlands, it was hardly surprising that his request had been thrown in the wastepaper basket.

Monique van de Ven suspects there was another motive for the producer's stubbornness. 'I don't think Rob wanted us to go to America at all. He was dead scared that we – or at least Paul and Rutger – would stay there, and he would lose his geese that lay the golden eggs – although he will always deny it.' She remembers Verhoeven's outburst of rage when his producer said he would not pay for the tickets. '*None* of us went – can you imagine?' What slightly calmed things down was Houwer's remark that they would not win the Oscar anyway. It was clear to him that François Truffaut was going to get the Academy Award – and indeed the French director did win. Paul Verhoeven went back to his usual activities. Hollywood seemed very far away to him, anyway.

Bread revolt in nineteenth-century
Amsterdam: Keetje (Monique van
de Ven) on the run.

From prostitute to artist's model.

From pauper to lady: Keetje meets
the banker, Hugo (Rutger Hauer).

Chapter 7

A Dutch Wave: *Keetje Tippel*

The success of *Wat Zien Ik*, *Blue Movie* and *Turks Fruit* had in only two years contradicted the long-standing claim that Dutch films could not attract a large audience – although the first two titles did it with a rather vulgar cocktail of humour and sex. With *Turks Fruit*, however, Paul Verhoeven showed that it is possible for a director to translate a best-seller into an individual cinematic language. The book had acquired value thanks to the fortunate casting of Rutger Hauer and Monique van de Ven. The film put a face to the characters on the page; whoever read the original novel after seeing the film would always see the blond locks of Rutger Hauer when reading the words of Wolkers's narrator, or hear the sad harmonica of Toots Thielemans during the rain scene on page 128. *Turks Fruit* had become part of the collective memory of the nation: twenty-two years later, the film was depicted on the Dutch commemorative stamp printed for the centenary of cinema.

The film also offered a new formula for home-grown producers. In the hopes of similar success, an enormous number of films based on successful literary works were produced. In addition to a film adaptation of three more novels by Jan Wolkers, Herbert Curiël made *Het Jaar van de Kreeft* (*Cancer Rising*) in 1975, based on the novel by the Flemish author Hugo Claus. In 1976 the second patriarch of Dutch film, Fons Rademakers, took on a film based on Multatuli's monumental *Max Havelaar* (script: Gerard Soeteman), a classic of Dutch literature from 1860 in which the nineteenth-century colonial regime of the Dutch East Indies – now Indonesia – was attacked.

Although the quality of what was on offer left something to be desired, by now it was clearly possible to speak of a budding feature-film industry. Verhoeven believes that the Filmacademie, which relentlessly churned out students, was a contributory factor. 'For the first time, there was a group of young Dutch people who thought, "Now *I* am going to film something." Soon it turned out to be, "Now we are all going to film something, because we are all very good." It was the start of a tough competition.'

In the period 1965–70 Dutch films only accounted for 1.3 per cent of the country's total cinema attendance. But 1971–78 showed very different statistics: 12.2 per cent of cinemagoers had seen a Dutch feature film, an average of 3.5 million people per year. These improvements were also evident in the annual reports of the Productiefonds. Between 1961 and 1968 the Fund financed precisely twenty-four feature films, but between 1971 and 1978 this number nearly trebled.

The Dutch film phenomenon was also noticed abroad. The prominent film journalist Peter Cowie, editor of the annual *International Film Guide* and biographer of Francis Ford Coppola, wrote about the new directors in his book *Dutch Cinema* (Tantivy Press, London, 1979): 'They are united in their determination to reject the documentary image of Holland as a country of dikes, cheese and tulips.' In reality, however, the Dutch film world was by no means as united as Cowie, an outsider, had portrayed it. Under the surface smouldered a conflict whose flames regularly broke through. The debate was about where the Dutch *auteur* film-makers were: directors who based their work on original scripts.

It was from this aspect that Paul Verhoeven was fiercely attacked by fellow film-maker Wim Verstappen, director of *Blue Movie*. Only a few weeks after the première of *Turks Fruit* on 3 March 1973, Verstappen wrote in the left-wing weekly *Vrij Nederland*: 'What has Paul Verhoeven done in *Turks Fruit*?' He claimed he could hardly find Verhoeven's signature; Verhoeven the *auteur* was missing. 'It looks as if the film has not been directed.' The writer of the article was honest enough to admit that he might be suffering from professional jealousy, but it was typical of the agitated atmosphere of the time.

Encouraged by their Filmacademie background, many of the newcomers mentioned by Cowie had placed themselves in the *auteur* category, following the example of the French and Italians, and they had a large number of critics on their side, also lovers of what Pier Paulo Pasolini had called 'the poetry of the cinema'. The highly individualistic Adriaan Ditvoorst was seen as the most promising exponent of the Dutch art film. He had shot *Paranoia* (1967) and *De Blinde Fotograaf* (*The Blind Photographer*, 1973) in an 'artistic' way based on the work of W. F. Hermans, and despite his lack of commercial success he was hailed as the Dutch Buñuel. Ditvoorst said of himself that he 'was the only one in the Netherlands who was not making bourgeois films, but films *about* the bourgeoisie.' Paul Verhoeven clearly belonged in the other camp; but neither he nor his producer Rob Houwer made any secret of it. Verhoeven provocatively said in an interview with the weekly *Haagse Post* in 1975: 'Every country gets the films it deserves. It is no good acting the artist here when it has been proved time and again that art films only appeal to a handful of film fanatics. There really is no point in trying to become a Dutch Fellini.' And as if to confirm his American outlook in advance: 'The first thing I demand from a film is tension.'

The conclusion was obvious: the relationship between Paul Verhoeven and the Dutch film press, between the commercial film and the art film, had been irreparably damaged. Although the director made it clear that he wished to address the public in the Hollywood way, his films were judged by the then-current artistic standards. In the Netherlands of the seventies 'never the twain would meet'. The schism would continue to dominate the film discussion until the late eighties and, on his departure for the United States in 1985, Verhoeven would mention it as a cause for his leaving.

Until that time his resistance to high culture consisted of describing the critics' exclusive preference for the art film as a muddy road, an impasse. The idea that they would allow a director to become well known only as a superior, universal artist, as an intellectual who, with the camera like a machine-gun on his shoulder, couldn't care less about petty bourgeois ideas of clarity, comprehensibility and craft, seemed to him a grotesque overrating of the medium, but still more an insult to the public. Of course, Jean-Luc Godard's *A Bout de Souffle* (*Breathless*, 1959) had been a revolution, but it did not mean that everyone was obliged to speak in 'artistic' tongues.

'I have been put on record as a demolisher of art,' he says, looking back on this period, 'but I have always made films I thought were worthwhile. But one should never lose sight of the relationship between investment and return. Surely film is both an artistic and a commercial product? I think that, if they invest millions in you as a director, you have a moral obligation to try to get that money back. That is why I have always chosen films which I thought would have a public. Of course, this meant you were soon labelled anti-élitist – this made you an object of suspicion, especially in the Netherlands in the 1970s. In literature it was just the same. I wanted my films to communicate with the rest of the world, not just a few critics. Actually, I still think *Turks Fruit* is a more artistic film than the whole lot put together.'

Despite his passionate tone in interviews, the success of *Turks Fruit* had surprised Paul Verhoeven as much as anyone. But he now saw a problem: how could his next film surpass even *Turks Fruit*? He was not uninfluenced by the fact that, despite his previous film's success, his fee had been only 20,000 guilders. Now that he was living with his wife and child in a more expensive house in Oegstgeest and they were expecting a second child (his daughter Heleen, born 22 June 1974), this sum was not much of an insulation against hard times. With feelings of shame, he signed on for unemployment benefit. The clerks were more than just surprised: 'He's not a sponger, is he?' Verhoeven decided to start a new project as soon as possible. But which?

In an article in the daily newspaper *De Telegraaf* of 29 December 1973, he put his anxieties into words:

Whenever during the first weeks I 'happened' to walk past the Amsterdam Tuschinski theatre and saw a queue of people stretching from the theatre to the Munt waiting to buy a ticket, I was very impressed. It is much more concrete than the 'more than 3 million spectators' proudly reported in the press adverts. Three million is just a number to me, but that queue is tangible: you can see it, you can walk past it and look at the faces of the people. When I saw that queue, I felt like running and leaping for sheer joy – which is what I did, but a few streets further on, of course . . .

That's how the first weeks passed. In a kind of pleasant glow. I went on holiday for a month, and when I got back, it was still showing and people were still queuing. But I did not enjoy it any more; I began to worry about what my next film should be. First the success of *Wat Zien Ik*, then the even bigger success of *Turks Fruit* – where do you go from there?

When the audiences kept on coming, I began to think that it could not have been my doing, that it was all due to the book, or the actors, or the position of the moon – anyway, something that had nothing to do with me. I started to get stomach ache, constipation or diarrhoea according to whichever project I tried. Because I kept thinking, 'It can never be the success *Turks Fruit* was – so it's no good.' And then I would look for something else.

Anyway, this went on for about six months, maybe until *Turks Fruit* disappeared from the cinemas. It did not dawn on me until then that I just had to take on a project which I felt like doing, without worrying about whether it would be a success.

The project which Verhoeven, in consultation with Gerard Soeteman and Rob Houwer, eventually chose, and which he mentioned for the first time in this article, was to be called *Keetje Tippel* (*Cathy Tippel*). It was a costume drama based on the memoirs of Neel Doff, a Dutchwoman of humble origins who lived from 1858 to 1942. She spent her childhood in the slums of Amsterdam, and later in Antwerp and Brussels. As a young girl she worked first as a prostitute, then as an artist's model. She married the rich socialist Fernand Brouez (called André in the book), but his early death made her a wealthy widow. Finally she married again, to a lawyer from Antwerp, and in 1909 began to write about her long journey up the social ladder. She chose to write in French, since as a schoolgirl she had never learnt to write good Dutch. Her book *Jours de Famine et de Détresse*, in which she reconstructed her poverty-stricken childhood, was published in 1911 and translated into Dutch as *Dagen van Honger en Ellende* (*Days of Hunger and Misery*). This book was followed by two more, *Keetje* (1919) and *Keetje Trottin* (1921) – later, she was mentioned as a possible Nobel Prize winner.

The work of Neel Doff had been brought to the attention of Soeteman and Houwer through a new translation of all three books by the writer and journalist Wim Zaal, published with great success in the early 1970s. On paper, the fragmented life-story of Keetje Tippel seemed good subject matter for a feature film. Like *Wat Zien Ik* and *Turks Fruit*, the production could have a Dutch setting, against which Keetje could be seen as an individual in a turbulent era – her childhood saw the emergence of the socialist movement on the streets of Amsterdam.

This is how the idea was presented to Verhoeven, but at first he was unenthusiastic about the sombreness and grim poverty. He had long tried to persuade both Houwer and Soeteman to shoot a much larger-scale film: *De Berg van Licht* (*The Mountain of Light*), based on the historical novel of 1905 by Louis Couperus. In this book, based on fact, the prominent Dutch author brings to life a tumultuous period of the Roman Empire; it is about a young homosexual priest who, thanks to the machinations of his grandmother, is pronounced emperor by the Roman army, although he is still only a boy. Verhoeven, who made no secret of his love for epic films, already had visions of the decadent Rome he could include in *De Berg van Licht*. The book has a brilliant finale in visual terms: the unfortunate demise of Emperor Helagabalus when a rebellion of the Roman people causes his extravagant regime to end in a bloodbath. 'Plenty of material for big scenes,' rejoiced Verhoeven. 'Unfortunately, much too expensive,' decided Rob Houwer.

Eventually, Verhoeven's strong urge to develop himself further as a director got the upper hand. *Wat Zien Ik* had been a drama in an attic, and although with *Turks Fruit* he had been able to extend his horizons, he had still not tackled a sizeable narrative universe. What reluctantly convinced him to film *Keetje Tippel* was a remark by Rob Houwer, who claimed that with this film Verhoeven would be able to achieve the grand scale he had always wanted – a comment that Verhoeven took as a promise. He received a budget of 2 million guilders to direct the most expensive Dutch feature film ever made; a film in which, Verhoeven decided, the entire screen would be highly coloured.

Towards the end of winter 1973 Gerard Soeteman started on the script. At Verhoeven's request he wrote sizeable scenes with steamboats and royalist Orange soirées. To counterbalance this he shows the Palingoproer ('Eel Rebellion') of 1886 in de Jordaan, the Amsterdam red-light district, when twenty-six people were killed during a police action. What Soeteman and Verhoeven found interesting was that most of the poorest members of the proletariat, such as Keetje's family, had long been supporters of the royal family, who were their greatest oppressors. Conversely, the prominent socialists who wanted to relieve the masses of their burdens were generally men and women of wealth an education. Keetje Tippel would live in both worlds, since she eventually marries a rich socialist. By then, she had already met King William III. In view of the historical fact that the king was, in Soeteman's words, something of a 'bum pincher', they devised a scene at an Orange party in which Keetje has to climb a flagpole – a popular game in those days. At the top of the mast is some food, but the pole has been greased with soap. As Keetje enthusiastically slides down with the food, she has the unpleasant sensation of someone putting his hand up her skirt. She turns round furiously, only to find it is King William III. The original script for *Keetje Tippel* breathed an atmosphere that vaguely resembled Bertolucci's epic film *Novecento* (*1900*), made at around the same time – 1976 – although Bertolucci's tribute to Marxism was absent from the Verhoeven–Soeteman story. They wanted to show the paradoxes of history without offering a ready-made political solution. The first draft of the script was 500 pages long. 'This is impossible. It looks like a political manifesto,' Rob Houwer growled as he rejected it in April 1974.

By then, preparations for *Keetje Tippel* were going full swing, as they had to shoot it in the summer. Without hesitation, the producer put on the brakes for what he called in the press 'a week of reflection'. Verhoeven and Soeteman would have to come up with a revised version or the entire project would be cancelled – although on the basis of an extensive synopsis, their application for a subsidy had already been approved by the Productiefonds. The commission said that the story had to be first and foremost about Keetje, and that the historical setting had to be pushed into the background. Gerard Soeteman thought this was a worrying development. It was not Neel Doff's testimonials as Keetje that were the most interesting, but the picture she painted of the period. In retrospect, this forced change of perspective was probably what made the film largely fail.

Verhoeven started shooting *Keetje Tippel* at the end of July 1974; the schedule was eleven weeks. Owing to the success of *Turks Fruit*, he had asked Monique van de Ven to play the lead, and Rutger Hauer would be one of her main co-stars. In addition, many renowned actors made their entry. The locations, edited together in the film as a single Amsterdam setting, included the stately Lang Voorhout in The Hague, the medieval Vismarkt and Oudegracht in Utrecht, and the old city centres of Amsterdam, Leiden and Brussels.

Giving *Keetje Tippel* its nineteenth-century atmosphere presented a number of problems. The wide shots had to be calculated down to the last centimetre, otherwise anachronistic parking meters, television aerials or supermarkets would destroy the period authenticity. In an attempt to distract the audience, they regularly brought on an old baker's cart or placed a couple of basket-weavers in the middle of the frame.

The progress of the shooting was threatened by more than just historical anachronisms. There was also a marital row within the camp. During the shooting of *Turks Fruit* cameraman Jan de Bont had fallen in love with Monique van de Ven, and they were married shortly afterwards. In *Keetje Tippel* de Bont did not seem too keen on the sequences – and there were many – in which his wife had to appear naked in front of the camera. Monique van der Ven vividly remembers the fuss. 'The openness and freedom of *Turks Fruit* were destroyed for *Keetje Tippel* by Jan's jealousy. If I was required to be naked in front of the camera, Jan would hiss from behind the camera, "Slut!"' Verhoeven hardly knew how to handle such a difficult situation. He normally flourished when there was an aggressive, alert atmosphere on the set, but he could feel that these marital rows were sabotaging the film. He tried to keep his troops in order, sometimes with a fatherly tone, sometimes in a rage. To little avail. They had to find a stand-in for Monique van de Ven's bottom, a woman the film crew picked off the street for a one-off performance. Verhoeven also called in his wife Martine who, with her experience as a group psychologist, tried to reduce the tension on the set. The chaos in the director's head was exacerbated by his hostile relationship with Rob Houwer. 'Artistic differences of opinion' were revealed when the Amsterdam newspaper *Het Parool* sent a reporter to the set. He recorded the following dialogue:

Rob Houwer: Paul, that fuck scene on the ship . . . I think it's disgusting. Disgusting. Throw it out. I don't want to see it again.

Paul Verhoeven (white with rage): No way. It's part of it. It's essential. And if you do chuck it out, you can go and direct it yourself. I'm not a child.

Although *Turks Fruit* had been an enjoyable adventure for cast and crew, *Keetje Tippel* regularly exploded into battles for control. Monique van de Ven says, 'I think we were all spoilt by the ease with which we had put together *Turks Fruit*.' In the same way as a writer can be plagued for a long time by a successful début, Verhoeven's breakthrough with his first real film, *Turks Fruit*, had now become a burden to him.

The scene which had caused so much tension between Verhoeven and Houwer was later to be the opening sequence of *Keetje Tippel*, which begins with Keetje's large family crossing the Dutch Zuider Zee from Frisia in search of a new and brighter future in Amsterdam. Her mother notices that Keetje's older sister Mina is absent from the lower deck of the ship. When Keetje goes to find her, she sees Mina making love to one of the sailors – in exchange for two bacon sandwiches, as Mina tells Keetje reproachfully when she has disturbed the pair.

The mood is set, the opening credits appear. Once in Amsterdam, it all becomes even more miserable. The basement flat they had been so looking forward to is damp, they have run out of money and food. To feed the family, Keetje's mother sends Mina out to work as a prostitute. Keetje gets a job in a laundry and later as a hat-maker's assistant. Then she too is told to find work on the street corner. This is how it is described in the book: '"Keetje child, the little ones have not been to school for two days – they can't, not without food. Couldn't you . . .?"' Torn between horror and a sense of duty, Keetje goes out on the streets. She is accompanied by her mother, who always walks ten paces behind her; during the physical transactions she waits on a nearby street corner.

When the opportunity to work as an artist's model presents itself, Keetje quits streetwalking; the painter, George, portrays her as a Dutch Joan of Arc and takes her to chic restaurants. She falls in love with the bank clerk Hugo (Rutger Hauer), a friend of the painter. Gradually the gap between Keetje and her parents widens. To accelerate her climb up the social ladder, she decides to move in with the bank clerk. When Hugo eventually dumps her – it is better for his career to have a woman from his own class – Keetje is on the streets again, but this time without a purpose. She ends up in a socialist demonstration which is crushed by the police. However, fate is kindly disposed towards her. During the demonstration she bumps into André (Eddy Brugman), a wealthy salon socialist and lawyer who has been secretly in love with her ever since she made her entry into the artists' circles. André is wounded during the clashes, and when Keetje takes him to his mansion, a kiss reveals that their love is mutual – the end credits disclose that they will be married and that Keetje will devote herself to her memoirs.

To give this costume drama its picture-book quality, Verhoeven chose colours reminiscent of the nineteenth-century painter George Hendrik Breitner, the leading figure in the Amsterdam school of Impressionists. Nevertheless, the atmospheric and – compared with *Turks Fruit* – calm camera movements could not conceal the weaknesses in the script. Although Monique van de Ven managed to give the young Keetje both innocence and rebelliousness, she looked more like a Cinderella than the Joan of Arc the director had wanted to make of her. The same was true of the scene in the Palingoproer riot, which was intended to be a large-scale demonstration. In the film it looks merely incidental, lacking in social realism.

Verhoeven was more successful in portraying the chilliness of human emotions. When the bank clerk Hugo (Rutger Hauer) comes to tell Keetje that their relationship is over, the director chose to use wide shots rather than close-ups. Verhoeven has Keetje standing in a doorway looking small and fragile. Hauer walks up to her and the camera follows him. After a number of cuts, Hauer's shoulder conceals most of her face from the viewer; we only see Keetje's eyes when he tells her the bad news.

Although this scene clearly shows that Verhoeven intended *Keetje Tippel* to be the serene mirror-image of the vigorous *Turks Fruit*, in some of the sex scenes he seems to forget this. The moment when Keetje is raped by the hat-maker Mr Pierre (Walter Kous) is rather explicit, although Gerard Soeteman had taken the event from Neel Doff's book. First we see a life-sized shadow of Mr Pierre's member on the wall. Like a kind of Big Bad Wolf, the silhouette sneaks up on the girl. The hat-maker takes her by surprise, then forces himself on her under the table. The bobbins on the table shake. 'Gosh,' says Mr Pierre as he wipes the blood off his member with a handkerchief, 'I was the first one.'

Verhoeven did not need the bad reviews to make his final judgement about the film. Gerard Soeteman had anticipated the critics' response: 'Well, this one's failed,' he muttered after the press première. And Verhoeven knew he was right. 'The film is full of mistakes and erroneous ideas. The performances are wrong. The accents are wrong. Because I was still too close to *Turks Fruit*, *Keetje Tippel* is full of sexual situations. Those do exist in the books, and we could have used them, but they needed much more distance.'

In retrospect, he thinks it would have been better to have given up after the row with Rob Houwer about the script. 'But we had already spent 20,000 guilders on pre-production, and in Holland that was sufficient reason to make the film anyway.' It was typical of the atmosphere of discord that the producer interfered with the film when it had already been showing in the cinemas for seven weeks. He decided to insert a new ending, one that he had at first rejected. The original version ends with a crane shot of Keetje striding across the mansion's moat towards a new future with the socialist André, who was wounded during the clashes. In the second version she walks on to his sick bed. 'You are bleeding again,' she says, 'you should suck it out – that's what I used to do as a child.' A kiss confirms their new-found happiness, fade out to black. At least this ending removed the rather confusing ambiguity of the original version.

Gerard Soeteman did not like either of these two versions. He had suggested they keep to the ending of the book. Through her marriage to André, Keetje has become a rich woman. Walking through town in her beautiful clothes, she is accosted by a hungry, drunken beggar woman. For a moment Keetje is face to face with her past, and realizes that this could have been her. 'Out of fright and shame,' Soeteman explains, 'she doesn't give the woman any money, but walks on. She walks quicker and quicker until she reaches her front door. Then she goes upstairs and puts her fingers in her ears to drown out the screams of the beggar woman. This is the ending I proposed. The circle is complete.'

This ending could not be used in the film because the producer had decided to show the main character mainly as she was between the ages of sixteen and twenty-two. This did not give Verhoeven the foundation he needed for *Keetje Tippel*. Although he and Soeteman had succeeded wonderfully well in making a continuous and rounded story out of the fragmentary episodes of *Wat Zien Ik* and *Turks Fruit*, the new film lacked dramatic structure. Rearranging a series of incidents from the early life of Keetje Tippel produced a colourful collage, but one without a solid foundation.

When the film was premièred in thirty cinemas on 6 March 1975, the reviews were harsh. Only the small Communist daily *De Waarheid* thought the film was good because of its attempt to write proletarian history. Charles Boost concluded in the weekly *De Groene Amsterdammer* that the film 'is uninteresting and shows a clumsiness we are not used to from the by now experienced threesome of Rob Houwer, Gerard Soeteman and Paul Verhoeven. The non-functional, pretty way of filming repeats itself throughout, so that poverty is given a golden tinge.'

In her review, Ellen Waller, critic on the quality daily *NRC/Handelsblad*, touched on the debate which was by now completely dominating the film press: 'Unfortunately, *Keetje Tippel* is a missed opportunity. It is a film without an *auteur*, that is to say, without vision, without character, without power of expression.'

The fact that Verhoeven's personal ambition to make large-scale movies could also be interpreted as part of his *auteur*ship, but within the genre of commercial films, was not discussed in the reviews. Commercially speaking, *Keetje Tippel* was less disappointing. With an audience of 1,829,068, it is still the seventh most popular Dutch film. Nevertheless, Verhoeven often says that if there is one film in his oeuvre which he'd like to be allowed to make again, it would most certainly be *Keetje Tippel*.

It was with mixed feelings that Paul Verhoeven went to the gala première of *Keetje Tippel* with his wife Martine and assistant Eefje Cornelis. The stately Tuschinski theatre in Amsterdam was festive with lights. The press and television were waiting in the foyer. Rob Houwer gave the occasion a touch of Hollywood panache – something he always did rather well. But this time Verhoeven did not feel like being the centre of attention. The party for *Turks Fruit* had been different; then, he really did have had something to celebrate as a director. Now he felt unstable. Insecure. In the interval he quietly headed for the men's room.

At the door he was accosted by a couple who announced themselves as the Bakkers from Utrecht. The director immediately sensed danger. 'Mr Verhoeven,' they said solemnly, 'we have a message from God for you.' Déjà vu made his temples throb. They told him they had seen him shooting *Keetje Tippel* at the Vismarkt in Utrecht. Out of interest they had bought the weekly *Haagse Post*. And they had understood the signals. Verhoeven knew exactly what the couple were referring to: his long interview with the journalist Ischa Meijer that was featured on the cover on 22 February. It had been a frank exchange, during which they had discussed not only his films but his religious crisis. 'And that is why we are here now. With a message. From God.'

Without waiting for further explanation, Verhoeven ran back to the cinema in a panic. 'I don't want to hear anything about it!' he shouted at them. 'I am a director.' The couple was not easily fazed, however. Further words were exchanged. Bystanders came to Verhoeven's rescue, and the couple were shown the door. They told him that they would certainly write to him – it was important! The lights went out in the auditorium. The show continued. The director sat crouched in his chair, wondering what diabolical plan was in store for him. He tried to concentrate on the film, but his head was buzzing with amazement at how these ominous incidents always hit him at moments of weakness. Compared with *Turks Fruit*, *Keetje Tippel* was perhaps a step backwards, but to him it was not a reason to doubt his vocation as a film-maker. No one, not even the Almighty, would be able to take that away from him now.

The élitist but naïve student club at the beginning of *Soldaat*, from left to right: Alex (Derek de Lint), Jan (Huib Rooymans), Erik (Rutger Hauer), President Guus (Jeroen Krabbé), Jacques (Dolf de Vries) and Nico (Lex van Delden).

The tango between Erik and Alex.

Verhoeven with Rob Houwer.

Chapter 8

Agent Provocateur: *Soldaat van Oranje*

Ever since he had filmed *Korps Mariniers* in 1965, Paul Verhoeven had toyed with the idea of a Dutch war epic – and not just because of its visual possibilities. In the recent history of the Netherlands the years 1940–45 represent a turning point, the only period in which an existential threat had been felt. So the Second World War offered plenty of drama for a feature film – and drama was something lacking in the usually tranquil history of the Netherlands. For the first time in a century and a half, the kingdom had been subjugated to foreign rule, and the deep imprint left by the German occupation was evident from the long period needed to come to terms with the trauma. Since the First World War had passed the Netherlands by as a result of its policy of strict neutrality, the unexpected German invasion of May 1940 struck twice as hard. This watershed in history developed into a litmus test for Right and Wrong. Its influence was to be felt until the late 1970s, when prominent politicians such as Josef Luns (the Dutch Secretary-General of NATO) and Willem Aantjes, Party Chairman of the Christian Democrats (one of the largest parties in the Netherlands) got into trouble because of revelations about the 'wrong' part they played in the war.

To Paul Verhoeven, the Second World War first of all meant the memories of his childhood. The V2s in the air over The Hague; the massive bombardment of the city on 3 March 1945; his father hiding in the cellar of the parental home; the dead bodies he had seen lying in the street – all these kept haunting him. With *Keetje Tippel* he had kept his distance from the subject, but to Verhoeven an epic story about the Netherlands in wartime was a theme he could taste, feel and breathe.

As the starting point for his new film, he chose a book published in 1971 under the title *Soldaat van Oranje*. It was the dramatized memories of Erik Hazelhoff Roelfzema, a wealthy student at the University of Leiden who during the war years had worked for the Resistance and flown for the British RAF, and had finally been appointed aide to Queen Wilhelmina, the Dutch monarch who together with her government had gone into exile in London. The book presents Hazelhoff Roelfzema as an adventurer, whose political convictions are for a long time secondary to the boyish excitement he finds in warfare. As well as sharing Hazelhoff Roelfzema's background as a Leiden University student – in different decades they had both been members of the Corps Minerva student association – Verhoeven also liked the author's initial naïvely romantic perception of the war years. The maxim *Beetje oorlog, best spannend* ('A spot of war might be exciting'), which Verhoeven has his leading actor and alter ego Rutger Hauer utter near the beginning of *Soldaat van Oranje*, expressed nothing less than his own childhood fantasy. From that moment on, Verhoeven is not constructing a *Boys' Own Paper* story, but a tale of how Hauer's maxim is overtaken by 'adult' reality.

The starting point for the story is an élitist but unworldly Leiden student club, whose members dismiss the news of the declaration of war by the British prime minister Chamberlain by serving a tennis ball. In the end, only the adventurer Erik and his friend Jacques (who stands aside from everything) survive the war. The other four members of the club, as well as some of their closest acquaintances, die during the Occupation – some as Resistance heroes, others as collaborators. The mental processes which underlie their choices between 'right' and 'wrong' are the real subject of the film. Although *Soldaat van Oranje* was shot in the style of a war spectacular, these life stories depicted the complex layers of reality of the Second World War in a way not seen before in Dutch cinemas. This is why Verhoeven felt that *Soldaat van Oranje* turned out to be not only his most personal but his best Dutch movie.

The fact that Paul Verhoeven tries to give a balanced account of the war was due to more than just Roelfzema's book. To him, there were no unblemished heroes; from his own observation he knew that, although it was easy to use the simplifications 'right' and 'wrong', these were inadequate to explain human behaviour at a time of crisis. This is why in *Soldaat van Oranje* he portrays the figure of Alex (Derek de Lint) with as much empathy as his mirror-image Erik (Rutger Hauer). In the story, however, Erik becomes a much-decorated hero, while his student friend Alex meets an inglorious end in the service of the Germans, as a volunteer in the Waffen SS on the Eastern Front.

This deeply rooted awareness of the ambiguity of human morality was something Verhoeven had acquired in his childhood. After the war he became friends with the boy next door, who was the son of the acting couple Ceesje Speenhoff and Piet Rienks. He was the child of 'wrong' parents, and for that reason he was shunned by the neighbourhood. His mother was the daughter of the eccentric poet and singer Koos 'the old bard with the young heart' Speenhoff, who had died in the bombing of the Bezuidenhout in The Hague on 3 March 1945. The boy's father was an actor who had never achieved much more than supporting roles in repertory theatre.

When the war broke out, the couple decided without hesitation to join the radio programme *Zondagmiddagcabaret van Paulus de Ruiter* (*Paulus de Ruiter's Sunday Afternoon Cabaret*). The broadcasts began on Sunday 19 October 1941, and from the start it was clear that the programme, from a broadcasting service which the Nazis had made subservient to the party line, identified with the ideals of the collaborating NSB, the Nationaal Socialistische Beweging (National Socialist Movement) of Anton Mussert. Behind the pseudonym 'Paulus de Ruiter' was Jacques van Tol, who before the war was known as the most talented writer of sketches and songs in the Dutch cabaret circuit. In his *Zondagmiddagcabaret*, Speenhoff and Rienks brought to life through the microphone the chatty duo Keuvel and Klessebes (Prattle and Chatterbox), who packaged anti-Semitic comments on current affairs in dialogue like this:

Keuvel: Morning, Miss Klessebes! What a fuss in Amsterdam, Miss!

Klessebes: Yes, those Allies of ours, I can't understand them anymore! It's beyond me!

Keuvel: Yes, it's safe beyond, Miss!

Klessebes: Yes, for the anti-aircraft guns! Apparently they have Yiddish pilots in America who are scared they might hurt themselves.

It was even more tragic that, during the war, van Tol rewrote in an anti-Semitic way the classic songs he had made in the 1930s for Jewish entertainers ('One of those crafty, half-baked, little Jewish men . . .'). Moreover, the *Zondagmiddagcabaret* particularly aimed at attacking the Americans, whom the majority of Dutch people saw as their future liberators from the Nazi régime. As Keuvel and Klessebes said: 'America? The highest skyscraper in the world, the richest millionaires, the most expensive bars, the hottest music and the biggest gangsters.'

The *Zondagmiddagcabaret* was on air until January 1944. Out of remorse, or perhaps because he saw that the tide was turning against the Germans, Jacques van Tol retired as a songwriter at the end of the war. For his collaboration, he was eventually condemned to three and a half years' imprisonment and the loss of his right to vote. He continued to write under various pseudonyms for the most important cabaret artists.

Ceesje Speenhoff and Piet Rienks were also interned, and thereby lost their right ever to earn their living as artists again. Piet Rienks, a fanatical NSB member, was given eight years' imprisonment on top of that.

So after the war, it was only the boy and his mother who came to live next door to Paul Verhoeven. They became buddies, partly because Verhoeven felt it his duty to stand up for the newcomer in his neighbourhood; eventually the boy became his best childhood friend. 'You could feel there was something the matter with that family. People pointed their finger at them everywhere. I thought that was really unfair. What in God's name did that boy have to do with his parents' NSB past? Why did they avoid him so much? That inverted bourgeois morality, just as much fed by feelings of hatred, disturbed me even then – but I could not put it into words at the time. It was more of an intuitive thing. How did I know that his father was not a valued member of society?'

At the age of thirteen Paul Verhoeven fell in love with Marijke, the girl next door. She turned out to be the daughter of A. J. Zondervan – lawyer, permanent aide to Mussert, and commander of his armed assault group the WA (De Weerbaarheidsafdeling). She was the first girl Paul Verhoeven kissed, which later led him to say mockingly: 'Of course, that is the moment when those fascist viruses of which I was often accused later got into my body.' But at such moments Verhoeven was in a teasing mood, enjoying making a politically incorrect remark. Behind it was the film-maker who wanted to reflect reality as realistically as possible on all levels.

The struggle between 'right' and 'wrong' can be found in most of his films – it is a consistent leitmotif. In the same way as his friend was the child of collaborating parents, Alex in *Soldaat van Oranje* turns out to be the son of a German mother and a Dutch NSB father, a fact which is also touched on in Hazelhoff Roelfzema's book. Although at the time of the German invasion Alex is dutifully serving with the Dutch army, his parents are interned by the same Dutch army on suspicion of treason. Alex shows solidarity with his parents and becomes isolated from his Leiden University friends. After the Dutch capitulation he tries his luck on the German side and joins the SS. 'His circumstances drive him in that direction,' Verhoeven says. 'Apart from Erik, none of his fellow students is interested in him any more. I could have portrayed Alex simply as a traitor, but I thought that was too easy. His choice is wrong, but human.'

Long before Paul Verhoeven tried to formulate the moral dilemmas of the Second World War in *Soldaat van Oranje*, these themes had preoccupied him as a film-maker. As early as the 'attic years', he had planned to shoot a documentary about Anton Mussert, leader of the NSB party, for the television channel VPRO. This was the period when Verhoeven was unable to get his feature films off the ground. A documentary about Anton Mussert was a remarkable idea in 1967, since it did not by any means fit into the historical debate then current. The official reading of this dark period in Dutch history came from the government historian Professor Lou de Jong. He achieved great celebrity with his twenty-one-part television series entitled *De Bezetting* (*The Occupation*), first shown in the period 1960–65 by the national broadcasting company NTS. As a matter of principle, no space in this epic narrative had been allowed for asking NSB members or other collaborators about their motives, since this was considered an insult to the viewers. Although the series made a great impression on the public – by now, television sets had reached two out of three Dutch households – the truth was that the underside of the historical reality remained undisclosed. Blame had not yet been apportioned to the precise Dutch bureaucracy which contributed to the deportation of 100,000 Jews to the extermination camps, the highest percentage in Western Europe. Moreover, the Dutch section of the SS had turned out to be the largest non-German one. But it was too early to talk about these and other painful facts.

The full extent of Dutch involvement in the persecution of the Jews was first recorded by the historian J. Presser, who in 1965 published his study *Ondergang. De Vervolging en Verdelging van het Nederlandse Jodendom 1940–1945* (*Extinction. The Persecution and Extermination of Dutch Jewry 1940–1945*) which, according to the reviewers, completely disposed of 'the fable of the Netherlands as a small country which behaved in an exemplary way towards "its" Jews.' The book initiated what might be called the second phase of coming to terms with the war.

A new generation of historians and journalists, unhindered by personal feelings, was considerably more critical about the way the historical account had been written so far. The pioneers among them went in search of the motives of Dutch people who had chosen to collaborate. The writer and journalist Wim Zaal, in his book *De Herstellers* (*The Restorers*, 1966), described the fortunes of the Dutch fascists, and in so doing immediately became suspect to the older generation. Something similar was experienced by the writer and artist Armando and the journalist Hans Sleutelaar on the publication of their book *De SS'ers* (*The Members of the SS*) in 1967, which caused a storm of protest; the book was seen as an 'incitement to anti-Semitic violence'. It contained exhaustive interviews with eight Dutch people who had joined the SS during the war. What was striking was that the interviews were printed in full, unaccompanied by any explanatory or condemnatory commentary. The compilers considered this a necessary task: 'How the people in the Resistance fared during and after the war is well known. We know nothing about the lives of the brutes who were their most bitter enemies . . . None of them was interrogated after the war; no historian considered it necessary to summon a member of the SS as a historical witness.'

It was along these lines that Paul Verhoeven wanted to make his documentary *Anton Adriaan Mussert*. Its central question was of why, during the Depression years, the otherwise sober Dutch people should have supported a fascist-inspired leader. Verhoeven wanted to know what kind of a man Mussert (born 1894) was, apart from being 'wrong'. 'People who out of complete conviction genuinely make a wrong choice have something beautiful and tragic about them,' the director said of the background to his film. Verhoeven did not mention that his curiosity about Anton Mussert went even further. Like himself, Mussert had been the son of a headmaster. Like himself, Mussert had struggled with a religious crisis. 'Mussert saw Hitler as an envoy from God who had come to save Europe, and saw himself as his prophet.'

During his research, Verhoeven discovered from photographs that as a young boy he had witnessed the moment when Anton Mussert was arrested by members of the Binnenlandse Strijdkrachten (Forces of the Interior) in The Hague. It was Monday 7 May. Young Paul was walking along the street with his mother when they passed a crowd which had formed to lynch the former leader and traitor. 'I remember a little bald man being led to a big building which obviously served as the headquarters of the Forces of the Interior, next to the Odeon cinema at the Herengracht. There were lots of pushing, shouting and cursing people. When my mother saw the scene, she said, "Oh, that's Mussert! They have captured Mussert!" As a young boy I did not understand the significance of it, although we were always told at home that Mussert was "very bad".'

Verhoeven's interest in Anton Mussert the historical figure was awakened when he began to read about the Second World War during his student days. The story of Mussert was a Shakespearean drama. As Verhoeven's documentary would recount, 'When Mussert is condemned to death in 1946, a former fellow student of his, Professor Willem Schermerhorn, is Prime Minister. A month before his execution Mussert sends a letter to Schermerhorn, in which he writes, "Now fate has decided that one of two childhood friends becomes Prime Minister and the other is shot dead as a traitor to his country; truly a theme for a great dramatist."'

Anton Mussert had known the later Prime Minister, Willem Schermerhorn, from the student world in Delft, where he had studied at the Technical University in 1912. After that, Mussert had earned his living as a talented engineer until 1931 when, inspired by the Italian Fascists, he founded the NSB. As a great admirer of Benito Mussolini, Mussert dreamed of becoming a leader of the nation himself.

Initially, Mussert's half-religious, half-mystical and very nationalistic message was very popular. His speeches and the party conventions attracted large audiences and, aided by the unstable political situation of the crisis years, the NSB received nearly 8 per cent of the vote in the elections of April 1935. His call for a powerful authority had, in his own words, 'shaken up the Dutch people'.

During his first visit to Berlin in November 1936, Mussert assured Adolf Hitler that in three or four years the time would be ripe to seize power in the Netherlands by the parliamentary route. The over-confident Mussert then began to insert anti-Semitic statements in his speeches, but this turned out to be a serious miscalculation, and the NSB slipped into political isolation.

Mussert's dreams of becoming a national leader were shattered when the Germans invaded the Netherlands in May 1940 and wanted to have little to do with him and his party. They regarded him as little more than a useful pawn, and pressed him to found a Dutch SS within the NSB. Eventually more than 20,000 Dutch SS volunteers left for the Eastern Front in June 1941 to fight Stalin's 'Bolshevik threat'.

Immediately after the war, Mussert was convicted as a traitor and was executed on 7 May 1946.

With his television portrait of the collaborator, Verhoeven planned to make marginal notes on the existing view of Mussert and the NSB. 'You might call it exploding the myth: Mussert and the NSB were not so much a cunning pack of wolves, more a collection of worried little bourgeois men. My film had to take a dialectical standpoint and look at both sides of the issue.'

For his project Verhoeven wrote to several survivors of the circle which had surrounded Mussert. The responses came quickly. On 12 February 1968 F. S. Rost van Tonningen-Heubel, known in the Netherlands as the 'Black Widow', wrote, 'Dear Mr Verhoeven, Many thanks for your letter. I will speak spontaneously, without written notes.'

She was the widow of Meinoud Rost van Tonningen, the man who during the war years had been President of the Nederlandsche Bank and who was a fanatical and fervent Nazi within the NSB.

Bringing the 'Black Widow' to the television screen was extremely provocative. As was to be expected, she proclaimed her husband's superiority over Mussert, but the real novelty of the situation lay in the fact that she was being publicly heard. Equally provocative was the appearance of farmers' leader E. J. Roskam, another former SS member, who displayed an almost religious adulation of Mussert. Moreover, a number of soldiers who had fought on the Eastern Front were interviewed, also for the first time on Dutch television. The journalistic balance of the film was maintained through interviews with former Prime Minister Schermerhorn and with jurist J. Zaaijer, the man who had prosecuted Mussert on behalf of the State, and who had also been a student friend of the fallen leader. In addition, a large amount of archive footage was shown.

Although the documentary was put together competently enough, Verhoeven's searching and, in the true sense, provocative angle gave the television station VPRO reason for doubt. The film had been ready for six months and was scheduled for broadcasting on 23 October 1968 when VPRO decided at the very last minute not to show it. Instead they showed an episode from a young people's concert. The VPRO press release said:

To apologize for the fact that the decision not to broadcast the film about Mussert by Paul Verhoeven was taken so late, Mr J. Kassies, member of the Executive Committee of the VPRO and temporarily in charge of supervising programme policy, yesterday afternoon showed the film to representatives of the press and explained the decision not to broadcast it. This decision was officially 'a lack of information value'. Although 'the VPRO does not doubt the integrity of the compiler in his intention to apply an historical-scientific approach devoid of emotional prejudices.'

The subsequent announcement in *Het Parool* revealed that the VPRO, represented by Jan Kassies, had asked the government historian Lou de Jong for advice. The authoritative professor condemned the portrait because he believed there was too little to counterbalance the effect of the NSB and SS members who appeared. Moreover, he was of the opinion that the documentary was 'redundant', since the history of Mussert and the NSB had already been dealt with adequately in his own television series *De Bezetting*. 'The irony', Verhoeven remembers, 'was that the VPRO let me make the film only on condition that this time the "mistakes" would be shown in front of the camera. They thought that would be really interesting. But at the critical moment they were frightened of my approach.'

The postponement was only temporary. Two years later, on 16 April 1970, the documentary was broadcast. There had been a changing of the guard at the VPRO, and the new head of documentaries was now the journalist and film critic Jan Blokker. This time, contact between the two was friendlier than usual. On 22 September 1969 Jan Blokker wrote:

Dear Paul, as I need not tell you, it has taken some time for the VPRO's television affairs to be put sufficiently in order for us seriously to begin catching up on the significant backlog . . . Your Mussert film is part of that backlog . . . It seems to me that the amendments and additions you propose are improvements on what is already a good documentary . . . The apologies for this late response on our part speak for themselves, so I hardly dare utter them. I hope it will be all right in the end.

The amendments proposed by Verhoeven were not of a drastic nature. With every interviewee, the image was freeze-framed for an instant while a voice-over added the personal details. Moreover, it was once again clearly stated that Mussert did not resist the deportation of Jews. In all, the additions increased the film's length by three minutes.

After all the previous commotion, the reviews were reasonable. Only the Communist daily *De Waarheid* sternly noted: 'The VPRO has taken the dishonourable task upon itself to rehabilitate posthumously the late NSB leader Mussert.' Verhoeven remembers how, during a preview arranged for the interviewed NSB members, E. J. Roskam had burst into tears because he was so moved by the portrait. 'The nice thing about the film was that those people who had thought from the start Mussert was an insignificant figure were content because that had been confirmed in the film. On the other hand, the supporters of Mussert were very moved, because in their eyes history had finally done justice to their former leader. So I would say it was clearly a neutral film.'

Mussert had not been presented as the incarnation of evil, but as a bourgeois whose patriotism had turned into a fatal religious mania and megalomania. The naïve idealist type. 'Of course, that is partly what caused the commotion,' Verhoeven says. 'The concept of an idealist is normally reserved for people who can say in all honesty that they mean humanity well. Nonsense. Obviously, an idealist can also support something that is completely immoral and destructive to many others – that is what history has shown us often enough. It could even be argued that Hitler was an idealist, couldn't it?'

The awareness of the ambiguity of history which Verhoeven acquired by making the documentary about Anton Mussert would nearly ten years later form the basis for his feature film *Soldaat van Oranje* (*Soldier of Orange*), for which shooting began on 25 September 1976.

'Not many film-makers would have dared to show the anti-Jewish feelings that existed in Holland, or the quasi-fascist initiation ceremonies among the university students in 1938, or the Dutch crowds pressing flowers into the hands of Nazi soldiers as they marched through the streets,' wrote Peter Cowie about *Soldier of Orange* in his 1979 book *Dutch Cinema* – and in so doing, put his finger for one moment on the suppressed Dutch wound.

The images of the marching SS members being greeted with flowers by the Dutch population was something Verhoeven had literally copied from the archive footage he had found for his Mussert documentary. The director was familiar from his own time at Leiden with the student types who are the main characters in *Soldaat van Oranje*. In the same way as he too was subjected to a similar initiation ritual two decades later, the film begins in August 1938 at the moment when the main character Erik (Rutger Hauer), a shaven-headed 'fresher', joins the Minerva student association. A humiliating yet warm welcome awaits him, ending in a soup tureen being smashed on his head – a joke initiated by Guus (Jeroen Krabbé), the president of the association. His actions fit perfectly with the mentality described by Hazelhoff Roelfzema in the opening chapter of his book *Soldaat van Oranje*:

The Leiden Student Association had only a few hundred active members, but as the heart of Leiden it naturally considered itself the heart of Europe, and since the Netherlands was the heart of Europe, and Europe was the centre of the world . . . anyway, the Corps was important. Furthermore, it was absolutely convinced that – if not in the eyes of God, then at least of every right-minded European and Dutchman – all people were created unequally. Everyone must know his place and accept it . . . In Leiden, style was considered the most important thing: not *what* you did, but *how* you did it, especially if you did nothing.

They also knew their wines, admired every kind of extravagance, impressed girls with their courtship behaviour, said *môge* ('morning') instead of 'cheers' and could talk endlessly, especially about things they knew nothing about. They also intended to graduate, sooner or later.

Pleased with himself in precisely this kind of way, Erik and the fellow Corps members from his year – Alex, son of a German mother; Jan, a Jewish boy; the slightly stuffy Jacques; the small Nico; and the arrogant president Guus – all have their photograph taken on the eve of the war. By the time the photograph turns up again at the end of the film, four out of the six friends have died. History has caught up with them, literally; when the Germans invade the country, Erik and Guus are coming back half-drunk from an association party on their motorbikes. German fighter planes marked with swastikas loom up behind them, firing live ammunition. The mood is set, the story can begin.

The script for *Soldaat van Oranje* was not a literal adaptation of the book. Some of the characters described by Hazelhoff Roelfzema were merged to improve the dramatic structure, and Verhoeven especially insisted on the mirror-image Erik–Alex. Together with Gerard Soeteman, and with some assistance from his previous scriptwriter Kees Holierhoek, Verhoeven created sufficient space within the story for some sizeable action scenes. The German attack on the Netherlands, the military parades through the streets of The Hague, the shootings on the beach of Scheveningen, and later the return of Queen Wilhelmina, these would have to become filmic events – ones which Verhoeven loved so much as a director, even though he still had to convince producer Rob Houwer of their necessity.

With a budget of 3.5 million guilders, *Soldaat van Oranje* was to be the most expensive feature film ever produced in the Netherlands up to that time. It would be even bigger than *Keetje Tippel*, the film for which Verhoeven felt the need to revenge himself. With *Soldaat van Oranje* he would have another chance to test his ability to work with large-scale sets – which had been deployed only half-successfully in *Keetje Tippel*.

Jeroen Krabbé (born 1944), who was cast by Verhoeven for the role of Guus, remembers how he had to get used to the director's working method. 'I came from the theatre and was not used to working with a director who did not come up with in-depth psychology about your role. There was no talk about: where does Guus come from? What did his parents do? Has Guus got a secret, a psychological wound? Paul left all that unresolved. At his command, you had to go and stand some-where and pull the face that went with the scene. Rutger, who had of course worked with Paul before, understood all that very well, but at the beginning I was deeply unhappy about it.'

What Jeroen Krabbé did not know was that Verhoeven had had grave doubts about the casting of Rutger Hauer as the refined, aristocratic Erik. Where Jeroen Krabbé had by nature brought with him the neces-sary sense of class, Verhoeven still saw his alter ego Rutger Hauer as the tough Floris or the wild painter from *Turks Fruit*. He had thought about letting Hauer play the role of Alex, but with his blond hair he would have looked too much like the cliché of a proto-Teuton, whereas Verhoeven wanted to give the Alex figure more nuances. For the role of Alex he chose the up-and-coming actor Derek de Lint, and after an extra screen test Rutger Hauer was given the role of Erik – which would eventually take him to America.

Convinced of his own ability, Hauer realized that the main role in *Sol-daat van Oranje* was perfectly suited to be a star vehicle. From the very beginning, he did not want to be overshadowed by the second leading man. As Krabbé wrote in his diary about the first week of shooting at the end of September 1976:

Rutger is more Oriental than ever today – does not say anything at all. Difficult to keep myself going next to him. He makes me dead nervous. Why is he doing this? Paul, however, was kind of glad to see me – which was better than I expected . . .

The rivalry between the two actors would reach a climax in a scene shot in the port of Den Helder. In the story, Guus and Erik have fled to England after the German invasion to join the Dutch government in exile and its secret service. In London, Erik and Guus offer to establish Contact Holland, an information network in the occupied home coun-try which was to prepare for a possible invasion by the Allies. From England they again cross the North Sea, arriving at the Dutch seaside resort of Scheveningen in the middle of the night armed with radio equipment.

Erik and Guus, who are sworn friends, cross to the Netherlands on board a motor torpedo boat (MTB): Rutger Hauer stands heroically at the prow, like a victorious Viking, while Krabbé seems to be wandering uninterestedly on deck. Later, Paul Verhoeven discovered that 'Jeroen had been deliberately told by Rutger that it was only a camera rehearsal.'

Jeroen Krabbé knew Rutger Hauer from the Amsterdamse Toneel-school (Amsterdam Theatre School) and was surprised at his very un-Dutch aggressiveness. 'I thought it peculiar that Rutger saw me as a threat, because he was cut out for the role of the adventurer Erik. He also had a tendency in front of the camera to push you out of the frame with his elbows. I did not kick up a row about that with Paul. I let it be, but I didn't really understand it. The only other actor from whom I would experience such rivalry was Jeremy Irons during the shooting of *Kafka*.'

While it may not have helped the atmosphere on the set, Rutger Hauer was certainly rewarded for his efforts. After the American première of *Soldaat van Oranje*, David Ansen of *Newsweek* cheered: 'The revelation of the film is the striking Rutger Hauer as Erik. Blond and blue-eyed, he cuts a classic romantic profile, but no mannequin could perform with such effortless authority and self-effacing wit. When an unknown actor can make his entrance with noodle soup pouring down his shaved head and *still* look good, you know you are in the presence of a movie star.'

Later, Rutger Hauer would say that he 'did not remember much of the rivalry'. During the shooting of *Soldaat van Oranje* Verhoeven had other things to worry about. Between all the scenes of spectacle, from the big ball-scenes shot in Hotel Huis ter Duin in Noordwijk to the German bombardment of the Willem II barracks in Amersfoort, he had to ensure that the complicated story line was never lost. Moreover, experience had taught him that every big production has its tensions.

In production stills, the director is regularly seen in a characteristic pose: sitting with his hands clasped around his head – tensed up, almost in pain, lost in deep thought – undoubtedly running through the film in his mind. Verhoeven had done story boards for large parts of the script. The pen sketches are very detailed. A scene in which an English seaplane makes an attempt to pick up the Dutch agents near the Frisian lake Tjeukermeer, and is taken by surprise by the Germans, is drawn shot-by-shot in the script. The notes speak for themselves: 'Better this way! Fade out the plane while the lights of the German patrol boat shine across the frame from behind the plane.'

Krabbé vividly remembers Verhoeven's struggle to recreate the Second World War. The actor tells how, in the scene where Erik and Guus approach on their motorbikes, the director wanted to capture the German fighter-bombers suddenly looming over the horizon in the same shot. Because there were a considerable number of formalities over hiring the planes and flying low over a densely populated area, it was only possible to shoot two takes of the scene. Krabbé: 'The planes would come flying over at twelve o'clock, make a wide curve and return in twenty minutes. The first time, something went wrong on the technical side. The second time, my engine failed to start. Paul, on top of the roof of the town hall in The Hague, exploded. I have never seen anyone so angry. He stood there cursing and yelling. It was primarily aimed at me, I was the moron, but they must have heard him through his megaphone as far away as Leiden.'

The coolly calculating advice of producer Rob Houwer did not make the director feel any better: 'Well then, you just matt those planes in. Continue shooting! Next scene.' 'Yes, but . . . THIS is what it says in the script!' Verhoeven riposted, whereupon Houwer grabbed the shooting script and tore out the complete episode. Krabbé: 'Of course he had read that in a book about some Hollywood mogul.' The collaboration between the producer and the director was characterized by endless fighting. In their attempt to make Dutch films with international appeal, every penny spent was one too many. Contractually, cast and crew had to be available twenty-four hours a day, and even on paper a production such as *Soldaat van Oranje* – which by Dutch standards was rather complicated – was impossible to shoot in twelve weeks. Houwer, who regularly declared in interviews that he 'gladly took on the role of the old Hollywood tycoon', appealed to the fact that the Dutch feature-film market had its limits; in a small country, 3.3 million spectators – which they had managed to attract with *Turks Fruit* – was a record. As a perfectionist, Verhoeven was unable to resign himself to a slipshod job: if the script said ten planes, then there had to be ten planes – and not two, as Houwer in turn would propose.

These huge differences of opinion were fought out on the set in full view of the other crew members, who usually watched in bewilderment. On Tuesday 9 November 1976, Krabbé's diary reports:

There is rather a hushed atmosphere on the set. It turns out that the shit has hit the fan. Rob Houwer was furious about not shooting a café scene . . . and it seems, at least according to Hans Kemna, the assistant to the director, that they even thought of stopping the whole thing. That seems rather exaggerated to me, but then again, if it's your millions they're talking about . . .

Rob Houwer immediately circulated a duplicated missive, which Krabbé still has in his scrapbook. 'It is gradually becoming clear that we are all biting off more than we can chew with *De Soldaat*. It appears to be more difficult than we ever imagined.' After seven weeks of filming, producer Houwer considered chucking it all in. He said there was no more money.

In the end it did not come to that. The first shooting period concluded with a party on Monday 15 November, and they shot for another five weeks from 17 April 1977. Houwer had received some extra money from the Rank Organisation, and had made an agreement with the Dutch television channel TROS to make a four-part television adaptation of *Soldaat van Oranje*. Thus the budget for the film was increased from 3.5 to 5 million guilders – although it was never clear what the exact figures for the production were, since Houwer never made any announcements about the precise budgets. Even Paul Verhoeven as the director did not know how much he was allowed to spend.

But the titanic struggle between Houwer and Verhoeven was a necessary evil. As Jeroen Krabbé observed, 'Rob had the power to curb and guide Paul's talent. That lava stream which would otherwise take up twenty metres of film, he was able to reduce to eighteen metres and sometimes to sixteen.'

Thus in April 1977 everyone cheerfully came back to work. It was necessary filmically to give depth to the images of Wilhelmina's royal household in exile in London. One of the most intriguing aspects of Dutch war history was the 'Affair van 't Sant'. Verhoeven had worked on this story line with great care, basing his character van der Zande on speculations that the Queen's special aide François van 't Sant had in fact been a double agent.

Initially van 't Sant had been asked by the Queen to cover up royal scandals, such as the illegitimate children of her husband Prince Hendrik. Once in London Wilhelmina appointed him as head of the Dutch Central Intelligence Service. One of his jobs was to screen newly arrived Dutch agents in England, but he was also involved in plotting missions in occupied territory. But after fifty-four Dutch parachute agents had been intercepted by the Germans, he was branded a traitor by the Resistance.

In *Soldaat van Oranje* Erik attempts on his arrival in London to eliminate van der Zande, the head of the intelligence service. But the old fox slips through his fingers, after which he coolly introduces Erik to the Queen. When Erik subsequently sees that van der Zande is completely trusted by the monarch, he abandons further assassination attempts. In this way the film does not give a definitive answer to the question of treason by van der Zande/van 't Sant. The matter was never solved in reality, and Verhoeven lets this ambiguity work for him throughout the film.

By playing with Dutch history in this way, Verhoeven lifted *Soldaat van Oranje* far beyond the usually rather limited genre of the war film. In addition, his eye for detail gives the film a special charm. This is evident, for example, is his casting of the actress Andrea Domburg as the resolute but unworldly Queen Wilhelmina, about whom Churchill apparently once said: 'I do not fear any man in the world, except Queen Wilhelmina.'

Soldaat van Oranje had its Dutch première on 23 September 1977. This time, Verhoeven was confident he had delivered an important film, and he was hurt by some of the reviews. 'The dramatic tension is limited to set pieces like in a James Bond film,' Ellen Waller wrote in a sour review for *NRC/Handelsblad*. 'The duo Rob Houwer/Paul Verhoeven consciously adopted their generation's personal view of the years 1940–45. And they equally consciously took the attitude of the majority of the current cinema-going public, who are much younger than Houwer (born 1937) and Verhoeven (born 1938) . . . The Netherlands' most expensive feature film does nothing for (film) culture; it might do something for the commercial credibility of Dutch films for a wider public. Which was the intention.'

'Films like *Soldaat van Oranje* are standard fare abroad,' *Trouw* reported sternly. Bob Bertina supported the film. On behalf of *De Volkskrant* he wrote: 'Paul Verhoeven has remained consistent. He proved before (especially in *Turks Fruit*) that he is capable of bringing to life characters from novels, and he never shies away from burlesque. Now he is in better form than ever. Here and there his approach to some of the scenes is so harsh and acutely unsentimental that you regret that he is filming merely the secret heroism of Hazelhoff Roelfzema.'

Although in later years (and especially after Verhoeven's departure to the United States), *Soldaat van Oranje* would be acclaimed as one of the best Dutch films ever, the unenthusiastic reception appeared to the director to be a denial of his professional accomplishment.

The film eventually attracted an audience of one and a half million in the Netherlands, but it was the American reviews which were the first to recognize the true value of the film after the première in August 1979. 'Verhoeven is a film-maker with enormous vitality, passion and a feeling for humor,' Kevin Thomas of the *Los Angeles Times* wrote. David Ansen of *Newsweek* excelled in his praise: 'Hundreds of novels and films have told a similar story: how a generation came of age on the battlefields of Europe. Few have done it as well as this superb Dutch-made epic. The screenplay is so crowded with character, adventure, intriguing moral quandaries and delightful humor that its two and a half hours fly by without a lull. Director Paul Verhoeven synthesizes the best of the European and American movie traditions: he can stage a tango with all the bravura of Bertolucci, but his stylistic flourishes are always employed in the service of his story. And what a story it is – an eight-course feast that leaves you hungry for more.'

The 'tango with bravura' to which the reviewer was referring had been for Verhoeven the crux of the film, in which the ambiguity of 'right' and 'wrong' was concentrated in one key scene. The main character Erik has sailed from England on a secret mission. Going ashore on the beach of Scheveningen, his cover is nearly broken. But because the dark British uniform he is wearing resembles that of the German *Kriegsmarine*, he is able to deceive the German guards. Against his will, he ends up at a dance held by the Germans, where he sees his friend Alex, by now a member of the SS. It becomes a confrontation on a chivalric level. Instead of reporting him, Alex takes Erik by the hand and pulls him on to the dance floor. As befits a stylized fight, a tango begins. With passion, they dance cheek to cheek. As they bend over to each other's side, the fine line between their choices in war is made tangible in the dance.

Verhoeven is suggesting that if the dice had fallen differently, it would have been Erik, not Alex, who would have become a member of the SS. 'Erik is not a Resistance fighter. He is an adventurer. History is on his side, and he embraces it in a carefree way.' But this flirting with danger causes people to die within the circle of his student friends. Paul Verhoeven has few illusions, not just about people in real life, but about the moral nature of his film characters.

Hans van Tongeren.

The actress and her coach: Renée Soutendijk and Verhoeven during *Spetters*.

Chapter 9

Better Dead than a Slave: *Spetters*

Wednesday 10 May 1978. A Mazda is tearing across the Dutch polders with true contempt for death – the driver is Paul Verhoeven. He is furious. Disappointed. He accelerates even more, needing to go even faster. Near the Frisian town of Stavoren he seems to be losing control of the wheel. An unexpected bend in a B-road forces him to slam on the brakes. When he has brought his car to a standstill in a cloud of burnt rubber, he realizes that he has nearly crashed into a boulder. It reads *1345 – Leaver dea as slaef*, which in the Frisian language means 'better dead than a slave'.

The stone is a memorial to the Battle of Warns, where the tough Frisians drove the Hollanders out of their territory. To Verhoeven the inscription means something entirely different. He reads it as a hint. Although he realizes that in a film this scene would be too improbable, the inscription concisely sums up his state of mind. His decision is made. He will no longer work with his producer Rob Houwer – the roles of servant and master have made him physically and mentally ill.

Feeling relieved about his decision and now driving considerably more slowly, he heads for Rutger Hauer's farm, far from the outside world in the Frisian town of Beetsterzwaag. They need to have a quiet talk. When Verhoeven sees the actor from a distance, he realizes the comic side of the situation. Rutger Hauer, the 'up-and-coming international star', is chopping wood in his garden, dressed in a blue overall, covered in dirt and with an untidy moustache. At present he has nothing better to do. The same situation applies to his visitor: unemployed. As far as film in the Netherlands is concerned – it's enough to drive you mad.

Not entirely to his surprise, Paul Verhoeven had for a long time found himself claiming unemployment benefit after each film. The fee had always been modest. For his successful film *Turks Fruit*, he had received exactly 20,000 guilders, and although with the subsequent productions his earnings had gradually increased, it seemed to Verhoeven that the producer–director relationship had gone badly wrong. His films had earned his producer Rob Houwer millions of guilders, while he himself had had to borrow money from his parents to buy a house. In view of the indisputable fact that a director in the Netherlands would not get a big production off the ground more than once every two or three years, filming gave him artistic but hardly any financial satisfaction. In order to avoid his children becoming the victims of his artistic ambitions, he had taken out an insurance policy to guarantee their university education. 'For a long time I thought I was on top of the world with Rob Houwer, because he let me make the films I wanted to make. That morning I realized in what an economically naïve way I had been operating.'

Verhoeven had reached breaking point because Rob Houwer had quietly left for Surinam with *Soldaat van Oranje* under his arm to stage a gala première there. This was not the first time this had happened; the producer had done something similar in Antwerp. With fireworks, but without Verhoeven. The director heard the news on the telephone from Jindra Markus, assistant to the director. Although Verhoeven had always been irritated by the fact that in interviews Rob Houwer emphasized that he made Rob Houwer films, devised by Rob Houwer, produced by Rob Houwer and delivered by Rob Houwer on Rob Houwer posters, the message about a première in Surinam, although unimportant in itself, was the last straw. He concluded that he had spent 'seven years with the devil'.

Verhoeven would later give this explanation when he was interviewed about the break by the Dutch magazine *Filmfan* in January 1979: 'I find it unpleasant when someone is constantly saying, "If it goes wrong, I'll take over." Whereas you know it's not true because it's not possible. With *Turks Fruit* Rob spent maybe five days on the set. I never consulted him about a shot or anything else, but in the publicity it was always Rob this and Rob that. That myth should be exploded.' He continued, 'Rob said in *De Telegraaf*, "Actually, Paul is Dr Jekyll and Mr Hyde, because he is very nice but when he starts working he is the devil." Well, I have now worked with Rob for seven years – that's the classic number of years you work with the devil, isn't it? It's very peculiar. I know a lot of fairy-tales about someone who sells his soul to the devil and for seven years all the treasures of the world are conjured up before his eyes, he sees everything, experiences everything, wonderful – and after seven years, *Boom!* He realizes he is standing in exactly the same place as where he started – everyone else has carried on with their lives, only he has stayed at exactly the same point.'

It was a feeling Verhoeven had earlier described in the diary which, on the recommendation of his wife Martine, he had started in June 1978:

In short, I think that Rob is using me in an unfair way, and is using my talent and commitment (and that of Gerard) to blow his own trumpet. We are no more than dumb employees, and we even let ourselves be treated that way . . . I want: more money, more respect and more enjoyment in my work.

It was in this mood that the director got into his car after receiving the bad news from Markus. During the journey, his seven-year collaboration with Rob Houwer passed before his mind's eye once more. Of course he was a skilful producer; Houwer knew how to find his way through the media jungle. They had often laughed at dinner parties about the way he had pulled off his latest financial success, but the atmosphere had become more strained when Rob Houwer told the press that *Soldaat van Oranje* had 'given him a black eye', meaning that Verhoeven's fanaticism had brought him to the verge of bankruptcy.

To break his dependency on Houwer required a drastic decision. Verhoeven would look for another producer, though in the Dutch film world this was not an easy task. On the recommendation of Jeroen Krabbé, he went to see Joop van den Ende, a wealthy television and theatre producer who seemed to have overcome his initial fear of the film industry. The repercussions of the meeting are recorded in Verhoeven's diary: '14 June 1978: Saw Joop van den Ende. Excellent conversation: there he is, the strong man fallen out of the sky. Depression has lifted. He wants to work with us, has apparently been planning for a long time to venture into the film world and sees this as an excellent opportunity. Which it is, I think.'

On 20 June 1978 another discussion followed, about which the diary says: 'Bit wearing; Joop tries too hard to sell his stuff, also made proposals for Gerard and me to make cheap (= silly) TV series in between. It's giving me quite a headache.'

A few days later he concludes: 'It sure is ridiculous (sad, frustrating) that after making four successful films you still have to plead with everyone . What a country!'

In the same period, in an attempt to make peace with Verhoeven, Rob Houwer proposed adapting the characters of police inspectors Grijpstra and De Gier from the detective novels by Jan Willem van de Wetering. It was with unusual poise that the director put his demands on the table: a fee of 100,000 guilders and 25 per cent of the profit. It did not take Houwer long to reply 'unacceptable'. Later, in an interview with the weekly *Vrij Nederland* on 22 September 1979, Houwer said about the matter: 'Suddenly Paul's whole attitude towards *Soldaat van Oranje* went down the wrong way with me. You simply cannot make a film of 6 million guilders in the Netherlands, you can't cover the production costs . . . The film was shot as it should have been. But I could no longer live with the thought that Paul did not at all realize what I had done for that film. That he had been allowed to work with international resources, but did not prove himself as a director.'

In Houwer's eyes Verhoeven had been ungrateful. He explained that without him the director would still be shooting *Floris*. And 'I am glad to be rid of Soeteman; he is Arrogance incarnate, and he thinks every word that flows from his pen is ingenious! You cannot work with someone like that. Effects on the level of blood and vomit, that is what he is good at, but don't ask him to create a character, because he can't do it.'

Houwer put his money on a collaboration with the director Wim Verstappen that was to have little success. Verhoeven and Gerard ('I don't work for Rob Houwer, I work for Paul') Soeteman had had enough. The deal with Joop van den Ende was quickly made. Verhoeven immediately put away his diary. The film-maker could start filming again.

The new logo simply said VSE Film BV, an abbreviation that stood for Verhoeven, Soeteman, van den Ende; the director, writer and producer were the directors of the company. The agreement was that VSE Film, in addition to cinema, would deliver material for television. The first project to be realized was *Voorbij, Voorbij* ('*Gone, Gone*'), from an original script by Gerard Soeteman, a film broadcast by the television channel KRO in May 1981. The prologue shows a group of Resistance workers at the end of the war burying a comrade who had been shot by a Dutch SS member a few days before the Liberation. The group swears revenge, after which the film moves to the present. By coincidence, the main character Ab (André van den Heuvel) sees the former SS member among a group of tourists, and thinks that the moment of revenge has come. He visits his old comrades-in-arms and proposes an attack. Nobody wants to know – Ab should leave the past alone.

The film, whose theme could be seen as a rounding-off of *Soldaat van Oranje* (how does a group of Resistance fighters experience the war after thirty-five years?), was told by Verhoeven in a calm tone. No big action scenes, but a great deal of dialogue. Since television seemed to him a more introverted medium than film, he shot *Voorbij, Voorbij* in an extremely economical way – an exception in his body of work. His decision to make such a 'simple dialogue film' was influenced by the knowledge that afterwards he would be shooting the dynamic production for the cinema *Spetters*.

This film was a break with the past in another sense. This time Verhoeven and Soeteman would not turn to a successful book as the basis for a script, but had decided to write the entire story themselves. The working title was *Buddies*, the story was about blue-collar circles in a village near Rotterdam, where young people occupied themselves with their love of girls and motorbikes. While *Soldaat van Oranje* had portrayed the ups and downs of a youthful élite, the idea behind *Buddies* was to give a similar portrait of a generation but this time about young working people at the bottom of the social ladder. It was to be a Dutch counterpart to *Saturday Night Fever* (John Badham, 1977) or *Grease* (Randal Kleiser, 1978). Verhoeven: 'More John Travolta than Robert Redford. Not candle-light, but neon light.' Thus *Buddies* could be the antithesis of *Soldaat van Oranje*. 'To us, it was a reaction against those highly intellectual, civilized student friends. Gerard and I thought that *every* milieu is special, so long as you see the special side of it.'

The protagonists of *Buddies* – the title would later be changed to *Spetters* (Dutch slang for 'good-looking young men'), thanks to an idea of Paul's wife Martine – are three friends of about twenty years old: Rien, Eef and Hans. The film is located in Maassluis, where the strict Calvinist Church still plays an important role in everyday life. Especially for Eef, whose father is an elder in the church and for whom every 'worldly aberration' of his son merits severe punishment.

Basing their approach on the idea that the working class might start their climb up the social ladder by way of crime, rock 'n' roll or sport, Verhoeven and Soeteman eventually chose the world of motocross racing for the main characters in *Spetters*. Verhoeven says, 'Sports such as boxing, cycling or football were also a possibility, but motocross has the advantage of being attractive to visualize.'

The three friends idolize the successful motocross rider, fellow-villager and dentist Gerrit Witkamp, who was modelled on the Dutch motocross rider Gerrit Wolsink – at that time a dental student on his way to becoming the world motocross champion. Between tinkering with their engines and cheering Witkamp, Rien, Eef and Hans become enthralled by the beautiful but opportunistic Fientje, who one day arrives in the village with a mobile fast-food stand.

Fientje has had more than enough of life among the meatballs and croquettes. The smell of frying makes her feel sick, but she sees no way out. As a form of escapism she starts going out with the three young men, one by one. First she chooses Rien, the smartest and most talented of the three. He is on his way to a career as a professional motocross rider, until an accident lands him in a wheelchair. Then she tries her charms on Eef, who works as a mechanic and petrol pump assistant, but he turns out to be homosexual. Hans is the dumb one, but as he might have enough money to start up a pub-cum-café, Fientje considers him a suitable match; she confirms this economic alliance with her body – an arrangement to their mutual benefit. 'Love?' she says. 'A bit of security, then love will follow automatically.'

Gerard Soeteman describes the basic idea of *Spetters* as a 'modern fairytale': three knights court a princess and eventually the youngest and clumsiest wins. 'The hero does not get a kingdom, but a chip shop and a girl with a (sexual) past. That does not mean to say she is not an acceptable match for a young man: it is real life. In our films, Paul and I have always resisted the odd idea that only romantic love can be real love.'

In order to reinforce the fairytale idea, the knights are put on motorbikes ('iron horses') and their clothes adapted to their roles. Rien, the hero, wears a white leather motorbike suit. Eef is a two-tone figure because of his ambivalent sexual feelings: his clothes are red and black. As Hans is rather cowardly, yellow is the colour of his suit.

The scriptwriter and film-maker distilled the backgrounds of the main characters from reality. Near Nieuwerkerk aan de IJssel, where Soeteman lived, was the village of Zevenhuizen, where they picked up the necessary atmosphere. It had a motorbike club; the local pub was on the corner of the high street; everything fitted. 'And in this small place everything was covered with a blanket of Calvinist religion.' Eef, the son of the strict Calvinist father, was based on a boy a friend of Soeteman knew from childhood, a pupil at the Christian *gymnasium* in The Hague. Eventually, he secretly started to take boxing lessons and defended himself successfully against his father's violence. Eef's curiosity about the behaviour of homosexuals, who in Rotterdam meet in and around the run-down shopping centre, was partly inspired by newspaper articles. The weekly *Haagse Post* had published a piece about 'queer-bashers', young men who attack male prostitutes and their clients. This is what Eef himself does in the film, although it gradually becomes clear that his hatred of 'queers' flows mostly from his doubts about his own sexual identity. In accepting the consequences – he is raped by four homosexual leather-boys, including Fientje's brother – he overcomes his uncertainties. This explicit scene was to meet with much criticism, but a similar event had once been described in minute detail in the evening newspaper *NRC/Handelsblad*, when a homosexual gang-rape took place in the Maas Tunnel in Rotterdam. The rape does not feature in the original script for *Spetters* – Eef was 'only' going to be beaten up. Verhoeven added it after seeing a similar incident in an American feature, set in the navy, at a gay film festival in Amsterdam. 'Really tough in its visualization. Compared to that film, things were fairly subdued in *Spetters*,' Verhoeven says. He thought of two other elements for the story. The character of Maja, Rien's girlfriend – who after the arrival of Fientje is carelessly abandoned by the up-and-coming motocross rider and seeks solace with the Pentecostal Church – was a condensing of his own experience of religious crisis. Moreover, the choice of subject matter was partly inspired by a change in Verhoeven's family situation. They had adopted Mariëlle, a fifteen-year-old girl from a similar working-class background, as their foster-child. Martine Verhoeven had met her in the course of her work as a school psychologist. 'Her presence gave the film's theme an instinctive line,' the director remembers.

The essentially nihilistic nature of *Spetters* showed a consciousness of the changing mood of the times. Now that the sexual revolution in Amsterdam and surrounding areas had come to an end, as hippy culture evaporated, the atmosphere in the big cities had become much more grim. By now, the dominant youth culture was punk music and no future. Tough leather jackets had pushed out the Paisley motifs. In sociological reports these kids were worriedly described as 'the lost generation'. The backlash against the 1960s, the time when 'love and peace' had made everything seem possible, climaxed in the large-scale street fights between police and squatters. The main issue of the squatter movement was young people's right to housing. Their actions had begun peacefully enough, pointing on the one hand to the financial speculators who left many buildings empty and the housing crisis among young people on the other. The movement had initially won public sympathy, but in the late 1970s and early 1980s much of this sympathy was dissipated by the militant and violent nature of their actions. Although the main characters in *Spetters* are neither particularly politically conscious, nor representatives of urban youth, they undoubtedly shared the embittered atmosphere of youth culture in the Netherlands at the end of the 1970s.

A script was put together which emphasized Soeteman and Verhoeven's tendency towards unaffected realism – a very earthy, Dionysian world took shape on paper. With a short introduction, *Spetters* was presented to the Productiefonds as a modern, realistic Dutch drama. It met with little approval. Chairman Anton Koolhaas immediately rejected it. Verhoeven: 'He thought the character of Fientje was that of a common whore – those were the words he used. How in God's name could we make a film about a whore? He was extremely indignant.' Producer Joop van den Ende became so angry that he slammed his fist furiously on the table, causing Anton Koolhaas to flinch in fright. Verhoeven: 'I got tears in my eyes, but I was too perplexed by this opposition to say anything.'

It was clear there had been a change of management at the Productiefonds. At the time of his association with Rob Houwer, Verhoeven needed only to mention the book's title in order to get a subsidy, but the atmosphere had changed with the arrival of the new chairman, Anton Koolhaas, in 1978. This writer and film-maker succeeded J. G. J. Bosman, formerly the driving force behind the Productiefonds and the 'godfather of Dutch film'. Having himself had a background in cinema, Bosman was of the same mind as Verhoeven in the debate about commercial versus art films, to the regret of the *auteurs* who in their turn accused Bosman of acting in an authoritarian way. Koolhaas's sympathies and antipathies were diametrically opposed to those of Bosman. As a prominent purveyor of Dutch culture, Koolhaas was more at home with the art film. Moreover, he knew Verhoeven from the Filmacademie, where as a student Verhoeven had never spoken very highly of Koolhaas – especially not his script lectures. For his part, the new director of the Productiefonds had regularly remarked that Verhoeven and Soeteman 'deserved capital punishment for the way they had adapted Neel Doff's *Keetje Tippel*.'

At the news of Anton Koolhaas's appointment, Verhoeven had anticipated slightly more resistance, but thought that with his reputation as a successful film-maker he would be on sure ground. His earlier films had managed to draw some nine million people to Dutch cinemas, and had more or less kept the entire Dutch film industry going. 'The insinuations about my integrity as a film-maker were an unexpected blow. Especially when it turned out that, at the meeting where *Spetters* was rejected, all the other applications were approved, including a proposal by Bert Haanstra based on a script by Chairman Anton Koolhaas himself.' In order not to have to fight the old chairman tooth and nail, it was decided to make a number of changes to the *Spetters* script.

This was largely camouflage, since Verhoeven had decided to shoot the first version anyway. 'When it turned out that I had used the original story they were really livid. It gave them a reason to tighten the screws on me even more with my next film, *De Vierde Man*.' The new version of the script was accompanied by an apology from Gerard Soeteman. After six months of pleading with the Productiefonds, funding for *Spetters* was obtained; with a subsidy of 750,000 guilders and money from producer van den Ende, the budget was set at 1.8 million guilders. In February 1979 preparations for the film began, arousing passions both inside and outside the offices of the Productiefonds.

The plan was to cast new faces for *Spetters*. For old times' sake Jeroen Krabbé and Rutger Hauer, the heroes of *Soldaat van Oranje*, were given supporting roles as a sports commentator and the motocross champion Gerrit Witkamp respectively, but were too old to play provincial teenagers. The search for fresh-faced new actors became a major undertaking. For several months casting director Hans Kemna visited nearly all the Dutch theatre, ballet and cabaret academies to select students for the forthcoming auditions. These would take place in Badhoevedorp, at the offices of producer Joop van den Ende. On the crucial day in March, 450 candidates turned up. Kemna remembers that, to make matters worse, the video installation packed up in the course of the morning, messing up the entire schedule.

Spoilt for choice, Kemna eventually decided on the punky Hans van Tongeren (born 1955), a student in the Mime Department of the Amsterdam Theatre School, for the role of Rien. The character of the latent homosexual Eef was given to Toon Agterberg, an actor with the De Soepgroep children's theatre. The role of clumsy Hans went to actor Maarten Spanjer, who had done some television work. As Maja, cashier in a supermarket and Rien's girlfriend, he cast Marianne Boyer. And the beautiful but selfish Fientje was to be played by the twenty-two-year-old Renée Soutendijk. She had become known for her role in Wim Verstappen's *Pastorale 1943* (1978) and for performances in television series. She was also involved in political theatre. Renée Soutendijk still remembers the surprise of her theatre friends when she announced that she was going to appear in a Paul Verhoeven film. 'He was seen as extremely commercial, and that was a charged, dirty word in those days. I thought that as a budding actress you should try as many different things as possible.' Once selected, she began her research at a mobile fast-food stand in the market of the working-class Albert Cuyp district of Amsterdam, so that on screen she would be throwing the meatballs into the frying fat with some credibility.

This was the cast which began shooting at Maassluis on 7 August 1979; the shooting would continue until 18 October. As with *Soldaat van Oranje*, Jost Vacano was the cameraman. It immediately became clear that Verhoeven was moving around the set in a provocative way. Like the main characters in the film, he was dressed in a tough leather jacket with lots of zips – but Verhoeven had long since lost the freshness of youth. After his row with Rob Houwer and his struggles with the Productiefonds, Verhoeven had 'the feeling I had to prove myself doubly, to show that I could make a good film without Rob Houwer, if only to make all the bragging about his important part in our productions sound ridiculous.'

The stress was clearly visible on the director's face. 'Paul was simply terrible,' Hans Kemna remembers. There was cursing, swearing and yelling. Kemna was aware of the change in the director's behaviour, as he had known Verhoeven since the days of *Floris* when he had been cast in a supporting role. The collaboration resulted in both friendship and a professional association – ranging from a role as the barman in *Wat Zien Ik* to doing the casting for most of Verhoeven's subsequent films. With *Soldaat van Oranje* and *Spetters* he was also given the task of assistant to the director. 'What I admire most in Paul is that in the middle of the greatest chaos he is able to withdraw into himself completely. I used to call, "Silence on the set! The director is thinking!" Within just a few seconds he would always have a solution for the most complicated visual problems, but with *Spetters* the stress soon got the upper hand.'

Because of the continuously roaring engines, the atmosphere was fairly aggressive anyway, but, Kemna continues, 'during the shooting of the races and in the presence of thousands of people Paul actually shouted through the megaphone that I was a moron and a fucking idiot, because a car wrongly moved into the shot from left to right. I really had to eat humble pie then.'

With the naïvety of an up-and-coming actress, Renée Soutendijk thought that all this aggro was simply part of 'Hollywood in Holland': 'As far as I was concerned, Paul's outbursts could be classified as professionalism, because I never felt there was anything nasty about them. Strangely enough, his shouting did not really disturb me, because I kept continuous eye contact with him and understood that he wanted to push everyone to the limit of their ability. Because of that driving enthusiasm, you are prepared to do much more for Paul than for other directors.'

Soutendijk's very first shot in *Spetters* was a car stunt, something she had never done before, partly because she had only just passed her driving test. 'I had to come tearing across a very small bridge in a gigantic American car, make a 180-degree turn in a skid and then get out really cool as if nothing had happened. Nowadays I would leave something like that to a qualified stunt man, but Paul knows how to manipulate you in such a way that refusing scenes or stunts would come across as very childish.'

After the long shooting days, always on location and sometimes involving sixteen hours of uninterrupted labour (Kemna says, 'We all lived on Benzedrine and cola tics'), personal disputes were usually resolved in the hotel. At these moments, the charming Paul Verhoeven eclipsed the angry director and it was possible to laugh about the film's progress. For example, how the security guards had to be misled on the night the gang-rape scene was filmed in a tunnel of the Rotterdam metro while it was still under construction. The guards were told that it involved a complicated chase scene, and a production assistant kept them away with brandy and cream cakes.

Meanwhile a small drama was taking place on location. In search of a person who would be able to have an erection in this scene on-screen, Verhoeven and Kemna had visited all the live clubs on the Amsterdam gay circuit, without any success. Finally, Hans Kemna had found a performer from Alkmaar, who together with his wife performed in an Amsterdam sex club. It transpired that the man was able to get into a state of excitement in front of the camera only if he saw a woman in front of him. His eye fell on a girl from the make-up department. 'If she looked at him,' Verhoeven remembers, 'he was able to "warm himself up". To top it all, the poor kid was a lesbian.'

As Verhoeven did not wish to make a distinction between the heterosexual actions shown in his earlier films and the homoeroticism of *Spetters*, he shot a scene of oral sex. The film shows clearly, not in semi-darkness, how a customer is served by a male prostitute, while Eef, full of curiosity, is secretly watching. Two prostitutes were hired for this scene. When, after a while, Verhoeven decided that he had enough footage, he called 'cut'. The men looked at the director furiously. 'He hasn't even come yet,' they muttered angrily.

There were not only problems with the shooting in and around the Rotterdam metro, but in broad daylight. The mobile fast-food stand, which also houses Fientje and her brother, was removed from the road by the police during the first take of a scene because of its dilapidated state. Meanwhile Verhoeven, unknowing, was standing on the roof of a high-rise block, ready to shoot take two. 'But the trailer never came back. They kept the thing at the police station for three days.'

Although the shooting time was considerably shorter than that of *Soldaat van Oranje*, to Hans Kemna the making of *Spetters* seemed much more exhausting. 'In the film, Paul rooted through so many things at the same time. He had to translate all those emotions with a cast of neophytes. They were enthusiastic. They were keen to learn. But they also needed a lot of time-consuming explanations and coaching.'

For Renée Soutendijk, *Spetters* was her début as a leading actress. The collaboration with Verhoeven would continue with *De Vierde Man*. 'What I learnt is that actors should ask themselves beforehand whether they want to do a film with Paul. It is a decision which needs to be made in advance, because *during* the shooting nothing else can be adjusted. Then he demands unconditional loyalty. Every obstacle is seen as a personal attack. If he senses mistrust, it drives him crazy. It gives him the feeling that he no longer has a grip on things. Paul is a perfectionist. Whoever goes on board has to meet the same requirements.'

The absence of Rob Houwer's iron fist on the set was more evident than expected. The eventual budget overrun was 1 million guilders. During the shooting, Joop van den Ende had had to divide his time between his company's theatre business, his television affairs and the film itself. Later it emerged that a crooked bookkeeper had amused himself in casinos and brothels with hundreds of thousands of guilders. Moreover, his fellow directors in VSE Film had found it difficult to stop Verhoeven's unbridled energy if it concerned budgetary restraints. If they tactfully suggested that *Spetters* was becoming too expensive, the director would shout, 'What's it to do with you? I'm the director of the firm making this film, so piss off!'

Verhoeven derived more enjoyment from the performance of Hans van Tongeren as the motocross rider Rien. On viewing the rushes, it became obvious that the young actor had a Hauer-like charisma, but was able to blend this with a convincing sensitivity. In the story, Rien has an accident with his motorbike and ends up paralysed in a wheelchair. Although there was a danger that the scenes would be flattened under the weight of too much pathos, Hans van Tongeren managed to portray convincingly the main character's disappointment with life in all its confusion and bitterness.

'In that take I let the camera ride ahead of Hans and his wheelchair,' Verhoeven says, 'and it struck me that his eyes had misted over. Initially I thought it was exaggerated, too overdone. But Hans had immersed himself so deeply that he could explain exactly how that guy must have felt at that moment. He said to me, "When that guy commits suicide, the whole world cries." He was not only furious, but scared – and he felt guilty about what it would do to his family and friends if he committed suicide. Later it became clear that he had consulted his own emotions for that scene.'

Hans van Tongeren committed suicide in August 1982. To Verhoeven, who had great plans for the talented but unstable actor, and had also built up a friendship with him outside filming, it would turn out to be the biggest legacy of *Spetters*.

After an extensive publicity campaign in the Netherlands' biggest morning newspaper *De Telegraaf*, a campaign especially aimed at young people – *Spetters. Tough & Romantic. Your film* – the film had its première in fifty-three Dutch cinemas on 25 February 1980. The director thought he'd 'made an interesting sociological statement'; however, the production immediately rebounded on him like a boomerang. '*Spetters* is a deep black pool for people whose mental growth stopped after three years of age,' the morning newspaper *De Volkskrant* wrote. 'A striking phallic fixation,' the *NRC Handelsblad* noted. 'Unashamed sexual exhibitions, in which their boldness is only exceeded by their tastelessness,' the morning paper *Trouw* concluded.

In an attempt to defend his work, Verhoeven appeared on the weekly talk show of Sonja Barend, the Dutch counterpart of Oprah Winfrey. Barend had a reputation for quickly jumping on the bandwagon of moral indignation, and immediately launched an attack. The broadcast almost got out of hand when militant homosexuals tried to kiss the director in front of the camera and, imitating a scene from the film, attempted to paint him with lipstick. The director was booed from the public gallery by disabled people in wheelchairs who believed that in *Spetters* Verhoeven 'had claimed that all disabled people should commit suicide because they were useless'. Explanations from a frantically gesticulating director were to no avail. He had just managed to escape a 'people's tribunal' – but that very week an action group was set up, Nederlandse Anti-*Spetters* Actie (Dutch Anti-*Spetters* Action) or NASA, which on the leaflets it handed out called *Spetters* a 'dangerous film', because it would only reinforce 'existing prejudices about women, homosexuals and other minority groups'.

Something had gone seriously wrong between Verhoeven, the press and a section of the public – but what? 'I knew I had filmed *Spetters* in a harsh way, but of course the story was partly about the opportunism and cynicism that clearly exists in society. My films are a heightened form of reality, because you are trying to portray a complete milieu in an hour and a half.'

Was the film really that bad?

It was an attempt at 'faction', a mixture of fact and fiction, something that had not often been done in Dutch film. The fact that the milieu of the working-class youth in *Spetters* is depressing and without hope cannot be blamed on the film-maker. The fact that they deal with their sexuality in a clumsy and immature way, with the exception of the slightly more experienced Fientje, is also realistic in view of their age. The main characters cannot express themselves well, but anyone who has been into a Dutch snack bar knows that the concept of a complete sentence is unknown in street language. *Spetters* seems to be about the typical Verhoeven–Soeteman dialectic: sons get on badly with their fathers, girls with boys, gays with straights, and as country bumpkins the main characters aspire to the worldly Big City. Viewed in this way, *Spetters* is a coming-of-age film, where the tone of the narrative is geared towards the not-so-spiritual world it tries to describe.

In Verhoeven's view, 'The dramatic drive of the film is lost when the Rien figure is paralysed by his motorcycle accident; the story loses its protagonist. Realistically speaking, there is nothing to be said against his accident: fate is always around the corner. In the cinema it struck me that young people like the film a lot until Rien falls off his motorbike. You can sense the audience thinking, "Is this really necessary?" The film suddenly tilts, and from that moment it is the figure of clumsy Hans, the youngest knight, who has to carry *Spetters*. Because we portrayed him too one-dimensionally, it does not work.'

Despite weaknesses in the script, Verhoeven has always seen *Spetters* as an 'interesting, progressive film. Very heavy too.' The way in which Rien's friends, including his sweetheart Fientje, immediately banish their former leader after his accident leaves little of the romantic perceptions about friendship intact. 'That's something I read in a German sociology book about young teenage dropouts. Apparently, if one of them makes a mistake, whether he goes to jail or ends up in hospital, the ones who stay behind do not want anything to do with him any more. Much of what the press calls a "deep black pool" results from a reality which the same newspapers rarely describe.'

The bitter-sweet ending of the film was a quotation from Céline's *Nord*, which Verhoeven had come across in a lecture. Immediately after the war, the controversial French writer had seen in Berlin how in the ruins of their former dwellings the residents drew lines on the ground with chalk to mark out their own territory and begin the reconstruction of their homes. In *Spetters* the café of Rien's father is smashed up by a group of Hell's Angels – and on the rubble of his former business, Fientje and Hans start a new future with a snack bar-cum-disco: destruction also leads to freedom. Nevertheless, the NASA group complained about the film's 'senseless violence' and was supported in this by a rainbow coalition of the Nederlandse Vereniging Seksuele Hervorming (Dutch Association for Sexual Reform) or NVSH, Partij van de Arbeid Homogroep (Gay Section of the Dutch Labour Party), Pacifistisch Socialistische Partij (Pacifist Socialist Party) or PSP, Vrouwen Tegen Porno (Women Against Porn), Rooie Flikkers en Paarse Potten (Red Gays and Purple Dikes), among others.

In the film Jeroen Krabbé has a supporting role as a sports commentator. With regard to the moral outrage, he observes, 'Sometimes Paul has the tendency to jump out of his own throat,' by which he means that the director has so much energy that he sometimes needs to be kept under control. 'In that sense he and Rob Houwer were well matched, because they were always cursing each other.' Joop van den Ende could not handle Verhoeven, and the actor believes that *Spetters* shows it. 'In *Soldaat*, Paul had managed sufficiently to curb his obsession with hyper-realism. It did have bits of brain lovingly stuck on the door when someone got a bullet through the head, but it was less *emphatically* filmed. The story was not thrown by the shock effects, as is the case with *Spetters*.' It is true that certain details from *Spetters* could be interpreted as tasteless, but Verhoeven argues that he just wanted to show what really happens when someone throws himself under a lorry, by allowing the male nurses to pick the crushed body parts from under the wheels in a Francis Bacon-like fashion.

In order to get as close as possible to reality, but lacking homosexual experience, Verhoeven often consulted Hans Kemna about the details of the action, and was given highly competent advice. 'If the script says that during the gang-rape the first guy grabs Eef from behind, I asked Hans, "What do they do then?" He explained to me that they would probably first spit on the anus as a way of lubrication. OK, I thought, if that is how they do it, then we will have to do it that way too. Even if nobody dares to do it, I'll film it that way. Also, Kemna always said that I talked about homosexuality in such a pathetically bourgeois way.'

Hans Kemna had had many discussions with Verhoeven about whether homosexuality could be shown in this way. That the rape scene is a punishment for Eef logically flowed from the story – but he thought the fact that Eef changes his mind about his own nature immediately afterwards occurred rather too quickly. 'I did say that to Paul. On the other hand, if I had felt that with *Spetters* he wanted to make an anti-gay film, I would never have taken part in it.'

Renée Soutendijk still remembers the deep disappointment: 'Nobody had expected that *Spetters* would provoke such an enormous hate campaign. Of course, the film has all the usual controversial Verhoeven elements – shocking images that make you think, "Gosh, I've never seen *that* before" – but *Spetters* was technically very well put together, and the story was about something different too. For a Dutch film, that was quite a lot really.'

The day after the devastating reviews, the makers of the film met in Amsterdam in sombre mood. To assuage their anguish, they filled their glasses, and someone suggested that it had perhaps not been a good idea to transport all the film critics by bus from Amsterdam to a theatre in Rotterdam for the press première. It had seemed a nice publicity stunt, since the film was largely set in Rotterdam, but it had given the critics the chance to put their heads together on the way back and arrive at a unanimous and devastating judgement. It looked very much as if they were all trying to surpass each other in formulating terms of deadly intent. Verhoeven believed that 'the reviews were so much along the same lines that after that bus journey it looked as if no one dared to utter any other opinion. As if on the way they had all goaded each other on.'

The box-office figures brought some relief: 1,124,000 people had been to see the film, less than to *Soldaat van Oranje*, but for the Netherlands this was still a respectable number. Strikingly, in the United States – where twelve years later similar arguments would be used against *Basic Instinct* – reactions were more positive. *Rolling Stone* talked about leading actress Renée Soutendijk as 'a Dietrich in glittering pants' – although the magazine thought that the film's shift from the comic to the melodramatic was too sentimental.

Spetters was especially successful on America's West Coast, where it ran for eight weeks and was mentioned in *Variety*'s box office charts. The *L.A. Examiner* praised Verhoeven as 'Holland's One-Man Wave' and labelled the film, not unjustly, as being in the genre of the exploitation movie – but in the sense of being a cult film. There had been a tradition of biker movies since Marlon Brando got on to a motorbike for *The Wild One* (Laslo Benedek, 1954). In the American experience, the genre stood for the modern Western, motorbikes being synonymous with horses. The definition in *Harper's Encyclopedia of Pop Culture* says, 'Biker movies – even the ones that try to be arty – always have the titillating look of cheap exploitation.' While opinions about the film have always remained divided, in that sense *Spetters* was fairly close to its origins.

The gang rape in *Spetters*.

The Verhoeven family at the time of *Spetters*: Martine, Heleen, Paul, Claudia, and foster daughter Mariëlle.

Spetters: a reference to Verhoeven's own religious experience.

Jeroen Krabbé as Gerard Reve during a lecture in the port of
Vlissingen. 'I lie the truth.' Renée Soutendijk is hatching
horrific plans.

Thom Hoffman as Christ in the 'first, psychosexual, religious thriller'.

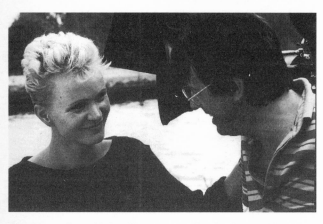

The film-maker with leading actress, Renée Soutendijk.

Chapter 10

The Femme Fatale: *The Fourth Man*

Paul Verhoeven emerged from the battle of *Spetters* with a sense of bewilderment. Whereas before, in addition to the usual criticism, there had been admiration for his audience-orientated and dynamic style of filming, this time the repulsion was unanimous. 'I may say that applied in both directions,' the director remembers.

Nor was Verhoeven's headache alleviated by the news that in February 1980 *Soldier of Orange* had received a Golden Globe for the best foreign film from the Hollywood Foreign Press Organization. 'Paul, you should simply *go* to America,' was the well-meaning advice from Joop van den Ende. The director, who was by now forty-one years old, had himself toyed with the idea of trying his luck in Hollywood, but the way in which his producer raised the question of this transition was too casual for his liking. 'I had the fearful suspicion that a transition would mean having to let go of my typically European themes. In short, I didn't want to go.'

Nevertheless, the call from the centre of the film industry was loud and clear. A key figure in the American appreciation of Verhoeven was Dan Ireland. Once he had been the programmer of a cinema in Vancouver, where they were trying to win back old ground by means of soft porn. Ireland recalls, 'I had to select the films and to my astonishment the package also included *Turks Fruit*. Towards the end I was in tears, I thought it was so powerful and beautiful. I went to see the managing director and told him that this film did not belong with us but a foreign language theatre, with subtitles.' The managing director did not agree with him. Ireland left and took *Turks Fruit* with him. He found a partner in Seattle, bought and refurbished a cinema and started the first Seattle International Film Festival – where he showed not only *Turks Fruit* but *Keetje Tippel*.

Struck by the quality of *Soldier of Orange*, he set out as an unsalaried, but indefatigable champion of Verhoeven. He approached producer Kathleen Kennedy, who worked with Steven Spielberg. 'I sent her *Turks Fruit* which she showed to Steven. A week later she called back. She said, "He was totally shocked. Is this porn?" "No," I answered, "it is powerful and explicit, but it's not porn."' Then Ireland gave her *Soldier of Orange*. The cinematographic wunderkind liked this much better: '"Steven has completely fallen in love with it, Dan," Kathleen said. "But are you sure it's the same director?" When I answered in the affirmative, she said that Spielberg had offered to help Paul in any way he could.'

And so, winning the Golden Globe was followed by a telephone call from Steven Spielberg. Verhoeven: 'Spielberg said, "Holland is too small for you . . . I'll introduce you to some studios here, so you can come and work here."'

The invitation was accepted in a spirit of curiosity. In the spring of 1980, with money from producer van den Ende, Verhoeven made his first journey to America's West Coast. He was accompanied by Gijs Versluys, van den Ende's Head of Production and a friend of the director since the late 1960s. In their luggage they carried a number of Gerard Soeteman's scripts. Spielberg received his European colleagues over lunch. What he was concretely able to offer them, he said, was that through his auspices they would be able to visit a number of major studios. Only later did Verhoeven hear from Dan Ireland that Spielberg had also considered advising his friend George Lucas to ask the Dutch director to make the third part of the Star Wars saga, *Return of the Jedi*, which was eventually filmed in 1983 by Richard Marquand. However, after seeing Verhoeven's latest film, the explicit *Spetters*, Steven Spielberg changed his mind: 'I suppose he was scared that the Jedi would immediately start fucking.'

The tour took Verhoeven and Versluys first of all to the Warner Studios in Burbank, Los Angeles. There the executives were given an adaptation of H. P. Lovecraft's *The Thing on the Doorstep*. Gerard Soeteman had set the story in the present and made the main character a presidential adviser who slowly loses his mind. As a member of the National Security Council he begins to believe in the inevitability of Armageddon, and intends to set this in motion himself by means of nuclear weapons. The schemes of Ronald Reagan and Oliver North over Iran and the Contras were yet to come, so the idea was eventually rejected as 'too improbable'.

Then it was on to Metro-Goldwyn-Mayer in Culver City – the company whose banner had once carried the slogan 'More stars than there are in heaven', but which in the early 1980s was almost moribund. They were especially interested in *Harry's Tale*, a Soeteman story based on an American study of the eighteenth-century slave trade with Africa. It was agreed that they would research the possibilities of the project.

At Columbia Pictures, also in Culver City, a project based on Agatha

Christie and entitled *Death Comes as the End* was discussed. The British scriptwriter Anthony Shaffer had devised an outline and put together a first script based on Christie's book. At Columbia's request, Soeteman had written an entirely new screenplay, and studio director Frank Price saw great possibilities for this thriller set in Egypt. In the following months he approved a budget of around $10 million; it really looked as if the project would become Verhoeven's first American–Dutch co-production. During the next few months the director, together with Gijs Versluys, went in search of locations in the Nile region – but when, not long afterwards, Frank Price moved to Universal, his successor immediately scrapped the whole idea.

The tour also led to Francis Ford Coppola's American Zoetrope studio in Hollywood. There Paul made a typical Verhoeven joke: he pointed out to his famous American colleague that it is not such an achievement to make a film like *Apocalypse Now* with such an enormous budget – no, what was really difficult was to make a quality film like *Soldaat van Oranje* with a small budget, as he had done. It did not result in collaboration between Coppola and Verhoeven.

In an attempt to land a serious American project, Verhoeven continued shuttling between the Netherlands and Hollywood. Many pats on the back and admiring words were received, but few signatures were put at the bottom of contracts. And yet the exploration of Hollywood also had its cheerful side. On one of the excursions Verhoeven was accompanied by Gerard Soeteman, who kept a diary of their adventures. He describes how he, Versluys and Verhoeven paid a visit to the villa of Barbra Streisand in Bel Air – the actress star had made it known she wanted to collaborate with them. In Hollywood, the stature of showbiz heroes was still many times greater than in the Netherlands:

We stepped inside a living museum. The entire interior is one gigantic collection of Jugendstil. Grand, grander, very grand. No time really to look around. We are quickly led down a staircase into a basement. We step into a dimly lit space. No art nouveau this time, but total Rietveld – New Realism. Everything grey, blue, red, white. Everything matching. Even the enormous jar of sweets is in the same colours and the carpet has a red stripe. Paul and Gijs greet Barbra with a kiss, I give her a firm handshake. We stand around talking for half an hour: about what we do, have done, are going to do. She talks about people and things she knows and very obviously knows a lot about. *Yentl*, *Soldaat*, *Turks Fruit* and Jane Fonda . . .

She gives us enormous mugs of coffee (stylish) and then fruit: strawberries, personally taking the stalks from us. Shall we watch a film? Because the basement is a projection area. Original drawings by Erté conceal an entire film projection installation, complete with operator. We fall straight into a film starring

John Cassavetes. After a quarter of an hour, nothing has happened except that the gentlemen have picked at, patted, brushed and dusted down each other . . . The film is stopped after general moaning and booing. La Streisand looks cross-eyed and desperately into the room, 'Can someone explain to me what in God's name this is all about, this fucking shit?' Nobody can. The conversation moves on to the fact that so many crappy films are made these days. And so expensive. Streisand is sad. In this situation she does not at all feel like going back to filming. Where can she get a good story? One with 'heart'. After *Yentl* she does not know where to go. So what will she do? Interior design! Do we understand why that Falk–Cassavetes film was praised so much in the newspapers? 'Oh, I hate critics.' I do not think it is pleasant when *she* hates someone. Now she exclaims that she loves our films. She has seen them all. They have 'heart'. And that is what she wants in a film (she beats her breast), 'heart'. As soon as she finds something with 'heart', she will act in a film again. She wants to make *Triangle* with us, about the founding of the trade unions around the turn of the century in the sweatshops manned mostly by Jewish children . . . We all get up from that projection room-cum-boudoir-cum-period room. As we walk through the hall I see the Jugendstil portrait of Queen Wilhelmina as a Dutch farmer's wife painted by Paul Berthon. I ask whether she knows who it is. Barbra hesitates. I say it is Wilhelmina. 'Oh yes! The Queen from the *Soldier of Orange*,' she exclaims with joy.

And so Verhoeven and Soeteman regularly returned to the Netherlands with a suitcase full of good intentions. It would not be until 1985 that their first American–European co-production would have its première: *Flesh + Blood*, in association with Orion Pictures.

Meanwhile, so as not to fall prey to inertia, Paul Verhoeven also looked for his next project in the Netherlands. Fortuitously, in April 1981 *De Vierde Man* was published, a novella by the celebrated Dutch writer Gerard Reve. Together with W. F. Hermans and Harry Mulisch, Reve (born 1923) was considered to be among the most important post-war writers in the Netherlands. But while many writers had tasted the commercial pleasures of a film adaptation by now, Reve's work – apart from the small production *Lieve Jongens* (*Dear Boys*, Paul de Lussanet) from 1980 – had fallen outside the horizon of cinema. Every director regretfully admitted that the problem with his books – full of irony, Mariolatry and homoeroticism – was that they were ingenious language games, but devoid of action. In Reve's novels, beginning with his début *De Avonden* from 1949, action was subordinate to feelings of hopelessness, sadness and doom. Mood instead of plot.

De Vierde Man was clearly different, as Verhoeven discovered on reading the novella. Originally, the work had been intended as the free give-away for anyone who'd spent a reasonable amount on books during the annual Book Week – an event organized by booksellers and publishers to publicize the book trade – and for this reason Reve used a more accessible language than usual. Even those unfamiliar with his fairly risqué oeuvre would be able to enjoy *De Vierde Man*. However, the tongue-in-cheek horror story, late nineteenth century in form, found no favour with the Book Week committee. The stumbling block was the main theme – love between men – and so *De Vierde Man* was published elsewhere.

At first sight, it seemed to Verhoeven that *De Vierde Man* would make a good television film, to be produced by VSE. He passed the novella on to Gerard Soeteman, who recognized that the central plot was sufficiently strong for a full-length feature film. Moreover, the entire idea had something tantalizing about it. How would the critics in the Netherlands react if the duo, so often accused of 'banality', ventured into filming a book by Reve, whose work had been the exclusive domain of the intelligentsia (although Reve had always spoken of himself as a people's writer)? After the devastating criticism of *Spetters*, Verhoeven was amused by the prospect of embarking on a film that was arty and deeply psychological.

De Vierde Man is the story of a rather shabby, alcoholic writer who, despite his homosexuality, is seduced by the female treasurer of a literary association during a talk in the harbour town of Vlissingen. The woman, named Christine Halslag, turns out to be a *femme fatale*. Like a black widow spider, she first forces herself on men and embarks on a sexual adventure with them, and then kills them without mercy. The second dimension of the story is that the entire plot may have taken place exclusively in the writer's head. As an artist and born dreamer, the Reve figure constantly creates fiction from banal facts. It is not for nothing that his motto is 'I lie the truth'. Seen from this perspective, Christine Halslag may in reality be an innocent widow whose path is regularly crossed by Fate. In any case, in both explanations she turns out to have lost three husbands. It is up to the reader to draw conclusions.

On page 102 of *De Vierde Man* Reve himself sighs ironically about the 'unfilmability' of the book: 'Which master of film could take this theme and make it plausible? . . . Even for an incomprehensible, "experimental" Italian film . . . the basic idea is too confused . . .'

In reality, Reve had written his Magic Realist thriller so transparently that new elements were easily added. Soeteman decided that it was possible to play on Reve's obsession with the worship of the Madonna by contrasting the *femme fatale* Christine Halslag with a *femme céleste* in the form of Mary herself. For the necessary surreal images the director was able to draw upon his own spell as a painter, since it was precisely in that style that he had painted and drawn as a student at Leiden.

In May–June 1981 Gerard Soeteman sat down to hammer out a script, while Paul Verhoeven went looking for an actor to play the main role of the alcoholic writer. He immediately thought of Jeroen Krabbé, whose performance in *Soldaat van Oranje* had pleased him so much. However, what Verhoeven did not know – or at least underestimated – was that Krabbé had fallen out with the intended producer, van den Ende, because of a prolonged financial dispute. So much so that the actor had been sitting at home in a depressive state for some time. Krabbé faced a dilemma. 'Paul came round and said, "I am offering you the main role." It was my dearest wish to play the figure of Gerard Reve, but when I heard that Joop van den Ende was the producer, I had to decline. A disastrous situation. Paul left, but at the bottom of the stairs he turned round, "What if it is with another producer?" I replied, "Then we can start tomorrow." Whereupon Paul said, "OK!" And simply walked out of the door.'

Unknowingly, Jeroen Krabbé brought about what Verhoeven was considering anyway: ending the collaboration within VSE Film. He had come to the conclusion that he was a film director first, and did not consider himself suitable as a part-time director of a company aiming to make a whole range of productions. The imminent death of VSE Film was regretted by few. 'Joop van den Ende realized that little would come of all the plans with Gerard and me which he had in his head, as we were primarily set on feature films.'

The next step was more remarkable. Because experienced producers were few and far between in the modest Dutch film industry, Verhoeven turned to Rob Houwer, the man he had cursed so much after *Soldaat van Oranje*. During a dinner party they ironed out difficulties which had previously seemed insurmountable. As fiercely as they had fought each other in various interviews, they lovingly posed on the showbiz page of *De Telegraaf* after the reconciliation. 'I felt I had expressed my irritation with Rob sufficiently,' the director said. For his part, Rob Houwer had had little success as a producer after the row with Verhoeven – all the more reason to restore the relationship to their mutual benefit. They agreed that Verhoeven would shoot his first 'art' film for Houwer. The fee was 75,000 guilders.

With this U-turn Verhoeven had safeguarded the main role of Jeroen Krabbé. The last hurdle to be surmounted before the filming of *De Vierde Man* was that Joop van den Ende still held the option on the book, an option which would run out on 31 December 1981. Since the director had not heard his former partner say anything more about the project, on New Year's Eve 1981 Verhoeven, accompanied by Rob Houwer's assistant Ineke van Wezel, travelled to Schiedam, where the writer lived with his partner Joop Schafthuizen, alias Matroos ('Sailor') Vosch. At exactly one minute past midnight, Gerard Reve was handed a cheque for 100,000 guilders. The popping of the champagne corks confirmed the festive atmosphere. Meanwhile, in a recess of the living room the statue of Mary, illuminated day and night, seemed to look on contentedly.

'Most of the women in Paul's films will not rest until they have got what they want. They usually win, and they let no one stand in their way.' Renée Soutendijk portrayed the *femme fatale* Christine Halslag in the same manner as Sharon Stone in *Basic Instinct*: ambiguous, cool and deadly destructive. 'It may be a Gerard Reve story, but it is typically Paul Verhoeven: the beautiful doll turns out to be a real bitch,' Soutendijk explains.

Her impressions were partly based on the role of Fientje she had played in *Spetters*. As Christine Halslag in *De Vierde Man* she would also have to use her sexuality as an instrument of power. In conversation, the director made it clear to her that showing women characters who were equal to men meant that his leading ladies also had to be able to play the bad guys. Not only from the point of view of emancipation, but because such a division of roles would come across as more surprising to the audience, trained in clichés as it is. He explained that as a director he could do little with the formula of 'good girls' long established in films.

In *De Vierde Man* Christine Halslag knows exactly what she wants, or at least gives that impression. From the moment that the writer Gerard Reve arrives for his lecture in Vlissingen, she decides to catch him in her web. She attracts his attention in a cunning way by constantly filming him with a Handycam; when the lecture lasts longer than expected, she invites him to spend the night at her place. The writer, who is always watching the pennies and has little enthusiasm for lonely hotel rooms ('What else can you do there but hang yourself, read the Bible or jack off?'), decides there is no point in doing things the hard way and goes with her.

Once inside, he allows himself to be seduced by Christine. In view of his homosexual preferences, this is quite an achievement for the apparently innocent treasurer of a literary association, who also turns out to be the manager of a beauty salon. The viewer realizes that only a witch can have that much power – although she buys, in Gerard Reve's words, 'a pig in a poke'.

What follows is an exciting love-making scene, in which Christine Halslag clearly shows her dominant traits. The writer instinctively feels he has stepped into a dangerous game. In a dream he sees Christine castrating him with a pair of scissors. In making his leading actress an attractive but dangerous woman, Verhoeven also had to avoid portraying her co-star as a sweetie. For the personality of Jeroen Krabbé as the alcoholic writer Gerard, he had both a villainous and an unpredictable character in mind.

Jeroen Krabbé's diary, starting at the time of the first rehearsals for *De Vierde Man*, speaks plainly:

31 March 1982

Discussion at the office with Paul Verhoeven and Gerard Soeteman. Gerard arrived first and we went through the script page by page. Paul came later, was ill and at the first thing I said started to curse, and called me every name in the book. I was flabbergasted and had to swallow hard to keep myself under control. At the same time I knew that this might be one of Paul's test cases to see how far he could go – but it was a nuisance. The rest of the meeting took place in a fucking awful mood.

Sunday 18 April 1982

Paul comes round and we chat about the role. In passing we touch on our row. Paul thinks that I should be able to take it. So it was to test me after all.

26 April 1982

Worked on the video with Paul for a long time. After a couple of hours we did get some results. Paul wants me to be hard all the time. I manage it only partly. He wants me to quit being soft-headed and superficial.

29 April 1982

Hard, hard, hard. Total metamorphosis. Only it causes me trouble. Working with Paul is pretty demanding. He is the absolute helmsman on the ship and tolerates no other.

Although from the beginning Paul Verhoeven had seen Krabbé as the Reve character, and had even begun a new association with Rob Houwer for the sake of it, the first screen test turned out to be a fiasco. Krabbé remembers: 'Later he phoned me and said, "You must come and have another look." Paul showed the video and suddenly the image froze. "That face!" he exclaimed. "That tormented face is the role – I don't care how you get it, but that is the look I want." That was very clever of Paul, because it was a basis to work from.'

Krabbé's success in *De Vierde Man* would eventually start him off on his international career (including *The Living Daylights* [John Glen, 1987], *A World Apart* [Chris Menges, 1987], *The Prince of Tides*, *Kafka* and *The Fugitive*) – in the same way that *Soldaat van Oranje* had done for Rutger Hauer. And yet Krabbé found the renewed collaboration with the director more difficult than expected.

'We had to shoot a scene at Amsterdam Central Station, and in Paul's view it wasn't going right. Among hundreds of onlookers, Verhoeven turned round and shouted, "Here we have that world-famous actor Jeroen Krabbé. The prick doesn't have a clue!"' Krabbé was greeted with howls of derision. The actor promptly walked off the set with the intention of never returning – but halfway towards the exit he changed his mind. 'In *De Vierde Man* Paul wanted me to be in a constant state of depression and aggressiveness. That is the reason for the ego-bashing. You are prepared to swallow a lot from that man. If Paul's genius had not beamed over Rutger and me, nobody outside Amsterdam would ever have heard of us.'

In the film the manic-depressive main character experiences a wave of good feeling with the arrival of Herman, the turning-point in the plot. Herman is a rather ordinary but good-looking guy. By then, the Reve figure had already seen him at Amsterdam Central Station, when he ran – driven by reckless feelings of lust – after him. But as is always the case with hopeless romantic love, the train containing Herman moved off agonizingly slowly.

Then it turns out that Christine Halslag herself – after all, it is a Magic Realist story – has a relationship with Herman. Gerard finds his photograph when he is nosing through Christine's post. It shows Herman, dressed only in red swimming trunks, posing with his tanned and muscled torso. 'God help me . . . what a body, what a hunk, I must have him . . . if it is the death of me . . . ,' the writer muses while caressing the photograph. Although he has only just decided to return to Amsterdam, the Reve figure persuades Christine to bring her lover to Vlissingen. Now Herman can make his entry.

Herman was played by Thom Hoffman, at that time the new young hero of the Dutch cinema. He had been given the role because he was the only one of forty young actors who during the casting had given Jeroen Krabbé a prolonged French kiss, whereas the actors preceding him had only given him an innocent embrace. Thom Hoffman admits that it was a cheekiness partly inspired by the fact that they were casting for a film adaptation of a Reve book, and his desire to help the writer who had been a favourite of his for a long time.

Seven years later, in 1989, Thom Hoffman was to play the leading role in the Dutch film based on Gerard Reve's first novel *De Avonden* (*Evenings*, Rudolf van den Berg), but now he met the writer he so admired for the first time. Prior to shooting, a press conference was organized on Tuesday 11 May 1982 in Amsterdam. It was attended not only by Verhoeven, Soeteman and the actors in provisional make-up but by Gerard Reve. The broad lines of the film were explained, and in the presence of the journalists the author grumbled about the autobiographical content of *De Vierde Man*: 'Look, I'm a healthy homosexual. I always felt my mother would not have approved of that relationship with Christine.'

Thom Hoffman remembers that there were drinks afterwards and Gerard Reve's partner Joop Schafthuizen immediately swapped shirts with him, as is customary after a football match. 'He said, "Give me your trashy T-shirt and you can have my Pierre Cardin." Then Reve himself joined us and muttered, "I hope he's not being mean. Otherwise I'll call him off."' A little later Thom Hoffman asked him to sign his copy of the book *De Vierde Man*. Reve fumbled around in his inside pocket. 'Very pompously he said, "With *this* pen I wrote *De Avonden* in 1949." Every-one could see that it was an ultra-modern, 1982 model pen from the Hema store. The sense of fantasy, which *De Vierde Man* is mainly about, was authentic with Reve – that much was obvious.' When Jeroen Krabbé later also received a blessing from the Catholic writer, it was clear that this occult thriller, peppered with religion, would be starting off under a lucky star.

Whereas Verhoeven had dressed completely in leather on the set of *Spetters*, for the 'artistic' *De Vierde Man* he had a more cosmopolitan look, modelled on his favourite singer Bryan Ferry. The director's working methods had changed little. 'Let's have a look. Where are we? We are now in week seven, and we're doing scene 35. Scene 34 we did in week one, and how did we approach that one again? Oh yes, it was medium close left, and a medium close right, and then a wide shot from the other side. We shot in total eight versions of the medium close left. During the first take a glass fell down, the second one had a textual mistake, and with the third one the boom appeared in the image. Take 5 was the best, so we'll take that as the starting point for the next shot. Right, Renée – you go and stand there. And Jeroen, you over there. Everybody ready? Action!'

Thom Hoffman watched Verhoeven at work on the set with some amazement. 'The man's inspiration, or you might call it professional madness, was obvious from the fact that he seemed to have *every* take of the film in his head, although Verhoeven himself said he had only "had another look at the rushes the night before."' The fact remained that the director did not know how to stop when others had long given up in total exhaustion. Shooting days of sixteen hours seemed more the rule than the exception.

Thom Hoffman arrived two-thirds of the way through the film, and he had thought of all kinds of effects to underline both his acting talent and his knowledge of Reve: long, pitying looks; long but meaningful silences. 'Paul said straight away, "Stop that immediately. I don't want any more psychology. We are more than halfway through the story and NOW we're going into the next gear." You couldn't argue with him.'

Hoffman remembers that the only thing which disturbed Verhoeven's blistering rhythm was the tragic news which reached the set in the coastal town of Noordwijk on 10 June 1982: Rainer Werner Fassbinder, the brilliant German director and wild man, had died. He was thirty-six years old and had been destroyed by his excesses. 'After the news there was despondency on the set, because everybody knew that Paul was burning himself out in the same way as Fassbinder. It seemed that the superhuman energy with which they both made their films would one day inevitably take its toll. That sudden realization was hanging over Verhoeven like a big thundercloud. And we could all see that cloud.'

There was no time for contemplation. There was a scene in the schedule with a white sports car, in which Herman and Gerard go cruising in the dunes. On the way, the writer will try to seduce the Adonis. For the film, the near-sighted Hoffman had exchanged his glasses for contact lenses, but had not anticipated the tough way in which he was expected to drive the car. It was not in the script. 'I thought, "Oh well, I suppose a stunt man will do that." Nothing was further from the truth. I had to thunder down the dune path at full speed and halfway along make a sharp turn. The first time I did it at thirty kilometres an hour. Verhoeven shouted, "Come on, man. Prick! You should be doing eighty." Jeroen was sitting next to me and simply said, "Poo!" Anyway, I accelerated to forty. No good. Paul was angry. "Fucking idiot, get out!" Then he jumped over the door into the sports car, threw the car into reverse . . . vrrrooooommm . . . took a run-up and flew like a madman round the bend. He then tore back up the same path in reverse. "And now you!" he shouted at me halfway up.'

The demonstration was so convincing that Thom Hoffman's heart sank into his boots. Verhoeven had another encouraging idea. 'He said, "I'll go and stand in the road, on the edge of frame. The moment I jump aside, you turn the wheel – but try to hit me, understood?" So I go for him at eighty kilometres an hour. Just in front of my bumper I saw him dive away. Jeroen and I thought the whole situation was so terrifying that afterwards we laughed hysterically for five minutes. Paul just looked at us glassy-eyed. He did not understand. When he is filming, Paul doesn't see any danger.'

Jeroen Krabbé also remembers many an oppressive moment from the shooting. He was worried about his phobia of big dogs. According to the script, his character is attacked by an Alsatian during a walk, so the actor was sent to the dog-training centre of the Amsterdam police force during pre-production. The test shoot with the dogs was not too bad, since he was allowed to wear a thick quilted overall. On the set, a man arrived with a dog from the circus. 'A monster! During the lunch breaks I had to take the beast out for a walk and feed him chicken legs.' The way the dog devoured the bones made Krabbé ask Verhoeven whether the animal could stay on a leash at least during the takes. This was allowed, partly because it had been decided to give the shot a more surreal atmosphere by having thousands of red flower petals flutter through the air driven by a wind machine.

Krabbé describes his moments of fear in his diary:

15 June 1982

I did not have much of a sense of humour today; with the prospect of being confronted by the dog, I was pretty scared. A stand-in had arrived, but the dog knew him and so the animal started to lick instead of attack. I sensed Paul's reproach towards me. In the sense of, 'You prick, you don't even dare to do that.' Fortunately, the dog suddenly made a lunge at Paul, who only just managed to jump clear. Only then did he understand my fear and say I was right. A little later it was time for the shot in which the dog would jump at me. I wet my pants, but it worked – with all those thousands of flower petals and the wind etcetera, that fucking dog came at me but was stopped by the leash. Not nice, but it was all right. Once more, there we go. He comes, but alas he does not stop, because the leash snapped – and he jumped at me. I went down, hitting the pavement with my thigh. The dog slipped, I jumped up. Consternation. Misery. The shot of the century, Paul cried! I wanted to go home, but Paul asked me whether I would do an additional shot because it was so good. Meanwhile, the totally disappointed dog-owner stood there bemoaning the situation with a broken and bleeding nose.

It turned out that the dog-owner had accidentally let the leash slip, and because of the power of the animal's leap the leash had smashed the owner's nose.

During the shooting of *De Vierde Man*, everyone's respect for the director's dynamism increased, if only because he was not afraid of exposing himself to the same torments as his leading actors. One such instance of setting an example was experienced by Thom Hoffman in a scene in which, during one of the writer's visions, he had to emerge from the sea in a white gown. 'It was one of those awful, ice-cold, grey Dutch days and I was standing up to my neck in water. Because of the waves I could not hear a word of Verhoeven's directions. But where another director would have let his assistant convey the message, he dived into the sea, clothes and all, and then stood next to me explaining exactly what I had to do. Then he swam back and called "Action!" Sometimes you think, that man is mad *and* dangerous. But at the same time you can't but admire so much passion.'

'Limited awareness' is how the director describes his mental state on the set. He *knows* that he does not know when to stop. But to him – certainly in view of those tight budgets in the Netherlands – it seemed the only way to shoot a film to his own rigorous standards. Because of Rob Houwer's strict régime, Verhoeven realized that only a few versions of every take could be shot. The atmosphere between the financial backer and the bulk consumer of money may have been described in the press as 'reconciled and happy', but in reality it looked more like an armed peace.

'The producer himself did not often appear,' Renée Soutendijk says, 'but we all had the feeling that Rob Houwer had spies on the set to check on the progress of the film. That's why the crew was split into two camps; we, the actors, had of course chosen Paul's side.'

With a budget of 2.5 million guilders, Verhoeven put the progress of the film before everything else – that is why the actors' objections to perilous actions had to be brushed aside. '*No* film stunt is devoid of danger,' Verhoeven regularly explains in interviews. As he told *NRC/Handelsblad* on 22 February 1985: 'Things can go a bit wrong sometimes. If time is against us and – just to take an example – a burning beam crashes down just a little too early, or a rearing horse throws off its rider, *a bit wrong* can be fatal. Such situations occur regularly, but usually I am so focused on the progress of the take that I don't realize it.' Sometimes things went really wrong.

The prelude to the climax of *De Vierde Man* takes place in a tomb. This is where Gerard has his way – he will let Herman make love to him. Outside there is thunder and lightning. As Herman begins embracing him, Reve is distracted by three urns; it turns out that they contain the mortal remains of Christine Halslag's earlier loves. With a shock he realizes that he himself could become 'the fourth man' – or else his beloved Herman. Gerard runs out in a panic, fleeing from impending doom. This scene of horror was shot at the Jewish cemetery in Muiden, and the lightning was contracted out to special effects wizard Harrie Wiessenhaan. He had developed a system for producing lightning, consisting of long tubes in which the air pressure was increased with gas. Thus it was possible to emit magnesium powder that would explode in the burners set up above it – a lightning effect reminiscent of the early days of photography, but which was capable of spreading across the full width of the cemetery.

In the rush to get the scene right, one of Wiessenhaan's assistants forgot to turn off the air pressure when he wanted to fill the tubes with magnesium powder for the next thunderbolt. An enormous flash shot from the tube. The boy had to be taken to hospital with third-degree burns. Five minutes later, Verhoeven was shooting again. These were moments when Jeroen Krabbé – entirely in character – thought, 'Mother Mary, please watch over us.'

Filmically, there is much to enjoy in *De Vierde Man*. The glossy camera work of Jan de Bont, shooting with Verhoeven for the first time since *Keetje Tippel*, rather suited the arty atmosphere which the director and cameraman had in mind. As usual, Verhoeven worked with considerable depth of field, but with *De Vierde Man* this style was taken to the extreme to achieve a hyper-realistic effect. 'I have always chosen to keep the depth of focus in my films, anyway. I like it because of the three-dimensional field it gives you. The background is as visible as the foreground, and in that sense clearly plays a part in the story. A lot of film-makers shoot their close-ups so that the surroundings look blurred. I think that is a cheap trick. It excludes the reality. It is claustrophobic. It regularly makes me feel sick.'

Verhoeven also found the alienation necessary for *De Vierde Man* in the use of colour filters. To illustrate this, Jan de Bont had looked to the work of the American artist Edward Hopper, to which Verhoeven added his knowledge of Salvador Dalí, Magritte and Delvaux. 'In those paint- ings *everything* is razor-sharp. The surrealism is in the objects, the combination of images and colours.' Thus in *De Vierde Man* the bluest blue is alternated with the reddest red, while the camera very slowly and 'artistically' pans round. It was an expensive conceit, thought producer Houwer, who would have preferred to see the easy, semi-documentary style of *Turks Fruit* for *De Vierde Man*, since it was he who received the huge bills for the special light filters.

To make it clear to the audience from the first moment that dream and action are intertwined, Verhoeven chose an opening sequence in which the delirium-ridden writer Reve wants to strangle his boyfriend, an appalling violinist. It turns out to be only morbid wish-fulfilment; in the sequence that follows, the gruff writer leaves for the lecture in Vlissin- gen without hurting a hair of his friend's head. Reve is continuously plagued by visions. In bed with Christine Halslag, his fear of castration even brings him a dream within a dream – not until the second time that he awakes does the writer return to reality. 'I pinched the idea of the double awakening from *An American Werewolf in London* by John Landis,' Verhoeven says. 'I did mention it to John later, and he said, "Gosh, I thought it looked familiar." "No wonder," I replied, "it's from your own film."'

So *De Vierde Man* is a continuous parade of quotations, filched from the style book of film history. When, during a train journey, the main character slips into a vision and thinks he is in a hotel, he sees a bleeding horse's eye protruding from the door of one of the rooms – a clear reference to *Un Chien Andalou*, the 1929 surrealist film by Luis Buñuel and Salvador Dalí, in which a razor blade is shown cutting through an eye. It was one of Verhoeven's memories from his student days, when *Un Chien Andalou* had been shown at the opening of the surrealist exhibition in Leiden where he had shown a painting.

Verhoeven and Soeteman also made a careful study of the dream sequence designed by Dalí for Hitchcock's *Spellbound* (1945), in which the main character's paranoia and fear of death is observed by enormous eyes. It is no coincidence that the eye is a dominant theme in *De Vierde Man*. In the myths surrounding the *femme fatale*, the eye plays a key role. Delilah burns out Samson's eyes after seducing him. This symbolism comes across most succinctly when Herman, with Gerard next to him in the white sports car, drives under some scaffolding, and due to an unfortunate set of circumstances is hit in the eye. An iron beam transported by a crane is hurled through the sky like a spear from Greek mythology and pierces Herman fatally.

It is a scene which still causes Thom Hoffman nightmares. 'That scene was produced in a typically Dutch way, which is to say that some ordinary son-of-a-bitch in a dirty overall, who in daily life was a crane operator, at that moment had power over life and death. My life and death.'

In the first take, the car containing Hoffman and Krabbé was supposed to miss the rod narrowly. In the second take, there would be a dummy in Hoffman's place which would be pierced by the rod. 'The crane operator moved the chain on which those rods were hanging up and down with four handles, but of course he only had to let those things come down three centimetres too low and he would have caused the most terrible accident. Anyway, it was touch and go – and Paul realized I was terribly anxious. He then walked to and fro with a broomstick under that crane five times to measure whether I would exactly fit under it with my car. Well, and then it was fingers crossed and accelerate. The final shot was of course done with a dummy. But it didn't matter, because at that moment the audience had put their heads between their knees with fright – and so had I, actually.'

Not only the recurring shock effects, but the quieter moments in the film were put together with care by Verhoeven. The sequence in which the Reve figure discovers the photograph of Herman in Christine's post, and quick as lightning makes his plans, is ingenious. 'Have a seat, then we can settle the bill,' says Christine Halslag when she takes the writer to her office in the hairdressing salon. He is to receive the fee for his lecture, and she takes a money box from her desk. On top of it are a letter and a photograph – Christine puts them to one side, clearly visible. From the corner of her eye she looks to see whether Gerard is watching her.

With satisfaction she concludes that he is. To taunt him, she throws far too many hundred-guilder notes on to the table. Then Christine is called away – she has to serve a customer in the shop – and Gerard goes for the photograph. It is Herman! Gerard gets excited and kisses the photograph, until he hears Christine come back. They then have a brief conversation. Christine laments her loneliness. Gerard offers to stay – but they both have a hidden agenda. Christine lures Gerard further into her web. Gerard wants Herman. While they embrace, Gerard looks at Herman's photograph.

Thom Hoffman says, 'The picture of Herman really becomes a third character in the room, because it seems as if the photograph comes to

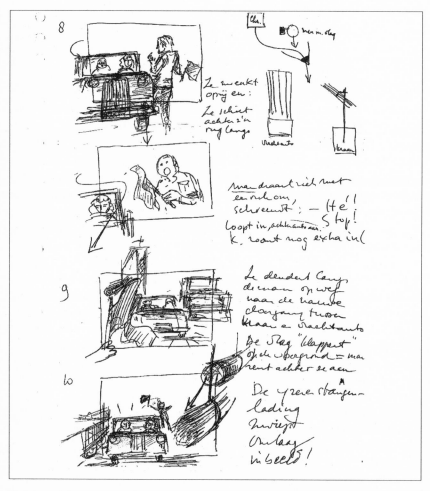

Storyboard for moment when iron beam hurls through air, killing Herman.

life. The way the scene is cut is a lesson in the grammar of film-making. Certainly, in collaboration with Jan de Bont, Verhoeven is an absolute master at that. Film is not choosing between a red or a black coat, film is speaking in images. As that shot across the shoulder when Christine and Gerard embrace draws your attention to the photograph of Herman, you think, "She put the photograph there deliberately, so that Gerard would discover it – although of course she could be genuinely pleased he is staying." Which is it exactly? Thus the images work very suggestively: it is a film language natural to no other Dutch director except Verhoeven.'

When, in the next exterior shot after a sharp cut, a rope ominously comes down from a crane in the shape of a noose, the viewer is given another indication of things to come. It is a moment in which the viewer already knows more than the main character – a much-used Hitchcockian device, borrowed by Verhoeven in admiration of the master.

The première of *De Vierde Man* was on Thursday 24 March 1983, and the film's structure and suspense brought Verhoeven positive reviews in the Netherlands, actually for the first time since *Turks Fruit*. *NRC/Handelsblad* reported: 'At the age of forty-four, Paul Verhoeven has delivered his first adult film, which is a healthy balance between film art and film entertainment . . . *De Vierde Man* has become a beautiful film, the first home-produced Magic Realist thriller *and* the first film by Soeteman and Verhoeven in which the banalities and crude effects are entirely at the service of a tight script and a visually charged narrative.'

And yet the layered complexity praised by the critics had been a great stumbling block during the shooting. Renée Soutendijk remembers how difficult she found it to give shape to a character with a hidden agenda. 'With *Spetters* I felt much surer about my role. With Christine, we never made a clear choice about where she stood exactly, because both explanations had to remain possible. Although I never normally do this, during the takes for *De Vierde Man* I had to keep looking at the rushes to see what kind of film we were making, and what exactly my role was.' We never see Christine actually killing anyone in the film, although it seems more than a coincidence that her three husbands had all died a horrible death.

Because of her character's ambiguity, Renée Soutendijk had to appear as both slightly naïve and very sophisticated. Jeroen Krabbé remembers how the actress struggled with this. 'At the end of the film we were lying on a bed together having a rest, when Renée suddenly burst out crying. "I've completely ruined it!" she exclaimed. "I don't know what I'm playing any more." I reassured her by saying that Paul would fix it on the cutting table, but to be honest nobody knew which explanation the film was going to give.'

Krabbé's diary says:

1 June
Today in Noordwijk again. Paul was very nice. Said that he too was very unsure. And he did not really know what he was making either. Fortunately, everybody has that feeling.

In the story as written, the Reve figure discovers Christine's turbulent love life when, looking in a cupboard, he finds an envelope with the death announcements of Johan, Henk and Gé. In the cinema version, Gerard finds in a similar cupboard three amateur ciné films. When he projects them, he sees the 'third man' Johan preparing for a parachute jump, the 'second man' Gé getting out of a car in a safari park to feed the lions, and the 'first man' Henk going fishing on the high seas. When the writer subsequently finds their mortal remains in Christine's family grave, he quickly draws his conclusions: the parachute did not work, the lions attacked, and the fishing boat was run down by a speedboat – the witch Christine has used her black magic to send her lovers to an early death.

Nevertheless, according to Verhoeven you could also maintain that Gerard's own imagination has got the better of him, and that it is not Christine at all who has arranged their fate. 'Gerard sees "signs" in everything, of course. During a walk along the beach, a dead gull falls at his feet, and he later connects this with the death of the parachutist. The dog which jumps at his throat is, in his imagination, a reference to the death of Gé in the safari park. And thus it goes on in Gerard's head.'

In *De Vierde Man* Verhoeven intended to play on what the psychologist Carl Jung called the sychronicity principle: the causal connection between events which seemingly have nothing to do with each other. Perhaps this was difficult for the actors to portray, but for Verhoeven, with his earlier interest in parapsychological phenomena, it was a fascinating theme. 'In old-fashioned terms we would call it black magic. In my view, if Christine had not been there those accidents would certainly not have happened. Her charisma is so strong that she does not have to lift a finger to influence events – she only needs to look in order to pull the characters into her Dark Realm. If you look at it that way, Christine is a reincarnation of the Devil.'

To make it clear to the audience which side Christine is on, during a night-time love-making scene on the beach she accidentally lies down on a piece of glass. She does not feel it: she has an insensitive spot on her back. According to medieval superstition, this was one of the ways to recognize a witch.

To support his fellow art colleagues struggling with Evil, the real writer Gerard Reve also appeared on set, accompanied by his inseparable mate, Joop 'Matroos Vosch' Schafthuizen. To support the synchronicity principle, Reve had worn exactly the same clothes, including the scarf and bracelet, as those in which he had appeared on the back cover of his book *De Vierde Man*. He had a friendly word for everyone and cheerfully walked through the takes, closely followed by the national press. The typically Revian black humour, which was the trademark of the writer, brought a smile to the stress-worn faces for the first time during the shooting. Krabbé recorded: '3 June – The press came. Gerard and Matroos Vosch were there too. Gerard thinks everything is fantastic and looks around like a happy child. I found Matroos Vosch an irritating twit. Gerard was very witty. When we told him that the food on the set was often very bad, he cheerfully answered, "Oh well, *I* live on Eucharists on some days."

In the spirit of Reve's work, a great deal of religious symbolism was added to *De Vierde Man*. Thus, in a Pasolini-like vision, the Christ on the Cross in a Catholic church changes into the beautiful Herman on the Cross, dressed only in red swimming trunks. Gerard immediately begins to pull the swimming costume from his body, but he is disturbed by an elderly lady who thinks it very curious that the writer is touching the holy relic in this way. When the camera zooms out, we see Christ on the Cross again.

Verhoeven: 'It was an image from my childhood that I used here. At Sunday school, which I attended for a year when I was eight, you were always given those brightly coloured pictures of biblical scenes with a perforated edge to tear off. One of these was the crucifixion of Christ, and I would stare at it for hours. I wondered what it would look like if they pulled off Christ's loincloths.'

Later the director thought that Christ must have been crucified naked, but that his followers found the fact too hard to accept. It was soon labelled blasphemy. 'When the Reve figure does it in *De Vierde Man*, it has, of course, much more explicit sexual connotations than I imagined at the time. The scene with Herman tied to the Cross relates to Gerard's perverse mind – it is a sadomasochistic scene. It fits well into the film because the entire narrative uses romantic-decadent symbolism – the nineteenth-century French writer Huysmans once wrote that he imagined Jesus hanging there with an erection, so in that sense my scene was not too bad.'

What seems to save the writer from being himself crucified by Christine is the continuous presence of Mary in the film. Although the Reve figure initially does not seem to recognize her, it is clear to the audience that Mary watches over the main character – she makes herself known by her dress. In medieval imagery, Mary has blue and white colours, which is why in the film she consistently wears a blue raincoat. Gerard sees her for the first time when he takes the train to Vlissingen and she shares a compartment with him. The little boy on her arm looks like baby Jesus, and when his mother peels him an apple and holds the long peel above him, he even has a halo above his head for a moment. During the story the *femme céleste* Mary regularly appears as a counterpoint to the *femme fatale*. In Gerard's dreams and visions she shows him the way to the Good. Finally she manifests herself as the nurse Ria when, after Herman's fatal accident, the writer ends up in hospital. It is there that the Reve figure recognizes his Mary in the comforter of the sick. Nobody believes him. The doctor says, 'Mr Reve . . . *Mary* in Vlissingen, among us . . .?' but Gerard is certain: without Mary's motherly protection he would have come to an unavoidably terrible end.

The device of the Queen of Heaven dressed in blue was for scriptwriter Gerard Soeteman a way of pulling Reve's Mariolatry out of the author's private universe. 'Gerard Reve is a clown who has merged with his make-up. He does not speak very highly of women, yet that is contrasted with his limitless admiration for Mary. You would think Reve is far too intelligent to lean on religion with such heart and soul. I wondered whether his Mariolatry might not be primarily a literary pose. That is why the main character Gerard does not recognize her in the film for a long time, even though the symbols are so clear.'

What Soeteman is driving at is that, in interviews, Gerard Reve had often explained how art and religion were twin sisters to him; as far as he was concerned, no artist has a rational view of the world. 'Every artist is religious,' he used to say, 'because he relies on metaphysical concepts. He doesn't have to go to church, but creation *is* interpretation, just like religion.'

At the time of the première of *De Vierde Man*, Gerard Reve reacted positively to the film. Even now, twelve years later, he still thinks it is the most convincing cinematographic adaptation of his work, better than the films *Lieve Jongens* (1980) or *De Avonden* (1989).

He had no objections to the elements added to the story. 'I was always aware that I write books and other people make films – their profession is not my profession. I said to director Verhoeven, "I will help you in every way I can if you want to know something from me, but I prefer to keep out of it because it is another work of art." If the film goes wrong, whose fault is it then, eh? Let the cobbler stick to his last.'

Reve explains how the director also demonstrated the difference between book and film. 'He said that a lot of things in the story are mysterious. You can make of it what you want, and that has a certain implication for someone who reads a book at his own pace and can go back a few pages – but that is not possible with film. In a film you have to say what there is to say in a few minutes. Then he gave an example: "In your book that guy Herman loses an eye, in my film he dies." I said, "No half-measures then."'

As a good Catholic, Reve had frowned for a moment at the scene of Thom Hoffman as the Jesus figure on the Cross. If they had asked him beforehand, he would certainly not have advised the director and scriptwriter to do it, but afterwards he thought it was 'an entirely justified linking of religious eroticism with bodily eroticism'.

Reve says, 'Look, you can't talk to people about eroticism, the word doesn't mean anything any more – it mainly creates confusion. Bodily eroticism is sexuality. Social eroticism is life in an association, a family, at school or in a sports club. Religious eroticism is the urge to become one with God. In the film the Saviour changes into the fancied young man on the Cross. I thought that was very impressive. The reason why it is not offensive but very good is because it fits naturally, organically into the film. A close shave, of course. These scenes often cause trouble, usually caused by a mistake in composition. You can ask Salman Rushdie about that.'

Reve was moved by the ending of the film. 'Christine did not have an antagonist, so the director came up with the woman who anyone with a bit of religious feeling recognizes: the Queen of Heaven. When at the end you get that discussion and the doctor says, "I am a Catholic myself, I have six children, but to think that Mary would consider it worth her while to appear in this dump is exaggerated. You are not *that* important . . .", it preserves the mystery!'

The writer said that Verhoeven knew his trade. The public automatically sides with those who are not believed. Reve considers it a reassuring thought. That way, at least, everybody knows that Mary is among us.

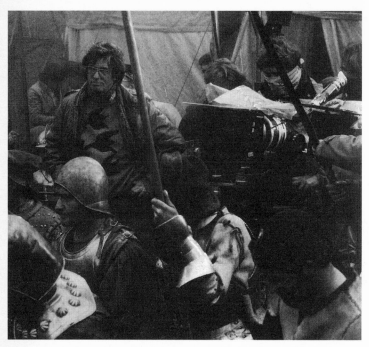

Flesh + Blood: the frustrated general and the mutinous army.

Flesh + Blood: Paul Verhoeven with Rutger Hauer.

Chapter 11

Flesh + Blood + Elbows

On the morning of 24 March 1983 Paul Verhoeven enjoyed breakfast more than usual. By now he had moved with his wife, two daughters and foster-daughter into a detached house at Beekestein 11, Leiderdorp. Today was the day of the Dutch première of *De Vierde Man*, and with some amusement he was looking at the good advance reviews. It surprised him somewhat that the film was being analysed in such a serious way. Verhoeven and Soeteman had put into the story everything they could think of in terms of hocus-pocus: religion, synchronicity, Magic Realism, fantasy, reality – there was no end to it. By giving these elements an artistic tone, they had made the story seem more layered than it really was. The director concluded that as long as the camera moved slowly, the light was filtered to glossy pink, purple and green, the main characters did not move too quickly and held each other enthralled with meaningful silences, the critics would write that film could also be art. Verhoeven himself thought that *Soldaat van Oranje* and *Spetters* were much more daring and interesting films, but with *De Vierde Man* he received all the applause these previous productions had been deprived of.

In some ways, he understood this. His commercial films had usually been assessed by the critics using artistic criteria, whereas Verhoeven had intended a more Hollywood tone. With *De Vierde Man*, the film and its critical reception were in agreement with each other for the first time, although Gerard Soeteman maintained that 'Reve must have written *De Vierde Man* with his left foot, just as we wrote the script with our left hand.' The newspapers and weeklies were publishing weighty articles about how much the film was a justification of the work of the great writer, and whether the Reve figure in the film could be compared to the real Reve.

At the same time, Verhoeven also realized the consequences: because of its literary tone, *De Vierde Man* would turn out to be a minor film in his oeuvre, as was later confirmed by the attendance figures of only 400,000. Thus *De Vierde Man* became his least popular feature film, but it did his reputation as a director a lot of good, especially in the United States, where the wittiness of the story, enlivened with high kitsch, was better understood than in the Netherlands. As *Newsweek* would write on 18 June 1984: 'What appears to be a death-obsessed, symbol-laden, dreamlike thriller turns out to be (among other things) a wickedly funny comedy ... The fascination of Verhoeven's dark and stylish riddle is its ability to work simultaneously as mystery and satire, to enter its hero's obsession and mock it as well.' The *Wall Street Journal* spoke of 'an eccentric blend of Hitchcock, Bergman and New Wave androgyny; a witty piece of work'. *De Vierde Man* would eventually receive many prizes, including an award for the best foreign production of 1984 from the film critics in Los Angeles.

His American contacts, the result of many overseas excursions, finally bore fruit. After *De Vierde Man* it seemed very likely that Verhoeven would make his first American–European co-production. After months of negotiating, Orion Pictures were prepared to let him shoot a story which he had presented under the title (and according to the new album of Bryan Ferry's Roxy Music) *Flesh + Blood*. The contracts were signed on 21 October 1983, and a long-running saga began.

Verhoeven realized that the proposal had been the result of desperation. The Orion executives kept asking for a film along the lines of *Soldaat van Oranje*; didn't he and Soeteman have something like that ready? In an excess of confidence, Verhoeven fell back on a project he had kept in a drawer since 1970 and which was to have become the adult version of his children's series *Floris*. At the time, Gerard Soeteman had written a fifty-page outline that had been given the working title *De Huurlingen* (*The Mercenaries*). The intended English title was *God's Own Butchers*. The story was about a troops of medieval mercenaries who are fired by their financial backer, nobleman Arnolfini, because a war has been settled. He keeps a few of the troops in his employment, mainly to chase the now-redundant mercenaries out of town.

This is how the former brothers in arms Captain De Jonker and Sergeant Maarten come to fight each other. According to the outline: 'De Jonker is an officer at the end of his career. Not because he can no longer physically cope, but because he is tired of war and wants to spend the rest of his days peacefully at his castle, which the council of trading town A. and the noble Arnolfini have put at his disposal.' De Jonker drops his friend Maarten in no uncertain terms when he realizes he is dependent upon the favours of the town council.

With a few faithful followers, Maarten leaves town, displaying his contempt for De Jonker in words and gesture. Now that winter is coming, Maarten – a flesh-and-blood contradiction, because in addition to being a well-oiled fighting machine he is also deeply religious – knows that he will be forced to live the life of an outlaw: robbery and looting are his only prospects. Shortly afterwards, Maarten's unruly army ambushes the convoy bringing Agnes, the bride for Arnolfini's son Jehan. Arnolfini demands revenge. De Jonker has to save the honour of the nobleman and his son's bride; the robbers must be punished. Under threat of losing his privileges, De Jonker puts on his weaponry with a heavy heart and sets off with Jehan and some soldiers. The knowledge that he is hunting the scalp of his former friend Maarten makes this punitive expedition even more distasteful to him.

Soeteman and Verhoeven had found the inspiration for *De Huurlingen* in a Western they greatly admired, *The Wild Bunch* (Sam Peckinpah, 1969). In that film, William Holden and Robert Ryan also belong to the same gang but are then compelled to fight each other from different sides of the law. '*The Wild Bunch* is a very good film,' Verhoeven explains, 'but it never manages a real confrontation between those two. I thought I could do better with *Flesh + Blood*.'

The outline of *De Huurlingen* does show the confrontation between De Jonker and Maarten. When Arnolfini's son Jehan falls into the hands of the mercenaries, De Jonker comes to the bath house to negotiate:

De Jonker and Maarten meet each other, an encounter full of mutual distrust. When the sergeant comes in naked with a bundle of clothes in his hand, De Jonker is already sitting in one of the baths. Maarten sits down opposite him. They are on their guard. And when the sergeant, in an unexpected move, reaches a little too obviously for the soap which has slipped into the water, De Jonker quick as a flash pulls out of the water a dagger that a little while earlier he had stuck into the wood under the surface. But the sergeant turns out not to have kept to the no-weapons agreement either: as soon as he sees the dagger, he stretches out his hand towards the bundle of clothes next to him and pulls out a long knife. With their weapons drawn, the men sit opposite each other, brooding.

The former friends decide to come to an agreement, but this is soon broken. The climax of the story is De Jonker's pursuit of Maarten, who has decided to go to the chapel of St Sebastian to thank God for the fortuitous way in which He has accompanied the mercenaries on their journey. The chapel is one day's journey away, in the middle of the marshy delta De Biesbos. Jehan is pulled along behind a cart. When they are caught in an ambush by De Jonker, there is only one way out: into the swamp. Jehan is dragged along and half-disappears under the water.

On an impulse, De Jonker decides to save the chained Jehan. Through lack of time, he has no choice but to cut off Jehan's hand – this is the only way he can free him. With the heavily bleeding, half-unconscious Jehan in front of him on his horse, De Jonker rides off. The stump of the arm is put into loose gunpowder and set on fire; the flash singes and closes the wound. In a classic showdown Maarten, Agnes, Jehan and De Jonker meet in the chapel. Maarten is killed by the sword which Jehan thrusts into him. De Jonker is crushed by a heavy statue of Mary. At the end of the story only Jehan and Agnes are still alive, more or less condemned to each other.

Because *De Huurlingen* resounded with the apocalyptic ideas of the Middle Ages – religion, superstition, waiting for the end of time, fear of the plague – at the meetings with Orion, Verhoeven spoke with passion about 'a story which deals with power and the lack of power, life and death, love and hate'. He emphasized that in the Middle Ages very few people died a natural death and that war was the order of the day. 'We all have the strange idea that the Middle Ages were romantic, but that is nonsense. This is due to heroic stories such as King Arthur, but that is literature, a feigned reality. *Flesh + Blood* is going to be a counter-fairytale.' In his summary he said that the film had to become a mirror set at a distance, dealing with the timeless theme of the human condition.

The Orion staff listened to the story with a mixture of amazement and admiration. In the same way as Verhoeven's father graphically used to portray in the classroom the adventures of the Crusaders or the turbulent voyages of the Dutch East India Company, so the director enthusiastically made the Middle Ages pass before the executives' eyes. Verhoeven explained that such an ambitious, million-dollar project could never be realized in the Netherlands, but that he foresaw great possibilities for a co-production. He was given $7 million, which at the exchange rate of the time meant to Verhoeven the unprecedented sum of 20 million Dutch guilders.

Orion also made a number of demands. Whereas on paper *De Huurlingen* had been set in a boggy river delta in the Netherlands, *Flesh + Blood* had a more continental appeal. More important, they wanted to see a love story incorporated into the plot, so that Americans could also identify with the main characters: unlike the original story, the kidnapped Princess Agnes had to be given a key role. Consequently, the confrontation between De Jonker and Maarten was pushed to the background.

Nevertheless, the director saw sufficient potential for the film to become 'a pleasant cocktail of the Western *Vera Cruz*, the adventure film *The Crimson Pirate*, my own *Floris* and a hint of *Star Wars*', and declared that he agreed with the suggested alterations. It was a rare compromise, partly inspired by the knowledge that he had found a possible escape route from the Dutch film climate he found so suffocating. Gijs Versluys would produce, because the renewed collaboration between Rob Houwer and Verhoeven had been short-lived. On 29 October 1982 Houwer said in a letter to the director, even before *De Vierde Man* was shown in the cinema, 'And as far as the future is concerned, I have had more than enough already. I am absolutely fed up with your neurotic behaviour and it makes me nervous to think I might ever have to have anything to do with it again.'

The distribution rights for *Flesh + Blood* had been sold in advance to twenty-five countries by Orion Pictures, which eliminated any investment risk. Moreover, they thought that a film crew in Europe would be much cheaper and work much faster than would ever be possible in Hollywood, with its strict trade-union regulations. Verhoeven realized that Orion was particularly interested in *Flesh + Blood* because as a director he had shown with *Soldaat van Oranje* and *Spetters* that he was capable of shooting a successful film for next to nothing. He was determined to pass this international test. But *Flesh + Blood* almost became his Waterloo.

Rutger Hauer's first memory of the shooting of *Flesh + Blood* dates from March 1984: while the rest of the crew look on pityingly, Verhoeven, with clenched fists, runs after a flock of geese and some pigs. They had come waddling into the shot uninvited, causing the take in the courtyard of the castle of Belmonte, in the Cordillera region of Spain, to be stopped. The livestock were not too impressed by this outburst of rage from the director, who is trying to catch them as best he can. Both dignified and offended, the animals take their time as they flee in the desired direction. Rutger Hauer remembers, 'That was how we felt as actors too.'

In *Flesh + Blood* Rutger Hauer played the main character Martin, leader of the troop of soldiers of fortune. The beginning of the film follows the original story line: the nobleman Arnolfini conquers the walled city, then disarms the majority of his men and chases them out of the gates. De Jonker, renamed Hawkwood in the American co-production, helps Arnolfini with this. There is no question of revolt, since there is no one to lead the unruly troop. Then the whore Céline gives birth to a stillborn child in the improvised encampment of the mercenaries. During the child's miserable burial in the mud, they discover a holy statue of Saint Martin, which is interpreted as a heavenly sign by a religious fanatic who calls himself the Cardinal. He promptly appoints the tough mercenary Martin as their leader – the similarity of name is sufficient reason for that. The statue of Saint Martin, the only Christian saint with a sword, is loaded on to a cart, and from then on serves as a godly compass – when it is convenient, they touch his arm to influence providence in the right direction.

Disguised as monks, Martin's men rob a company of travellers which includes the bride-to-be Agnes – after which she takes over the story line of *Flesh + Blood*. The beautiful, virginal Agnes is raped by Martin, but nevertheless falls for his almost bestial charms. It is a calculated romance, since by making herself known as the leader's sweetheart, she realizes she will be able to keep the rest of the troop away from her. Martin falls in love with Agnes, and tries to attain her level of civilization by learning to eat with a knife and fork and dressing better. The other members of his troop watch with mixed feelings – they think that Martin is developing into a dictator. Although they have founded a 'commune' based on equality in a castle they have conquered, they now realize that some are apparently more equal than others.

Meanwhile, Agnes and Martin are making passionate love in a bathtub (which would later re-emerge in *Showgirls*); this time the princess is doing it of her own volition. Like a Patty Hearst *avant la lettre* she seems to be able to reconcile herself to her kidnappers, until her intended bridegroom Steven (called Jehan in *De Huurlingen*) appears at the gates. Agnes has to choose between Steven and Martin, between security and adventure.

Over the fourteen weeks of the shoot, Verhoeven felt the film slipping through his fingers. 'It was agony all the way. What a mess! I have never felt so unhappy as with *Flesh + Blood*. It just made me livid if something did not work – and hardly anything did. The computer in my head became completely overloaded.'

Spain had seemed an eminently suitable setting for *Flesh + Blood*. Research had discovered four locations: the towns of Cáceres and Oviedo, the old fortified town of Avila and the impressive castle of Belmonte (where in 1961 *El Cid* had been shot by Anthony Mann, with Charlton Heston and Sophia Loren in the leading roles). At Verhoeven's instigation, Rutger Hauer was cast as Martin. Now that he had acquired some fame in Hollywood in *The Osterman Weekend* (Sam Peckinpah, 1983), *Nighthawks* (Bruce Malmuth, 1981) and *Blade Runner* (Ridley Scott, 1982), there were no objections from Orion Pictures to letting the Dutchman carry the film. Moreover, as the former Floris, Hauer had experience of playing a knight.

The role of Agnes caused more problems. Extensive screen-tests were carried out in New York: Orion thought of Nastassja Kinski and Rebecca de Mornay, while Verhoeven felt more strongly about the up-and-coming actress Jennifer Jason Leigh (born 1958), who had impressed him with her role in the high-school drama *Fast Times at Ridgemont High* (a.k.a. *Fast Times*, Amy Heckerling, 1982). Verhoeven got his way, partly because Rebecca de Mornay's acceptance was conditional on the casting of her then boyfriend Tom Cruise in the role of Steven. Verhoeven dismissed this 'conditional casting' and decided on the young Australian actor Tom Burlinson for Steven. His father, the nobleman Arnolfini, is played by the Spanish actor Fernando Hillbeck.

The small army of mercenaries primarily consisted of second-division American actors (including Brian James and John Dennis Johnston), with the Brit Ronald Lacey as the Cardinal, Susan Tyrrell as the whore Céline, and the prominent Dutch actress Kitty Courbois as Anna, a kind of Mother Courage. The role of the old fighter Hawkwood, who is first Rutger Hauer's friend and later his enemy, was given to the Australian Jack Thompson. It is fair to say that with American–European money, a cast from all over the world and Spanish and Dutch technicians, it really was an international co-production.

Naturally, it took some doing to set this up. With the Orion agreement in their pocket, Verhoeven and Versluys went to the Productiefonds to safeguard a Dutch contribution of between 750,000 and 1 million guilders for the film. It was no longer Anton Koolhaas wielding the chairman's hammer, but that other well-known name from the past, Jan Blokker, who had been appointed on 1 June 1983. On accepting the job, he had declared in interviews his love of *auteurs* among film-makers, and had characterized Verhoeven as a 'shrewd guy': 'I think I would have stopped *Spetters*. I think that it is (a) an exceptionally bad film, and (b) I am sure that even at the script stage it reeked of extremity.' The chairman added, 'If those guys want to make that kind of production, they will just have to finance it themselves.' The Productiefonds existed for nobler purposes: criteria such as taste and traditional methods were crucial factors in the decision-making, Blokker explained, to ensure that 'talent is protected with government money'.

Although Verhoeven had easily been able to pay back the loan for each of his films, and was regarded as by far the most successful Dutch director, the script for *Flesh + Blood* was initially rejected by the chairman of the Productiefonds. Too much rape, murder and slaughter, was his judgement – which, after Blokker's utterances in the press, was not entirely unexpected. The money did eventually materialize after all, but it was, the Fonds declared grinding its teeth, a 'decision made on completely non-artistic grounds'. It would be a good way for the Dutch technical crew to gain experience, Blokker decided, and with a gesture intended to be generous he put up one-twentieth of the cost.

When shooting began in March 1984, Paul Verhoeven was relying on his inspiration. Whereas he normally shot strictly according to storyboards, he thought *Flesh + Blood* was particularly suited to a slightly looser style of directing. He had been familiar with medieval subjects since primary school, and by now he had wide experience as a film-maker. In retrospect, however, there could have been no worse moment for such a decision. 'The film immediately turned out to be far too complex for such an approach. Horses, castles, so many cameos, and all so complicated to shoot. I should have drawn up a detailed shooting script, but I thought, "I'll fix it on the set." Well, I did fix it, but not well enough I think.'

Once on the set it turned out to be impossible to reach acceptable working agreements with so many different nationalities. The Spanish technicians usually said *mañana*; every weekend they went back to their wives and children in Madrid. Their colleagues from production promised 120 horses, but came back with only 15. The Spanish make-up people thought the Dutch were a strange, impolite people, and made this known with 'go-slow' actions. Some of the American actors over-indulged in drink and drugs. Thus, as early as rehearsals, the crew of some 150 people had split into hostile cliques.

The director was caught in the middle. Although he was able to rely on his director of photography, Jan de Bont, he saw the rest of the crew as mutinous. What made matters worse was that they had been promised sun in the Spanish interior, but all they got was thick packs of snow and mud. Although spring was coming, the temperature regularly fell to twenty below zero.

Kitty Courbois noticed that, as early as the start of rehearsals, Verhoeven was very worried about the lack of discipline on the set. 'Many of the Americans were in Europe for the first time, and after a week's rehearsals they wanted to get to the beach as quickly as possible. They saw the film mainly as a job on the side. The one who really had it made was "party animal" Jack Thompson, although the Australian was not one of the troublemakers. With his well-filled refrigerator he was the life and soul of the party, and had contractually negotiated that his two lovers – cheerful sisters – would be accommodated in the hotel. Lucky guy.'

Journalists who had been invited to the shooting brought home ominous reports. Verhoeven, as always with his heart on his sleeve, expressed in these articles his irritation with the Americans, who thought that the Spanish hotels were awful by Hollywood standards. Or told how actor Brian James had thrown a chair at producer Gijs Versluys's head after being criticized for his constantly late arrival on the set. Not only in front of the camera but off screen, the unruly army of Rutger Hauer turned out to be 'maladjusted riff-raff' who refused to subject themselves to any form of discipline.

Verhoeven told the newspapers plainly, 'I am getting sick to death of that bunch. You can't even look through the camera without seeing them. They form a group within the film, but also outside it. I mean, if one of them thinks the toilet is dirty, they all think it's dirty. I already knew that actors are sometimes just like children, but it simply isn't funny any more. If you forget for one moment to give them all the same amount of attention, trouble starts.'

In the same way as a class of schoolchildren unerringly senses when a teacher has lost his way, the behaviour of the actors became more and more provocative. Verhoeven knew it, but was powerless. 'With those kinds of group behaviour, it's inevitable they choose a bogeyman. And that was me.'

Uninvited, the actors came up with their own ideas for every scene, which considerably delayed shooting progress. If these consultations took too long, the Spanish crew would spontaneously call a lunch break, so that the director was without technicians. Then the food was not good enough. 'There was a fucking awful atmosphere on the set all the time.'

Kitty Courbois confirms these tortured observations. 'I really enjoyed the peripheral aspects of an enormous production like that, such as the special effects, but as far as the actors were concerned, they begrudged each other the bread they ate. I had good relations with the British, the Dutch and the Australians, but the American actors were so used to fighting for their lives that they started to use their elbows. The Dutch actor Hans Veerman, who plays the role of the doctor, immediately started to talk about flesh, blood and elbows. Meanwhile, the rushes were being viewed in Holland, and from there I was told not to let myself be pushed out of the shot every time. Literally. With every take it was the same. They called action and the first thing you knew was, Whammm, you were thrown out of the shot. So I started to hit back.'

Because *Flesh + Blood* is set against a background of continuous destruction, it was Verhoeven's intention to let a great deal of thick black smoke pass across the screen. For this purpose, piles of car tyres were set on fire, but as soon as the wind was starting to blow from the wrong direction, shooting had to stop instantly or the actors would be exposed to poisonous fumes – after which the grumbling merrily continued.

Verhoeven's childhood dream was slowly turning into a nightmare. In the Netherlands he was only used to being closely watched by the producer, but here he had a complete staff of Orion people around him – and it made him pretty nervous. Verhoeven set up every shot with three or four cameras at the same time. Not because he liked doing it that way, but merely to gain time. Often there was no time to do different takes. He shot three times as many shots per day as in the Netherlands, and they were complicated: shooting, fighting, scenes with horses, troop movements, 300 cameos. Verhoeven realized he was permanently teetering on the edge of an abyss. 'I have never lost myself so much as with this film.'

The people from Orion had descended on the set after six weeks, when the first reports of chaos and delay had reached Hollywood. For a moment, the director feared he would be fired and replaced by a 'butcher', a director for hire whose only concern is to finish the film. The delegation was headed by someone from the completion bond – an insurance company which pays out to production companies if a film, for whatever reason, cannot be completed. Fortunately, Verhoeven says, they were not after his life but his success. The person in question even managed to negotiate extra shooting days for Verhoeven with Orion – though the budget eventually overran by 1 million dollars. 'But it did not give me any less of a headache. I cursed the day I had decided to become a film director.'

Jan de Bont clearly remembers the cataclysmic shooting. 'Paul always starts a film very optimistically, but then discovers that the people he is working with cannot do everything the way he would like them to. Then he explodes. He simply cannot imagine why other people are slow and sloppy, since he always prepares so well. Then he thinks, "They get paid well for it, don't they, why don't they do their work properly then?" I think it's wonderful that he is so obsessed with filming, but perhaps it's also a bit naïve of him to think that everyone is as obsessed as he is. Some directors do not think it worthwhile to get so heated about the details – scared as they are of having a heart attack. I think Paul would rather die than deliver a product he cannot support.'

The greatest source of annoyance and disappointment to the director was Rutger Hauer, whom he had catapulted to an international career with *Turks Fruit* and *Soldaat van Oranje*. For a long time they had talked about each other as alter ego and 'father figure', but with *Flesh + Blood* that professional idyll suddenly came to an end.

By now Hauer, almost forty, had worked in America with directors such as Sam Peckinpah (*The Osterman Weekend*) and Ridley Scott (*Blade Runner*). Whereas before he had naturally followed Verhoeven's lead, he now considered every suggestion at length. 'It is my career, and I would like it to go on. Without scars. All Paul's films have given me scars, except this one,' he would later explain.

The conversations on the set went something like this: 'Rutger, if you could jump off that horse' – 'Sorry, Paul, but in Hollywood we really do that very differently.'

The director was overcome by confusion. Although at the time of *Floris* Hauer had insisted on doing all the stunts himself (such as diving into a moat from a castle drawbridge when everyone knew the water must be full of wrecked bicycles), he now declined the honour. 'Of course in America they ask for a stand-in as soon as there is a drop of water on the ground,' Verhoeven slowly began to realize.

If Verhoeven and Hauer talked at all on the set, it was in an argumentative tone. And also in English, because the rest of the crew had made it known they did not appreciate it when the two conducted their affairs in Dutch. In view of the accents they both had, these clashes must have been tragi-comic. Jan de Bont: 'Paul wanted to give a realistic picture of the Middle Ages and Rutger wanted to be very artistic. Rutger has been gigantically ruined by Hollywood. He kept referring to his role as the android in *Blade Runner*, but the remarkable thing is that Ridley Scott is only interested in the visual style of his films. The actors have to immerse themselves in that style, which very often means that they simply have to sit still and are hardly allowed to move. I know that because I shot *Black Rain* with Ridley Scott – but you can also see it on the screen. Like that famous scene in *Blade Runner* with Rutger and the white pigeon on the roof, that was filmed very cerebrally. But Rutger thought *that* was real acting. That was his big mistake.'

Jan de Bont portrays the clash between the egos of Verhoeven and Hauer as a turbulent divorce with slamming doors. They never made up. In an interview which appeared in the weekly *Haagse Post* on 22 December 1984, long before *Flesh + Blood* was shown in the cinema, Rutger Hauer said unusually bitingly, 'If you want to develop a good relationship with an actor, you have to take the time for it. And Paul does not do that. During the preparations for *Flesh + Blood* he ignored me, ignored my wishes. What he does is use my charisma and personality for his smut. It really is two-dimensional. It is fucking, beer-drinking and fucking. Other than that, nothing happens. Not in one of his films. That *Soldaat van Oranje* rises above that level can be easily attributed to me.'

Hauer voiced these sentiments immediately after his return from Spain after the shooting of *Flesh + Blood*. The magazine did a second interview with the actor a few months later, when the fury had diminished. Hauer continued, 'Perhaps we did not understand each other very well this time. But what has been shot still shows Paul Verhoeven and Rutger Hauer together. Paul means a lot to my career. I have always had a love–hate relationship with Paul. On the one hand I know that I need him, on the other hand I could sometimes beat him up. We were very close to that in Spain. It went too far then. We had to let the matter rest.'

For Verhoeven, the damage had been done. The director thinks it was a deliberate act of revenge on the part of Hauer. 'I was dismissed by him. Maybe in Rutger's eyes I had denied him three times. For *Floris* I had a different actor in mind for the main role at first. Later I told him I did not consider him suitable for the role of the artist in *Turks Fruit*, which in the event he played fantastically. And the third time I believed that Rutger was a bit too rough to play the somewhat refined aristocratic Erik Hazelhoff Roelfzema.'

Verhoeven realizes that the actor has never forgotten this. In the same way as he cannot forget Rutger's blabbing about *Flesh + Blood*. 'Particularly *before* a film has been released. I don't think you do a thing like that. The interview was the kiss of Judas from Rutger. A knife in my back. I don't think I will ever forgive him for that.'

Exactly ten years later, on his farm at Beetsterzwaag, Rutger Hauer still believes that *Flesh + Blood* is a painful story. 'I thought the script was a weak, pornographic medieval adventure – I thought it should have been done differently. I wanted to have better scenes, and I was promised them too. But because the wife of scriptwriter Gerard Soeteman fell ill, those improvements never materialized. It all became very malicious, and at one point I said, "If we are not going to have other scenes, I will not be shooting *Flesh + Blood* at all." That was during a meeting with Paul and producer Gijs Versluys. My agent turned to me and said, "Rutger, I think you have misunderstood that clause about complete script approval." But my lawyer was there too and he said, "No, no, no . . . Rutger has understood that *very well*." All in all, it was becoming a bit embarrassing, so I thought, "Oh well, I'll manage. I'll get through it, because I did not feel like having lawyers on my backside, endlessly messing about. We began shooting, but in my view the story was not quite right. And it never was.'

Kitty Courbois has another explanation for Rutger Hauer's rebellion on the set. The actor was working in the realization that he needed a hit to safeguard his career in Hollywood. 'If I was observing things correctly during the shooting, Rutger wanted to be rid of his image as a villain – the role he always had to play in America. What he tried to do was to make Martin into a real hero, but because of the story that was not possible. It was this difference of opinion that led to the terrible rows between Paul and Rutger.'

After almost four months of shooting, the agonizing task was nearly completed. The work of the gang was finished, and Kitty Courbois was also allowed to go home. When she went to say goodbye to the director, with whom she had built up a friendship amidst all the chaos, she was amazed. 'They were shooting in a beautiful location with a small cast. The sun was shining. I heard birds whistling. Paul was sitting on the ground in the lotus position. Jennifer Jason Leigh and Tom Burlinson were acting out a very tender love scene. An unimaginably harmonious scene. No more screaming "GET THOSE HENS OUT OF THE WAY!" and "CAN YOU KILL THOSE GOATS!" After all we had been through, I simply did not think it possible that Paul was also capable of directing in peace and quiet. You could see by his happy face how much he had longed for this kind of moment.'

Flesh + Blood looked very much like a return to Verhoeven's original starting point, but in an intensified form: undiluted realism – a slap in the face for those who had thought *De Vierde Man* so tasteful. Even some of the director's circle of friends had carefully enquired whether he would continue in this new, more 'artistic' path, and whether such nasty stories as *Spetters* now belonged to the past.

'Just wait and see,' he had replied. And on 30 August 1985 *Flesh + Blood* had its world première at the prestigious Venice Film Festival. The reactions were very mixed. What surprised the Italian public more than anything else was that a woman emerged from the arena victorious. However, amidst the whistling there were also noises of approval. Strip the film of its violence and pools of blood, and the viewer is left with a clash between two views of the world: fatalistic Christianity versus the progressive thinking of Renaissance man. Whereas Martin and the Cardinal are guided by superstition, by fear of the Devil and the wrath of God, Steven tries, like a young Leonardo da Vinci, to solve problems in a scientific way.

Gerard Soeteman explains the reason why he and Verhoeven found the period around 1500 such an interesting time. 'The old dogmas of the Church were subject to debate – Anabaptists and other reformers emerged. It is the eve of the Renaissance, and its breakthrough from Italy to the North is imminent. Whereas before, the human body is considered the temple of God, the Renaissance man tries to improve health with medical science. Those developments were taking place on many different fronts.'

Thus, behind the fire, flesh and blood there is a story – which was not recognized by everyone at the time. 'The vision of a cynical man, one with a very sombre outlook on life, who considers every idealism as naïve and thinks that people are worse than animals,' *de Volkskrant* wrote in a devastating review on 12 September 1985 after the Dutch première. The weekly *Haagse Post* noted: 'If ever a film was sold under false pretences, it is *not* Paul Verhoeven's *Flesh + Blood*. That is exactly what the viewer is shown for some two hours: much human and animal flesh, and much blood, also from humans and animals. In the form of severed body parts, chopped into pieces, torn apart, rotting, partly decayed, in a state of total decomposition, and whatever else the director and special effects team managed to dream up.'

But although *Spetters* had been unanimously condemned, *Flesh + Blood* was not, as the review in the *NRC/Handelsblad* testifies: 'Now that he has visibly crossed the boundaries of Dutch chamber drama, Verhoeven's pessimistic vision becomes less threatening and more recognizable as a stylistic device, an idiom. Those who admire the films of Brian de Palma and George Romero cannot accuse Verhoeven of hatred of men or women. The comparison with Erich von Stroheim suggested by the director himself is going a little too far, but *Flesh + Blood* has undoubtedly had ingenuity, intelligence, humour, a sense of style, and erudition invested in it.'

The film was certainly sombre. Soeteman says that was intentional.

'When I wrote the outline in 1970, I felt a strong hostility towards religion and any other messianic teaching aimed at blaming someone else for your problems.' His father had been a pacifist, Utopian and Communist, and his son had found that all these -isms provided little edification at home. Although he denies no one the right 'to be unhappy in his own way', his father's naïve idealism had always made him feel an automatic urge to pull the rug from under every new movement. 'Every ideology promises a paradise that is unbearable to anyone with civilized taste.'

Soeteman knows that it is different for Verhoeven. They share the same morbid sense of humour, they have a similar fascination for history, but at the same time Soeteman finds Paul a very peculiar man. 'Because of his mathematical background he is capable of perfectly abstract, clear thinking, but you only need to knock on his door and say, "You are the resurrected Christ" and you will see something in his eyes that says, "Maybe they are right!" – whereas someone else would answer, "Would you like one or two guilders in your collection tin, because I assume that is what you are after?"'

Viewed in this way, *Flesh + Blood* is a crucial Verhoeven film, because the fight between logic and spirituality is one that is very familiar to the director; these are the elements still fighting for priority in his own mind. 'For all its pessimism, its delight in the perverse, its fixation on disease and vice, *Flesh + Blood* has one glorious merit: it's alive . . . If the movie is a failure, it's the sort of failure one would gladly trade for dozens of pallid, reasonable, predictable successes. It's offensive, but it surges at you, upsets you, forces out contradictory responses,' the *Los Angeles Times* wrote immediately after the American première on Friday 30 August 1985.

The film-maker himself was not half so contented with the final result of *Flesh + Blood*. Years later, he wanted to make amends with *Crusade*, a script written by Walon Green – the man who had created *The Wild Bunch*, the film on which *Flesh + Blood* had been partly modelled.

The theme of old friends becoming rivals had been overwhelmed by the focus on Princess Agnes that the American financiers had wanted so much. 'The triangular relationship Martin–Agnes–Steven is now the main story line, but in retrospect I think we should have stuck with Hawkwood and Martin. The failure of *Flesh + Blood* was a lesson for me: never again compromise on the main story line of a script.'

Nevertheless, it was not without some pride that he had entered *Flesh + Blood* for competition in the Dutch Film Days Festival at Utrecht in September 1985. He had fulfilled the prediction he had once made at the Filmacademie, that one day he would shoot an epic which would overwhelm the viewer with an infernal noise. *Flesh + Blood* may not have been a *Ben-Hur*, but composed as it was of 1660 shots, in its two hours there was at least never a dull moment – which could not be said of all Dutch films. Moreover, it was a farewell present, because after hesitating for a very long time, Verhoeven had decided to go to America. He had come to the conclusion that he could no longer work in the Netherlands.

At the Dutch Film Days Festival, *Flesh + Blood* was awarded two Golden Calves, the well-meaning Dutch equivalent of the Oscar. One for best direction and one for best film – but the way in which these had been awarded to Verhoeven caused controversy. Some members of the jury of seven made public their objections to the result, saying that the decision to honour Verhoeven had not been made unanimously but by majority. In the auditorium and at the party afterwards, the film community grumbled a great deal – opinions which the newspapers reported extensively the following morning.

Verhoeven did not see these articles. That morning he was already on his way to Schiphol Airport to catch his KLM flight. Destination: Hollywood. A camera crew followed behind. The images were intended for inclusion in a documentary, *The History of Dutch Film, Episode 5: Tomorrow will be better.* A little sullenly, the director looks at the conveyor belt in the departure hall. His shirt is half-open, on his shoulder hangs a green travel bag. With emotion, he gives the reason for his departure in one thunderous statement: 'At the moment there is too much negative feedback about my work in the Netherlands. You waste so much time and energy setting up a film in the teeth of the moralizing prejudices of all the committees you have to face in this country in order to get your money – 70 per cent of your energy goes not into making your film, but into overcoming the difficulties of financing it. It is totally unbalanced.'

His fury was aimed at the Productiefonds, where he had regularly been obliged to back down, first by chairman Anton Koolhaas and later by his successor Jan Blokker. 'I cannot bring myself to appear before that committee again to say, "I meant it in this and this way, because I think it would be nice, but if you see it differently, maybe it should be done that way." Those people don't know the first thing about it. It is a senseless situation and fighting against it has become too hard for me.'

Rob Houwer, the producer with whom Verhoeven had made five successful films, said in a 1985 interview with the weekly *Vrij Nederland*, 'As regards Verhoeven making it in America, I'll believe it when I see it. You can't give me a single example of a foreigner who has made it in America. Louis Malle, Antonioni. You are tied to your European roots.' The Dutch film press also waved Verhoeven goodbye with the usual ambivalence. 'A professional; but also a confused, moralistic, provocative, dubious, pessimistic and resistible observer of society,' the morning paper *de Volkskrant* concluded in its review of *Flesh + Blood*.

The television images of Verhoeven's departure conclude with a voice-over: 'With mixed feelings, the director who has lured the largest number of people into the cinema so far leaves for Hollywood. He goes to shoot the film *RoboCop* there.' In pronouncing the film's title, the inflection of the voice betrays a certain irony. There was much less irony in the last, oppressed look of Paul Verhoeven into the camera.

III Film making: America

The Hollywood film-maker.

A drawing of RoboCop.

RoboCop: Verhoeven with writer Ed Neumeier.

RoboCop: Its realization on film.

RoboCop: Verhoeven with RoboCop.

RoboCop: Peter Weller – the machine man at his most vulnerable.

Chapter 12

The Americanization of the Bible: *RoboCop*

The room in the Beverly Hills Hotel had everything a visitor would expect for $190 per night, concluded Paul Verhoeven as he unpacked his bag on Saturday 28 September 1985. He had just arrived from Amsterdam. He put aside the address book that he had found in his luggage; it was not going to be of much use in the United States, where he only knew Jan de Bont and Monique van de Ven – the cameraman and actress who had left the Netherlands for Hollywood nine years ago – his agent Marion Rosenberg and lawyer Thomas Hansen.

Verhoeven realized that he had taken an irreversible step. He was forty-seven years old, weary of both film and the social climate in the Netherlands, and he now would have to start all over again as a director. Although Hollywood's inner circle knew his work and had been very enthusiastic about *Turks Fruit*, *Soldaat van Oranje* and *De Vierde Man*, he was practically unknown to the wider American film-going public. There was little awareness of a Dutch cinematographic tradition in America: perhaps Joris Ivens and Bert Haanstra enjoyed some fame as documentary film-makers, and one or two people knew that Audrey Hepburn was the daughter of a Dutch baroness. Since the early 1960s the actor John van Dreelen, a pseudonym for Jack Grimberg, had often been mentioned in his native country in connection with Hollywood, but he was not listed in any current *Who's Who* in the United States. In addition, Verhoeven's own credentials had not been sufficient to gain the respect of the American actors with whom he had worked on *Flesh + Blood*. Their conduct during the shooting in Spain had been close to mutiny – and how could he be certain that the Americans would be any more sympathetic to his next film?

Verhoeven had come over to shoot *RoboCop*, a science-fiction story about a cop who is turned into a destructive machine. This invitation from Orion Pictures had made him decide it was time to make a definite move to the United States. At the time of the Oscar nomination for *Turks Fruit* in 1973, various people had strongly recommended him to take this step, but it seemed such a drastic one that he had hesitated. The working method he had sampled with *Flesh + Blood* had seemed ideal: making a film of international appeal with American money, while staying in his dull but familiar native country, where his wife worked and his children went to school. But the combination of the constant criticism of his films in the Netherlands and the fact that, as far as he was concerned, *Flesh + Blood* had failed as an experiment in international co-production finally made him take the plunge. It may have been possible for an actor to live in the Old World and work in the New World, as Rutger Hauer was attempting to do. A director, however, would have to live in the country itself, if only to understand the sensibilities of the American public. This was the only way a film-maker could become familiar with the tastes and attitudes of the Americans, and get to know the market in which he was now going to work. As soon as the children had finished their school year in the Netherlands, his family would also emigrate. Until then, he would have to cope on his own.

In October, between the discussions about *RoboCop*, Verhoeven would have to travel to Vancouver at the invitation of the TV channel HBO to shoot (in seven days) an episode of the thriller series *The Hitchhiker*. He had been asked on the strength of *De Vierde Man*; the script HBO had sent him was about a director who threatens his female lead to get her into the right mood for a horror movie. At the end of the twenty-five-minute episode, the actress reverses the roles. The director was to be played by Peter Coyote and the title of the story was *The Last Scene*. To Verhoeven it seemed a nice routine job, a warm-up for the real test: *RoboCop*.

For now, he had decided to ignore his jet lag and have a drink in the Polo Lounge, the bar of the Beverly Hills hotel where many a film deal had been struck. After that, he would go for a walk on the Rodeo Drive, for it was time to explore his new home town. As he closed the door of his hotel room behind him, he smiled and thought of one of his Dutch comic-strip heroes, the ever-adventurous Tom Poes. 'This', thought Paul Verhoeven, 'was Tom Poes's most adventurous adventure – and it had better all end well too.'

The Hollywood where Paul Verhoeven was about to make his entrance was ruled by pop culture, as he had realized after his previous visits. In 1975, as if by magic, twenty-eight-year-old Steven Spielberg had come up with *Jaws*, the spectacle with which the 'boy wonder' had shown the major studios that there was a whole new cinema-going public to be tapped – the twelve- to twenty-four-year-olds, an audience with very specific tastes. Youngsters were no longer interested in the realism, laced with social comment, of *The Graduate* (Mike Nichols, 1967), *Midnight Cowboy* (John Schlesinger, 1969) or *The Godfather* (Francis Ford Coppola, 1972). They wanted action, excitement, sensation, sex and humour – the ideal ingredients for an evening out in the shopping mall.

Films such as *Ghostbusters* (Ivan Reitman, 1984), *Back to the Future* (Robert Zemeckis, 1985), *Indiana Jones and the Temple of Doom* (Steven Spielberg, 1984) and *The Terminator* (James Cameron, 1984) had few intellectual pretensions, but offered stylish visual entertainment for young people. The box office returns were impressive:

E.T. The Extra-Terrestrial (1982), directed by Steven Spielberg: $228 million
Star Wars (1977), directed by George Lucas: $194 million
Return of the Jedi (1983), directed by Richard Marquand: $169 million
The Empire Strikes Back (1980), directed by Irvin Kershner: $142 million
Ghostbusters (1984), directed by Ivan Reitman: $132 million

In Hollywood this was called the 'juvenilization' of the movies – in fact, the juvenilization of the world. Because of its leading position in the film industry, the United States developed more than ever into a world-wide exporter of pop culture.

Thus Paul Verhoeven was not surprised when the script sent to him by Orion's Barbara Boyle in the summer of 1985 appeared to have a 'cyborg crimefighter' as its main character: 50 per cent human, 50 per cent machine, 100 per cent cop. Initially, it did not appeal to him in the slightest. On the front page of the script was written in huge letters 'The future of law enforcement', and the director promptly concluded that this was not the level at which he wished to live his intellectual life. Only when his wife Martine and the film company insisted did the director study the script more closely, with an English–Dutch dictionary to hand. While looking up all the unfamiliar slang – 'At first I did not understand why the black villains kept calling their white colleagues "brother" when they were clearly not related' – he gained a new perspective on the RoboCop story, a perspective with depths that surprised him. From that moment the film began to rise in his estimation above the platitudes of the action formula, but without abandoning the idiom of the genre. Moreover, the idea appealed to his pragmatic side. If he was to make the transition to America, maybe a science-fiction story was not such a bad idea. As a newcomer in the United States, Paul Verhoeven had to guard against over-confidence. 'To start straight away with, say, a story about New Orleans, full of racial issues and social comment, seemed a bit too ambitious to me. Science-fiction gives you a great deal of freedom. And besides, when that science-fiction layer is stripped away, you are left with a story about a man who has lost his identity. RoboCop goes in search of his past and gradually discovers that he was once born as Murphy, a human. That seemed to me a universal theme.'

Paul Verhoeven had made another resolution on his arrival in Hollywood: he would avoid the trap that had led to the failure of so many European directors before him. At the time of the great wave of émigré film-makers in the 1930s, the non-Anglo-Saxons such as Fritz Lang, Billy Wilder, Otto Preminger and Ernst Lubitsch were regarded as culturally enriching, and Hollywood looked up to their supposedly European sophistication. But a list made today would record the less pleasant experiences of European directors such as Michelangelo Antonioni and Wim Wenders, who went home with their heads spinning. Ingmar Bergman progressed no further than the announcement of American film plans during his visit to Hollywood in 1976.

These film-makers had probably underestimated the fact that in the United States a director could not make a film with a European narrative and the rhythm and pace of the Old World. Verhoeven realized that, for the American public, film was first and foremost a circus. A story had to be divided into three parts: a beginning, a middle and a grand finale – preferably with orgiastic explosions, or at least a universal shoot-out. He could not point to a three-act structure in the work of Federico Fellini and Alain Resnais that he had so admired in the past, or even in his own films, but he had decided in advance to submit himself to the iron law of Hollywood. His survival tactic was 'Go with the flow'.

In his American adventure Verhoeven would be assisted by Mike Medavoy, the forty-five-year-old executive vice-president of Orion Pictures. Verhoeven knew Medavoy to be a resolute man, an old hand in the film industry who had started in the post room of Universal Studios – and a man who also knew the quirks of European directors. In 1984 Wim Wenders had made *Hammett* for him, a project which started at Coppola's Zoetrope Studio as a disaster, and ended at Orion Pictures as a fiasco. But Medavoy had confidence in Paul Verhoeven: 'Wim could have made it here if only he had listened to somebody. Paul is smart.' Medavoy had managed to convince the board of directors that despite the failure of *Flesh + Blood*, in which Orion Pictures had invested $7 million, the Dutch film-maker was the right man for *RoboCop*.

'The first of Paul's films that I saw was *Soldier of Orange*,' recalls Medavoy, 'and I thought it was extremely well made, and for very little money by American standards. When his name came up for a project, I thought, "He can do it." There is an intelligence about his work, a bit of sensationalism – or the other word you could use is that he provokes the audience. We then proceeded to make a film with him, which was *Flesh + Blood*, and it was a disaster, commercially speaking. Nevertheless, you could see the talent, and his taste for action and eroticism. So we were willing to give Paul a second chance.'

That decision was easily taken, since Orion Pictures Corporation did not exactly see the *RoboCop* project as the spearhead of its activities. The company was the new kid on the block in Hollywood. Founded in 1978 by Arthur Krim – who together with four kindred spirits, including Mike Medavoy, had left United Artists Studios – Orion particularly concerned itself with 'quality' films: Woody Allen's work, Miloš Forman's *Amadeus*; Oliver Stone's *Platoon* and later Jonathan Demme's *The Silence of the Lambs*. The television series *Cagney and Lacey* was an Orion production, and the same company gave the young director Susan Seidelman permission to shoot *Desperately Seeking Susan* in 1985, followed by Kevin Costner with *Dances with Wolves* in 1990.

The dream of the founders was to make Orion into a 'film-maker's studio', a counterpoint to the majors, where any artistic motives for film-making seemed to have been permanently abandoned. That trend was reinforced by the fact that, one by one, the majors were being taken over by big corporations: Columbia was bought by Coca-Cola and sold on to Sony; MCA/Universal came into the hands of the Matsushita Electrical Industrial Company; Paramount was already the property of Gulf and Western; and Time Inc. was to acquire Warner Brothers in 1989. For these big corporations the film industry became more than ever an investment, a money-spinner. Unlike Orion, the majors did not care what kind of films they released as long as the box-office figures showed an annual growth.

The attempt of Orion Pictures to offer Hollywood a creative way out was courageous; the harsh reality was, however, a constant lack of money. In desperation, the company in 1984 allowed James Cameron to make *The Terminator* with Arnold Schwarzenegger. Although Orion loathed the genre, artistic objections soon evaporated when the film became a success, with profits of some $50 million.

The company's reasoning was that if *RoboCop* were able to bring about a similar cash-flow, the noble goal of the 'better film' would be safeguarded for a few more years. Thanks to Medavoy's intervention – and the fact that several other directors, such as Jonathan Kaplan, had pulled out earlier – it was left to Paul Verhoeven. The experienced producer Jon Davison – *Airplane!* (Jim Abrahams, David Zucker, Jerry Zucker, 1980), *White Dog* (Sam Fuller, 1982) and *Twilight Zone: The Movie* (John Landis, Steven Spielberg, Joe Dante, George Miller, 1983) – was expected to keep the Dutch director under control. This also applied to the budget, which was modest by Hollywood standards: $13 million dollars. Of this, $300,000 was for the director – but the film would have to be shot in thirteen weeks.

The original script for *RoboCop* had been written in 1984 according to the conventions of the American comic strips in which improbable heroes such as Iron Man or Spiderman ruled. Ingredients: an upbeat narrative, with archetypal villains and an unapproachable, albeit slightly neurotic, super-hero. The setting: a violent metropolis in the near future.

The creators of *RoboCop* were Michael Miner and Ed Neumeier. Miner had made a name for himself as an experimental film-maker: he had worked with the British director Alex Cox, who shot *Repo Man* in 1984, and had made several music videos. He had also filmed one of his own scripts with the less than subtle title of *Deadly Weapons*. Ed Neumeier, a good-natured cowboy in appearance, had once made a living as a studio reader, reading other people's scripts. Later he was allowed to call himself a development executive, but it remained an existence that only mildly satisfied him. It was the twenty-something Neumeier who had approached the thirty-something Miner with the suggestion of writing a script together. He already had an idea for it.

'When I worked for Warner Brothers as a reader, they were shooting *Blade Runner*. At night I used to leave my office and go over to this amazing set they had, and I would just say, "Hey, what can I do?" They were so busy that they would go, "Oh, we need to take this prop over there," and I ended up doing little things like that. It was very inspiring and I kept thinking, "This is a movie about robots who look like people. Wouldn't it be cool if there was this thing that looked like a robot and that was a cop?" My original notion was that it was a robot and it was trying to understand why people were so fucked up. A notion of a purer intelligence trying to figure out the corrupted intelligence of human beings.'

After that, the problem was how to glue the audience to their seats. 'I figured out that what would shock them most was if the hero of the story got killed right away – like ten minutes into the movie, so you think, "O-ho, the movie is over!" I suddenly realized that it has to be a story about a guy who becomes a machine.'

This is why policeman Alex J. Murphy, on the first day of his transfer to the unpleasant district of Old Detroit – barely four pages into the script – is shot to pieces by a group of gangsters led by the villain Clarence Boddicker. After a thorough electro-surgical overhaul, Murphy returns to the streets of Detroit as a machine man – RoboCop. His destructive journey through the china shop of crime is ready to begin.

Once the original idea had been formulated, Miner and Neumeier wasted little time. Although this was to be a genre film, in the best tradition of the comic strip it was also intended to spice it with satirical comment on contemporary America. In the same way as the science-fiction films of the 1950s dealt not with the future but with the Cold War – men from Mars *always* turned out to be Russians – *RoboCop* had to say as much about the 1980s as about the future. References to the

Reagan era – the era of Michael Milken and the junk bonds swindle – are evident throughout. The origin of this satire dated back to when Neumeier, as a development executive for Universal Studios, became acquainted with the mores of yuppie life. At that time he was surrounded by – as he now calls them – 'stupid people in suits who were always working out of greed and getting away with it'.

In the Detroit of RoboCop, the multinational Omni Consumer Products (OCP) is in charge of a society where privatization seems to be a religion. Even police work is contracted out to this company. Omni Consumer Products looks after the safety of citizens as well as 'Travel Concepts, Community Concepts, Entertainment Concepts – the products and degree of specialization are endless'. The corporate crooks have their headquarters in an impressive skyscraper far away from the dangerous life on the street. Inside, careers are made and broken. OCP's hidden agenda is to enhance the old part of Detroit with a prestigious development project.

In order to achieve this, crime must first be dealt with. This is why OCP is busy developing two types of invulnerable enforcer. The company president, simply referred to as the Old Man, prefers the security robot Enforcement Droid 209. During a presentation at headquarters by deputy director Dick Jones (played by Ronny Cox), the prototype unfortunately loses its head and riddles a young executive with bullets from its 20mm machine-gun, after which it hopelessly expires in a power cut.

The initiator of the rival plan seizes his opportunity. The ambitious and unscrupulous Bob Morton (played by Miguel Ferrer) manages to push through his RoboCop project. Only one vital component is missing: the corpse of a well-built man. By some whim of fate, their wish is fulfilled at that very moment. In another part of the city, Officer Murphy and his new partner Ann Lewis (Nancy Allen) try to arrest Clarence Boddicker's gang. A shoot-out follows. Officer Murphy is no more; RoboCop can be born. This takes place quietly, because the rest of the police force has gone on strike in protest against the dangerous working conditions. If they had known that their battered bodies would be remodelled into invulnerable machines, they would never go back on to the streets.

'What the story particularly needed was clarity,' Paul Verhoeven remembers. He had initially suggested several drastic amendments to the script. For instance, to provide romantic interest, Officer Murphy was to have an extra-marital relationship with Ann Lewis. Moreover, the tone of the story was to be made considerably more realistic. But that was precisely what Ed Neumeier wanted to avoid at all costs. 'Michael and I got to do

187

the second draft with the full support of Jon Davison – the second draft is more or less the movie. We were all very excited about it, but then we had a whole period where the project kept falling apart. The people who wanted to do it and who were kinda good always had other commitments, and then some awful people wanted to do it, and Orion would go with them – but looking back, I can only say, "Thank God that didn't happen." They were people who didn't have any finesse, they tended not to see RoboCop as funny, they tended to see it as . . . really serious. Which isn't comic-book-like at all. I mean, it is a film about the guy in a suit walking around – it is silly. So it should be a funny movie.'

Yet both writers were prepared, albeit hesitantly, to carry out Verhoeven's wishes. After all, it had seemed for a long time that RoboCop might never come to life at all. Now, Jon Davison had made a clear agreement with Verhoeven – 'a pretty big deal' in his words. It was significant that Davison had commanded, 'Whatever Paul wants, we'll do it.' So they deleted and rewrote. They had two months in which to do it. An additional problem was that Miner fell seriously ill. Meanwhile, Ed Neumeier allowed Verhoeven to sample the atmosphere by handing him a pile of American comic strips. 'He obviously fell in love with them. I almost got through the next draft, but I felt that it wasn't working very well. After he read the script Paul did an amazing thing. He just said, "This is terrible! We go back to the old one . . ." And that was that. In my experience of the film business I had never seen anybody do that. To be able to look at something and just sort of go, "Oh, I don't like this" – and also, not to blame somebody else for it. I do believe that the comic books definitely had something to do with the way he suddenly started looking at this project.'

Finally, after some polishing, Verhoeven decided it was now possible to shoot the original script. *RoboCop* had to become first and foremost a real American film. Moreover, once he had overcome his intellectual distrust of the story, Verhoeven realized it gave him a chance to return to the world of which he had such fond memories, the comic strips of his childhood. In *RoboCop* he suddenly recognized the image from *Tom Poes in het land van de blikken mannen* (*Tom Poes in the land of the tin men*), where his childhood hero disguises himself with metal limbs and a helmet, and looks half-creature, half-machine.

The subtle satire so typical of the better comic strips was partly put over in the Media Breaks, when two newsreaders report in a light-hearted tone on riots in Acapulco, the progress of the Star Wars Project or, in CNN style, the arrival of RoboCop. 'Give us three minutes – we'll give you the world!' the news flashes say, alternating with commercials for artificial hearts and Nuke 'Em, a vicious family board game. Despite the excessive and detailed violence Verhoeven portrayed, *RoboCop* never lost its comic-strip tone. The audience is always aware that this is a story to be taken tongue-in-cheek – a feeling reinforced by the sometimes blatantly cheap production methods. Just as comic strips should always be printed on cheap paper, this small budget suited the film perfectly. When *RoboCop* was released in 1585 American theatres in the second week of July 1987, the reviews were decidedly positive.

To be convinced, the reviewers did not need to go to the grand *Robo-Cop* party held at the 9:30 Club in Washington on the occasion of the première. The *Washington Post*, which reported the film on its front page, had as its headline HARDWARE WITH A HEART – PAUL VERHOEVEN'S RIVETING ROBOCOP. And *Newsweek* said, 'The triumph of Verhoeven's slick, lively movie is that it never loses its soul to its hardware. It's got a fresh, B-movie spirit; even as it slams you against the wall, it's tickling your ribs.' The *New York Times* concluded that the Dutch director 'doesn't let the furiously futuristic plot get in the way of the flaming explosions, shattering glass and hurtling bodies. If you glance away, chances are you'll miss somebody blown away.' But even if the critics reviewed the film light-heartedly, it had not been so easy for Verhoeven to shoot *RoboCop*.

In November 1985, while awaiting the arrival of his family, Verhoeven took a flat in West Los Angeles, on 1171 Granville Avenue. When not occupied with the *RoboCop* project or with going to the cinema himself, he killed time by watching television. Fascinated by the overwhelming amount of choice available, he realized he had ended up in a country where world news seemed made on a conveyor belt – and broadcast live too. If there wasn't a summit between Reagan and Gorbachev, there was probably another space-shuttle explosion. Television seemed to be the shortest route to getting to know the emotions of the Americans – and how they flaunted them on the screen!

The culture shock Verhoeven experienced is perhaps best explained by talking about its reverse. In 1992 Paul Schrader, the American film-maker of Dutch descent – scriptwriter of *Taxi Driver*, *Raging Bull* and *The Last Temptation of Christ* (Martin Scorsese, 1976, 1980, 1988), writer and director of *American Gigolo* (1980), *Cat People* (1982), *Mishima* (1985) and *Light Sleeper* (1992) – gave a lecture in Utrecht as part of the Dutch Film Days Festival. He kept a diary of his experiences for the evening newspaper *NRC/Handelsblad*. It was a journey of discovery on the head of a pin: 'Lost my way after [the village of] Giethoorn. Fortunately, getting lost in the Netherlands is like getting lost in Manhattan – it is awkward but it is never for very long. I keep having the feeling that the Netherlands is a sparklingly clean toy country which has been put together by very good little children. Somebody said

189

that I should go and look at a miniature model of the Netherlands, but why should I? I'm right in the middle of it now.'

By contrast, Los Angeles seemed to Verhoeven to be a collection of extremes, a truly metropolitan inferno. A drive through the different conurbations that make up the city showed the greatest imaginable contrasts, from the inexhaustible wealth of Beverly Hills, through the studentish, laid-back atmosphere of Venice, to the deep poverty of the inner city, where gang violence had been elevated into a life-style. The city seemed to be the ultimate Now society, full of enterprise and consumer appetite; this is what gave Los Angeles its special dynamism – certainly compared with the Netherlands. Its inhabitants lived their lives as if they might be struck down by the Seven Plagues at any moment.

For Verhoeven everything was upbeat in LA. Loud music in fast cars. Big buildings and short stories – a meeting with a studio executive at the offices of a film company would take an average of twenty minutes. Everyone in Los Angeles seemed to have another appointment. And a hidden agenda; there were numerous taxi drivers who, without being asked, would point to a recently completed script in their inside pocket and there were waitresses on the terraces of Sunset Boulevard who, without being asked, would tell you that they had come to the city to make it as an actress – without knowing who they were talking to. Hollywood was a hype society – Hollyweird, as its inhabitants sometimes called it.

Meanwhile, the situation regarding Verhoeven's own film was that RoboCop was to be played by Peter Weller, an actor who had acquired cult status with his role in *The Adventures of Buckaroo Banzai across the 8th Dimension* (W. D. Richter, 1984), described by the critics as 'off-the-wall pulp fiction'. Weller was a tough guy and a Method actor as well. His co-star was to be Nancy Allen, known from her work with ex-husband Brian de Palma in, among other films, *Carrie* (1976), *Dressed to Kill* (1980) and *Blow Out* (1981).

For the design of the RoboCop suit, producer Jon Davison first thought of Rick Baker, the most famous special effects make-up artist in Hollywood. He was fully booked, however, and so the job went to Rob Bottin, a former pupil of Rick Baker, who had made his name with his work on *The Howling* (Joe Dante, 1981), *The Thing* (John Carpenter, 1982) and *Legend* (Ridley Scott, 1985). Jon Davison knew him from an earlier collaboration on *Twilight Zone: The Movie* and was very enthusiastic about the results of Bottin's perfectionism, although the producer also knew that meeting deadlines was usually a difficult task for the designer.

Rob Bottin appeared to be an archetypal sci-fi freak, nearly six and a half feet tall and the kind of boy who at the age of five walked around with a cardboard box on his head pretending he was Frankenstein. Never having let go of his admiration for the better-class B-movie, he was in a state of utter euphoria when, at the age of twenty-five, he was commissioned to design the Robo suit. His brief was clear; the audience must not immediately burst out laughing when Peter Weller makes his entrance as the robot. Verhoeven had decided that it had to be in the spirit of the female robot from *Metropolis* (Fritz Lang, 1927).

To Rob Bottin, the first meeting with the director was memorable in every respect. At the request of Davison, he had brought the provisional sketches for the robot to the office. Verhoeven was content, except about that part of the suit which made it look as if RoboCop was wearing a bow-tie.

'So I said to Paul that I would take the drawings back to the studio and draw up various solutions to the problem area. Because of his storyboards I knew that Paul could draw quite well himself, and I gave him a very nice sketchbook with transparent paper. This way he could sketch some of his own ideas for the robot on top of my designs as soon as something new came to him. Paul's reaction was different from what I had expected. First he stared at me for a moment, then he grabbed a pile of photocopying paper and shouted, "Paper? Paper! I've got more than enough paper!" – throwing the sheets around the office. So I left.'

Paul Verhoeven also remembers that first meeting, albeit in a completely different way. 'It was not at all a friendly gesture from Rob Bottin, but an undisguised power game,' he said. 'By making that suggestion in the presence of the producer and the writer, he was saying: "You prick, if you know it so well, you can do it yourself." It was a classic case from the Hollywood style book and nothing else.'

It would certainly not be the last time that Bottin and Verhoeven would come to a confrontation during the preparations for *RoboCop*. 'Rob and I argued a lot about the costume,' Verhoeven confirms. 'At one point it was so bad that he did not want to talk to me any more. In the first instance his design was 90 per cent perfect, but I wanted it 100 per cent – and then it went off in completely the wrong direction. We dragged all sorts of robots from Japanese comic books into it and so the original idea was nearly strangled.'

Meanwhile, Rob Bottin and his team in the studio had created both a miniature RoboCop and a life-sized copy in clay. Verhoeven regularly came to check the progress. 'He always seemed to be concerned for the public not to see RoboCop as a person charged with sexuality. He wanted to be sure that you couldn't see his private parts. One day Paul came round again and immediately burst out: "This is wrong and that's no good. Will you never get it right?"'

Bottin, irritated, asked whether he knew how to do it any better. I sure do, Verhoeven replied, and jumped on to the stage with a spatula in his hand. Amazed, the designer wondered, 'What the hell was wrong with this guy? When I got over my first amazement, I went after him. We literally came face to face. I could feel his breath. "It's crap!" he shouted in my face. It was the first time that I was convinced I would have a fist fight with a director.'

Paul Verhoeven: 'Rob Bottin gave me the spatula and asked me to make the changes which I considered necessary. He probably thought that I would be scared of that, but I simply started to cut into his clay model, taking pieces off it. Apparently it was the only language he understood at that moment.'

In their urge for perfectionism they at least agreed about one thing: the suit for RoboCop would be the key to the film's success. The costume could make or break the machine man. 'That's why,' Ed Neumeier remembers, 'we went to Rob's studio so often. We were *all* a bit concerned about it. On that one afternoon it did all get terribly out of hand. Eventually, in addition to Paul, the two producers and myself also climbed on to the stage. We were standing there wielding our knives and cutting into the clay model. It looked more like gang rape. Afterwards, I did think that we went too far. Paul as the director had the right to stick his nose in, but actually we didn't know what we were talking about.'

Finally, Verhoeven and Bottin decided to go back to the original design with a high-tech element added here and there. RoboCop had been given his definitive form. 'A lot of the arguments,' Ed Neumeier concludes, 'had to do with Paul saying in his driven way: "Hey, get out of my way, this is my film!" while Rob was used to being addressed as a boy wonder and had never met anyone who had not given him free rein. But anyway, in an unorthodox way they managed to work out something quite good in the end.'

However, due to the delay, another problem was looming on the horizon. By now it was June 1986, time to travel to Dallas, Texas. Because the suit was still not finished, Verhoeven devoted his shooting time to the scenes without the robot. When the costume finally arrived two weeks later, leading actor Peter Weller was more shocked than relieved. He had practised at home in New York with an American football outfit. In this he had been assisted by Moni Yakim, Professor of Movement at the New York Juilliard School, but neither of them had counted on the suit being so heavy. While Rob Bottin pulled the actor into the suit at four in the morning, he sensed that Weller's uncertainty was turning into irritation: 'He just sat there, muttering: "This ain't cool, man. This ain't cool at all!"' The feet were too big and the arms were too bulky. Weller felt ridiculous and clearly showed it. 'So I said, "Take it easy. It's not an Armani made-to-measure suit. You're walking inside a steel construction."'

It did not help.

After twelve hours of lugging, fitting and measuring, Peter Weller would not come out of his trailer. Verhoeven was asked to go and see him, he went immediately, in a thunderous rage. He was ready to murder someone when his eye fell on the robot, and his anger instantly evaporated. With a huge grin and cries of delight, he walked around the machine man, looked at him from different camera angles and spontaneously gave the designer a kiss. 'This is great!' Verhoeven rejoiced. 'Come on! We're going to start shooting!'

This blissful moment lasted exactly thirty seconds. 'Well, I *hate* it,' the man in the suit itself snarled. Disbelief. Confusion. Was Peter making a joke? The actor explained that he had planned to move very loosely, but now he felt like a monolith. 'I look like a goddamn robot – I look like Gort in *The Day the Earth Stood Still* and, goddammit, I don't want to look like Gort. I'm not going to make a fool of myself.' The director explained that it was not his intention to have a 'floating ballerina' in his film. The idea was for RoboCop to move in an angular way: 'Trust me, it's going to be terrific!' And Verhoeven began to talk enthusiastically about how he planned to let Weller overact; it could rival *Ivan the Terrible*, the Eisenstein classic, which he had carefully studied beforehand.

But Peter Weller did not answer. Nor did he move. As a Method actor he was able to play a character only if he believed in it unconditionally. Shaking his head, the director walked away again. 'I didn't understand Peter's attitude at all at the time, but it was, of course, total stress. He had not had a single minute to walk around in the costume, to look in the mirror, to make a video of it. It was not his fault that the suit arrived too late.'

Equally under stress and in fear of losing even more shooting days, Jon Davison decided to make an issue of it. With the support of Orion chief Mike Medavoy he decided to make a typical Hollywood-style gesture. Peter Weller was fired – instantly. For insurance reasons, Bottin and Neumeier recall, the fatal dispute between Verhoeven and Weller was secretly recorded on video by the second producer, Arnie Schmidt. If it came to it, they would be able to produce the tape as a last resort, but in the meantime they faced a tricky deadlock.

'Peter', Ed Neumeier explained, 'was the only one who fitted the $600,000 suit. The idea that we would let someone else walk around in it was a total fantasy. That dismissal was pure bluff. I do not think that anyone, including Jon, seriously intended to throw Peter out, but we all pretended we would. As soon as the news broke, everyone in Hollywood frantically started looking for a replacement actor, but what they were really looking for was someone with the right shoe size.'

Because they had to resume shooting the next day, a stuntman was called in to play the robot. Peter Weller saw this and began to have serious worries. Neumeier: 'Although we were all grown men, of course, the scene was more like a quarrel in a nursery class. And we had taken Peter's nicest toy away.' There followed a string of telephone calls between the actor, agent, lawyers, studio and producers, after which the provoked actor promised to mend his ways: 'Sorry, Paul. I'll be cool.' The director was not yet convinced, but accepted the apologies.

Peter Weller: 'The problem was that there were four heavyweights on the set. Nobody was anybody's friend there. To start with, I don't let anyone walk over me. And Paul, he is so driven. Then you have the dom-ineering Rob Bottin, as well as that self-willed little kid, the writer, Ed Neumeier. So when the suit was not ready, everyone panicked. There was a really shitty atmosphere – everyone was cursing everyone else. Eventually we realized that this was too crazy for words, that we had either to call off the whole film or work on it together. I assured Paul that I would do my best, but it took a while before I had convinced him. The battle was on Thursday. On Friday night everyone was talking again. On Saturday and Sunday we were testing the suit. And on Monday we were ready to start shooting.'

Paul Verhoeven had understood that there was some ground for Weller's complaint about the suit. At the advice of Verhoeven's wife, Martine, who was staying on location for a few days, Moni Yakim, the Professor of Movement, was flown over to Dallas. Weller was given the weekend to practise his movements.

Peter Weller: 'Moni said, "Listen, we'll slow everything down. We'll let the weight of the suit work for us." That turned out to be a brilliant idea, because this made RoboCop much more pathetic. Because I started to walk on the ball of my foot, instead of on the heel, his step changed. He was no longer a streamlined, ultra-hip man of steel, but a somewhat unsure, more human character. And so Paul sculpted his film around this sad metal creature.'

'Sad creature' is a description Verhoeven rather likes. He has grown to love *RoboCop* and now calls it his best American film. 'We shot the last part of the story in Pittsburgh, Pennsylvania, on the site of a derelict steelworks. As you can see at the end of the film, this is where the big shoot-out between RoboCop and the villain Clarence Boddicker takes place. I would drive to the set early in the morning when it was still cold and misty, and I could hear Peter Weller as I arrived. Clad in his Robo-Cop suit and completely made-up, he would be playing his trumpet, sitting there half-hidden in a corner. Lyrical, heavenly notes played by the sad robot resounded between the twisted steel. I often watched in silence.'

What is so sad about the robot is that he tries to accept his new exis-tence, but cannot forget the old one – although it is practically wiped out, both mentally and physically. 'This struggle is expressed most clearly at the end of the film. RoboCop has finished his job with a last shoot-out. "Nice shooting, son!" says the chief. "What's your name?" After a short silence, RoboCop replies, "Murphy!" The first time I saw the film I was part of an audience in a rather heavy district of New York. That was very interesting, because the people were so engrossed in the film; before RoboCop had time to react to "What's your name, son?", the whole audience was already shouting "MURRRR-PPPHHHYYYY". I found that very moving. They too felt that the circle had finally been completed.'

Verhoeven is willing to go one step further. 'It's pure resurrection. For me, *RoboCop* is a Christian fairytale. First, Murphy is gunned down in the most horrific way: that is the Crucifixion. And it has to be so violent, because the audience has to remember him. Before that, he has not done anything in the film. He comes to the police station to put on his uniform, then he goes after the villains with his partner, and bang! he is dead. That shooting is the only thing we know about him – I did that deliberately. Next, the film makes a steep descent into the finite, after which he experiences his Resurrection, in a modern way.

'In the scene at the old steelworks, at the climax of the fight between Clarence and RoboCop, you see those almost Trojan walls. There is also a gigantic puddle. If you look closely, you will see that RoboCop does not go through it but over it. I did not want to do it too obviously – otherwise it would look silly – but I had a grid put under the water so that he would not sink but rather glide across the water, as it were. RoboCop is a Jesus figure – an American Jesus. Entirely in tune with current ideas here, he says, "I don't arrest you any more." He has done with Clarence, the time of turning the other cheek is over. Americans want to be humane, but if they think it takes too long, Christian morality is pushed aside for the moment and they go for their weapons – just like RoboCop.'

So the machine man led Verhoeven to familiar territory: Christian symbolism and a fascination with the figure of Jesus. From *Turks Fruit* to *Flesh + Blood* the director had been playing with religious iconography: for example, the presence of the Virgin Mary in *De Vierde Man* and Rutger Hauer's halo in *Flesh + Blood*. For the perceptive viewer, those references were more than just visual puns. They bore witness to Verhoeven's predilection for mysticism: an obsession which since his arrival in the United States had found an outlet not only in *RoboCop*, but in the meetings of the Jesus Seminar.

Since 1985 a group of seventy-seven progressive theologians had been meeting at six-monthly intervals with the aim of reconstructing the life of Jesus in a purely scientific way. Verhoeven read about the seminar in a newspaper and immediately decided to be a member of the audience. He took a seat in the back row of the auditorium at Salem, Washington state, to listen to the discussions led by Professor Robert W. Funk. Verhoeven had his own Bible to hand; it was a Bible in Ancient Greek, the language in which the New Testament was first recorded, the language Verhoeven had learnt at secondary school.

Professor Funk explained to his audience the aim of the seminar. 'It isn't about Jesus-bashing – we want to liberate Jesus. The only Jesus most people know is the mythic one. They don't want the real Jesus, they want the one they can worship, the cult Jesus.' After eight years of study, the results of the research were published under the title *The Five Gospels* at the end of 1993. It also included the Gospel of Thomas, only discovered this century. This edition of the New Testament by Robert W. Funk, Roy W. Hoover and the Jesus Seminar gives a portrait of a Jesus nobody has ever met at Sunday school. According to the theologians, only 18 per cent of Jesus's pronouncements in the New Testament can actually be attributed to the historical figure. Verhoeven: 'We have, for example, analysed the entire prayer "Our Father", and of this we can attribute to him only the words "Our Father".'

The historical Jesus is characterized by the Jesus Seminar as a rebel who strove for a peaceful liberation of Israel. He wandered through the country and preached that the long-awaited Kingdom of God already existed on earth. He cured the sick by faith healing, positioned himself on the fringes of society by spending time with those rejected by society, expressed his criticisms of Jewish religious laws, unjust taxation and the subservient role of women. He was a charismatic speaker, and after causing a riot in Jerusalem, he was tried by the Jewish authorities and crucified by the Roman occupiers some time between AD 30 and 33.

After his death, Christians building their new faith overpainted the historical Jesus with a mythical Jesus, the son of God. In doing so, the testimonies of Matthew, Mark, Luke and John were distorted more and more by the processes of oral history.

The seminar's view was that Jesus was no more than a simple Jewish farmer – probably not the first-born in his family, and quite possibly illiterate. He was not of divine descent, nor is there any historical evidence for his Resurrection. After Jesus was taken from the Cross, he was buried in a shallow grave, and his body may have been eaten by stray dogs.

These conclusions were arrived at after a line-by-line assessment of the authenticity of New Testament texts during the study meetings. After the discussion, there was always voting by acclamation, carried out by colour coding. For each question, the scholars at the seminar were allowed to choose from four different-coloured pebbles. Red meant 'he undoubtedly said it, or something very like it'; pink meant 'probably authentic'; grey meant 'well, maybe'; and black 'definitely not true'. The pebbles were thrown into a tray; most votes were valid.

The director, who had managed to amaze the gathering with his extensive knowledge of the Bible ('I get along quite well'), had by now been allowed to cast his vote as the only lay person. He was the odd man in, and he still is – the seminar is now researching the doings of Jesus. Verhoeven regularly writes papers, and has set up a working group entitled the Jesus Cinema Seminar.

All this relates to the film about the real life of Jesus he wants to make. Provisional release date is Christmas 2000. By then, Verhoeven will have worked on the project for fifteen years. At every six-monthly meeting, the working group talks about the film for two hours on the basis of an agenda formulated by Verhoeven. 'Some people are doing research into the dress of the period. Or into how you should visualize a healing. What did exorcism in the Jewish tradition look like? What is the role of Lazarus or Judas? How should you place the rebels historically? What exactly was Jesus's relationship with John the Baptist? I usually bring a paper with me in which I recreate part of the Bible story. Then I say, "This is how I think these events took place. What do you think?" We then discuss the matter. Ideas, thoughts, chronologies – but always set in psychologically dramatic narrative structures.'

The reason behind his planned film, says Verhoeven, is twofold. First of all, there is his dissatisfaction with earlier attempts to describe the life of Jesus on film. 'They usually just stick some elements together. For me, even Scorsese's *The Last Temptation of Christ* was disappointing. It was a fairytale. A serious film about the life of Jesus has never been made, directors have never really gone into the subject matter. The political and economic situation, for example, is usually left out. The most historically correct image of Jesus and his time is to be found in *The Life of Brian*, the comedy by the Monty Python team.'

According to Jewish law, rabbis and other spiritual leaders were not allowed to earn money from their religious teachings, so Jesus earned his living as a carpenter – this is Verhoeven's conclusion. He not only made chairs and tables, but probably fortifications and city walls. His activities covered a wide area. 'Nazareth was only an hour's walk from Sepphoris, a city very influenced by Hellenism. Jesus spoke Aramaic, but he probably also knew Greek. So it is also quite possible that Jesus had a knowledge of Greek philosophy, which in turn must have had a great influence on his thinking.'

His second reason for participating in the research and planning the Jesus film was recorded by the *Vancouver Sun* on Saturday 2 November 1991, when a meeting of the Jesus Seminar took place in Edmonton. Under the heading 'The Modern Doubting Thomas', Verhoeven was interviewed about his fascination with the theme. The newspaper stated: 'Verhoeven thinks Christ has become a Jungian archetype, a mythic symbol of the collective human unconscious, for those who hope to survive death. Because Verhoeven fears death, he'd like to believe the same. "I just don't want to cheat," he says, "I don't want to believe something if it's not true."' The fact that the findings of the Jesus Seminar on which the intended film will be based do not tally with current opinion is evident from an article published in the *Los Angeles Times* on 24 February 1994. It cites a recent national survey of adults by the Barna Research Centre in Pasadena, which found that of those questioned 90 per cent believe Jesus did live on earth; 80 per cent believe he was a human like the rest of us; 40 per cent believe he made mistakes; 80 per cent believe he rose from the dead and 36 per cent believe they'll meet Jesus in heaven. The members of the Jesus Seminar agree that Jesus lived on earth and was a human being, however 80 per cent of them are convinced that he made mistakes, while only 10 per cent believe that he rose from the grave, according to Verhoeven.

At a time when fundamentalist Christianity was spreading rapidly in the United States, it was hardly surprising that the first papers of the Jesus Seminar were burnt in public by members of the New Hope Baptist Church near Hobart in 1991. With the demonstrations against Scorsese's *The Last Temptation of Christ* still fresh in his memory, Verhoeven knows that his planned film will stir up many emotions. 'Blasphemy is a term resorted to very quickly in the United States, because the figure of Jesus is claimed by so many different groups – and they go hard at it. Nothing new, of course, because throughout the centuries a lot of death and destruction has been caused in the name of Jesus. As a symbol of a merciful nature, Christians have chosen a figure on a cross – which after all is the most refined torture there is. And that hangs above everybody's sideboard as a symbol of our spiritual frame of mind. No wonder something has gone wrong with Western civilization ever since. It's a history of crusades, inquisitions, Hitler and the Holocaust.'

In view of the nature of his project, with the working title *Christ the Man,* it could well be his last film in the United States, a possibility Verhoeven takes seriously. But this knowledge will not prevent him from filming it.

Meanwhile, Verhoeven had his hands full with his first American film. Thirteen weeks' shooting time had been planned for *RoboCop*; eventually, it became fourteen, an acceptable overrun in view of all the problems. It was awkward, however, when it turned out that RoboCop was not able to walk up and down stairs. In the scene in which the machine man has to settle a hostage case in the town hall, he is expected to walk up the steps with authority.

Verhoeven explains: 'For an upward step, we filmed the first movement from behind; the downward movement of his foot we filmed from above. We omitted the actual movement in the middle.'

Moreover, RoboCop did not fit into his car. The shots behind the wheel are all medium-shots, as Weller was wearing only the top part of his suit. To reinforce this impression they also filmed RoboCop stepping out of the car, but then the viewer only saw his steel feet. After the earlier problems surrounding the costume, the director also had to get used to Peter Weller's Method acting. Verhoeven regarded an actor as someone who, at his command, would walk from A to B – and who, when he snapped his fingers, would promptly turn back. Method actors were different. When Verhoeven said: 'OK, Peter, now walk into the room,' the leading actor did not move an inch. So someone whispered in his ear, 'Peter is a Method actor. You have to call him Robo.' Only when Verhoeven did this did Robo begin to move.

For their part, the actors also had to get used to Verhoeven, and especially to his philosophy of real-time acting – the secret of the dynamism of his films. Bottin explains: 'First Paul reads a scene from the script and what he consequently puts on film never lasts longer on the screen than the time it takes him to read the scene in "paper form". In other words, Paul uses only real time, he does not draw anything out – something which actors usually love to do. Some actors will say, "Yes, but *how* should I be coming through that door?" Or "*What* are my thoughts in the meantime? Shouldn't I be moving very slowly now, because in the story I am unhappy?" "No," Paul would answer. "Read the script. Don't worry about the way in which you pull your pistol. Just pull your pistol. That's what it says." He then shoots the action, and goes on to the next scene.'

So it is not the actor, but the cameras which do most of the work in Verhoeven's films. This was evident to the film crew when they saw the rushes: even without editing, the images already had a dramatic impact. 'Everything is constantly on the move in this film,' the *New York Times* wrote about *RoboCop*, an apt observation. The camera walks through the corridors of the police station following someone, and then in one movement swerves along to follow the person coming from the opposite direction – the image never stands still.

Editor Frank Urioste, who previously worked with Robert Aldrich and Vincente Minnelli, edited Verhoeven's first three American films and received Oscar nominations for editing *RoboCop* and *Basic Instinct*. 'While most directors after editing a scene say, "It's too short", you can always hear Paul worriedly saying, "Too long. Still far too long!"' In order not to lose pace even the dialogue in *RoboCop* was shot with the steadycam, says Urioste. 'If the background image in a scene stays the same, it gives the viewer a feeling of delay, a sort of resting point in the film. Paul wanted to avoid that with *RoboCop*. By letting the steadycam consistently wander through the corridors, the audience never gets time to get its breath back. The camera technique and the hard editing give *RoboCop* its blistering tempo.'

Verhoeven had picked up these fast action sequences from James Cameron's *The Terminator*; the industrial atmosphere of *RoboCop*, with the hard, fluorescent neon light, was something he remembered from the post-modernist French thriller *Subway* (1985) by Luc Besson. Besides giving the film a harsh futuristic setting, this way of using lights would grant Robo maximum freedom of movement. Cameraman Jost Vacano saw possibilities for the idea, but designer Rob Bottin did not. Trained as he was in the old Hollywood school, where a continuous shadow was standard for science fiction, he feared that the viewer would immediately spot the weaknesses in the costume – it would spoil the fun.

Long discussions followed. Vacano argued that it was not semi-darkness, but a great deal of extra light that would give RoboCop his mythical proportions – the suit would work as a mirror, the environment would be reflected in it. Hesitantly, Bottin agreed with the advice of the director and the director of photography. 'And yet', Verhoeven remembers, 'during the entire film he kept hammering on about his fear that the lighting would be wrong. But I really trusted Jost, because I had worked with him on *Soldaat* and *Spetters*. Jost knows exactly what he is doing, but I believe that Rob really started to hate him on the set. And me, of course.'

Their difference of opinion came to a head during the shooting of the third act of the film. RoboCop takes off his helmet; he is no longer a machine but Murphy again. With his head full of wires and contact points he turns to the camera. The viewer sees how the electrodes have become flesh. Because Murphy's third-act face was a prosthesis of rubber, Bottin pushed even more for shadow.

'Paul decided to make a test shot,' he recalls, 'which was shown in a viewing room. Because our relationship was not very good anyway at that time, it did not surprise me to hear Paul squawking from the back row: "Well ... Rob? What do you think of it? I think it looks very good." As if he wanted to say, "For God's sake, let's stop going on about it." But the point was that I still thought the mask looked too pale. So very I carefully said, "Paul ... all I am going to do now is tell you what I see, and I sincerely believe that there is some room for improvement." He then burst out: "Improvement? Improvement! THIS LOOKS FINE TO ME! I think you want to make it into one of your space monsters, Rob, but this is a police cop!"'

His pride hurt, Bottin left the viewing room, considering handing in his resignation. In the lobby he waited for transport. A moment later the door swung open behind him. He heard threatening footsteps in the corridor. It was Verhoeven and he was angry. 'Paul came up to me like a hurricane. He was trembling with rage and said: "Why are you so ridiculously pig-headed?" I answered that I was just as obsessed with the film as he was, but that it bothered me that I wasn't able to discuss it. He then growled dangerously, kicked against a glass table and walked out. "Take it easy, Paul," I called after him. "Don't you tell me when to calm down!" he shouted back, after which he left with Ed Neumeier in the car. Meanwhile, Jon Davison had come up behind me in the corridor. "What's the matter with Paul?" I asked. Jon answered: "Well, maybe he is a bit hot-headed, but he's a terrific director, don't you think?"'

The next day the scene was shot after all, without any further discussion or comment. The rubber face was made up a little more, the always calm Jost Vacano had found a suitable colour filter. At night the dailies were shown. 'The scene looked fantastic. It caught my breath,' said Rob Bottin. Verhoeven agreed with him, but these discussions had taken them to breaking point.

The realization that in Verhoeven they had a very different captain was something which the crew became aware of more and more during the shooting. Ed Neumeier remembers how some of the Americans on the set were making sour jokes about it in the beginning, along the lines of, 'We'll show these Europeans how to make a movie' – or how, behind the director's back, they doubted *RoboCop*'s significance in film history. And yet during the fourteen weeks in which the shooting took place, practically everyone succumbed to Verhoeven's overwhelming energy. The film contains a shot of not more than three seconds, which was put in by editor Frank Urioste as a joke, and which speaks volumes about Verhoeven's passion. In this shot RoboCop goes to a disco to look for Clarence Boddicker's stooges. Among the people dancing we see the director for one brief moment. He is dancing ecstatically, with his head almost in camera, to the loud techno-pop. It shows that, as far as he was concerned, there was no need for reservations about the standard of *RoboCop*.

Peter Weller acknowledges Verhoeven's energy. 'I wouldn't want him for my wife but, man, his desire to get this thing beyond perfect turns me on. It's in your face movie-making. You don't feel like it's just a movie you are shooting, you feel that this guy has this vision and it's gonna happen, or else he is gonna die. People on the set would say he is nuts. But then I got it. He is not nuts, he just starts in fifth gear.'

Paul has an operatic sense about him, Weller diagnoses. 'During *Robo-Cop* I had some time off, and a friend of mine wanted to go to the set. The shooting was about the bad guys, who are testing the Big Gun – they are blowing the shit out of the street, right? I drive up, and for the first time I see Paul happy! He is talking to all the camera guys and he shouts, "Way to go!" – but the rest of the set is like glass, everywhere, as far as the eye could see. So I talk to one of the guys. He says, "Paul set up four cameras and then the explosion was so overwhelming, so huge, that a fireball literally ran down the street." You can see that in the movie, where one of the actors is ducking out of this shot. Actually, one of the cameras burnt down. Then Paul walks up to me: "Oh, you've missed it! We had this big boom, and it was fantastic." He was ecstatic. Since Paul didn't have a lot of experience with special effects, he was kind of at the experts' mercy. For a long, long time he didn't get what he wanted, but this time they finally gave him the Armageddon that he envisioned.'

There is another spectacular scene in *RoboCop* which stands out from all the other violent events – the scene at the petrol station. The script reads:

204: EXTERIOR SELF-SERVICE SHELL GAS STATION – NIGHT
A lonely place in the middle of the night near a freeway overpass lit by a huge electric sign spells out 'Shell'.
Someone riding a battered grey motorcycle roars into the station.

205: ATTENDANT BOOTH
The ATTENDANT, glasses and pimples, concentrates hard on his analytic geometry textbook. He looks up when hears a tap-tap-tap on the booth's glass window.

206: WHAT HE SEES
Emil, Clarence's wheel man, stands there, leering, using the barrel of his MAC-10 to get the attendant's attention.
Emil: 'Gimme all your money, bookworm, or I'll blow your brains out.'

The person in the booth who finds himself in this awkward situation is a personification of the young director himself – the Paul Verhoeven from Leiden, a mathematics student with glasses. When RoboCop receives a message about the robbery and comes to the rescue, things quickly get out of hand: the garage attendant realizes just in time that the whole lot is about to explode, grabs his textbook in terror and runs out as fast as he can. It looks like a quotation from the work of Kurt Vonnegut: the director fleeing his own nightmare.

This dimension was not noticed by everyone. *Time* was apparently blinded by the fierce light of the explosions when on 17 July 1987 the magazine wrote about *RoboCop*: 'No wonder this film was almost X-rated for violence: it is crazy in love with the imagination of disaster. *RoboCop*'s pleasures are cold comfort. The laughter it provokes catches in the throat like a nettle from the bottom of a popcorn box.' The review did not touch on the fact that the robot has subtle human traits that can move the viewer. Plagued by flashes of memory, and the fact that his partner has said, 'Murphy, it's you!' RoboCop trembles in his chair half-way through the film. He breaks loose to find his past. When he plugs into the computer, it says under his own name 'Deceased', together with a photograph and an address.

Verhoeven: 'Then his house turns out to be up for sale – to make it more dramatic, of course. I toyed with the idea of having his family still living there, and his young son walking out of the house, but not recognizing RoboCop as his father. The only one who does recognize him is the dog, just like the story of Odysseus. The dog has been waiting for his boss, and once Odysseus has returned the animal dies instantly. That is a very good detail in Homer. Very clever. I remember Mike Medavoy asking me for a long time, "Did you include that dog?" because he thought it was fantastic too. In the end he was very disappointed that I left the dog out. I thought it was perhaps a bit too pathetic, too European.' But it would have sounded a personal note, because when he is back in the Netherlands, Verhoeven always has this irresistible urge to return to his old haunts, to revisit the reality of his youth – which of course no longer exists.

'It is a feeling that goes deeper than the playground of your childhood. It is a longing for resurrection – the wish for it to be the way Christianity makes it out to be, that the dead will rise again – and the rational anger that of course it isn't true – even if someone with my mathematics background can speculate that, according to Einstein's laws, travelling through time might one day be possible. Not now, of course. I am not psychically gifted or anything, but when I place my hands upon the houses of my youth, the images from the past come floating to the surface with great clarity. This is why the moment when RoboCop returns to his past has an enormous emotional impact on me. I had no problems whatsoever in filming that scene, awkward though it may have been. It was very close to me.'

RoboCop became the hit of summer 1987, both in the USA and the rest of the world. Immediately after release, the film jumped to number one in *Variety*'s Movie Top Ten. In the first weekend the profits reached $8 million, after seventeen days this had risen to $26 million, and after a year's circulation the total was $55 million (which in the following twelve months was to be doubled on the international circuit). In addition to good reviews and profits that were satisfactory in every respect, this success was reflected in the merchandizing. There were RoboCop dolls, video games, T-shirts, pinball machines and a cartoon series. In the eyes of the public, RoboCop entered the major league of American pop culture. RoboCop became an icon. Everyone knows what he stands for:

justice. RoboCop is the avenging angel in a hostile universe. He cannot be corrupted, and is more or less the only one in our time who takes his prime directives seriously: 1. Serve the Public, 2. Protect the Innocent, 3. Uphold the Law.

Ed Neumeier believes that *RoboCop* was made at exactly the right time: 'The film just happened to come along at a time when crime was becoming a big problem in America. People were, and still are, very frightened. I didn't realize that when I was writing this character; I thought I was making a satire about Reagan's America. But the audience locked on to it because RoboCop was a guy who was going to shoot down criminals in the street. FINALLY. Even my old Catholic aunt loved it.'

The film critic Rita Kempley pointed out in the *Washington Post*, in a reference to 'Irangate' and the Wall Street insider trading affair, that at a time when American heroes of flesh and blood were rather disappointing, people of flesh and steel were rising up to show us the right path. 'This world needs RoboCops!'

In his native country, Verhoeven got reviews such as he had never had before – it was as if the Prodigal Son, who was suddenly having such success in that faraway country, was being embraced after all. The film was premièred at the Dutch Film Days Festival on 17 September 1987: 'It is not only a superbly made and very American action movie, but an intelligent, witty and rock-hard cynical vision of the near future. Those who during the film festival had the opportunity to see both *RoboCop* and the short, poetic student films *Eén Hagedis Teveel* and *De Lifters*, which Verhoeven made in Leiden in the early 1960s, were amazed to see the extent to which a film-maker can develop,' the national quality newspaper *NRC/Handelsblad* recorded.

'*RoboCop* is the glorious realization of a boy's dream. Verhoeven's first American film is also a vital expression of what Hollywood is still capable of,' wrote *Trouw*.

RoboCop had been interesting in every respect. A European director had given the USA a brand new pop icon – one which, as a young boy and a teenager, he himself would have very much admired had he seen it at the cinema in the Boekhorststraat in The Hague. 'There, in that old cinema, lie *RoboCop*'s true roots,' the director stresses. 'That is where I saw *Attack* and *Vera Cruz* by Robert Aldrich in the 1950s; Byron Haskin and George Pal's *The War of the Worlds*; the films of John Ford, and later of Sam Peckinpah – everything which was then considered a B-movie.' That experience equipped him to create the right tongue-in-cheek tone, of which perhaps the best example is when RoboCop exactly hits the crotch of a villain by firing between the legs of a woman he is holding hostage. 'Vintage Verhoeven,' the American press noted with a mixture of horror and admiration. That was a misunderstanding. What they were shown in *RoboCop* was nothing but the American imagery which he as a child had absorbed in the cinema. Now, in his own way, he had returned it to its source.

Total Recall.

Total Recall: Verhoeven with Arnold Schwarzenegger
and Sharon Stone.

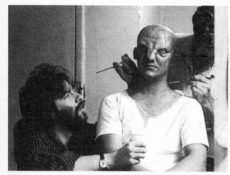

Total Recall: Oscar-winner, Rob Bottin.

Total Recall: with cameraman Jost Vacano
in the Martian tunnel.

Chapter 13

More Lines than Ever for Arnold:
Total Recall

'Watch out, Arnold. Behind you!' In the summer of 1990, the forty-two-year-old Arnold Schwarzenegger was at the height of his popularity. He was the champion of the 'don't mess with me' genre, and had been described by *Time* as 'a star whose body is its own stunning special effect'. In films such as *Conan the Barbarian* (John Milius, 1982) and *The Terminator* (James Cameron, 1984) his muscles had done most of the talking, but the language was strong.

In the eyes of his public, Arnold Schwarzenegger was no longer an actor; he had become a persona. Like Elvis, James Dean and Marilyn Monroe before him, the character of 'Arnold' overshadowed the roles the screenwriters had devised for him. He walked through his films as Arnold, independent of the story, and in the shadow of his own persona he lugged along the character he was supposed to play.

'Watch out, Arnold. In front of you!' The exuberant behaviour of his fans at a screening of Paul Verhoeven's *Total Recall* in the United Artists theatre in Westwood, Los Angeles, illustrated what Schwarzenegger himself had claimed in the *New York Times*: 'In the last five years most people haven't really talked about the characters that I play.' The actor too was aware that he represented a hologram on to which American youngsters projected their fantasies. Although in *Total Recall* he was called Doug Quaid, during the screening the audience simply called him by his own first name – and this in a way that Europeans only know from children watching Punch and Judy shows.

'Watch out, Arnold. Above you!' Part and parcel of the action genre was talking back to the screen. The viewer was invited to do this by the on-screen witticisms of the hero, who when convenient would step out of his character in an almost post-modern way and address the audience directly over the heads of his co-stars. Irony was the key. 'Consider this a divorce,' Arnold says laconically as he shoots his wife (Sharon Stone) through the head in *Total Recall*. She had understood the message a long time before, but the audience was given an extra nudge.

From the lips of any other actor this remark would have sounded either misplaced or stupid, but from the lips of the gentle giant it made many people laugh, even in such a serious adventure as *Total Recall*. This effect was reinforced by Schwarzenegger's rather obvious Austrian accent: 'After twenty years in this country, I could be speaking American English properly. But long ago I realized that I needed something "off", a flaw to remind everyone that I am indeed a mortal human being.'

As with every American cartoon character, whether it was Bugs Bunny or Popeye, the self-mockery with which Schwarzenegger put things into perspective had become his trade mark. His one-liners, known as 'Arnie-isms', were specially written for him. They made the excessive violence of his persona digestible: Arnold was really a big softie, not a deadly fascist to give you nightmares.

In 1968, during his first visit as a bodybuilder to the USA, Schwarzenegger was announced rather unflatteringly as the 'Austrian Oak'. Nor was his feature film début *Hercules Goes to New York* (1970) much of a success. Mr World, Mr Universe (five times) and Mr Olympia (six times) was not taken seriously as an actor. He fared better on his own territory in the 1977 documentary *Pumping Iron*, which gave an insight into the competitiveness of the world of body building. In his ambition to win one more Mr Olympia title, Schwarzenegger's main rival was Lou Ferrigno, later the Incredible Hulk.

Schwarzenegger's charming performance in *Pumping Iron* gave the film industry confidence that they could create a new pop icon out of the man who talked of himself as an artist : 'I feel like I am Leonardo da Vinci; I am a sculptor shaping my body.' He certainly did not lack ambition. In his adolescence, he had felt he was meant 'for something big'. By 1990, he ranked among the ten most powerful men in Hollywood.

Arnold became a guarantee of a good return on investment. Once his name had been linked to a production, the budget shot up. In return for the success he guaranteed, the star was given more and more control over the production. Schwarzenegger began to choose his films and his directors. After seeing *RoboCop*, he personally instructed the production company Carolco to ask Paul Verhoeven to direct *Total Recall*. Schwarzenegger thought that the comic-strip language used by the Dutch director in his first American film was particularly suited to this large project.

Thus the businessman Schwarzenegger gave Paul Verhoeven the task of delivering the product Arnold to the public in the most effective way. Verhoeven realized that this would not be an easy task: 'For Americans

Total Recall was not going to be a Paul Verhoeven film but an Arnold movie.' Yet from the very beginning he intended to lift Schwarzenegger's acting on to a higher plane than his audience had seen up to then.

Verhoeven had worked before with a leading actor who in professional circles was called 'the Russian actor'. His former leading man, Rutger Hauer, was an example of this. The term referred to a psychological experiment which had been carried out at the Moscow Film Academy in the twenties by cinema professor Lev Kuleshov. An actor was asked to look without any expression into a camera. The same shot was then inserted between three different film fragments: a delicious plate of warm food, a very attractive woman and a dead baby in a crib. When the students were asked about the quality of the acting performance, they waxed lyrical about the variation in human emotions. 'Truly a great actor!' they are said to have exclaimed. Only later they were told that it was a single take. The viewers had been seduced by the arrangement of the images, by the juxtaposition.

Verhoeven's presentation of the young Rutger Hauer in the television series *Floris* and in *Turks Fruit* had been largely based on this principle. He deleted large parts of Hauer's dialogue, but still managed to present him as a full character by means of montage. And now he was able to make good use of this technique again with *Total Recall*.

As Verhoeven explained, with affection tempered by realism, 'We must not regard Arnold as the new Laurence Olivier. He is more of a Charlton Heston. His strength is his charisma. The public is very sympathetic to Arnold because he started with all manner of handicaps: that strange, large body, that cliché which equates muscles with stupidity, that heavy accent, that funny jaw. People think of him as a role model, but as an actor he is definitely improving. Arnold is eager to learn. In my film he got more lines than in all his previous films put together.'

Schwarzenegger was hardly conscious of Verhoeven's plans for him, or at least tried to give that impression. He did not count his lines. 'I don't keep statistics,' Arnold says coldly and lights a black Cuban Davidoff in the manner so familiar from his films. 'People always bring me statistics. They go, "Arnold, do you know that in *Total Recall* you kill more people than ever before?" Or, "Is it true that in this picture you have more close-ups than in all your previous ones?" It is all up to the director. I wouldn't know.'

Nor did he need to, since other people were keeping track of the facts for him – and not just the box-office figures. *The Guinness Book of Movie Facts and Feats* says of *Total Recall*: 'The film offered gore fans 110 acts of violence an hour and thirty-five slayings, eighteen of them performed by muscleman Arnold Schwarzenegger in a bad mood.'

Nothing was left to chance in the 'product placing' of such a major

Hollywood phenomenon. The première of *Total Recall* on Friday 1 June 1990 was accompanied by a survey carried out by the National Research Group Inc. of Hollywood. The findings were based on 3245 questionnaires completed by audiences in cinemas in Atlanta, Kansas City, Sacramento and Washington.

The survey showed that 61 per cent of Arnold fans were men – the largest proportion of them were under twenty-one and white (only 20 per cent Afro-Americans); 72 per cent of all spectators said that 'the dominant reason for coming to see the movie was Arnold Schwarzenegger'. Director Verhoeven was mentioned by 9 per cent of the audience as the main reason for going to see *Total Recall;* this was due to the reputation he gained from *RoboCop.* The audience had an essentially middle-class educational background: 35 per cent had completed a university course, 37 per cent were still studying, and most of the rest were high-school kids.

The report's conclusion was clear: 'The movie played very well to these audiences, receiving well above average ratings and "definitive" recommend scores. Younger (under 21) males were the most enthusiastic audience segment, followed by younger females and older males. Older females were the least enthusiastic group; their ratings and recommend scores were still somewhat above average levels.'

Movie Ratings:	Total	Males		Females	
		21 under	21 over	21 under	21 over
Excellent	48%	65%	44%	52%	39%
Very Good	37%	29%	42%	33%	40%
Average	9%	4%	10%	9%	12%
Fair	4%	1%	3%	4%	6%
Poor	2%	1%	1%	2%	3%
Index rating score	81.4	89.0	80.9	82.1	76.6

The rating of 81.4 out of 100 which the audience gave *Total Recall* during the opening weekend was a reliable foretaste of the film's potential. *Total Recall* became the hit of the summer season, the period when American cinemas have to bring in the bulk of their revenue. By the end of the summer, the film's profits in the USA alone were $120 million, which far exceeded the competing titles *Die Hard 2* (Renny Harlin, 1990), *Back to the Future Part III* (Robert Zemeckis, 1989), *Gremlins 2: The New Batch* (Joe Dante, 1990), *Dick Tracy* (Warren Beatty, 1990) and *Days of Thunder* (Tony Scott, 1990). World-wide, the profits would more than double to $270 million.

Satisfying as this was, Paul Verhoeven derived more pleasure from this observation in *Newsweek* on 11 June 1990: 'While an action icon like Chuck Norris is strictly a creature of the pow-zap school, Schwarzenegger, under the aegis of film-makers like James Cameron (*The Terminator*), Ivan Reitman (*Twins*) and Dutch director Paul Verhoeven (*Total Recall*) has become a more complex and engaging figure.' In the James Cameron film, Arnold had still been a robot. The light-hearted comedy *Twins* (1988) had given him an opportunity to exploit his self-mockery. In *Total Recall* the hero still looked tough and shot his opponents to pieces, but something had changed. He had doubts. He showed feelings. He spoke in more than monosyllables. The Arnie-isms had been decimated. Under Paul Verhoeven's direction, the 'Russian actor' Arnold had become Schwarzenegger the human being.

One morning in the autumn of 1988 Verhoeven was expecting the arrival of a motorcycle courier; instead, a van stopped in front of 2922 Bottlebrush Drive, Beverly Glen, where the family was now living. To the director's dismay, not five but *forty-five* versions of the *Total Recall* script were unloaded.

The telephone call from Mario Kassar of Carolco had certainly whetted Verhoeven's appetite. The head of the major independent had politely enquired whether Verhoeven might like to make a film with Arnold Schwarzenegger. Perhaps he would like to read the script some time? A meeting followed, and Verhoeven – who after the success of *RoboCop* had been offered a new film almost every day, and had for a long time considered filming the police thriller *Black Rain* (Ridley Scott, 1989) – now set to work. It was to take him days to struggle through the mountain of paper totalling about 5000 pages.

At that stage, Verhoeven did not know that at least six directors had been involved with the project since 1980. Russell Mulcahy, who made *Highlander* (1986), was the first. David Cronenberg, cult hero of *The Dead Zone* (1983) and *The Fly* (1986), was number two. Fred Schepisi (*A Cry in the Dark*, 1988), Lewis Teague (*The Jewel of the Nile*, 1985) and Richard Rush (*The Stunt Man*, 1979) had all struggled with the script. The leading role had been assigned at various times to Richard Dreyfuss, Christopher Reeve and Jeff Bridges, but the film had never come off.

The person most conversant with these false starts was Ron Shusett, the main author of the *Total Recall* script. He was a fifty-something with an almost childlike fascination for science fiction; at school, he had eagerly read every comic strip featuring 'weird flying creatures'. In 1974 Shusett had come across the short story 'We can remember it for you wholesale' by the American science-fiction writer Philip K. Dick. In the idea of a man who 'is not who he thinks he is', Shusett immediately recognized an intriguing starting point for a film. For $1000 he took out an option on the story. With his permanent partner Dan O'Bannon, Shusett began writing a script, but progress was slow. They put aside the plan, and meanwhile wrote the mega hit *Alien*, directed by Ridley Scott in 1979.

The first draft of *Total Recall* was not completed until 1980. It seemed to have been born under an unlucky star. The Disney studios initially had the rights, but after a period of rewriting, pre-production and changing directors they concluded that the project was becoming too expensive. Moreover, the scriptwriters seemed unable to think of a good ending for the story. So Disney gave over *Total Recall* to Dino de Laurentiis's DEG Studios. 'After that, we tried every ending we could think of,' Shusett remembers, 'and then Dan O'Bannon dropped out because he was sick of the whole project.'

In the spring of 1988, and forty-five versions of the script later – Shusett had had to put up with a procession of script doctors but had found a new partner in Steven Pressfield – it looked as if *Total Recall* was finally going be produced by De Laurentiis. Bruce Beresford had been asked to direct, and the leading role had been given to Patrick Swayze. A complete film set had been built in Australia, an investment of $6 million.

A month before shooting was to begin, Ron Shusett received the message of doom: the DEG Studio was going bankrupt. With his flops *Dune* (David Lynch, 1984) and *Tai-Pan* (Daryl Duke, 1986), Dino de Laurentiis had overplayed his hand. *Total Recall* seemed total history. Ron Shusett: 'The script was ice cold, it was a joke in Hollywood. People felt it was doomed, there was too much money against it without even a frame of footage shot. Who's gonna do this ? It was like an Egyptian curse on it, and people began to think I was a lunatic, because I spent 80 per cent of my time trying to make this movie. So they thought, this guy can't cope with reality. And I guess they were almost right.'

Shusett was not the only one who had read the message of doom in *Variety*. Schwarzenegger too read the share index of the film industry every day, but the message made him feel considerably more cheerful. The actor had come across the script of *Total Recall* in 1985, and the moment De Laurentiis went bankrupt, he immediately told Carolco, 'Buy it!' His command set in motion a chain of events that led to the by now rather weary Paul Verhoeven.

The new director realized that many of the problems with *Total Recall* were to do with the fact that the original Philip K. Dick story had only twenty pages. This contained the concept of the film, but it was no more than a first act, while Hollywood's magic formula is three acts and a conflict.

Philip K. Dick's opening was promising enough. 'He awoke – and wanted Mars. The valleys, he thought. What would it be like to trudge among them? Great and greater yet: the dream grew as he became fully conscious, the dream and the yearning. He could almost feel the enveloping presence of the other world, which only government agents and high officials had seen. A clerk like himself? Not likely.'

The main character no longer knows that in the past he had been a government agent with the Martian secret service. Although the memories of that existence have been wiped out, there remains an inexplicable desire to go to the red planet. Driven by homesickness and longing, he decides to follow the current trend of that year – 2085 – and books a journey to Mars in his head with Rekall Incorporated. He is promised 'the memory of a lifetime', but something goes wrong with the chip implant. By accident, his original memory is activated. The past, which had been deleted, now slowly comes back. In utter confusion, he turns to his wife for support.

'Did I go to Mars?' he asked her. 'You would know.'

'No, of course you didn't go to Mars; you would know that, I would think. Aren't you always bleating about going?'

He said, 'By God, I think I went.' After a pause he added, 'And simultaneously I think I didn't go.'

'Make up your mind.'

'How can I?' He gestured. 'I have both memory tracks grafted inside my head; one is real and one isn't, but I can't tell which is which. I am in trouble.' His voice came out husky and coarse. And shaking. 'Probably I'm heading into a psychotic episode; I hope not, but – maybe that's it. It would explain everything, anyhow.'

While Verhoeven was working through the many versions of the script with the original story by Philip K. Dick to hand, he was struck by the continuously open border between fact and fiction – and by the continual fear of psychosis that burdens the protagonist. Verhoeven realized that, as with his own film *De Vierde Man*, this script could be interpreted on two levels: either everything that happens to the main character Quaid is reality, or it takes place only in his head.

In the first act of the film, the script retains the theme of the confused man, after which Ron Shusett and Dan O'Bannon took over the helm from Philip K. Dick. They let Quaid leave for Mars in search of his own past. This is where the forty-five variations of the script begin. The writers' search for the continuation of the story resulted in the most diverse story lines. In one of the rejected options, Quaid discovers that he is the incarnation of a Martian in a synthetic body. In another variant he develops into the dictator of planet Earth. None of these solutions worked. For Ron Shusett just one theme remained intact: 'I always knew that overwhelming feelings of fear should dominate it.'

Verhoeven agreed with him. When he accepted the invitation to tackle *Total Recall*, his first task was to reorganize the script. For this purpose he brought in an additional screenwriter, the academic Gary Goldman. Verhoeven particularly wanted to make the two narrative levels, fantasy and reality, more equal. Goldman had earlier written *Big Trouble in Little China*, filmed by John Carpenter in 1986. He had got to know the Dutch director while working with him on *Warrior* – one of the many projects Verhoeven had had a taste of before *Total Recall*. The introduction of an intermediary for a script that had been altered as often as *Total Recall* seemed a logical step, but Ron Shusett still had to swallow when he heard the news.

Gary Goldman understood that feeling. 'In Hollywood, rewriting is usually a kind of massacre, where the subsequent writer tries to destroy the work of the previous writer; his one and foremost goal is to take the original writer's name off the screenplay. This is standard practice.' Goldman had no intention of doing this, because the quality of the script itself was not at issue. Everyone in Hollywood agreed that the first act was brilliant. 'After its strong opening it kind of collapsed, and so my job was to see what we could do to make the whole movie work. To a certain extent Paul and I were even handicapped, because there were restrictions: Ron had so many versions of the script, but he also had in his contract things we weren't allowed to change.'

In addition to the arrival of the new script doctor, another development worried the long-suffering Shusett: the entrance of Arnold Schwarzenegger. On the one hand, it was good that Schwarzenegger still wanted to do the film after all this time, because without the involvement of a star of his calibre *Total Recall* would never be made at all. On the other hand, Shusett realized that having Arnold on board, particularly as captain, would undoubtedly have consequences for the narrative. For example, the office worker originally portrayed by Philip K. Dick was a somewhat mousy man, a Walter Mitty type who appeared to possess enormous powers without knowing it, and who had been trained as a secret agent in a previous life. Significantly, in the book his name is Quail, a synonym for fearful (which the film-makers changed to Quaid to avoid any associations with Dan Quayle, then Vice-president of the USA).

Shusett was afraid that this idea of the little man who hits the big time would be jeopardized. 'When Arnold got involved, I was wondering, wouldn't that ruin the whole surprise? Arnold is too powerful to play a meek guy, the audience knows he is a super agent to begin with. Because of his persona, you can't say to him, "This is your character" and then have him play it.'

After consultation, the main character was changed from an office worker to a construction worker, a question of physique. Although the original story had had a dark, serious tone, more action and adventure were written in. It was all meant to make the story fit Arnold.

The credits in the final version of *Total Recall* betray the long route the 117-page script had travelled: 'Written by Ronald Shusett & Dan O'Bannon, revisions by Ronald Shusett, Steven Pressfield and Gary Goldman.' Paul Verhoeven was ready to start his second American movie, for a fee of $3 million. The call sheet included Sharon Stone, at that time still fairly unknown, and three veterans from *RoboCop*: actor Ronny Cox, cameraman Jost Vacano and special effects magician Rob Bottin. Thanks to Arnold, the budget was $55 million, which made *Total Recall* at the time one of the most expensive films ever produced. For example, it cost more than Verhoeven's entire Dutch oeuvre and *Robo-Cop* put together.

'Arnold, don't walk like that. It looks silly!' From April 1989, Verhoeven's strict instructions to his leading man resounded daily through the Estudios Churubusco just outside Mexico City. Determined not to let the megastar slip into his usual routines, Verhoeven refused to go easy on him. He had deleted some of the Arnie-isms specially devised by Goldman and Shusett (such as the philosophical remark 'I don't believe in violence') because they seemed nonsensical to him, and would have undermined the realism Verhoeven wanted so much.

'Don't talk like that, Arnold, it's over the top, *ja*!' To his relief, Verhoeven had noticed that on the set Schwarzenegger did not display the dreaded ego that actors had inflicted on him in the past. When in a small group, Schwarzenegger would sometimes let slip, 'Oh ho, Paul is pissing glass again!' when Verhoeven was about to have an outburst, but apart from that he meekly did what the director asked of him. Schwarzenegger realized he was clay in the director's hands: 'On the set Paul yells all day, but you don't have to take it personally – it's just the way he works. It's an outburst of energy, it brings all the creativity out. That's good.'

He soon realized that Verhoeven had a precise idea of what he wanted to see on the screen. 'We did a lot of rehearsals, because Paul does only four takes of every scene. On Sundays we would work on the things to come that week, especially the stunts, and Paul participated in every one of them – whenever it was necessary, he threw himself straight in the fighting scenes.'

What the Dutch director was showing his star were the ju-jitsu moves of Dick Bos: shoulder throws, somersaults and other tricks he remembered from the Alfred Mazure comic strips that still had a prominent place in his bookcase. And this passionate approach worked, Schwarzenegger concluded. 'A lot of critics wrote that my acting in *Total Recall* had dramatically improved. Well, that's not because of me, but because of Paul.'

This brotherly relationship sometimes gave the Americans on the set reason to chuckle. As Sharon Stone, who plays Quaid's wife Lori, later said in an interview with *Playboy*, 'I made fun of Arnold and Paul right off the bat. We were doing rehearsals in a hotel room. Arnold was lying on the bed and Paul Verhoeven was on top of him, straddling him, caressing his hair, explaining to me how he thought the scene ought to go. I said, "I think I'll leave you two guys alone. You're so darn cute together."'

Together, Verhoeven and Schwarzenegger seemed to have found a European solidarity that the Americans had difficulty understanding. Each in their distinctive accent, the masculine Austrian and the 'Dutch madman' frequently had heated debates about how they were going to surprise the American public with *Total Recall*. It is an image that Schwarzenegger also treasures: 'Sometimes Paul had a little difficulty with his English in explaining to the American crew what to do. I didn't – I guess that because I am also European I could read his mind. The point is, Americans are what you call "language lazy": they only respond to perfectly correct English. When you are at work, that can be very irritating – especially for the director, who has so many other things on his mind.'

In this case, 'other things' meant a cast and crew totalling 300 people. So for budgetary reasons, the location was shifted to Mexico in April 1989. The shooting schedule for *Total Recall* was twenty weeks, the average costs some $150,000 per production day. To keep the pace up, eight sound stages were erected in the large halls of the studios, as well as more than thirty-five separate sets of miniatures, so that it was easy to switch from one location to another. In addition, they regularly went outside. The first part of the film was set on Earth, and although Verhoeven had initially wanted to shoot in Houston, the makers noticed that Mexican architecture had futuristic qualities too, so that it was possible to incorporate several locations into the film's total concept without any problems. Moreover, near the studios was a large mining district with predominantly red and brown tints that could serve as the exterior for the Mars panoramas.

It is relatively easy to do an illustration on paper of Mars as a colony of Earth, but film makes different demands. The 'blue screen' technique played a particularly important role: enormous scenes were shot against blue screens which, after shooting, would be filled in at the laboratory with separately filmed matte paintings (painted backgrounds) and miniatures.

Since Verhoeven insisted that his high-impact action sequences should not be subservient to these complicated background effects, and that his cameraman Jost Vacano had to be able to make flowing, circling manoeuvres, they used real-time motion control, at that time the latest thing in computer technology and developed by George Lucas. This made it possible to animate the Martian views in the correct perspective later, a three-dimensional precision job that was contracted out to Dream Quest Images. Under the guidance of visual effects supervisor Eric Brevig, this is also where the volcanic Martian landscape and its crucial features – such as the landing platform for the Mars shuttle on which Quaid arrives from Earth – were made. The wide shot of the landing, the overture to Act 2, is one of the most impressive in the film. The carefully constructed panorama from Mars, which includes the two moons in the background, has the same kind of appeal that made Ridley Scott's *Blade Runner* (1982) – also from a Philip K. Dick story – into such a striking visual spectacle.

Equally striking are the mutants that play an important role in the complex story of the film. Quaid meets them in Venusville, the red-light district of Mars – modelled by Verhoeven on the Amsterdam red-light district where his film *Wat Zien Ik* (1971) was set. Venusville is the breeding ground for the Martian resistance. Quaid comes there to find Melina, his former lover. He has by now discovered that in his previous life he had gone undercover with the armed opposition as a secret agent for the Martian dictator Vilos Cohaagen. His task was to find and destroy their charismatic leader Kuato. As Quaid wins the trust of the resistance fighters, he gains more and more understanding of their motives: the mutants no longer wanted to be slaves labouring for Cohaagen, whose power was based on his monopoly of the oxygen supply. Quaid fell in love with Melina and 'went native' – sufficient reason for the dictator to take him off the job immediately and exile him to Earth. There his mind was wiped blank and he was given a new identity, including a house, a job and a wife from the Agency. But as a result of his visit to the dream factory Rekall Inc., fragments of his old existence return. In Venusville, Quaid hopes to piece together the jigsaw of his life.

He finds a procession of deformed characters, mutants created by Rob Bottin. As special-effects make-up designer, he was given free rein. A woman with three breasts was one of the more recognizable items in his cabinet of curiosities. 'A mutant can be anything, but I felt that if I made them too outrageous, the audience would go, "Oh, of course this is a dream." So I had to think in terms of everything being real, without losing the imaginative aspects: it is what I call surreal-based realism. It was Paul's approach that, as we revealed each mutant, the deformities would be progressively more shocking.'

The crown of Bottin's efforts was Kuato, the Che Guevara of Mars. This creature, a human head looking like an angry baby with little arms, grows out of his brother George's stomach – which is why Cohaagen finds it so difficult to track the resistance leader down. Screenwriter Ron Shusett had the idea for Kuato when he saw photographs of Siamese twins during his research. 'I originally thought of it like this: Quaid was knocked unconscious, and then he would wake up with blurred vision, as in the old detective movies where they get slipped a Mickey Finn. Quaid would see this guy bending over him with two heads, but he and we would think it was because of the blow to his head. But as he becomes fully conscious, this guy would still have two heads! That was the first time I thought of Kuato, and from then on he grew into a key character.'

In the end, it took twenty on-set operators and a computer to get the mechanical prosthesis Kuato to talk – especially since Bottin had suggested that an inspirational leader should be capable of gesticulating with Shakespearean grandeur. 'In other words, he had to be something more than just a talking face.' The takes became so complicated that they decided to complete them during post-production in Los Angeles.

Naturally, this 'surreal-based realism' also included actors. The key role of dictator Vilos Cohaagen went to Ronny Cox, who had played the corrupt executive Dick Jones in *RoboCop*. The part of Cohaagen's right-hand man Richter went to Michael Ironside because of his ruthless appearance. Melina, Quaid's mistress on Mars, was played by actress Rachel Ticotin; her appearance was somewhat reminiscent of Sigourney Weaver's in *Alien* (Ridley Scott, 1979). For Quaid's wife Lori, Verhoeven came up with Sharon Stone, a cool thirty-one-year-old blonde who had a background as a model and could have been described as a star actress long in the making. In Hollywood jargon, she was a 'nearly girl', because she had just missed important roles in, for example, *Dick Tracy* (Warren Beatty, 1990) and *Batman* (Tim Burton, 1989). She could only point to her share in such easily forgotten films as *King Solomon's Mines* (the remake by J. Lee Thompson, 1985) and *Police Academy IV: Citizens on Patrol* (Jim Drake, 1987), although she had made her début in Woody Allen's *Stardust Memories* (1980). Her remuneration for *Total Recall* was $50,000.

Although as an adolescent Paul Verhoeven had dreamed of making epic films on the scale of *Total Recall* – and with *Flesh + Blood* he had already taken a step in that direction – the reality turned out to be a nightmare. With almost clockwork regularity, an average of twenty crew members a day reported to the specially hired set doctor in the Estudios Churubusco. The symptoms all pointed to food poisoning. The Mexican catering was upsetting the cast and crew, and only Arnold Schwarzenegger, in view of his star status and the fact that the film was largely dependent on his presence, was allowed to have a cool-box full of fresh fruit and vegetables flown in from Los Angeles every day. Moreover, the many technically complicated and time-consuming shots caused the budget and the shooting time to overrun considerably.

Paul Verhoeven is not the type to dwell on past calamities, but in *The Making of . . . Total Recall*, a documentary produced by Carolco, the emaciated face of the director clearly showed his fatigue and stress. It even came to the point where Verhoeven had to be put on a drip at night; owing to persistent nausea and vomiting, he had begun to show signs of dehydration.

Ron Shusett, who was on the set throughout the shooting, remembers the atmosphere of mounting crisis: 'One day, Paul got sick. He had gotten sick before, but his time it was the worst; he couldn't stand up, and should have been in the hospital. I told him so, and said, "The insurance will cover it." But Paul said, "No, the insurance doesn't cover the first three days. I have talked to Carolco, and they have to pay in full out of their pocket." Now at the time we were already $12 million over budget – not because of Paul, but because this project was awesome; it was uncontrollable, actually. So he went on, "They're gonna cut $150,000 dollars a day off the budget if we don't shoot. If I make it through one more night, I might recover."'

Thus the director was transported by minibus to the outdoor night shoot, where he continued to direct the film, mostly from a stretcher on the roof of the vehicle. 'He looked like a corpse. His whole face was white – it was five in the morning and raining heavily. He could hardly stand up, people were holding him. And he said, "Unless I am dying, we are not gonna stop shooting." Nobody dared to laugh.'

When the night shoots were finished Verhoeven recovered, with the help of vitamin injections and a drip, but this was not the end of his problems. There were daily arguments about budget cuts with producer Buzz Feitshans ('Make that hourly,' Feitshans later said in an interview), with Schwarzenegger mediating as best he could. After all, it was an Arnold film. In addition to his fee of $10 million, he had insisted on a percentage of the box-office receipts.

Ron Shusett stresses the importance of Schwarzenegger's enlightened self-interest: 'Whenever we needed more money Arnold flew back to Carolco and got it. He would just say, "I demand it" – and they had no choice. So it was more or less like a football game where you just follow the full back and he blocks everybody out in front of you. Paul would be right behind him and run ahead.'

With some six months of filming behind him and another six months of post-production ahead of him, Verhoeven flew back to Los Angeles at the end of August 1989 – the first time he had been back since the shooting of *Total Recall* began in April. Martine came to meet him, which was perhaps just as well: Verhoeven had buried himself in the film and the

Mexican locations to such an extent that he had almost forgotten that he lived in Los Angeles and had a wife and children. 'Mexico struck me as a very seductive country. I thought about starting a whole new life there. What was really appealing was to be confronted by a world full of magical and religious emblems – something I am highly sensitive to because of my background.'

The story of the Aztecs, their bloody human sacrifices, their defeat by the Spaniards – the whole apocalyptic history that hovers like a shadow over Mexico's culture, as well as its passionate population – all this touched Verhoeven far more than his somewhat sterile existence in Hollywood. On the journey back he was accompanied by Ron Shusett, the only person who had not left Verhoeven's side during the entire shooting time. Even during public holidays, when all the others had travelled back to familiar Los Angeles, the two of them had stayed behind in an empty hotel, their heads full of Martian mutants. Shusett, the director's equal in obsessiveness, had not wanted to miss a single minute of the process. He had waited quite long enough for his brainchild to be captured on film. 'We were like two convicts, two jailbirds there in Mexico, getting together through it all.'

At the première of *Total Recall* in June 1990 at the Griffith Observatory in Los Angeles Verhoeven was back to his normal weight, which was more than could be said for the financial reserves of Carolco. In the end the film cost nearly $60 million, and it was not just Verhoeven's reputation that depended on it making a profit. It soon became clear, however, that not Carolco, or Arnold, or Verhoeven had overplayed their hand. The film's reception was extra-terrestrial. The *San Francisco Chronicle* reported on Friday 1 June 1990: '*Total Recall* is a first-rate action movie, slickly done and with so many imaginative extras that, for a time, it feels like a classic in the making. It's not, but it's still solid and entertaining and deserves to be the blockbuster hit it's bound to become.' And *Time* wrote on 11 June: 'Verhoeven seems to have assumed that today's moviegoers have a megabyte media intelligence; then he worked like crazy to overload it. When *Total Recall* is cooking, it induces visual vertigo . . . In today's market $60 million movies can buy you a sloppy-looking sequel like *Rambo III* which puts nothing on the screen but bloat. Or as here, the fat bankroll can allow canny artists and artisans to put a mammoth, teeming fantasy on film. "Open your mind," says the mutant guru, and *Total Recall* does just that for moviegoers at the start of a blockbuster summer.'

The reviewers had not been put off by the fact that this was by far the most complex 'juvenilized' film to be produced in Hollywood in more than a decade. Throughout *Total Recall*'s 109 minutes, viewers constantly have to decide for themselves whether they are watching fantasy or reality. As soon as the main character Quaid sits down at Rekall to have his virtual journey to Mars implanted, fact and fantasy become intertwined. Although Quaid, like a real Superman, saves the entire planet at the end of the film, the question remains as to whether we are watching his dream or his deeds.

'Because it is all filmed so hyper-realistically,' Paul Verhoeven explains, 'it seems plausible to the audience that Quaid's adventures are real. The only thing is that, when you analyse the story, you could equally maintain that they are not.' This is the crux of the matter: when Quaid orders his journey to Mars, the employees of Rekall Inc. make an exact prediction of the entire course of his quest. 'Take a vacation from yourself,' they suggest, giving him four options for a travel identity. In his head, he can go to Mars as (a) a millionaire playboy, (b) a sports hero, (c) an industrial tycoon, or (d) a secret agent. Quaid chooses the last option, and the Rekall salesman congratulates him on his imaginative choice. Verhoeven: 'The man literally says, "By the time the trip is over you'll get the girl, kill the bad guys, and save the entire planet." And this is exactly what happens. In fact, it is clear after ten minutes what is going to happen in the film. All Quaid's adventures are the result of his choosing the secret agent travel package. He has simply paid for it.'

The climax of this clash between fantasy and reality is the moment when, on behalf of Rekall Inc., Doctor Edgemar gives Doug Quaid an important message in his Martian Hilton hotel room. 'This is going to be very difficult for you to accept, Mr Quaid. You're not here, and neither am I.' An almost *Nouvelle Vague* dialogue follows, in which Edgemar explains that, as a doctor, he has been artificially implanted as an emergency measure in the dream trip Quaid ordered at Rekall.

Quaid: 'Bullshit.'
Dr Edgemar: 'What's bullshit, Mr Quaid? That you're having a paranoid episode triggered by acute neurochemical trauma? Or that you're really an invincible secret agent from Mars who's the victim of an interplanetary conspiracy to make him think he's a lowly construction worker?'
Quaid's certainty is undermined.
Edgemar looks at him with great sympathy and kindness.
Dr Edgemar: 'Stop punishing yourself, Doug. You're a fine, upstanding man. Your whole life is ahead of you . . . But you've really got to want to return to reality.'
Quaid is half-convinced, but doesn't want to show it.
He says, 'Suppose I do . . . then what?'
Dr Edgemar: 'Swallow this.'
He opens his hand, revealing a small pill.
Quaid: 'What is it?'

Edgemar: 'It's a symbol. Of your desire to return to reality. Inside your dream, you'll fall asleep.'

Quaid picks up the pill and examines it.

He says, 'All right. Let's say you're telling the truth, and this is all a dream . . . (realizing something, Quaid raises his gun to Edgemar's head) . . . then I can pull the trigger, and it won't matter.'

Edgemar remains preternaturally calm. His eyes and voice express his unselfish concern for Quaid. 'It won't make the slightest difference to me, Doug, but the consequences to you would be devastating. In your mind, I'll be dead. And with no one to guide you out, you'll be stuck in permanent psychosis.'

Finger on the trigger, Quaid is torn with doubt.

Edgemar: 'The walls of reality will come crashing down. One minute you'll be the saviour of the rebel cause, then the next thing you know you'll be Cohaagen's bosom buddy. You'll even have ridiculous fantasies about alien civilization – as you requested. But in the end, back on Earth . . . you'll be lobotomized.'

Quaid becomes totally demoralized.

Edgemar: 'So get a grip on yourself, Doug. And put down the gun.'

Edgemar stares hard.

Quaid hesitantly lowers the gun.

Edgemar: 'Good . . . Now take the pill and put it in your mouth.'

Quaid puts the pill in his mouth.

Edgemar: 'Swallow it.'

Edgemar and Quaid's wife Lori watch with great anticipation. Quaid is wracked with indecision. Then he sees a single drop of sweat trickle down from Edgemar's brow. Abruptly, he swings his gun at Edgemar and fires. Edgemar's blood splatters in a dense circle on the wall. Quaid spits the pill out on to Edgemar's bloodstained body.

And so the story abruptly moves on again. It is Verhoeven's trade mark to tempt us with a striking image, or in this case an intriguing idea, and then to take an almost perverse pleasure in knocking it down. The viewer is left disengaged. It only becomes clear afterwards how the director has managed to keep all the strands together. The last image of *Total Recall* shows how the second narrative thread has been consistently pursued to its conclusion. By then, Quaid has saved the red planet by activating the Martian reactor. This results in a huge displacement of air: Mars receives its own atmosphere and the mutants slowly recover from their lack of oxygen. Quaid is holding Melina in his arms. He kisses her in a *Gone with the Wind* fashion. Happy ending? Contrary to our expectations, the final image does not fade to black, but turns into a blinding light. Doctor Edgemar's last warning ('But in the end, back on earth, you'll be lobotomized') has come true: Quaid's mind has blown up. At least, for those who wish to interpret it that way.

The director is sure of it. 'The quintessence of the film is that Quaid likes the dream so much he does not want to wake up. He does not hesitate to pull the wool over his own eyes.' So the drop of perspiration trickling down the doctor's face is a wilful projection by Quaid to enable him to stay in the dream. It gives him a reason to decide that the doctor is no good. 'And the funny thing is that the public wants it too. I have noticed in the cinema that during the scene in the hotel room, the audience are watching very quietly, almost grinding their teeth, as if to say, "Damn, we haven't been watching a dream for an hour, have we? Surely we're not going back to the beginning?" And to their relief Arnold then takes them further on his journey by shooting the doctor. But it remains a dream.'

This is a detail Verhoeven greatly enjoyed, and so he encouraged scriptwriters Shusett and Goldman to emphasize Doctor Edgemar's monologue. 'In the original versions it wasn't written that way, but I thought it was a good joke to tell the audience exactly what is going to happen and then to con them again. A Brechtian theatre technique, with one of those teasing, omniscient narrators – but in 1990s fashion, geared towards America and so hocus-pocus that they instantly forget that you did it.' Because they *want* to forget, Verhoeven concludes with devilish delight.

The planet Mars, as the director remembers from studying astronomy at university, was in the human imagination traditionally associated with blood, danger and violence – even with hell. This fascination had everything to do with the threatening way in which Mars glowed in the heavens. Among the five planets that attracted attention because of their brightness and motion across the starry sky – the others are Mercury, Venus, Jupiter and Saturn – Mars was an exception: unlike the others, which radiated a bright white light, Mars glowed with an unexplained red light. The planet inspired fear as early as 3500 BC, when the Sumerians were studying the skies. Unaware that the red glow was caused by oxydized iron on the surface, they associated it with blood. This is why the Sumerians called the planet Nergal, the Greeks named it Ares, and finally the Romans called it Mars – they were all naming it after their own god of war.

When in the seventeenth century Mars was viewed through telescopes, its reputation was permanently damaged. Polar caps were clearly visible and a thin atmosphere was suspected. Mars seemed to resemble Earth more than any other planet and the fear of a competing civilization in an unreachable world increased. While attempting to map the red planet, the Italian astronomer Giovanni Virginio Schiaparelli claimed in 1877 to have observed an ingenious network of channels. His idea was taken by H. G. Wells, who in 1895 wrote *The War of the Worlds*, an epoch-making story in which the Martians attack Earth.

In the next century, Hollywood did not want to fall behind. After the 1922 silent film *The Man from Mars*, came the film version of *War of the Worlds* (Byron Haskin, 1953) in which the Martians were the sons of an evil empire intent on spreading death and destruction in California. In *Invaders from Mars* (1953) the men from Mars were again given the role of the bad guys; unfortunately director William Cameron Menzies had to keep showing the same fighting scenes due to lack of money. To satisfy people's curiosity earthlings were sent in the opposite direction. In *Flight to Mars* (Lesley Selander, 1951), the first colour production about the red planet, a scientist and journalist set out to investigate and find the remains of a lost civilization. Mars was also honoured with a visit from Robinson Crusoe in *Robinson Crusoe on Mars* (Byron Haskins, 1964): the story of an astronaut whose spaceship breaks down and who becomes stranded on the planet. His 'Friday' is an alien coping with similar problems, after which a beautiful interplanetary friendship develops.

Verhoeven had studied many of these films prior to *Totall Recall*. As with *RoboCop*, it was Fritz Lang's *Metropolis* (1927) which inspired many of Verhoeven's ideas for *Total Recall*. This applied particularly to the structure of his film, but there was also an obvious parallel to the climax in *Metropolis* – the sequence in which the entire underworld, the domain of the labourers, is flooded. This spectacular scene was transposed in all its chaos to *Total Recall* and reversed; it is the moment when Quaid activates the nuclear reactor. This results in a turbulent influx of oxygen: the Martian atmosphere which saves the planet is created.

To give meaning to the reassuring blue that follows, Verhoeven first wanted to drown the viewer in red. 'Red as far as the eye can see. Red through the windows. Red in the light. The colour of danger. The colour of "Watch out, fragile!" – which of course applies to the glass domes in which they all live . . . In that sense *Total Recall* is playing with the idea of an apocalyptic story.' When everyone is expecting a Martian meltdown, an interplanetary Chernobyl, the mysterious nuclear power station once deserted by the aliens turns out to be a blessing in disguise. 'I'm totally comfortable with that as a scientist. *Total Recall* can be seen as my plea for nuclear energy – although I haven't got a solution for the waste disposal problem. Beyond that is the realization that Einstein's formulas to obtain energy in that way are ingenious. Really a godsend, as you can see in the film, although in this case the gods are aliens.'

There is a sharp contrast between *Total Recall* and *RoboCop*. In Verhoeven's first sci-fi film, the technology of the future was presented as a source of fear. The borderline between man and machine seemed completely eroded, until the moment when RoboCop becomes Murphy again. In 1990 Martin Amis wrote in *Première*: '*RoboCop* was doubly futuristic. As a movie, and as a vision. It wasn't just state-of-the-art. It was also state-of-the-science; when you see its twirling rivets and burnished heat-exchangers, when you hear its venomous shunts and succulent fizzes, you suspect that the future really might feel like this – that it will act this way on your nerve-ends. Technology is god in *RoboCop*, but it is also the villain, with its triumphant humourlessness, its puerile ingenuity, its dumb glamour.'

In *Total Recall*, however, science wins on all fronts. It is a nuclear power station which saves civilization. The scientific gauntlet which Verhoeven threw into the ring was picked up by the prominent sci-fi writer and astronomer Arthur C. Clarke, author of *2001: A Space Odyssey*. In his book *The Snows of Olympus*, Clarke gives his vision of the colonization of the red planet, which he expects to take place in the twenty-first century. In chapter eight he refers to Verhoeven's film:

At the climax of the movie *Total Recall*, the life-support system of a Martian colony is sabotaged. In the nick of time, our hero (Arnold Schwarzenegger) discovers a gigantic buried machine built by some vanished race and is able to switch it on. Form a standing start it gives Mars a breathable atmosphere in about sixty seconds flat. Ridiculous! Even the most optimistic planetary engineers believe that to replenish the atmosphere of Mars would take not seconds but centuries – and more likely millennia.

What Arthur C. Clarke underestimates, Verhoeven ripostes, is that Hollywood laws regarding spectacular entertainment will, of course, always exceed scientific reality in a film of 109 minutes. And yet, as a qualified physicist, Verhoeven tried to maximize the scientific element in *Total Recall*. The people involved with the script before him had made light of it. In the version nearly filmed by Bruce Beresford, for example, the inheritance of the aliens was a tree with an underground root system containing nuclear material. 'I thought that really was complete nonsense. I thought it should be something technical – an enormous reactor.'

Verhoeven asked designer Ron Cobb – who had also worked on *Alien* (Ridley Scott, 1979) – to design a Martian nuclear power station. He came up with a construction that looked like a gigantic metal spider, but Verhoeven thought it was still too small. At some point, production designer and *RoboCop* veteran Bill Sandell brought in a book of futuristic designs from the 1920s and 1930s. 'It was full of skyscrapers, and because we couldn't find a solution, we turned the book upside-down. That really was Eureka! Upside-down, those skyscrapers were hanging down as if from a ceiling, and went straight into the ground. That's the idea we used.'

When Quaid switches on the reactor, the nuclear fuel rods emerge from their tubes and push down through the Martian polar ice. The ensuing radiation melts the ice and so the atmosphere is created. 'What you see is the O_2 component blown into the atmosphere, and in terms of physics that is correct. What is not correct is that no nitrogen is added to the atmosphere, which is as much as to say that if someone lights a cigarette, the entire planet would explode. But anyway, the explanation in *Total Recall* does not go that far. It's Mars – they might have different ice there, mightn't they? What concerned me was to be scientifically correct *up to a certain point*, namely above the Hollywood level. And within the space allowed by film narrative, I think it worked quite well.'

The criticisms of the explicit violence in *Total Recall* were harsher than the comments about its scientific content. After the première, the *New York Times* wrote: 'Paul Verhoeven has come up with a vigorous, super-violent interplanetary thriller that packs in wallops with metronomic regularity. Mr Verhoeven is much better at drumming up this sort of artificial excitement than he is at knowing when to stop.'

Dan O'Bannon, who with Ron Shusett had worked on the first versions of the script, also complained in a 1992 collection of interviews entitled *The New Screenwriter looks at the New Screenwriters*: 'The way the violence plays in *Total Recall* is as though there wasn't enough there to support the excitement without it. And I feel that there was. I don't think it needed that level of violence, and I think that, in order to make the time and space for the violence, they lost some good things in the way of humor and surprise and character.'

Verhoeven's violence was too 'exaggerated' and 'baroque' for him. Of course, O'Bannon continued, the first versions of the script of *Total Recall* were not without blood either. 'There was certainly violence; you can't have an action thriller, a James Bond-ish type of spy thriller, without having people killed and violence and blood. But I was surprised at the length to which it was carried. It was as though the director had no confidence in the script.'

Verhoeven believes O'Bannon's criticism ignores the fact that Schwarzenegger is playing the lead, and that the script therefore had to be adapted – which is not to say that he had not been subjected to this type of remark before. Criticism of his explicit portrayal of violence has been a constant in his film-making career since the days of *Floris*. It had been a bone of contention with *Flesh + Blood*, and *RoboCop* had had to go back to the cutting room seven times before it received its R rating. As was to be expected, it was no different with *Total Recall*.

'But I think every human being enjoys destruction. Why else do we all go and look when two cars have crashed at a street corner? Even though we know the victims may be lying there bleeding, without limbs, and completely messed up. Laurel and Hardy are also destructive, but we have a good laugh about it. I remember a film with them and, I think,

Ben Turpin, in which they are selling Christmas trees. They get into an argument with a customer, who in his anger begins to demolish their car, to which they respond by destroying his house. Well, things escalate, of course, so the house and car are gone in no time. But because we are all born with a malicious streak, we can have a really good laugh at that.

'We've simply got something sadistic, some very dubious things, in us. Jung talked about the shadow we always carry with us. That is a rather undangerous, euphemistic, mild psychoanalytical term, because he meant a demon, of course, a devil whom we always project on to the other person, in the sense of 'that shadow belongs to you'. We have been struggling with that idea for a few thousand years; we hardly dare ask ourselves whether our good intentions are really meant that sympathetically, that positively.

'The writer Walker Percy has a beautiful parable about that. He saw his neighbour jogging and thought, "Hey, I thought that guy had a heart condition." So he speaks to him and expresses his surprise. No, no, the man says, the doctors made a mistake. It was not his heart but his back, and jogging was good for him. Moreover, he felt fine because he had just received a pay rise and could now buy that beautiful house across the road, with that superb swimming pool and that big garage. The question then is, "How much do you not begrudge that man?" You think it is OK that his heart is good, but the pay rise bothers you. Or you do not begrudge him the pay rise as long as he keeps his heart condition. Or worse. We don't wish anyone too much luck. We are jealous. Malicious. Destructive. But we do not want to deal with it. So I make films with a shadowy side.'

The most criticized scene in *Total Recall* (also condemned by the audience survey as 'too violent/bloody/gory') is the one where Quaid gets into a fight with Richter, tyrant Cohaagen's hit man. They are fighting on a lift platform which shoots up; Richter is hanging off the edge and becomes trapped between the lift and the next floor. The result is as inevitable as it is explicit: his arms are chopped off.

Verhoeven: 'It may seem a horrific or, if you like, sick black fantasy, but it is an autobiographical image. When I was about seven, my father sent me to the town hall to deliver a letter. They had those paternoster lifts there which go round continuously. I found them so impressive that I thought, "I'll just sit down and let myself be carried up all the way" – with my legs trailing over the edge. I did not see that the next floor was rapidly approaching, and before I knew it my legs had got stuck. For a moment I thought I had really lost them, but fortunately the edge of the floor turned out to be hinged – they had thought of it beforehand. I got away with a fright, but I'll never forget it. That is why that scene in *Total Recall* is so good, because it is based on reality – that is why it feels honest in its associations and has much more impact.'

At the beginning of the 1990s the debate about the excessive violence in action films flared up again. In 1992 the American journalist Michael Medved published his book *Hollywood versus America*, in which he noisily argued that the film industry was ignoring traditional family values and, in fact, inciting violence. 'America's long-running romance with Hollywood is over,' the first sentence ominously announced. 'Tens of millions of Americans now see the entertainment industry as an all-powerful enemy, an alien force that assaults our most cherished values and corrupts our children. The dream factory has become the poison factory.' It is no surprise that the book discusses Paul Verhoeven at length: 'Mr Verhoeven is surely entitled to bring to the screen his warped and feverish fantasies (just so long as the studios support him in these endeavors), but it strains credibility for him to suggest that his work simply recreates the horrors of everyday life.'

And: 'Actually, Verhoeven's recent body of work demonstrates Hollywood's own basic instinct, which is to paint America with a decidedly dark palette in which the favorite color is always deep red.'

The director is familiar with these statements; he is often asked to give talks on the subject. 'I have found a saying, not by Medved, but rather Medvedian in character, namely: "Art that cannot rely on the joyous, heartfelt assent of the broad and healthy mass of the people is intolerable." When I read that out during one of those talks, the audience usually nods approvingly, until I say whose quote it is: Adolf Hitler in 1937, at the opening of the Munich exhibition where the Nazis showed the art they thought was "degenerate". As far as I'm concerned, Medved is making use of veiled fascist rhetoric.'

The point is, says Verhoeven, that the link between film violence and real violence has never been scientifically proved. He quotes from the work of leading psychologist Stanley Milgram who, without wasting words, concludes: 'There is no evidence that subjects imitate anti-social acts observed on television.' Verhoeven has also read a 1986 report by Professor Jonathan L. Freedman, who analysed many studies of violence. Freedman says, 'There is no field study that clearly shows that television violence increases aggressive behaviour.' And he writes: '. . . it does not support the hypothesis that viewing [aggressive] television causes an increase in aggressiveness in the real world.'

The director believes that in Europe the 'shadow' aspect of human nature is taken much more into account, a lesson they have learnt from the many wars on that continent. 'Here, it is un-American to point that out. Americans believe in their own goodness, their chosen status as God's Own People. Hence the gigantic hang-up about Vietnam. They cannot accept that they made a mistake: that's the Utopian thinking this country was built on. Right is right – that's us – and wrong is wrong – that's the others.'

For eighty years, Hollywood has been confirming this view. The classic good guy (always an American) takes on the archetypal bad guy (preferably a European) and always wins. 'In my films I try to put that cliché into perspective. And that bothers them.'

Verhoeven believes that the debate on violence serves mostly as a smoke screen, and points to the presidential aspirations of Bob Dole, the most recent critic of Hollywood. The comparison with the McCarthy era comes up: 'Initially I saw America as an open society, but the longer I'm here, the more I begin to notice the hypocrisy – especially in cultural politics. We are heading for a time when you could go straight to prison if you made a particular type of film: the film industry will then serve as a scapegoat for society's distress. The debate distracts attention from America's real problems – where the violence is caused by economic decline, drugs and that idiotic firearms law. As long as you can buy a revolver here for next to nothing, people will continue to shoot each other – but they would rather not talk about that.'

By now, it was no longer merely through television images that the immigrant Paul Verhoeven had become acquainted with the ways of American society. When *Total Recall* was released, he had been in the United States for five years, and his unbridled fascination for the country had been replaced by a more modified perception. Here in the Beverly Glen everyday life looked like an idyllic suburb from a Spielberg film, but an enormous gate was needed to protect them. Outside the house, the district's private security guards were constantly patrolling; they were clearly visible and promised every potential intruder an 'armed response' – as if Verhoeven's RoboCop himself was on guard.

On their arrival in the United States, his daughters Claudia and Heleen had been sent to a state school, but this turned out to be something rather different from the Dutch idea of state education. At school, the girls got to know about the gang phenomenon; some of their so-called friends turned out to be criminals who were sent to prison for drug-dealing or car theft; parties were sometimes rudely interrupted by a drive-by shooting, when a rival gang aimed at some of the guests. This was not television. This was real.

Verhoeven's diagnosis of American society – that it would improve with a hefty increase in taxes – annoyed his Republican neighbours. Meanwhile, on his way to the cinema on Third Street, Santa Monica, he would stumble across emaciated tramps, or would be nearly knocked down by embittered and forgotten Vietnam veterans in wheelchairs. These were paradoxes his European eye would never completely understand. 'In the Netherlands I only half-followed the social debate because the point at issue was usually something silly like a 1 per cent wage increase or a row between a mayor and an alderman. Here I devour the papers. The flaws in the system grab your attention. Survival of the fittest is the norm. Economic gain always takes precedence. And the existence of things like sex and violence is simply ignored by puritans. The USA is a laboratory for human behaviour.'

What fascinates him above all is that *everything* in America is presented as entertainment, that reality is only comprehensible when shown on television, as was evident at the time of the 'Rodney King riots' in April 1992. Verhoeven happened to be having lunch at the Bel Age Hotel with a splendid view; the riots were reaching their height a short distance away, and as he saw the plumes of smoke drift across the city, the other people in the restaurant were watching the television reports of the disturbances with a cocktail in their hands. It was an image that would not have been out of place during the last days of Rome. And yet Verhoeven realized that if he wanted to function as a film-maker, he had to embrace American culture in all its extremes – because it had been for that reason, and for that reason alone, that he had come. Where else in the world could you find a city where they gave millions to people like himself – where else but here in Hollywood, the circus of hope and failure.

With *Total Recall*, despite the criticism from conservative circles, Paul Verhoeven had managed to establish himself as an influential director. In *Première* magazine's Power List, which gives the hundred most powerful Hollywood personalities each year, he came in at number fifty. 'The most successful formerly obscure European art film director going,' read his description. His work was also noticed by the Academy, although not as much as Verhoeven would have liked. *Total Recall* had received two nominations, in the categories Sound and Sound Effects Editing, but won only a Special Achievement Award (for visual effects) for Eric Brevig, Rob Bottin, Tim McGovern and Alex Funke.

Philip K. Dick did not benefit from the success. He had died aged fifty-three on 2 March 1982, plagued by paranoia. His heirs, however, harvested the fruits of his labour. As a result of *Total Recall*, Dick's work suddenly became very popular in Hollywood. Although Ron Shusett had only paid $1000 for an option on the story 'We can remember it for you wholesale', the price for a story of similar length (under thirty pages) rose to $500,000. Philip K. Dick's novels and short stories were very successfully reprinted. As Ron Shusett pointed out, *Total Recall* had turned him into 'a mini-version of Van Gogh'.

To screenwriter Shusett, the Oscar nominations were a vindication of his struggles to get the film off the ground. In a rather unusual gesture for Hollywood, he gives Verhoeven the credit. 'The truth is, *Total Recall* was a very difficult movie to pull off, because the audience could easily get lost in it. As a matter of fact, that is what happened with Arnold's next movie, *The Last Action Hero* – on paper, it had some of the same multi-layered qualities of *Total Recall* and yet the audience turned its back on it completely. After the bombing of The *Last Action Hero* I thought to myself, we were lucky that didn't happen to us. It could have happened if Paul had made mistakes in the storytelling, but he never lost control.'

Shusett's comparison between *Total Recall* and *The Last Action Hero*, the 1993 Arnold Schwarzenegger fiasco orchestrated by John McTiernan, is illuminating. Although as a story *The Last Action Hero* hangs together remarkably well: little boy admires film hero, jumps through the screen and lands in his world, after which he in turn shows the star the real world – a post-modernist pastiche that attacked Hollywood's mystique – it became Arnold's first box-office flop.

The fans who had so appreciated the layered reality in *Total Recall* were totally confused by *The Last Action Hero*. This was to do with the tone and pace of the narrative – a conclusion that Schwarzenegger, perhaps subconsciously, had already drawn himself. Asked in 1990 why he had wanted Paul Verhoeven as director for *Total Recall* – so much so that he personally introduced him to Carolco – Schwarzenegger said that, after seeing *RoboCop* as well as *Soldaat van Oranje* and *De Vierde Man*, he realized Paul was a terrific storyteller. 'A star doesn't make a blockbuster all by himself. He attracts attention in the first week, but from the second week on it's the story that has to do it.'

The businessman in Schwarzenegger knew that, if the storytelling failed, nobody would come and watch. 'Not even for Arnold.'

Basic Instinct: Verhoeven's homage to Hitchcock – George Dzundza, Michael Douglas and Sharon Stone.

Basic Instinct: Sharon Stone and 'the Flash' – the three seconds that shook the world.

Basic Instinct: Verhoeven with Michael Douglas – 'Paul is living his movie.'

Basic Instinct: Verhoeven with Jan de Bont.

Chapter 14

Under the Spell of the Blonde Devil:
Basic Instinct

Leiden, 1958. Paul Verhoeven is spending Saturday night at a slightly seedy student party in the company of his good friend and room-mate Robert Haverschmidt. They are both about twenty years old and dressed in existentialist black. Robert is the more forward of the two. He is the one who dares to speak to the girls, who always seems to find the right words, while Paul meekly follows in his footsteps. He lacks the ease with which Robert moves around the partying guests, where the girls are wearing their hair like Juliette Gréco and gently swinging to the rhythm of jazz, glasses of white wine in their hands. Verhoeven is gazing in front of him when Robert abruptly pokes him in the ribs. He has a grin on his face. 'There,' he says, 'there! Look at that!'

Paul Verhoeven looks in the direction Robert is pointing. He sees a woman, no longer young, sitting in a chair. He knows that she is the steady girlfriend of a journalist, an art critic on the *Leidsch Dagblad* newspaper – they have all been moving in the same cultural and student circles for as long as Verhoeven can remember. The woman recognizes him too, and smiles. Then, very slowly, she changes position and crosses her legs, allowing the two astonished young men to see right up her skirt. She is not wearing any underwear.

'Come on,' says Robert enthusiastically. He takes the hesitating Paul by the arm and goes up to the woman. 'Hey, did you know,' he whispers to her, 'did you know that we can see *everything*?' She nods. 'But of course,' she replies unmoved, 'that's why I'm doing it.' Giggling, the boys slink off again. The incident has made *them* blush, not *her*.

Exactly twenty-four years later, 60 million viewers were to experience a similar sensation while watching Verhoeven's *Basic Instinct*, in the scene that went down in history as the Flash. The actress was Sharon Stone, and although the audience had learnt in the course of the story that this *femme fatale* did not wear anything under her figure-hugging white dress, the sudden view of her femininity still hit the interviewers at the police station with the force of a sledge-hammer. They sat there like schoolboys peering through the keyhole of the girls' changing rooms, unaware that this was how their suspect expressed her contempt for them.

With this scene, Sharon Stone was catapulted into the major league of Hollywood divas. World-wide, Verhoeven's film attracted more viewers than any other film in 1992; and from then on, from Afghanistan to Zanzibar, Sharon Stone was mentioned in the same breath as Marilyn Monroe, Ava Gardner, Greta Garbo, Lauren Bacall and Bette Davis. She had grown into what the American monthly *Vanity Fair* called 'our first post-modern goddamn goddess.' After *Basic Instinct*, Sharon Stone's fee rose to $6 million per film – but the odd fact that the key to her success was to be found at a seedy student party in Leiden in 1958 was something only Paul Verhoeven knew.

Basic Instinct is the third in Paul Verhoeven's 'psychosis trilogy,' as he now calls his American films. What the three films have in common is that they each deal with two parallel realities. Officer Murphy became RoboCop, but deep in his soul he remained the human being he had once been. Arnold Schwarzenegger in *Total Recall* went through life as the construction worker Doug Quaid, but then turned out to be secret agent Hauser. And Sharon Stone's Catherine Tramell in *Basic Instinct* was also an ambiguous character who, as the story developed, kept provoking the question: was she only a writer, or also a cool calculating murderess? Michael Douglas as detective Nick Curran tried to penetrate this world of make-believe, but failed because Catherine Tramell hid behind her manipulative sexuality. Until the very end, both explanations remain a possibility for the viewer – while it is also suggested that if the murderess is not Catherine, it might be police psychologist Beth Garner (played by Jeanne Tripplehorn).

Paul Verhoeven had played with the idea of parallel realities before in *De Vierde Man*, but since working in the United States he had become more conscious of the theme. 'Maybe it's got something to do with my coming here from Holland and having two realities myself, which are of equal importance to me. In my films it is not a question of choosing between those two threads, but of handling them equally. You could say, in view of my scientific interests, that the idea has been adapted from quantum mechanics, where the starting point for current thinking is multiple universes and multiple reality. In the way I organize everyday realities, such arguments always play a role.'

In the past, he had long abstained from such metaphysical reflections in his work, for fear of once more relapsing into psychosis. This is why, in *Turks Fruit*, *Soldaat van Oranje* and *Spetters*, he chose to portray raw reality as realistically as possible. Now, in his fifties, with a solid marriage, two grown-up children, three dogs, and enough professional success to be able to call himself economically independent, he had exorcized these fears. It was time to re-examine what had always fascinated him: ambiguous reality. This is what he had done as an adolescent, when he became interested in surrealist painting and had translated that interest into cinematographic form with *Eén Hagedis Teveel* and *Niets Bijzonders*, his very first films.

It was an attack of religious fervour that had pushed him off that track in 1966. 'A psychosis is a state in which you think that life is created by your brain. A psychedelic state without drugs; as if you have fallen into a black hole from which there is no escape. The fear of becoming a prisoner of my own thoughts has played tricks on me for a long time. For example, it would still not be impossible for this room where I am now sitting in such a relaxed way to change suddenly and for me to see the most terrible monsters coming out of the walls; they all want to eat me, a bit like in Polanski's *Repulsion*. My head is still full of those kinds of fears, but now that I am so firmly rooted in reality, I have dared to let the gates of my mind swing ajar again. That is why I let the main characters in *RoboCop*, *Total Recall* and *Basic Instinct* struggle with schizophrenia and psychosis, the feelings I know so well myself. And yet I know that those gates must only stay *ajar*, because once they swing wide open, it is very difficult to close them again.'

By now, Verhoeven's everyday reality could have been called ordered, even by outsiders. The family moved to a fine wooden house in the Pacific Palisades. His wife Martine had found her niche as leader of the Santa Monica College Symphony Orchestra, and in addition gave private tuition to budding violinists. The children were studying: Claudia at the University of California in Berkeley, Heleen at the art academy in San Francisco. With his record of three box-office hits in a row Paul Verhoeven no longer needed to worry about his stature as a director, an anxiety that had long plagued him in the Netherlands.

The position he had managed to achieve was once again evident from *Première*'s Power List, where by May 1993 he had risen to number thirty-two. Although he ranked below people like Steven Spielberg, Kevin Costner, Arnold Schwarzenegger and Oliver Stone, he was above Jodie Foster, Robert Zemeckis, Jack Nicholson, Harrison Ford and Martin Scorsese. Verhoeven's status was further enhanced by the independent position he had adopted within the Hollywood community. Directors of his calibre would normally have turned to power-blocs such as International Creative Management (ICM) or Creative Artists Agency (CAA), agencies sometimes described as 'the grease in the Hollywood machine'. They have been the most significant factor in forcing up film budgets, by ensuring that 'packaging' – studios can only say Yes or No to a package of actors, writer and director put together by one of the agencies – has become the norm.

Although, as a new arrival, Verhoeven could simply have ended up on the client list of CAA founder Michael Ovitz – who, not without reason, appeared at number three on *Première*'s Power List in 1993 – the director decided to remain loyal to Marion Rosenberg, the agent who had assisted his first uncertain steps in the New World. He had met her in 1980 when *Soldaat van Oranje* had been such a success in the United States and he had needed an agent. At that time she was already looking after Rutger Hauer's interests, and after some searching, Verhoeven too recognized her as suitable. She was a sophisticated woman with thirty years' experience in the industry, during which she had co-produced some fifty films, including three with Marlon Brando.

Since the 1970s Marion Rosenberg had built up a reputation as an agent for the up-and-coming people, and from her office on Melrose she had helped many a budding talent climb the Hollywood ladder. This is exactly what she did with Paul Verhoeven – and now that he has planted his flag on Sunset Boulevard, Marion Rosenberg still represents him.

It is rare for a medium-sized agency such as hers to have such a big fish on its list; she explains. 'It is a very provocative thing to say, because it obviously alienates him from the Hollywood establishment, but Paul feels he has to stay independent. That is the way he functions best. He can then take material and actors from any source and doesn't have to rely on the big agencies, who normally dictate what is and what isn't made. I think a lot of directors envy him for that, because he has achieved a control that a lot of them don't have – they see that Paul is a maverick and how he does a lot to his own drumming.'

Rosenberg believes Paul Verhoeven needs someone like Mario Kassar, the former president of Carolco. 'Someone who will say, "Here's the cheque, go make the movie" – but that's all. As long as Paul's films make money like they do – naturally, *that* is Hollywood's bottom line – he can fly on his own radar.'

Nearly all the top directors have set up their own company in Hollywood, or have exclusive contracts with the majors, or attach their name as executive producer to other people's films, or make commercials in between, or are supervisors on television series – all ways of reinforcing their reputation. 'None of this for Paul. All he wants to do is to direct his own movies; he is a film-maker first and foremost, and the rest he is not remotely interested in.'

As an outsider, Verhoeven did not often appear at cocktail parties; the only director whom he befriended in Hollywood was John Landis. Over the years the latter has offered him many a cameo appearance in his films, but Verhoeven has always politely refused. He thinks acting is for actors. His aim is simply to maximize his hard-won artistic freedom so that he can put one of his own productions into his list of all-time favourite films – or at least the list he thought up for the celebrations of the centenary of cinema in 1995:

1. *La Dolce Vita*, Federico Fellini (1960)
2. *Some Like it Hot*, Billy Wilder (1959)
3. *Lawrence of Arabia,* David Lean (1962)
4. *Doctor Zhivago,* David Lean (1965)
5. *Touch of Evil*, Orson Welles (1958)
6. *Ivan the Terrible*, Sergei Eisenstein (1945)
7. *North by Northwest*, Alfred Hitchcock (1959)
8. *Ben-Hur*, William Wyler (1959)
9. *Metropolis*, Fritz Lang (1927)
10. *Gone with the Wind*, Fleming, Selznick (1939)

Akira Kurosawa's epic *Rashomon* (1950) might be added, Verhoeven says, as his list clearly shows his passion for big films, very big films, 'deserts in wide screen, snow as far as the eye can see, made by directors with big reputations'. This unbridled enthusiasm was what fuelled his energies, and always had done – as his teachers had noticed during the short time he studied at the Filmacademie in Amsterdam, the time he had cheekily declared that one day he wanted to make his own *Ben-Hur* or a film about Alexander the Great.

Paul Verhoeven has never made a secret of his sources of inspiration. He is happy to quote Buñuel on the 'hidden continuity of film history'. When Verhoeven surveys his own oeuvre, he has no difficulty in finding quotations from other people's work, and derives much pleasure from visually instructing himself about these with the help of his laser disc player. 'With every new project I think a long time about the visual style I am going to use. To orientate myself, I dig deep into my memory, remembering the films I saw as a boy, most of which I have on my shelves by now.'

The screen in his living room is of impressive dimensions, and the volume control is always set at ten, 'otherwise it's no fun'. Images from *Metropolis* (Fritz Lang, 1927), *North by Northwest* (Alfred Hitchcock, 1959), *Touch of Evil* (Orson Welles, 1958) and *Vertigo* (Alfred Hitchcock, 1958) flash past. Enraptured, he points to details which have stayed with him since childhood. 'You see those skeletons lying there in the underground vaults?' He points to the screen showing *Metropolis*. 'That's exactly how they are in *Total Recall*.' As proof, he shows the shot from his own movie where, deep in the caverns of the red planet, Arnold Schwarzenegger and the Martian resistance fighters are heading in the direction of rebel leader Kuato. They are indeed very similar.

The scene in the chariot race from *Ben-Hur* where the wheels crash into each other has been transferred, almost completely, to *Spetters*, where the motocross riders race side by side along the track. *Flesh + Blood* was an attempt to imitate, and perhaps even surpass, Sam Peckinpah's *The Wild Bunch* (1969), while the angular walk of Peter Weller as the half-human, half-machine in *RoboCop* was nothing more than the exaggerated acting of Eisenstein's *Ivan the Terrible* – just as the robot suit had obviously been inspired by the robot Maria from *Metropolis*. And *Basic Instinct*? This is Verhoeven's homage to Hitchcock, with a touch of Orson Welles.

He shows the famous opening sequence from *Touch of Evil*. The location is a small Mexican–American border town where a bomb attack is being carried out. First we see an anonymous hand setting the timer of a bomb; then the camera, in one fluid movement, pans silently up and down, following the villain as he puts his bomb in the back of a convertible, after which the circling camera's eye describes the surroundings, from left to right and back again – we see cameos flow uninterruptedly past the screen, we hear bits of dialogue, until Susan (Janet Leigh) and Mike Vargas (Charlton Heston) walk on to the screen. This immaculately executed crane shot takes exactly three minutes and twenty seconds. '*Basic Instinct* is highly influenced by *Touch of Evil* – especially the camera movements. The technique of the fluid, continuous camera was already evident in *film noir*, of course, but in *Touch of Evil* that fluidity reached its apogee. Not editing, but *mise en scène* – that is what I have tried to approach with *Basic Instinct*.'

With this fluid visual approach, Verhoeven broke away from the style of his previous work with its staccato, upbeat montage; although he remembers he had tried those long, uninterrupted sequences before in episode twelve of *Floris* – and of course in *De Vierde Man*. 'But in *De Vierde Man* it was even more artificial: you can clearly see that the camera is doing things that have no motives. In *Basic Instinct* the camera has a fixed position during all the scenes at the police station, and it looks as if it is led by the people who are moving around in that space, because when they turn round, the camera turns with them; in this way, all the characters at the police station are filmed almost continuously from the back. This is why it looks to the viewer as if the camera is following them everywhere, but that's all fake. *I* am leading the camera. The actors are walking past it according to a fixed pattern. From A to B to C. It is a choreography for the camera and is not determined by the people. The effect is reinforced because the actors continue to talk off screen, and the camera only returns to them later on.'

He stops the film, winds back and says, 'You watch, especially in the background. They may be moving from left to right and diagonally, but in fact they are not walking *anywhere* – they are moving around aimlessly.' This ever-moving background gives the film its pace.

The dialogues in *Basic Instinct*, however, have been filmed in a very Hitchcockian way. 'All the psychological scenes between Michael Douglas and Sharon Stone are based on quick screen changes: tak-tak-tak-tak, looking, looking back, speaking, listening.'

He takes *North by Northwest* from the shelf and talks about the dialogue between Cary Grant and Eva Marie Saint in the restaurant car of a train heading for Chicago. He, Roger Thornhill, is unjustly suspected of murder and is fleeing from the police. She, Eve Kendall, recognizes his photograph from the newspaper (and actually belongs to the camp of spy James Mason, the villain of the film). The quintessence of that dialogue, Verhoeven says, is the same erotic word game he was to use later between Sharon Stone and Michael Douglas – dialogue very daring for its time, in which Eve Kendall takes on the traditionally masculine text.

He: You feel you have seen me somewhere before? Anyhow, I have that effect on people, it is something about my face . . .

She: It's a nice face.

He: You think so?

She: I wouldn't say it if I didn't.

He: Oh, you are that type!

She: What type?

He: Honest.

She: Not really.

He: Good, because honest women frighten me.

She: Why?

He: I don't know, somehow they seem to put me at a disadvantage.

She: Because you are not honest with them?

He: Exactly . . . What I mean is, the moment I meet an attractive woman I have to start pretending I have no desire to make love to her.

She: What makes you think you have to conceal it?

He: She might find the idea objectionable.

She: But then again, she might not.

He: Think how lucky I am for being seated here.

She: Luck had nothing to do with it.

He: Fate?

She: I tipped the steward five dollars to seat you here, in case you would come in.

He: Is that a proposition?

He introduces himself as Jack Philips, western sales manager for King Bee Electronics. It then appears that Eve (who introduces herself as twenty-six and unmarried) had known all along who he really is: Roger Thornhill, wanted for murder, whose photograph is printed on the front page of every newspaper in the USA. But he need not worry.

She: Don't worry, I won't say a word.

He: How come?

She: I told you – it is a nice face.

He: Is that the only reason?

She: It's gonna be a long night.

He: True.

She: I don't particularly like the book I've started, you know what I mean?

He: Now let me think . . . Yes, I know exactly what you mean.

She takes a cigarette. He gives her a light. She takes his hand. And invites him to her cabin – E3901.

In *Basic Instinct* the conversation between Michael Douglas and Sharon Stone unfolds according to the same principle. She knows more about him than he knows about her – and she exploits it. This becomes evident when detective Nick (Michael Douglas) and his sidekick Gus come to interview Catherine Tramell on the terrace of her beach house. The Hitchcockian effect is further reinforced by the view of the cliffs, the immeasurable heights which, as the British director knew, give the viewer a vague feeling of anxiety. Transposed to the 1990s and spiced up by Verhoeven, the dialogue proceeds as follows:

Nick: Ms Tramell? I'm detecti . . .

Catherine: I know who you are. How did he die?

Gus: He was murdered.

Catherine: Obviously. How was he . . .

Nick: With an ice pick. How long were you dating him?

Catherine: I wasn't dating him. I was fucking him.

Gus: What are you – a pro?

Catherine: No. I'm an amateur.

Nick: How long were you having sex with him?

Catherine: About a year and a half.

Nick: Let me ask you something, Ms Tramell. Are you sorry he's dead?

Catherine: Yes. I liked fucking him.

And during the interrogation at the police station things are no different. Four detectives and assistant district attorney John Corelli are waiting for Catherine Tramell. When Corelli begins to talk, even the cigarette returns as a weapon.

Corelli: There's no smoking in this building, Ms Tramell.

Catherine: What are you going to do? Charge me with smoking?

After this, the role reversal is complete.

Corelli: Would you tell us the nature of your relationship with Mr Boz?

Catherine: I had sex with him for about a year and a half. I liked having sex with him. He wasn't afraid of experimenting. I like men like that. Men who give me pleasure. He gave me a lot of pleasure.

Corelli: Did you ever engage in sadomasochistic activity with him?

Catherine: Exactly what do you have in mind, Mr Corelli?

The superiority of the cool, blonde Catherine Tramell is the same as the superiority of Eva Marie Saint in *North by Northwest* – or of Kim Novak, Grace Kelly and Janet Leigh, the other unapproachable blondes who populate Hitchcock's films. 'It is nothing new to say this, but in Hitchcock's oeuvre students of film can find everything about cinematographic technique. Similarly, *Touch of Evil* should be compulsory, because the way Welles leads the camera makes the film the most interesting production of the last forty years.'

When he's as inspired as this, with his remote-control in his hand, Paul Verhoeven would not make a bad impression as a visiting lecturer at a film seminar. It is in any case interesting to hear him discuss the influence of his own films on other directors. How the water plane from *Soldaat van Oranje* turned up in *Indiana Jones and the Temple of Doom* (Steven Spielberg, 1984), for example. Or how the French director Jean-

Jacques Beineix with *Betty Blue* (*37.2° au matin*, 1986) was making an almost literal remake of *Turks Fruit*, and Beineix too received an Oscar nomination in 1987. The ironic comic-strip tone of *RoboCop*, which was copied all round, and Robovision as a way of toppling the narrative perspective. And how, ever since Sharon Stone and Rachel Ticotin in *Total Recall* didn't, as was traditional, pull at each other's hair or roll about in the mud but exhausted themselves in Dick Bos-like ju-jitsu, every fight between women in American films began to look like that macho duel filmed by Verhoeven. Not to mention the string of followers of the cop and copulation thriller, *Basic Instinct*.

With a budget of $45 million, *Basic Instinct* was originally intended to be no more than a medium-sized production. In tone and look, the script by Joe Eszterhas resembled a B-film in the tradition of *Touch of Evil*, and cameraman Jan de Bont was to shoot it in a glossy way. At first sight it was a classic whodunit, and in keeping with that genre, the protagonist has a tormented personality. Like, for example, James Stewart in his role of John 'Scottie' Ferguson in Hitchcock's *Vertigo*, Michael Douglas as police detective Nick Curran is haunted by his past. Whereas Scottie is at critical moments overcome by his pathological fear of heights – brought on by a rooftop chase where he saw his police partner fall to his death – Nick Curran's reputation is damaged by the fact that on a previous case he shot down two tourists, innocent bystanders. He is sent to police psychologist Beth Garner for therapy. Meanwhile, Nick has been given the nickname Shooter at the station because of his alcohol and cocaine abuse and his trigger-happy way of operating.

At the beginning of the film Curran has to go and investigate the murder of Johnny Boz, an ageing pop star who has been killed with an ice pick. The fact that Curran falls in love with the chief suspect, the beautiful (and bisexual) writer Catherine Tramell, does not improve his standing within the force. What makes her a suspect is the fact that, by way of research for her books, she appears to be sleeping around with real people whom she later presents as fictitious characters. The problem is that the violent way in which they usually meet their end in her books is suspiciously similar to what happens to them in real life. Coincidence?

The story had the charm of archetypal pulp fiction and was full of Hitchcockian twists. Verhoeven thought it would be a nice counterpoint to those technically complicated productions *RoboCop* and *Total Recall*. A handful of leading players, a small crew, a manageable shooting period – it seemed a sunny prospect to him. But he might have known by now that no Paul Verhoeven film is ever a small film, not even if he himself insists on it. *Basic Instinct* was to cause more commotion than any other Verhoeven film to date.

It all started with the battle for the Joe Eszterhas script. Typical of Hollywood, two former associates were trying to outbid each other. On the one hand there was the flamboyant Mario Kassar, of Italian–Arabic descent; on the other there was the former hairdresser and wigmaker Andrew Vajna, a Hungarian. In 1976 they had set up Carolco Pictures together, a company initially intended to be a film distributor. After a while, however, it began increasingly to operate as an independent film production company. Its first great success was the Sylvester Stallone vehicle *First Blood* (Ted Kotcheff, 1982), followed by two equally lucrative sequels; they also produced Verhoeven's hit *Total Recall*.

In the press, Carolco was described as a 'model indie', a shining example of a successful independent company, until financial problems began to get the upper hand; the company's sidelines in the video, music and television industries turned out to be considerably less successful. Shareholders and creditors began to complain. Andrew Vajna allowed Kassar to buy him out for $106 million, then started his own production company Cinergi. He promptly started bidding for the script Kassar wanted.

Kassar's Carolco won the contest in June 1990, but not without a struggle. The $3 million they had to pay for *Basic Instinct* was a painfully record sum. The only person looking on with a smile while the price went up was Joe Eszterhas himself, a forty-something who was well over six feet tall and had impressively long hair. Rugged in word and gesture, Eszterhas was a former *Rolling Stone* journalist, and had been the screenwriter of *Flashdance* (Adrian Lyne, 1983), *Jagged Edge* (Richard Marquand, 1985), *Betrayed* (Costa-Gavras, 1988) and *Music Box* (Costa-Gavras, 1989); he was sometimes called Hollywood's 'burliest answer to Hemingway'.

Eszterhas was more than satisfied with the record sum. 'For years and years I had been saying that a writer deserves as much money as the principals, because the writer is where it all begins – but we have always been on the bottom of the totem pole. When *Basic Instinct* was sold for $3 million it suddenly elevated the writer into an entirely new position.'

The price generated much publicity. Eszterhas thinks this was natural but exaggerated. 'The fact that Michael Douglas was paid $15 million for *Basic Instinct* didn't gather an enormous amount of publicity, because people are used to actors getting paid that well. The fact that Paul Verhoeven was paid $5 million to do *Basic* nobody wrote about, because directors get that kind of money. But the $3 million for the script was big headlines across the top of the page. And from that moment the whole project was in the middle of a goldfish bowl – it became a very, very public project.'

Carolco put producer Irwin Winkler, a friend of Joe Eszterhas, on the project. Writer and producer both thought of Miloš Forman (*One Flew Over the Cuckoo's Nest*, 1975, and *Amadeus*, 1984) to direct the film, but Mario Kassar had other ideas. On 19 July 1990 Paul Verhoeven signed the contract to make *Basic Instinct;* from *De Vierde Man*, Kassar knew that the director was adept at the psychological thriller. For his part, Verhoeven had by now acclimatized himself sufficiently to direct an American film set in the present, and thus free himself from the science-fiction label attached to him since *RoboCop* and *Total Recall*.

The news about Paul Verhoeven's involvement caused confusion to Joe Eszterhas: 'I had never met Paul; I liked *RoboCop*, but hated *Total Recall*. So I called Mario and asked him why. I wanted Miloš Forman to do it, because we had worked together before. Actually, the script had been flown to Europe, where Miloš was in the south of France on a bicycle trip. He read it, said he loved it and that he was very, very interested, but by the time we let Carolco know that Miloš wanted to do it, they said, "Forget it, we already signed Paul." It was a *fait accompli*.'

This was the beginning of what was to be a long struggle. Eszterhas went to Florida on holiday, came back in September and met Paul Verhoeven and Michael Douglas at Irwin Winkler's home. The forty-six-year-old actor had been chosen for the leading role over Mel Gibson, Kevin Costner and Richard Gere because in films such as *Fatal Attraction* (Adrian Lyne, 1987) and *Wall Street* (Oliver Stone, 1987), Douglas had shown himself particularly skilled at playing characters plagued by moral questions.

The discussions between writer and producer on the one hand, and between director and star actor on the other, turned into disasters. Paul Verhoeven proposed some amendments to the script which did not go down well with Eszterhas. What he explained to Eszterhas, Verhoeven recalls, was that as a director he had to put it together on the set and that it certainly would not work if he could not believe in the story; so they 'had better agree beforehand'. The director believed it was dramatically necessary to have a scene in which Catherine Tramell makes love to her girlfriend Roxy. Beneath the surface the entire story of *Basic Instinct* is about bisexuality, but the audience never gets to see anything about it. 'Prudish and moralistic' was Verhoeven's judgement, and without hesitation he proposed a lesbian love scene. Joe Eszterhas was not enthusiastic: 'No way, Paul, that's sensationalism.'

Eszterhas: 'It was the first time I had met the man and we got into a very, very heated argument. He saw that I was really pissed off and at one point said, "Look, I am the director, *ja*? And you are the writer. So I am right and you are wrong, *ja*?" He said it with a very aggressive tone of voice, so I yelled, "If you say that to me one more fucking time I will come across the table and hit you!" It was a bad, bad meeting.'

Michael Douglas and Verhoeven ('It was also meant to test them a bit, of course') left the room. Joe Eszterhas did too, but not before he had decided in consultation with Irwin Winkler that they would both pull out of the project. The announcement to Carolco was to be worded: 'We want to be paid our full price, but we want to have nothing to do with this movie.'

Michael Douglas felt rather unhappy about this nerve-racking meeting, but was clearly behind Verhoeven: 'I think that Irwin, being a very respectable producer, felt that, with the director already decided upon and the actor already decided upon, he was a bit trapped. He had mentioned Miloš Forman. I think he is a great director, but I told Irwin that I didn't think that *Basic Instinct* was his kind of movie; this movie is what I call a slamdance, and that is completely Paul's style. So I guess he was very disappointed.'

This news also reached the press at the point when Verhoeven still thought that within two weeks – after he had returned from a holiday – a second round of talks would follow: 'That is what had been agreed, but they simply waited until we had gone. After that Joe and Irwin were immediately bandying it around. Apparently, that's how it works in Hollywood.' Again there were big headlines in *Variety*: 'Winkler and Eszterhas pull out.' Meanwhile, Paul Verhoeven called on Gary Goldman, the writer who had been such a help to him on *Total Recall*. Together they worked on four versions of the script in accordance with the director's ideas.

At different points in the story, Goldman and Verhoeven tried to write in the lesbian love scene. 'It seemed that this lesbian relationship was being suppressed out of a kind of delicacy,' recalls Goldman, but to Paul it seemed very natural to the story. After a while we found out that putting it in would have impeded the flow of the narrative, and that the screenplay was in fact constructed so tightly that there was no place to put it in. It would slow the movie down.'

The most suitable moment seemed to be one-third of the way through the film, when Nick Curran discovers during a conversation at Catherine's home that she knows everything about him – including the conclusions of the police psychiatrist's report. Nick immediately suspects that his psychologist Beth has passed on this confidential information. Furious, he goes to settle scores with her. Then the camera was going to linger with Catherine and her girlfriend Roxy. Verhoeven explains: 'They were going to start kissing and making love, as if to say, "We don't need you, Nick, we've got each other." But when I read it again, I thought, "We can't do that." Not for moral reasons, but because the viewer's attention is not there, plot-wise that is. The viewer wants to see how Nick, in a state of fury, goes to call Beth to account. It fits better in the story, because it shows how well Catherine can manipulate and set people up against each other.'

At the end of February 1991 Joe Eszterhas received a telephone call. The slightly rewritten version of *Basic Instinct* – a number of locations had been changed, and some of the dialogue had been rewritten in the style of *North by Northwest* – was on its way to him. Would he like to read it?

He'd rather not, the writer replied – they wouldn't want him to have a heart attack, would they? It was with great suspicion that at three o'clock that afternoon he accepted delivery of the script at his home. 'I decided to read it the next morning and was thunderstruck to see that it was literally the very first draft that we had had the argument about. So I called Paul and said, "Listen, I got the script – what is going on?"'

Verhoeven cheerfully explained that this vivisection of a film script was his way of getting more familiar with the material he had to film. For *RoboCop*, for example, he had done just the same with Ed Neumeier. Verhoeven could also have mentioned his way of working with Gerard Soeteman, the scriptwriter on his Dutch films, where they sent each other versions they had rewritten separately, in the hope of meeting somewhere in the middle. Verhoeven was very familiar with this way of working, but in Hollywood, that city of large egos, it seemed impossible. The director did not give such a lengthy explanation in his conversation with Eszterhas. He simply said, 'Gary Goldman and I tried different things and none of them worked. I was wrong – how would you feel about coming back on the movie, Joe?'

Eszterhas was perplexed: 'I said, "I would be thrilled." And so one of the things I will always respect Paul for is that he publicly said, to more big headlines, "I was wrong – I didn't understand the basement of the script and I had to work through four different drafts to understand what the basement was." Now that is a very rare, ego-less thing to do in Hollywood – and I really admire the man for it.' A big reconciliatory dinner followed with Eszterhas, Verhoeven and Michael Douglas. With the exception of Irwin Winkler, who in the meantime had been replaced by the British producer Alan Marshall, everyone was back on board and smiling again. Or so it seemed.

As a result of all this publicity, the Hollywood watchers had turned their full attention to *Basic Instinct*. A month later panic broke out again. Somehow a copy of the script had got into the hands of some American groups campaigning for homosexual rights. Shocked, they concluded that the story portrayed bisexual women as psychotic murderers – and that, in their view, this had been done deliberately. There was only one word for it: homophobia. They demanded a full explanation. During preparations for shooting in San Francisco's Bay Area, the epicentre of gay America, the Queer Nation group staged a demonstration on 10 April 1991. The police arrived and put a cordon around the set. Although shooting began in the next few days, the action group GLAAD (Gay and Lesbian Alliance Against Defamation) issued a statement in which they claimed that the film would send out a dangerous message: 'The film industry bears a grave responsibility for the perpetuation of stereotypes and the dramatic increase in homophobic violence over the past few years.'

This charged language gave Paul Verhoeven the feeling he was back in the Netherlands for a moment. His work had become the target of campaigning groups as early as 1973, when the feminist-inspired Vrouwen Bevrijdings Front (Women's Liberation Front) had organized a picketline at theatres showing *Turks Fruit*; later, with *Spetters*, it had been NASA – the Nederlandse Anti-Spetters Aktie (Dutch Anti-*Spetters* Action). In addition to his cinematic talent, he had taken with him to the USA his knack for antagonizing sections of society. Although only a few people there knew of Verhoeven's reputation for this kind of thing, once again he had made it on to the front page of the newspapers, even before a single frame of the film had been shown in the cinema.

He explained that he was in no way hostile towards any form of sexual orientation, pointing to the fact that in his film *De Vierde Man* he had portrayed the homosexuality of the main character as completely natural. This achieved little. 'Not unless the script is completely rewritten and the premise changed will we stop the demonstrations,' spokesman Jonathan Katz declared on behalf of Queer Nation. Activists visited the set to shine torches into the camera. Paint was thrown and cables were cut. Demonstrators also waved American flags to encourage passing motorists to honk; they in their turn thought it was a show of support for the American troops in Kuwait, or that it had something to do with the local Forty-niners football team, and so they responded with obvious enthusiasm.

As yet, the political-correctness offensive had made little impression on the director, but scriptwriter Joe Eszterhas publicly started to have his doubts. In an attempt to make peace, the film-makers and activists met on neutral ground. On the evening of 24 April 1992, in the conference hall of the San Francisco Hyatt Hotel, director Verhoeven, scriptwriter Joe Eszterhas and producer Alan Marshall sat around the table with representatives of GLAAD, Queer Nation, ACT UP, Community United Against Violence and San Francisco's Supervisor for Homosexual Affairs, Harry Britt. The meeting took two hours. It became a bizarre show, Verhoeven remembers. 'We had agreed to stick to our guns and point to the fact that the activists were drawing rather premature conclusions. But once we were there, Joe Eszterhas made a complete U-turn.'

The proposals put forward by the activists included, among other things, that the leading role played by Michael Douglas should be rewritten for Kathleen Turner as a lesbian police inspector. In addition, Catherine Tramell and her girlfriend Roxy should murder not only men but women, to prevent the public from viewing them as archetypal man-haters. Paul Verhoeven shook his head as he listened to these suggestions, but Joe Eszterhas said that he was sympathetic to the arguments.

The writer now says, 'I had convinced Paul to do the meeting, and I found that some of the changes these people suggested could be done without hurting the plot. For every good idea at the meeting, there were ten totally crazy ones, but I particularly refer to what Harry Britt had to say – I found him a very sensitive, intelligent, interesting man and not a militant at all, so when he took offence to certain pieces of dialogue I was willing to change it.'

The reason for his sympathy was rooted in the fact that Eszterhas had emigrated to America from Hungary in 1950 as a five-year-old full of expectations, but on arrival in Ohio he had been bullied at school. His accent and culture were ridiculed, and at the age of fourteen, in the agony of being an outcast, he nearly killed another teenager with a baseball bat.

It was the same rage, he says, that he later put to paper. 'Because of that great prejudice I always had a lot of affinity with the minorities. I actually wrote two films – Betrayed and Music Box – dealing with prejudice against Jews, so I didn't want anything that I had written to cause harm, especially to a minority group like gay people. And I said, "Let's make some changes." But Paul said, "We don't have to make the changes. The way I shoot it, I promise you, is not gonna harm anyone."'

Verhoeven saw Eszterhas's changed views as desertion. The evening concluded with Verhoeven stating that at the very most, and without any further commitment, he would be prepared to look at Eszterhas's script changes. Five days later, Eszterhas presented his proposals. He had included a remark which Michael Douglas had to make to his partner Gus when they take a close look at the potential suspect, Catherine Tramell: 'A lot of the best people I've met in this town are gay.' In addition, Eszterhas wanted to tone down the scene in which Michael Douglas more or less indecently assaults his police psychiatrist and former girlfriend Beth (out of frustration over his failed advances to Catherine) – as well as a notice on the screen beforehand: 'The movie you are about to see is fiction. Its gay and bisexual characters are fictional and not based on reality.' The director did not like the changes at all.

Thus Eszterhas suddenly found himself in a painful as well as ironic position. 'I was arguing to make changes to my own script and it was the director who was saying, "No, your script is fine, we won't make any changes."' Again the writer retired. Again with doors slamming.

The affair became so heated that Verhoeven decided to defend his artistic freedom, and on his behalf Carolco took the matter to court. A week later, San Francisco Superior Court Judge John Dearman ruled that the activists had to stay approximately one hundred yards from the film locations, and were in addition forbidden to use torches. Nevertheless, Verhoeven was barracked on his daily trip to the set. Producer Alan Marshall tried to shield him as much as possible. Accompanied by police, Marshall took up his position in front of the activists. Whenever he deemed it necessary, he made a citizen's arrest. The court decision gave him the power to have activists who came too close to the set removed.

To Michael Douglas it was a most unpleasant situation, and not just because of the death threats he received. 'For me it was hard, because for four years I did this television series *The Streets of San Francisco*. It was where my career began – so I didn't enjoy militant people screaming at me. There we were, making what was meant to be a little psycho thriller and all of a sudden we were of sociological importance – we made it to the nightly news headlines. It was just wild. After Joe's chickening out, I felt that I had to support Paul – and the funny thing is that part of Paul got really excited. He loves debate, he loves controversy. We also realized that their demonstrations would help the film a lot – and that is exactly what happened.'

Verhoeven: 'I was so annoyed that I shot the date-rape scene between Nick and Beth so that there was very little leeway – only to show how far you can go as a film-maker before it becomes banal. The script only touches on that meeting – but I thought, "If they want to take offence at something that much, then I'll give them something to take offence at!"' Thus we see in the film how the frustrated Nick brutishly throws the police psychiatrist over a chair and tears off her clothes. Michael Douglas followed the director's vision – as early as the rehearsals he went into another gear for this scene. Verhoeven: 'Very brave of Michael Douglas to play that so explicitly, because at that moment he did not say, as so many stars in Hollywood would have done, "This is too risky, I have to think of my audience, I mustn't alienate them."'

The outdoor shoots in San Francisco were completed on 9 May 1991, and then filming continued for another two months behind closed doors at the Warner Hollywood studios. The activists did not find another opportunity until a year later: at the première of *Basic Instinct* on 20 March 1992. They handed out leaflets saying 'Catherine did it!' and again referred to the film's supposedly homophobic character. The activity soon died down, however, when it appeared that none of the audiences had found any basis for the accusations.

Verhoeven received support from the reviews: 'This film is far too bizarre and singular to be constructed as homophobic, but the bisexuality helps to undermine any possibility of real closeness between the story's men and women, which is apparently the point,' the *New York Times* wrote.

Even Joe Eszterhas, who had been to see the film in his local cinema – after all the rows he had not been invited to the screenings or to the gala première – had to admit to the television crew who had followed him closely: 'I think Paul Verhoeven was absolutely right that it hurt no one. I am happy that he had the wisdom to turn down my changes. It is a dazzling piece of entertainment, with many great layers and I think that ultimately the movie will be judged as a classic of the genre. I am proud of the movie, and as soon as I get home I will congratulate him and send him a case of champagne the next morning.' And so he did.

The director himself had thought from the beginning that all the commotion was a load of nonsense. At some point, he remembers, they even tried to pin it on him that the film was 'anti-obese people', because Nick's voluminous sidekick Gus (George Dzundza) comes to such a sticky end. It seemed to Verhoeven that all these criticisms came from outsiders who in their hankering after politically correct action had lost all sight of reality. 'But what I was most disappointed by is that, after seeing the film, the activists did not even take the trouble to write a note, as if to say, "Sorry, we were wrong." In my eyes that would have done them considerable honour.'

The troubled relationship between Paul Verhoeven and Joe Eszterhas had a happier ending. Eszterhas simply wrote another script for the director entitled *Showgirls*. Both value their relationship. As Joe Eszterhas says, 'I guess I am Paul's favourite enemy.'

'Ultimate evil to ultimate charm' was how Paul Verhoeven wanted to present his leading lady Sharon Stone as Catherine Tramell. This idea was based on a short moment in *Total Recall*, just before the scene in which Quaid shoots her through the head with a 'Consider this a divorce'. Sharon Stone as Lori has just been in a fight with her rival Melina and has a grim, determined look on her face. When she notices that Quaid wants to liquidate her, her expression changes in two seconds from extremely vicious to silky smooth. She says, 'Doug . . . you wouldn't hurt me, would you, honey?'

Verhoeven thought that if Sharon Stone could put this much ambiguity into a scene, she might also be able to maintain such changing moods throughout a film. When an 'airplane version' of *Total Recall* had to be made for intercontinental flights, and the sound track had to be adapted because of the language used, he invited the thirty-three-year-old actress to do a screen test.

The tape of the screen test for *Basic Instinct* is still in Verhoeven's possession. The director can be seen in the role of Michael Douglas, and Sharon Stone plays Catherine Tramell. The scene is the detective's interview with the suspect: Sharon Stone makes eyes at him, smokes, flirts, is silent, sighs, but remains equally untouchable under all circumstances – while off screen Verhoeven tries to tighten the screws on her: 'Let me ask you something, Ms Tramell. Are you sorry he's dead?'

The way in which Sharon Stone is prepared to follow all the director's instructions unintentionally betrays how desperate she was to play the role of Catherine – despite the inferior quality of the home video, she radiates blonde ambition. 'Sharon knows exactly what she wants,' Paul Verhoeven explains, 'and she also knows exactly how to get it.' This is something she had in common with the character of Catherine Tramell, or as the director told the American press at the time of the première, 'Sharon is Catherine without the killing, *ja*?'

Initially, other people were less convinced of this. Michael Douglas had rather hesitated to begin with: 'I always hoped for an actress of equal stature – I wanted two names up there to share the risk, because I knew from the beginning that it would be a very realistic and graphic movie.' Geena Davis was asked. Michelle Pfeiffer. Lena Olin. Ellen Barkin. Julia Roberts. Greta Scacchi. But none of these ladies wanted to be filmed completely in the nude, partly because the director had made the intention of his film quite clear. 'You know Paul . . . [does an imitation of a Dutch accent] . . . it's like "YAH, YAH, there is nud-it-ty, nud-it-ty, *ja*? Show your breasts." He is like an X-ray machine.'

Verhoeven got his way. But before the decision was taken to cast Sharon Stone, he had considered giving the role of Catherine Tramell to the Dutch actress Renée Soutendijk, his leading lady in *De Vierde Man*. This film had made her familiar with the role of the *femme fatale*, as was evident from the successful screen test she had made in Hollywood. However, she was not given cast because Verhoeven realized more and more that this particular role would not have been such a surprise to Americans if a European actress had played it. 'They would have reacted along the lines of "Sure, she is a slightly crazy, weird and dangerous lady, but she comes from decadent Europe, so what else do you expect?"'

Verhoeven decided it had to be an intelligent Californian beach-babe, a girl next door, with whom the American public could completely identify. He kept coming back to Sharon Stone. 'After every test with another actress I said to the people at Carolco, "Have another look at Sharon as well." And then they always said, "Yes, she is more suited, but we can't cast her because she is not well known." Finally they had their backs to the wall, because we were about to start shooting.'

Now that Michael Douglas and Sharon Stone had been cast, Verhoeven was able to explain, with the help of storyboards he had sketched himself, what kind of film he wanted to make. Sharon Stone was particularly struck by the acrobatic content of the love scenes. 'When Paul showed me the storyboards, I thought, "Jesus Christ, I'm going to be sitting on my shins." I not only have to do a complete back-bend, but I also have to pull myself back up without using my hands. And then make it look as if I'm getting off. This athletic feat would take a lot of work. It took some training to get my quadriceps strong enough so that I could manage it. I also had to be flexible enough to be able to do it fifty billion times so we could do all the takes,' the actress told *Playboy* at the première of *Basic Instinct*.

It was a relaxed interview, in which reporter David Sheff treated Sharon Stone with respect. What the new star had forgotten to tell him was that at the beginning of the ninety-four shooting days for *Basic Instinct*, they had seriously considered firing her. The breaking point came when the dialogue in the house by the sea had to be shot – the scene where the detectives Nick and Gus try to question Catherine about the murder of her friend Johnny Boz.

Verhoeven: 'She was so good on the test tape, but this was a disaster! We had to shoot that dialogue again and again. At one point she was completely in tears, and we thought about giving up Sharon altogether. Then I talked to her all night, along the lines of, "Of course you can act, Sharon. We made that tape, remember?" And the next morning it went click! As if by magic she had turned back into the cool and cunning ice princess which she had to be as Catherine Tramell.'

As director of photography, Jan de Bont was responsible for the camera work on *Basic Instinct*. He remembers: 'With Sharon, Paul was remarkably patient in explaining what he had in mind. He was so convinced she had to play that role that he invested all his energy in it. That meeting by the sea had to be done about twenty times – it didn't look like anything at all. But Paul persisted while the rest were looking at their feet in embarrassment. To help him, I sometimes said, "Sorry, Paul, it was out of focus" – also not to offend Michael Douglas too much, because he always recorded his takes effortlessly.'

Verhoeven: 'The point is Sharon *can* act, but she does not know how to get at her own talent. I was the first director who was able to press the right buttons with her. And she knows it. There had never been anybody with so much vision of her, no one who was prepared to climb that entire mountain with her. There had not been anyone who cared enough about her to draw out the talent within her, like a sculptor does with a piece of stone.'

During the shooting, Michael Douglas became irritated by this unequal distribution of Verhoeven's attention. 'They had this very complicated relationship going on that I never understood exactly.

Meanwhile, I felt I was being taken for granted. All the focus was on her part, but for me it was a very hard shoot too, because my character is almost in every single scene of the movie.' Or to put it more graphically: 'The hardest thing was the physical exhaustion of trying to create what in the script was called "the fuck of the century" over eight complete shooting days. It had to be like a dance. A choreography. A fight sequence. All the moves have to be natural, look real. When you do a love scene, everybody in the audience becomes a judge. When you see an ice pick or somebody gets shot, it probably never happens in your life – but love-making is something we all do.' Sharon Stone also recalls the shooting of the sex scenes with mixed feelings, although initially she had no hesitations. 'It took me a while to realize that everybody in the room knew me better than my gynaecologist does.' Paul Verhoeven realized that for all concerned the love scenes were a trial, both physically and psychologically. During the shooting, the number of people present – in terms of lighting, camera, sound, director and actors – had been kept to a minimum. His directions, however, sounded less well prepared. For days he exhausted himself with encouragements like 'Fine, go and lie on top of each other. Start moving. OK, stick your tongue out. Can you lick her? Can you lick her nipple a little bit more? Or his nipple?'

The reason for filming the love-making so extensively was because Verhoeven, who had got wise after earlier experiences, felt that the American film board MPAA might have difficulty with the explicit images. For every close shot he also took a medium one just in case, and for every medium shot he also recorded a wide shot. Thus he would have sufficient material on the editing table to be able to deal with the film censorship in a subtle way. To the actors this meant three times as much work. To Michael Douglas, three times as much annoyance. 'Still I would not hear anything from Paul. Towards the end that became very frustrating.'

Tensions rose so high that it was rumoured Michael Douglas had punched the director in the face. The crew had seen Verhoeven enter the actor's trailer, and the next thing they saw was the director in a blood-stained shirt leave by ambulance in the direction of the hospital.

Verhoeven: 'We had been shooting for about twelve weeks and I had a meeting with Michael that morning. He was livid because he had never heard from me what I thought of his acting. Which is true, because I am not someone who keeps exclaiming, "Fantastic! – we'll do it once more!" I'm more like "Yes, that's good. Next shot." If an actor hears something from me, it usually means *that it is not good*. Michael became very unsure about the lack of compliments. It was such a strange role, anyway – one in which he had to expose himself completely. The reality was that he always acted so on target that I thought, what a professional! Where

Sharon needed ten takes, he did it in two. Actually, I thought it would be a bit patronizing to keep congratulating him on that. I thought, "That guy knows his job so well, he really does not need my applause to understand that he is doing it right." That was also because I was used to Arnold as a star. As a European, he doesn't at all want to hear from me how good he is. So whenever I said to him, "OK, next shot," Arnold naturally thought, "Great, that's going nice and quick!"'

Douglas interpreted the director's signals, or lack of them, completely differently. Verhoeven's remark in the trailer that the rushes looked great was interpreted by him merely as a compliment to Jan de Bont. For weeks, he had been grinding his teeth while Verhoeven gave all his attention and affection to Sharon Stone. Douglas and Verhoeven did not hit each other in the face, but they did strike their fists on the table. When Verhoeven walked back to his own trailer, a vein in his nose broke as a result of the tension and he was unable to stop the bleeding. He was kept in hospital for a few days' observation. In the Netherlands, Verhoeven would have been sent home the same day, but in America he had to submit to a situation in which the hospital's fear of a court case far outweighed the demands of a Hollywood production. 'The funny thing was that my nose is not usually my weak spot. Normally I get nauseous and start to vomit because of the tension.'

The row with Douglas was resolved, although the tabloids insisted that they would be happy to drink each other's blood. 'We talked it through. Michael performs perfectly in *Basic Instinct* – every time I watch the film he becomes better and better. Part of his own persona is, of course, exactly the shadowy side which Joe Eszterhas had written for his character.'

But the fact remained that Michael Douglas had had to get used to Verhoeven's distinctive way of working from the very first take. 'The most difficult aspect of being an actor with him is that Paul hears the rhythm and the melody of the movie in his head. All he wants to do is to replicate this pace in the picture. Anything different from that he is not interested in. Paul is living his movie. It is classic European, where as an actor your job and role is not so much to interpret, but to try to fulfil the director's vision. He would say, "Just trust me, *ja*."'

Then Verhoeven would once more act out what he meant in front of the amazed Douglas. Sometimes, when he had had enough, the actor would say, 'You do the part, Paul, I'll give you my voice, OK?' The other thing that worried him during shooting was whether the audience would find the story credible. 'In all of his stories Joe Eszterhas plays this great chess game – back and forth, back and forth – but most of the time he doesn't know how to finish it.'

Douglas's worries were understandable. The plot, which Verhoeven called 'the game of two parallel realities', hinged on the possibility that either the brunette police psychologist Beth or the blonde writer Catherine Tramell was the killer. At the end of the film it is suggested that Beth, dressed in a blond wig, is the killer; but as we see Catherine Tramell again making love to detective Nick, her hand gropes around under the bed for the dreaded ice pick, which the viewer knows to be the murder weapon.

The ambiguity of the ending went too far for reviewer David Hansen, as is obvious from his remarks in *Newsweek*: 'It's hard to believe the man who made *The Fourth Man* (a good film about a murderous *femme fatale*) found a shred of psychological plausibility in the ham-fisted Eszterhas script . . . Funniest of all is that this whodunit gets so tangled up in its twists that half the audience can't figure out who did dunit when it's over.' His criticism turned out to be the exception. The *New York Times* said, '*Basic Instinct* transfers Mr Verhoeven's flair for action-orientated material to the realm of Hitchcockian intrigue, and the results are viscerally effective even when they don't make sense. Drawing powerfully on the seductiveness of his actors and the intensity of their situation, Mr Verhoeven easily suspends all disbelief.'

And that is what it was all about: suspending disbelief. From Hitchcock to Brian de Palma, from Orson Welles to Paul Verhoeven, directors of thrillers were always tested by this one criterion. Whoever failed was laughed at. Whoever succeeded would prove himself a professional. The principle is enunciated on page 21 of the *Basic Instinct* script, when Catherine summarizes her job as a writer: 'It teaches you to lie. You make things up, but they have to be believable; it's called suspension of disbelief.'

It was down to the director and to the director alone, Michael Douglas believes, that the critics and the public wanted to follow the 'chess game' in *Basic Instinct*, although the discussions about who was guilty continued for months after the première. Before and during the shooting, the director and leading actor had often talked about the inconclusive ending. When Verhoeven had been trying to rewrite the script with Goldman, they had looked for less ambiguity, but they realized that the obvious options – Sharon kills Douglas or Douglas kills Sharon – would not help the story. The viewer had to decide, although Verhoeven never had any doubt. Catherine was the murderer because Catherine was the Devil.

Michael Douglas: 'What Paul did so well with *Basic Instinct* was he told the audience that the Devil doesn't carry big horns or a tail, nor does he have bad breath. No, the Devil comes as the most seductive, sexy, wonderful and evil thing on earth – and then it kills you! I mean, people take liquor and drugs that in the end make them puke, but they'll take it anyway because in the beginning it makes them feel good. During the shoot Paul spoke strongly about good and evil, and about Sharon being the representation of the Devil. His directing gave *Basic Instinct* this gothic, slightly larger-than-life quality. Naturally, there is no woman like Catherine Tramell, so brilliant, so beautiful and so exciting. She's a metaphor, a moral dilemma. Nick is trying to recover, to rehabilitate himself – but the darker part of his soul still wants to be seduced by everything that is bad for him. That is where all the fury comes from. Nick is torn apart.'

Sharon Stone had already explained in an interview in *Playboy* how she saw Catherine: a sociopath driven by the need for power. A bird of prey. 'She is so raw and willing to go anywhere to pull Nick into her web. She'll seduce him in her mind, she'll seduce him with her sexuality. And when she sees that something "gets" him, it makes her all the more excited.' Above all, she concluded, the creation of Catherine was 'a male sexual fantasy. I don't know any woman who is gonna like jump down on the bed and have three orgasms in four minutes.' In her view, Paul, Michael and scriptwriter Joe Eszterhas were all macho men who were extremely wellmatched. And in April 1992 in *Entertainment Weekly* she said of 'the fuck of the century': 'I think they should have cut to Michael at the end of the sex scene and he should have been smoking an *entire* pack of cigarettes, like twenty of them all around his mouth.'

Sharon Stone says it laughingly but also in the knowledge that because of the masculine way in which she had played Catherine Tramell, she had become one of the guys. From *Sliver* (1993) to the Cannes Festival in 1995 she would continue to wave her skirt on request.

'A complex, compelling, Nietzschean *Überfräulein* who owns everything about her own power,' said Naomi Wolf, author of *The Beauty Myth*, in April 1993 when asked by *Vanity Fair* what she thought of Sharon Stone as Catherine Tramell. In the same article, Camille Paglia, the influential post-feminist essayist, also spoke enthusiastically about Verhoeven's new image of woman: '*Basic Instinct* has to be seen as the return of the *femme fatale*, which points up woman's dominance of the sexual realm, and Sharon Stone's performance was one of the great performances by a woman in screen history. That interrogation scene in the police station became one of the classic scenes in Hollywood cinema! There you see it all: all those men around her, and a fully sexual woman turns them to jelly. The men are enslaved by their own sexuality.'

In all their simplicity, these were the Three Seconds that Shook the World – the shot which made the police interrogation in *Basic Instinct* one of the most sniggered-at scenes in film history. To put Sharon Stone in a hostile environment without underwear was a decidedly Paul

Verhoeven-type stunt, with acknowledgements to the woman in Leiden in 1958. Verhoeven knew that if he inserted at least one ground-breaking element into the film – an image that everyone would talk about – the public would also be prepared to come and view the rest of the story. He surprised even the writer of *Basic Instinct*. Joe Eszterhas: 'What he did so brilliantly – because this whole scene is about using her sexuality to beat these guys up – is that he made it much more direct with that flash. When I saw the movie for the first time, the entire theatre went "Ooooooooooh, my God!" when that happened. They couldn't believe what they were seeing – including my sixteen-year-old son who was sitting next to me. After the show, we walked out of the theatre and my son, who had really loved the movie, said, "God, dad, God, that scene – how did you come up with the idea of doing that scene where she flashes?" And I said, "Sorry son, it was all Paul Verhoeven's idea." And I felt that it was gonna break his heart.'

Whatever the cultural or philosophical terms in which Naomi Wolf and Camille Paglia explained the scene, or however dramatically important it was in the eyes of Joe Eszterhas, it was Sharon Stone who most objected to it. During the publicizing of *Basic Instinct* at the Cannes Festival in May 1992 – the film was scheduled to open the festival – she was still seen cheerfully posing arm-in-arm with Verhoeven in front of the cameras, but in interviews she gave off very different signals. Stone said she had been misled by Verhoeven. He had promised her that the shot would be taken in semi-darkness. He had proved to be a liar. The reporters wanted to know whether this was one of those typical love–hate relationships between star and director. 'Yes,' Stone had answered, 'Paul loves me and I hate him.'

Meanwhile, Paul Verhoeven watched from the sidelines with a mixture of amusement and amazement. As he remembered it, there had been consultation between star and director before and after the take, and Sharon Stone had said that the shot was a very good idea. She had asked if it could be shot at the end of the day for reasons of privacy. 'Before the take she gave me her pants, as if to say, "There you are, Paul, that's for you."' Sharon Stone did not regret her gift until a private screening at Carolco when, surrounded by her manager Chuck Binder and some of her friends, she was again confronted by the shot, and the others made denigrating remarks about it. The cliché appeared to be true: in Europe, sexuality was treated in a much more candid way than in the United States, where it remained obstinately taboo. In the American version of *Basic Instinct*, four important scenes were cut after seven reapprovals, or the MPAA would not have given its usual R rating. In comparison with the uncut European version, it was the opening shot (the murder of Johnny Boz), the so-called 'date rape' scene between Michael Douglas and his psychiatrist Beth, the long love scene between Douglas and Stone, as well as the murder of Nick's partner Gus, which were drastically cut – despite the fact that many a 'European' medium shot had already been replaced by an 'American' wide shot. It was not only the board of film censors that was in puritan mood. Verhoeven had noticed that even in the original Joe Eszterhas script, it said before the three long love scenes, 'It is dark. We cannot see clearly.' 'I asked him, "What do you mean by that? Do I have to film six pages from the script in the dark or something?" Surely that's enough to drive anyone round the bend? Surely people can leave the light on when they make love? I don't like making love in semi-darkness either. The more light the better, actually. It is quite nice to see what you are doing.'

Both in his films and in his personal life, Paul Verhoeven has always practised a free sexual morality of which he makes no secret. What shocked Hollywood, he says, is that Catherine Tramell is capable of sex without love, an attitude at odds with the romanticism that the film industry had propagated for so long. 'All chaste nonsense, of course. Surely fucking is an underrated form of expression, of communication? I've been to bed with enough women who thought sex without love was fine.' Later Verhoeven would add in the gay magazine *The Advocate*: 'Sex is a form of play – doing what you did when you were four or five years old and were playing in the street with your friends. Once you are grown up, it is difficult to be playful, but one of the ways you can is with sex. It is a way of showing yourself: That's how I'm made. This is what I like. Caress me here. Tickle me there.'

The once-timid student from Leiden, who had blushed at the exhibitionist partygoer in 1958, and his wife Martine had initially had an 'open marriage', as was fashionable during the sexual revolution of the 1970s. 'In the circles in which we moved, that was the norm at the time; the experiments were an inextricable part of being an artist. That sudden openness suited me quite well. I knew very little about women, and in this way I could catch up; also there was no fear of AIDS then, of course.' With their move to the United States, both partners returned to monogamy, aware that short-lived affairs often led to painful court cases and compensation claims.

Paul Verhoeven brought in another rule. Although it was quite possible to fall in love during the days of shooting, in the hot-house atmosphere of highs and lows shared with the crew, a director should never court his leading lady: 'It destroys the magic.' It is a lesson history taught him. 'After Roberto Rossellini married Ingrid Bergman in 1950, nothing more became of her.' There had certainly been a deep relationship between him and Sharon, but in the interests of the film it had never been physically consummated – although that was certainly what was being written at the time. 'The film is so good because our interest in each other was sublimated into an artistic performance. And I also think that an affair with Sharon would have absolutely led me to the Devil.'

For Verhoeven, the devilish sex and the flirtation with sadomasochism indulged in by Sharon Stone in *Basic Instinct,* and later described by her as 'macho male sexual fantasies', were based on reality. 'I know a woman who told me, after we had had a drink, that she was so aggressive with sex that she had to put gloves on when she was going to make love, otherwise she would completely rip her lover's body apart. She said, "I can't understand it, but at the moment I get my orgasm, I actually want to kill him." That intertwining of love and death is an age-old phenomenon.'

The businesslike tone in which the director talked about sex tallied with the nonchalance he displayed on the evening after the famous shot, when he presented Sharon Stone's pants to his wife Martine. With Dutch soberness, she put them in the laundry basket; they thought their daughters might make good use of them.

28 April 1995. Paul Verhoeven with his wife, Martine, as he receives a knighthood from Mattie Peters, the Consul General of the Netherlands, in Los Angeles. 'I believe the Queen has always been a fan of mine.'

Showgirls: the goddess number.

Showgirls: Paul Verhoeven with Elizabeth Berkley and Glenn Plummer.

Chapter 15

Gambling in Vegas: *Showgirls*

'Okido!' – he means *'Action!'* With the tip of his tongue showing, Paul Verhoeven is standing in the back of a pick-up truck. He is surrounded by lights, cameras and monitors. The archaic filler word 'okido' is part of his personal film vocabulary, but everyone seems to understand his instructions.

Kyle MacLachlan, the cool leading man of Verhoeven's new film *Showgirls*, gets into a red Ferrari and drives off into the night with leading lady Elizabeth Berkley. The truck with Verhoeven also starts to move. The camera is rolling and with the Ferrari in view they are on their way to a scene on the Strip. 'Where are we going? You'll have to give me directions,' says MacLachlan disingenuously; he plays entertainment director Zack Carey in the film. 'Your place,' Berkley replies. In *Showgirls* she's the young dancer Nomi Malone who intends to use her sexuality to benefit her career.

It is November 1994. Paul Verhoeven has descended with his crew on Las Vegas, Nevada, the world headquarters of bad taste. This is where *Showgirls* is set, a story which will make Verhoeven's previous film *Basic Instinct* look like *Bambi*, as one of the director's assistants put it. The Joe Eszterhas script faintly resembles *All About Eve*, the classic 1950 backstage movie by Joseph L. Mankiewicz – so Verhoeven tends to refer to *Showgirls* as 'All About Evil'.

In the film, Nomi is a runaway who hitchhikes to Las Vegas to find a new life. She lands a job in a grubby strip-club, the Cheetah, but she wants to work in the Stardust, the luxurious casino show. She will pursue her ambition unscrupulously to the top, culminating in the moment when she literally throws her main rival Cristal Connors (Gina Gershon) down the stairs. None of the other dancers says anything. The realization that everyone will now move up one place pushes all moral objections to the background. At most they think, 'Shit happens.' 'There is always somebody younger and hungrier than you coming down the stairs after you. How else do you think I got my first lead?' Cristal forgives her rival

261

Nomi at the end of the film, after the two dancers have waged a life-and-death battle.

This is the gist of the story, but *Showgirls* is in fact a realistic portrait of Las Vegas the 'sin city', where the typically American cocktail of money and sex rules – even if much of it happens under a veil of hypocrisy. With great pleasure, Verhoeven has come here to lift the veil: 'Telling is showing, isn't it?' Now that he has completed his imaginative 'psychosis trilogy' of *RoboCop*, *Total Recall* and *Basic Instinct*, he thinks it would be interesting this time to film an unflinchingly realistic portrait of present-day America. And where can you find a sharper enlargement of the New World than in Las Vegas?

In the American experience, Las Vegas is not just a city. It is a psychological experiment. Just like Nomi in the film, everyone who passes through thinks they are cleverer, more beautiful, richer and luckier in gambling and love than they really are. In 1994 gamblers gambled away $5 billion there. Every year, the highest suicide rate in the USA is recorded there.

These statistics do not diminish the mythic proportions of this desert city. Although, geographically speaking, Las Vegas should have been nothing more than a railroad whistle-stop, it grew into a metropolis where hundreds of aircraft land every day. To the arriving partygoers Las Vegas feels like the last real frontier of the United States, a mental borderland of which Mario Puzo once said in his book *Inside Las Vegas*, 'On a three-day visit to Vegas you can have one of the best times of your life. To do that you have to forget about great museums, the pleasure of reading, great theatre, great music, stimulating lectures by great philosophers, great food, great wine and true love.'

And yet, Puzo concluded, Las Vegas is the most effective dream democratic capitalism has managed to produce. The fact that this occurred thanks to the bankroll of the noted murderer and gangster Ben 'Bugsy' Siegel only increases the mythic content. And it does not apply only to men, because the female equivalent of the fortune-hunter is the Weekend Call Girl. She has a respectable job in Los Angeles or New York during the week and takes a flight to Vegas on Friday night to spend the weekend searching for her probably old but certainly wealthy dream prince.

Meanwhile, the film crew have moved to the Riviera Casino on the Strip. A corner of the auditorium has been reserved and Paul Verhoeven is busy with his leading lady Elizabeth Berkley. A patient mentor, he explains what he intends to do with the scene, and is not ashamed to whisper words of encouragement into the actress's ear. He caresses and embraces her, cracks jokes with her – all of which is intended to put Elizabeth, his material, at her ease. If necessary, Verhoeven does exactly the same with her opposite number Gina Gershon. The rivalry between the two actresses can be sensed both on and off the screen, but Verhoeven realizes this can only help the film. It is now one o'clock in the morning. Page 5 of the script reads:

They are in the casino. There are hundreds of people even at this hour. There are slot machines everywhere – the pulsating hum and ever-present jingle of machine and money that is Vegas. She (Nomi) stares wide-eyed at this glittering, swirling world.

While technicians lay down cables and put up lights, the numerous Elvis imitators continue crooning outside the casino. They take in all manner of variations: from the young Elvis to the one with the side whiskers and the paunch. Inside, the Bill & Mary Sixpacks shuffle through the hall from fruit machine to fruit machine. They are holding plastic cups full of quarters and will not be distracted from their search for happiness.

Only ten years ago, the Strip was a centre for more carnal pleasures, but Las Vegas has changed its image. They now want to bring respectable family entertainment here, as if it were a Disney theme park for gambling-crazy people. Superficially, this has been achieved. In 1994 *Time* called Las Vegas 'a hyper-eclectic, twenty-four-hour-a-day party machine' and in Caesar's Palace alone the sun sets six times an hour by means of light effects. The MGM Grand – with five thousand rooms the biggest hotel in the world – opened in 1993. Its competitor, the Luxor, was erected in 1994 as an enormous pyramid of dark glass – larger, of course, than the Cheops original and including a reproduction of Tutankhamen's tomb.

Only two blocks behind the glossy façades of the new hotels, the grubby dance clubs have not changed. The advertising leaflets handed out everywhere show dazzling, half-naked dancers, strippers and escorts. They promise 'the hottest completely nude girls in Vegas' and invite you to 'discover the secret pleasures of the Orient'. During their excursion to prepare *Showgirls*, Verhoeven and Eszterhas saw that the reality of Las Vegas was to be found in clubs such as the Cheetah ('Come rumble in our jungle – be wild'), the Crazy Horse and the Palomino. 'The general idea about Las Vegas', says Eszterhas, 'is that it is solely about money, but that is puritan hypocrisy. Vegas is about sex. And the casino hotels know it, because they run coach trips to this sexual wilderness.'

It was in these obscure places of entertainment that Eszterhas and Verhoeven found the working mothers, derailed students, dumped weekend call girls and runaway teenagers who would serve as a model for *Showgirls*. They all made a living by stripping night after night or by treating visiting businessmen to a 'lap dance' in their private cabins. This consists of a stripper wiggling her bottom on the lap of a client. She is allowed to be naked, but he is not. The other rules are that the client cannot touch the girl or seek genital relief with his zip undone. If he does this an angry rebuke awaits him, which only a big tip can make up. 'The first time I saw a lap dance,' Joe Eszterhas says, 'I immediately realized that it is the manifestation of consumer sex in the era of AIDS. It is intercourse without intercourse.'

By letting the character of Nomi make the transition from the underbelly of the city to the glamorous casinos of the Strip, *Showgirls* is able to portray both milieux. From the outside it is the difference between night and day, but from the inside it is no less base – with the only difference that in clubs such as the Cheetah the pretensions have been shed along with the clothes a long time ago.

'I trust Paul completely,' says Elizabeth Berkley when asked about the many nude scenes she will have to play. Meanwhile, the director discusses the camera movements of the steadycam with Jost Vacano, his director of photography. 'Circle around Elizabeth's face,' he says, and illustrates the idea by making a frame with his thumbs and index fingers. Gesticulating, Verhoeven goes up to his leading lady with the camera running after him. Now that he has tied his blue sweater around his waist, the crew know that the director is in his element. 'Paul is the circus director,' a female camera assistant says, 'and we are the clowns. His clowns.' It is meant as a compliment.

'Rolling. We're rolling,' someone says, and the scene comes to life. In the background a number of cameos, dressed up in Halloween horror-clothes, cross the frame. Elizabeth Berkley walks up to a fruit machine. She pushes coins into the machine and pulls the handle. 'Cut!' Verhoeven suddenly orders, with the tone of a general. Everyone looks up, surprised. The New York actor Michael Cooke, who has flown in specially to portray a greasy type who addresses four sentences to Nomi at the gambling machine ('You lose all your money, honey?') is thrown off balance for a moment. Since nine o'clock this evening he has been rehearsing to anyone who wants to hear ('You wanna make some more – it won't take us longer than fifteen minutes?'), but now that it's his turn, he has a mental block. 'I thought take six was the best, Paul,' Cooke remarks, still cheerful after numerous takes. Verhoeven looks at him searchingly. Outside, morning has broken.

After Verhoeven had completed *Basic Instinct*, *Showgirls* had not been his only option. Mike Medavoy, the man who had invited him to the USA to make *RoboCop*, had once explained to him that it was wise to work on several projects at the same time – in Hollywood, projects come and go. Verhoeven realized how sound this advice was when he saw two projects collapse in a short space of time. First there was *Mistress of the*

Sea, a pirate saga with a leading role intended for Geena Davis and with finance from Columbia. The story was specially written by Michael Christopher for a female protagonist, the privateer Ann Bonney; she was strong, sensual and, when necessary, opportunistic. Because of his childhood fondness for Errol Flynn spectacles, Verhoeven was particularly looking forward to the project. He remembers that Columbia initially had no objection to the explicit script, but when it became clear that the film needed a budget of at least $75 million, the mood changed. According to the rules of Hollywood, the film now needed an equal male lead, since a woman alone would not guarantee a box-office hit. Harrison Ford was mentioned, but the director did not want to compromise. 'It was essential to make Ann Bonney superior to the men. The chaos surrounding *Flesh + Blood* taught me never to tamper with the basic outline of a story.'

Ironically, a similar pirate project entitled *Cutthroat Island* (with the very same Geena Davis and directed by her husband Renny Harlin) then led to Verhoeven's other film option, *Crusade*, being called off. This epic project with a budget of $120 million had been thought up on the set of *Total Recall* by Arnold Schwarzenegger and Verhoeven, after which Walon Green, author of *The Wild Bunch*, had written the script. Arnold was to play Hagen the slave who, after being condemned to death, in 1095 bails himself out by volunteering to join the First Crusade led by Godfrey of Bouillon. Godfrey's army leaves to free Jerusalem from the hands of the Muslims. Gradually, Hagen begins to doubt the morality of this holy mission.

But although by the summer of 1994 the swords had already been polished, the locations chosen, the 22,000 costumes made and the contracts signed, at the last minute Carolco Pictures did not proceed with the project. The production company, as ever experiencing liquidity problems, put the director who had helped it to million-dollar profits with *Total Recall* and *Basic Instinct* on hold – it would be too expensive to produce both *Cutthroat Island* and *Crusade*. The rights to the project would later be given to Schwarzenegger, as part of the 'play or pay' deal he had made with Carolco. When asked whether *Crusade* will ever be made, Verhoeven hesitates; he now knows from experience that, in Hollywood, projects come and go. *Showgirls* and *Crusade* have one thing in common. Richard the Lionheart lost the next Crusade to Saladin because his soldiers were too busy gambling.

On the set of *Showgirls* Paul Verhoeven seems miraculously to have forgotten all his previous worries. It had been too long before he was able to start work again, and in his more sombre moments he thought back to the Netherlands, where the most interesting projects often collapsed at the last minute too. 'It's better to work than to wait for the ideal project – which never comes anyway,' his guide and philosopher Martine had said, and after ample consideration Verhoeven had agreed with her. *Showgirls* had to be his next film, the story Joe Eszterhas had outlined to him over lunch at the Ivy, the trendy Beverly Hills restaurant. The meeting had originally been planned to settle the disagreements surrounding *Basic Instinct* – but they were soon exchanging memories of the big MGM musicals across the table and their mutual distrust evaporated.

The many dance scenes in *Showgirls* are not to be shot in Las Vegas. This is why the crew leave the city straight after the night shoot and take the plane to Lake Tahoe. Paul Verhoeven, Jost Vacano, producer Alan Marshall and the leading ladies Elizabeth Berkley and Gina Gershon choose the private jet. The rest of the crew take a charter flight. These are the people responsible for production, camera, technical matters, electricity, make-up and hair, wardrobe, sound, editing, continuity, props, gofers, choreography, lighting, video control, catering, security, nursing, location, transport and special effects – not counting the actors and dancers, some 150 people. Although shooting will take four months, 90 per cent of the crew will never speak to Paul Verhoeven. Showing a talent for team building, these 'foot soldiers' launch into a loud sing-song. Thus the director misses what is a beautiful moment from his own production. Someone had brought a ghetto-blaster and had put on Sheryl Crow's CD *Tuesday Night Music Club* – which contains the hit 'Leaving Las Vegas', an encapsulation of the film's theme:

Quit my job as a dancer
At the Lido des Girls
Dealing blackjack until one or two
Such a muddy line between
The things you want
And the things you have to do
Leaving Las Vegas
Leaving Las Vegas . . .

The next shooting day, Verhoeven is the first on the set. On the stage, in the party room of the Horizon casino, a large set has been built representing the Stardust, the chic casino in Las Vegas where Cristal Connors is star of the dance routine 'The Goddess'. The location is described by Eszterhas as 'a hectic, loud, hip Vegas show, the opposite of the musicals from the past'. A smoking volcano, activated by 'lava guy' on the work schedule, forms the background to twenty-five dancers warming up with stretching movements. Some of these muscular bodies have worked with Madonna and Janet Jackson, but this time they have to move across the stage almost entirely naked. This is the cause of much giggling among them. The film crew has other problems. Nude bodies are one thing, but they also have to be lit in such a way that they look attractive. Meanwhile, Verhoeven involves himself with absolutely everything. He talks to the dancers, consults the choreographer Marguerite Derricks, jumps on and off the stage, goes through the camera positions – four are in position for this scene – deliberates about the lenses to be used. It never seems to stop.

Then a strong rhythm track is heard: music by the British pop composer Dave Stewart. It is the 'Goddess' theme, the show's central number, and the dancers now come running from all directions. Diva Cristal Connors, announced to the sound of explosions, ascends from the volcano. At the back of the hall Nomi watches open-mouthed because, according to the story, this is the first time she sees the star of the show. Connors is now being carried on the dancers' hands. The almost-naked Gina Gershon, eyes heavily made-up, sensually but distantly looks into the camera – 'Don't mess with me, honey' – despite the fact that she is *au naturel*.

And yet this type of dancing is a miracle of taste and chasteness compared with what the Cheetah shows on its catwalk. The loudly cheering audience slips dollar notes into knickers, and those who want to spend more go to the back room in the company of a lady dancer. 'You like her?' the demonic Cristal Connors asks her friend Zack Carey when she sees he is obviously enjoying Nomi's stripping. 'I'll buy her for you.' The subsequent dance scene alone would turn out to be sufficient to give the film its NC-17 rating.

From the moment the director made it known he was going to do *Showgirls*, the American press had not stopped talking about the new Verhoeven–Eszterhas project – not so much because of the 'dark mirror' they thought the duo would be holding up to American life, more because Verhoeven would be the first major Hollywood director contractually allowed to deliver a film rated NC-17. This rating was created in 1990 by the Motion Picture Association of America (MPAA) as a more neutral alternative to the X label, which in the public mind was synonymous with pornography. After earlier brushes with the American film board, Verhoeven had agreed to shoot *Showgirls* only if he was given complete creative control. In order to portray the Las Vegas dance world realistically, a fair amount of frontal nudity was inevitable. 'I am not a crusader,' the director explained to the *New York Times*. 'I am too amoral to care. And it's not to shock. I just don't want to shock myself by cutting my film.'

It was the distribution company MGM that declared itself willing to release the film according to Verhoeven's wishes. As President Frank Mancuso said in *Variety*, 'We accept the verdict of the censors. It is also the right rating – *Showgirls* is an adult film for an adult public.' With this,

MGM became the first major Hollywood distributor to enter the 'adults only' arena with open eyes, trusting to Verhoeven's always controversial 'touch of evil'. In return for complete creative control, the director handed back 70 per cent of his $6 million fee. It was agreed that the difference would be returned only if the film, which had a $38 million budget, turned out to be a success.

'We do what we do in Vegas.'

'What's that?'

'We gamble . . .' With these words, entertainment director Kyle MacLachlan pushes Nomi forward as the new star of the Stardust while the fallen diva Cristal Connors is on her way to hospital. Everyone on the set of *Showgirls* knows that the film is a gamble too. The British producer Alan Marshall explains that by Hollywood standards Verhoeven is taking a big risk by filming this dark story. Why he is doing it can only be guessed. *Showgirls* is peopled exclusively by charlatans, crooks, hypocrites, near-whores, ordinary whores, scroungers and people with hidden agendas, and they all seem to be competing to find the biggest sucker of all. 'Can you spell MGM backwards?' producer Tony Moss (Alan Rachins) mockingly asks a nervous dancer at the audition for the 'Goddess' show. 'Judging by the intelligent look on your face – not. Dismissed!'

Because of her opportunistic attitude to life, protagonist Nomi Malone does not have anything admirable to offer either. Only when her friend Molly, the only warm character in the film, is raped by pop star Andrew Carver (a kind of Axl Rose on heroin) does Nomi realize that during her climb to the top she has sold her soul. When it also turns out that the rape is being covered up by Zack Carey, she decides to avenge Molly, her conscience.

Thus, Alan Marshall explains, *Showgirls* cannot derive strength from the audience's identification with a sympathetic main character. The film will have to depend mainly on its frank approach to the subject. It does make *Showgirls* into a typical Verhoeven film, he says. 'Paul is working with American money, but he is certainly not an American film-maker. His ideas about what he wants to say in his films prevent him from being a crowd-pleaser. That makes him an exception in Hollywood.'

Alan Marshall knows no other director of Verhoeven's calibre in the USA who would dare put his reputation on the line with a film that gives such a bleak view of Las Vegas, and which has no stars. Twenty-one-year-old Elizabeth Berkley can only point to her previous role in *Saved by the Bell*, an American sitcom about college kids. Her co-star Gina Gershon appeared in *Cocktail* and *The Player*, as well as in Schwarzenegger's *Red Heat*, but for this thirty-something actress *Showgirls* is just as much her first big role. And while Kyle MacLachlan (born

1960) managed to attract a cult following as special agent Cooper in *Twin Peaks*, he describes himself – despite big roles in *Blue Velvet* and *The Doors* – as 'someone from the Hollywood periphery'.

For the time being, Paul Verhoeven is happy with this. It resembles the way he put together *Turks Fruit* and *Spetters*: working with relatively unknown actors at least means there will be no tantrums. A benevolent 'Okido!' resounds from the stage.

'Gentlemen, please . . .!' The conductor taps his music-stand impatiently. By now it is June 1995, and Paul Verhoeven has flown to London with the rough cut of *Showgirls* under his arm to finish the soundtrack with Dave Stewart. At the Whitfield Studio, the conductor is now trying to call to order the sixty musicians of the London Metropolitan Orchestra which will be playing the score today. For the moment, however, the musicians are gathered round the monitor showing a clip from *Showgirls*. 'And this . . . is my latest love scene,' Verhoeven had said with an undertone of self-mockery. His reputation turned the remark into a marching order.

The orchestra is now seeing the swimming pool sequence – a transposition of the bathtub scene from *Flesh + Blood* to a kitsch Las Vegas setting. Zack has taken Nomi to his house in his red Ferrari, and more especially to his pool lit by neon palm trees. What initially seems to have been intended as a nocturnal swim soon turns into passionate lovemaking. Naked, Nomi walks into the swimming pool and Zack follows with champagne and glasses. They kiss. He pours champagne over her. She slowly sinks underwater and just as Zack is expecting her to give him oral sex, he suddenly loses her. She re-emerges voluptuously in a corner of the pool. Then follows a shot borrowed from Polanski's *Repulsion*: pretending to frighten her, Zack comes with raised hands through the curve of water spouting from a fountain shaped like a dolphin. For a moment, the fierce blue light gives the scene an eerie atmosphere, but when Nomi crawls on top of him the suspense is replaced by eroticism. On the soundtrack being played simultaneously, the drums beat a driven ostinato rhythm, culminating in a climax which is visible on the monitor. 'Gentlemen . . .?' Like a sniggering bunch of pupils after a sex education film, the members of the orchestra take their seats in the studio.

In the control room, Paul Verhoeven smiles at the effect of the scene. Post-production has never been his favourite part of the film-making process, but for *Showgirls* he has chosen to be present from the beginning to the end. The way in which the soundtrack for *Showgirls* is being put together here in London is, as Verhoeven says, 'an interesting, but slow process'. Prior to shooting, Dave Stewart had already produced a number of basic tracks, which were used during the big dance scenes such as 'Goddess' (the volcano dance number) and 'The Avenging Angel' (a grand S & M dance) in Las Vegas and Lake Tahoe. Now it is a matter of synchronizing image and music for the entire film. The main musical themes return in different arrangements, sometimes with a big orchestra, sometimes fragmentarily on acoustic guitar and piano. While doing so, the composer, musicians and director keep a constant eye on the image. 'Instant composing gives me complete control,' Verhoeven points out.

This is no exaggeration. Although the director is not a musician, he grew up with Stravinsky and Debussy and learnt to understand complex compositions. So he says to Dave Stewart, 'That scene is not meant in a sentimental way – it should go more like grrrrr!' Or 'The African hand drums should go ta-ta-ti-ta-ta-ti-dom.' He explains how the surging bass themes should arouse vague feelings of unease in the viewer, and suggests turning the drum rhythms around or fitting in an extra beat. Verhoeven regularly asks to hear the dialogue on another soundtrack, to test whether it and the music fit together. Thus the final soundtrack is built up layer by layer. At the end of each track Dave Stewart picks up his twelve-string Rickenbacker and accentuates with a single lick or tremolo the link between image and music. After a well-placed sostenuto he concludes, 'That'll keep the kettle boiling, won't it?'

Meanwhile, they are also busy preparing for *Showgirls* in Los Angeles. A sixteen-minute trailer has been made to convince American distributors of the qualities of this modern musical. Eventually, 1388 theatres will agree to show *Showgirls* – almost as many as with *Basic Instinct* – thus allaying the initial worries about a boycott. In the knowledge that several newspapers and television channels have declared in advance that, as a matter of principle, they will not give space to an NC-17 film, it is felt that the Internet might be a good alternative source of publicity: on a special page, Elizabeth Berkley will personally answer questions about the film. In addition, 250,000 free promotional videos of *Showgirls* will be made available through the video library chains. All this is an attempt to escape the fate which has befallen smaller NC-17 films: to meet an inglorious and anonymous end. Director Philip Kaufman, for example, knows all about that, since his NC-17 film *Henry & June* (1990), about the Parisian years of the writer Henry Miller, brought in only $11 million owing to the lack of cinemas and advertising. Even so many decades after Henry Miller, sexuality seemed not to have lost its dangerous overtones in the USA.

To Verhoeven, it is a different matter. 'Sorry, Paul, *that* sound we don't have in stock.' 'One moment . . .' They are working on the 'Avenging Angel', the S & M dance number from the film. They have the music, but the technicians at the mixing table are unable to provide a suitable sound for the shot in which a male dancer pretends to lick leading lady Nomi between her legs. Without fuss, Paul Verhoeven goes up to the microphone specially set up for this kind of problem. When the clip is shown again, he clears his throat. A sound is heard: 'SLURPPP!' While the technicians look at each other out of the corner of their eyes, Verhoeven sits down again. 'Okido!' you can see him thinking.

In the interviews preceding *Showgirls*, the director had reminisced about his secondary-school teacher who, in discussing Manet's nudes, had remarked that the breasts of a woman were among the high points of aesthetics, a statement he could only endorse. Also indelibly printed in his memory is the scene in which sex kitten Françoise Arnoul – a Brigitte Bardot *avant la lettre* – showed her bosom for three seconds in Ralph Habib's 1953 film about prostitution *Les Compagnes de la Nuit* – a film that made the young Verhoeven blush during his adolescence in The Hague. 'The only thing I could imagine with regard to *Showgirls* is that part of the audience will go home in a state of excitement and, thinking of the film, make love or masturbate. That's not so bad.'

Remarks like this in American publications are normally accompanied by the comment that this is a European speaking; in other words, enlightened but decadent, mad but not dangerous. 'Paul is in the luxurious position that he works here, but does not come from the United States,' Kyle MacLachlan said on the set. 'As a European, he doesn't really need to take the slightest notice of anything. He has no reputation to lose, because Europeans are seen as eccentric anyway. So he can simply continue in his own style – he is more or less outside the social control prevalent in Hollywood.' Nicely put, but nothing could have been farther from the truth.

'It's going to be impossible to keep my food down for the next twenty-four hours,' someone said. 'This is the end of the world as we know it,' said someone else. The mood at Paul Verhoeven's office is far from buoyant this afternoon. Tomorrow, 21 September, is the première of *Showgirls*, but the director is describing how the press has reacted. As usual, the reviewers were asked for their first impressions. Well, *if* they had been able to sit through the entire showing . . . the destructive criticisms were unanimous. In passing, the churches in the state of Washington have announced that they will be condemning *Showgirls* next Sunday. 'The reviews will be terrible,' Paul Verhoeven sighs to Elizabeth Berkley, who has just put her head round the door with an enquiring expression on her face, on her way to the Internet promotional meeting. The young star bites her lip. Verhoeven consoles her for a moment. When she has gone, he says that the whole situation reminds him of *Spetters*. 'Every time I really want to say something in a film, it seems to go wrong. Martine said that this time maybe we should move to France.'

He is still able to laugh at this remark, but the omens were not lying. The morning after the première party at the MGM Academy Theatre in Beverly Hills, the verdict arrives like a monster with a thousand heads. 'The strain of trying to make America's dirtiest big-studio movie', Janet Maslin wrote in the *New York Times*, 'has led Mr Verhoeven and Mr Eszterhas to create an instant camp classic. And the surprise is that despite the intense steaminess of *Basic Instinct*, *Showgirls* is, in every sense, not so hot. The film-makers had declared they were bravely exploring new levels of licentiousness, but the biggest risk they've taken here is in making a nearly $40 million movie without anyone who can act . . . Mr Verhoeven, trying to fuse the rawness of his early Dutch films (including *Spetters* and *Keetje Tippel*) with the slick proficiency of his American hits (*RoboCop*, *Total Recall*) becomes a man without a country this time . . . Elvis has left the building, in the words of the screenplay's favorite cliché.'

Kenneth Turan of the *Los Angeles Times* did not lag far behind. 'First off, this nominally risqué story of naked ambition among Las Vegas showgirls has somehow managed to make extensive nudity exquisitely boring. Then it has beaten some stiff competition to set new low standards for demeaning treatment of women on film. And, perhaps most mind-boggling of all, it has made it possible for viewers to look longingly back on *Basic Instinct* as the golden age of the director Paul Verhoeven/screenwriter Joe Eszterhas collaboration. Everything you feared it might be and less, *Showgirls* is a movie made to be exploited, not seen.'

Time noted, 'We don't blame Verhoeven, the director of two sleek, inventive Hollywood fantasies (*RoboCop*, *Total Recall*), for making this movie – though we're surprised he can bear to watch it. The real culprit is Eszterhas, swami of the high concept.' *Newsweek* commented, 'For all its sex and nudity, *Showgirls* is for the most part fiercely unerotic . . . Offered as a blow for artistic and sexual liberation, *Showgirls* if it succeeds will really be a triumph of Hollywood cynicism. And there's nothing titillating about that.' *Variety* insisted that 'the only positive thing there is to say about *Showgirls* is that the sensibility of the film perfectly matches that of its milieu. Impossibly vulgar, tawdry and coarse . . . With the exception of Molly, everyone in this picture is a selfish, heartless, unsympathetic user. There is no reason whatever to take an interest in any of these people, who are provided with no human dimensions. Most annoying of all is Nomi, who, as Berkley plays her, is harsh, graceless and quickly tiresome: the character is so hard she's not attractive or sexy at all.'

The *Hollywood Reporter* saw the only redeeming feature as the dance numbers, 'particularly the large production numbers, although most viewers will be distracted by bouncing body parts.' Only Vivian Holland of *Playgirl* called *Showgirls* 'one of the best films of the year'. All the other reviewers were irritated by the level of Eszterhas's dialogue or his 'masturbation fantasies', as the critic Roger Ebert called them. The overall verdict in the press was that, by letting bad taste sink to new depths, Paul Verhoeven had given the NC-17 rating a very dubious name.

While television crews left for Las Vegas to hear the dancers explain that the reality of their lives was much more positive than is shown in *Showgirls* (although the script was based on interviews with the same dancers), David Letterman and Jay Leno were making cruel jokes about the film in their late night television shows. The features pages of the *Los Angeles Times* were full of articles ridiculing the production, and even the weather forecasters and sports commentators referred unflatteringly to *Showgirls* in their daily slots. This broad debate would not be pushed aside until the verdict in the O. J. Simpson trial. Paul Verhoeven scratched his ear. After a good start – $8.3 million dollars in the opening weekend – he saw how *Showgirls* had faded in the theatres: the profits would not exceed $25 million dollars. (Though due to overseas revenue, the breakeven point of $38 million was soon reached – and the very successful video sales would eventually make *Showgirls* a profitable project.) Explanations of the fiasco had been given left, right and centre. It was suggested that MGM's marketing department had made too much of the racy qualities of the story: 'Leave your inhibitions at the door' was the slogan with which *Showgirls* was launched. But this was not to the liking of Joe Eszterhas, who on the day of the première had on his own initiative published an open letter in *Variety* addressed especially to women.

Among other things, he wrote: '*Showgirls* is set in Las Vegas, in a world of nude lap dancing and topless casino dancing. My script is based on extensive interviews with the young women who are Vegas's dancers. The movie shows that dancers in Vegas are often victimized, humiliated, used, verbally and physically raped by the men who are at the power centers of that world . . . The studio releasing *Showgirls*, in its infinite corporate wisdom, has decided to place some of the advertising for the movie on the sports pages . . . Their advertising people have devised a tag line "Leave your inhibitions at the door" to sell a movie which is about a young woman who leaves her ambitions at the door to save her soul . . . I implore you not to let . . . either misguided, fast-buck advertising . . . nor politically correct axe-grinding influence your feelings about *Showgirls*. I implore you to form your own conclusions . . . I believe deeply that you will like *Showgirls*.'

This remarkable appeal by Joe Eszterhas had no effect, which did not entirely surprise Verhoeven. Only the week before Eszterhas had said in an interview that 'young people under seventeen should all get false means of identification so that they too could see the NC-17 film', which did not particularly help the publicity campaign for *Showgirls*. Perhaps it was not up to Eszterhas to play the card of integrity, notorious as he is for quarrelsomeness – as Verhoeven himself had noticed at the time of *Basic Instinct*. Eszterhas should have known that, because of the astronomical amounts he received for his scripts compared to other scriptwriters, he was one of the most hated people in Hollywood; the day of reckoning was always imminent. 'I can go with his statement that the film was launched in the wrong way. But not that he then wages the battle on his own. He could also have sat round the table with us earlier on.' None of this diminishes his qualities as a writer, says the director, continuing to defend his partner in crime. 'Moreover, I did of course decide myself to shoot *Showgirls*, so the final responsibility for the film is with me.'

Verhoeven had waited long before daring to tackle such a contemporary theme in his newly adopted country. His *RoboCop* and *Total Recall* had been science-fiction stories, while *Basic Instinct,* though set in the present, was a timeless metaphor: Sharon Stone was nothing less than the Devil in a miniskirt. What he learnt from the mounting indignation at *Showgirls* was how sensible he had been as a newcomer to the United States in 'not starting straight away with films full of social comment.' But he had now tumbled into that dreaded trap for European directors. 'Verhoeven never gets past the vantage point of an outsider looking in,' the *New York Times* said sternly about the film, implying that non-Americans will never understand America. Perhaps this is true. To him, *Showgirls* had seemed harsh but honest, yet now it seemed as if he stood with a bloody axe at the roots of American civilization. 'They expected a sexy film, but what they got was a portrayal of mores. Behind all the nudity is a mudstream of egotism and gloom – and it is precisely Nomi who is the least sympathetic character of all. I had thought that I could get away with something like that in an "adult film", but they almost blamed Elizabeth for it personally.'

Verhoeven's observing of the rather untempting reality of behind-the-scenes Las Vegas also seemed to get in the way of any judgement about *Showgirls* as a piece of cinema. Few words were spent on the remarkable steadycam filming of the dressing-room scenes, a camera language for which he had especially studied Fellini's *8 1/2* (1963). He was discussed as a film-maker in quite another way. In an advance review of *Showgirls* in the magazine *Première,* he had still been the 'underrated' and 'underestimated' craftsman and director Verhoeven. The day after the première, however, the *Los Angeles Reader* called him the 'once-mighty' Paul Verhoeven, whose 'American trajectory – from *RoboCop* to *Total Recall* to *Basic Instinct* – has been steadily downhill.' Unwittingly, this showed there was probably more truth in Verhoeven's unflattering view of American showbiz than could be admitted on paper.

Epilogue

Myth, Poetry and Prose

It is a late July evening and Paul Verhoeven is celebrating his birthday on the garden terrace of Michael's restaurant in Santa Monica. Earlier he had been telling his guests about the day he decided to become a film-maker and the conversation now turns to what makes a script a good film script.

After five short productions (*Eén Hagedis Teveel, De Lifters, Niets Bijzonders, Feest, De Worstelaar*), two television films (*Gone, Gone*; an episode for *The Hitchhiker*), a twelve-part television series (*Floris*), two documentaries (*Het Korps Mariniers* and *Mussert*), as well as eleven full-length feature films (from *Wat Zien Ik* to *Showgirls*), and with the twelfth – *Starship Troopers* – on the way, Paul Verhoeven's answer is firm. He is less concerned with what is written, than with what he is able to project on to a text: 'To me, a script is a Rorschach test.' In other words, when he is reading a script, do film images spontaneously come into his head? Can he put himself into the shoes of the main character, or add something to the story from his own experience or imagination? 'Gerard Soeteman had the ability to come up with subjects which immediately interested me. In Hollywood I am offered a hundred and fifty scripts a year, of which perhaps three are worthwhile.'

One of those was Walon Green's *Crusade*, where galoping horses and Jerusalem in flames immediately appeared in his mind's eye. With Ed Neumeier, too, Verhoeven is able to have a fruitful exchange of ideas, which is why after *RoboCop* they worked together on the sci-fi spectacle *Starship Troopers*. And then, of course, there is Joe Eszterhas, the writer of *Basic Instinct* and *Showgirls*: 'His prose is clear and open. That's why the script for *Basic Instinct* allowed a maximum projection of my vision on to the story.' Although Verhoeven had initially thought that the idea of a female serial killer who kills people with an ice pick as research for a book highly unlikely, as was the case with *RoboCop* and with *Showgirls*, it had been Martine who had suggested shooting the film. Verhoeven says, 'As far as she was concerned, she thought that with my sensibilities and love for Hitchcock, I would be able to make a very plausible story of *Basic*

Instinct. The framework which Joe handed to me turned out to be much better constructed than I had at first thought. That is the quality of a script: to write it in such a way that it leaves the director with enough room for interpretation. Joe has that talent, at least for me.'

Despite the credit the director gives to his scriptwriters, Verhoeven's films are very much his own. Everything he touches receives *his* signature, whether the story is written by Gerard Soeteman, Ed Neumeier, Ron Shusett, Walon Green or Joe Eszterhas. *Showgirls* is a good example of this. It has become a typical Verhoeven film not only because of Nomi's trust in her basic instincts, but because half-hidden behind the main characters is the religious symbolism with which the director has imbued the story. The film starts around Hallowe'en (31 October, the eve of All Saints' Day) when Nomi walks into a casino in which people are dressed up in seasonal costumes. There is a gradual ascent up until Christmas: she escapes the world of the lap dance and lands in the 'Goddess' show. After her début she receives flowers from Zack Carey, which she proudly carries across the car park, while a Salvation Army band quietly plays hymns in the background. She is buoyant, life seems to be flourishing, but Christmas is not yet over before the moral decay sets in.

This evolution is clear during the 'Bliss' dance number, when Cristal ascends to heaven like a Messiah on a cross. As the 'white goddess' she is surrounded by a cloud of light; meanwhile the black dancer Annie is writhing on the stage, tripped up by a fellow dancer. The scene's Christian mythology is evident, and it is a recurring element which Verhoeven lovingly adds to his films. On different levels – because when Nomi goes to visit her boyfriend James, the frame above shows the flashing neon advertisement: 'Jesus is coming soon', alternated with 'Jesus is coming ... on' – a visual joke which Verhoeven borrowed from *De Vierde Man* (the neon sign 'Sphinx' becomes 'Spin', meaning spider).

In an article about the shooting of *Showgirls* that appeared on 12 February 1995, the *New York Times* had some difficulty in placing Verhoeven as a film-maker. It points out the similarities between *The Fourth Man* and *Basic Instinct* and the 'satiric touches' in *RoboCop*. The article says that he has an 'original, subversive streak' and continues: 'Readers might be surprised to know that Mr Verhoeven's films include historical dramas about a poor family in nineteenth-century Amsterdam (*Keetje Tippel*) and Dutch Resistance fighters during World War II (*Soldier of Orange*), a swashbuckler set in sixteenth-century Europe (*Flesh + Blood*) and a gritty look at a Dutch motorcycle gang (*Spetters*). In *The Fourth Man* Mr Verhoeven created a new genre, the psycho-sexual religious thriller.'

The confusion is not entirely surprising. At first sight Verhoeven's films seem to be an eclectic mixture. In this regard he himself says:

'Within an *oeuvre* the differences are often more noticeable than the similarities. When you listen to Stravinsky, you are overwhelmed by the differences. The compositions are sometimes neo-classical, sometimes expressionistic; at the end of his life he even started to use twelve-tone music. When you first let your untrained ears listen to *L'Oiseau de Feu* and you then put on *Canticum Sacrum*, you would conclude that they are by two entirely different composers.' Verhoeven believes that the reason for experimenting with so many different styles as a film-maker should not be given too much significance: 'I just don't feel like repeating myself, so I always try something new.'

For those who are not satisfied by this, it is possible to point out more similarities in his work than mere elements of style or visual jokes. For example, what Paul Verhoeven must have recognized during the Rorschach test with the script of *Showgirls* are the parallels between the main character Nomi and his earlier protagonists from *Keetje Tippel* and *Spetters*, films which were similarly about youngsters without education, power or money. Although they are set in different locations and periods, Keetje, Fientje and Nomi could be seen as daughters from the same family. They are all three on a journey of survival, and in their pragmatism they have already pushed aside any high, romantic expectations about life.

Quoting the German poet Rainer Maria Rilke, Verhoeven says, 'If as an artist you analyse your motives too much, you lose not only your demons but your angels.' When asked for a definition of his own work, he adds, 'It's up to other people to do that.'

In any case it is important to remember that Verhoeven's thinking was shaped by the Second World War and its aftermath. At night he still regularly dreams of himself in the role of hero 'with a short carbine and hopefully on the side of the good guys'. In his dreams he is untouchable, which can be explained by the fact that his parents returned unscathed from the bombing of The Hague. Here speaks the mythic Paul Verhoeven, under the spell of larger-than-life feelings, ideas nourished by the favourite adventure films of his youth, such as *Captain Blood* (Michael Curtiz, 1935) or *War of the Worlds* (Byron Haskin, 1953).

In his later boyhood and student years Paul Verhoeven developed a surrealist perception of reality, expressed in his interest in hypnosis, UFOs and magic. He started to paint, and in his head created a hermetic universe, in which everything is interconnected and coincidence does not exist. This has resulted in a poetic perspective: the artist controls reality, in the same way as the mathematician in him tries to do this with formulas encompassing the cosmos.

After his mental crisis in 1966, Verhoeven's sense of reality became stronger. Allegory gave way to a precise description. From then on, things were called by their name: a poetic alibi no longer existed. This was when Verhoeven grounded his prosaic realism in the sixteenth- and seventeenth-century Dutch School of Painting. These three phases – myth, poetry and prose – show the palette from which Paul Verhoeven chooses his film language.

The mythic film-maker can be found first in *Het Korps Mariniers*, then in his children's series *Floris*, the films *Flesh + Blood*, *RoboCop* and *Total Recall* and now *Starship Troopers*, as well as in his plans for *Mistress of the Sea* and *Crusade*. To a certain extent these are all fairytales, with a clearer contrast between good and evil than is usual in Verhoeven's other films. None of the villains in *RoboCop*, for example, has balanced character traits. In these films the archetypes of Western culture are liberally used, especially Christian metaphors. It could be argued that these real heroes are the wish-fulfilment of the boy in Verhoeven. The actors do things which he himself does not dare to do, or is not capable of doing, but would like to. The heroes from these films know no limits: Arnold Schwarzenegger saves the entire planet Mars with a movement of his hand. In *Starship Troopers* Johny Rico saves the entire human race from the evil bugs. RoboCop walks on water like Jesus and brings strife-torn Detroit to its senses; Floris did the same for the Middle Ages in the name of Oldenstein. Thus the heroes all have something of the celestial: they are saviours. Even Martin in *Flesh + Blood* thinks he is sent by God, although he shamefully abuses it. No wonder that his opponent, Steven, is finally able to free himself from his distressing imprisonment with the help of a mythic, well-directed flash of lightning by way of a hint.

The poetic–surreal Verhoeven is apparent in: *De Lepeltjes* (*The Teaspoons*), the film which got him the commission for *Eén Hagedis Teveel*; in *Eén Hagedis Teveel* itself; in *Niets Bijzonders*, *De Lifters*, *Feest*, *De Vierde Man* and *Basic Instinct* – these films all juggle fantasy and reality, because, as in a Maurits Escher litho, perspective is constantly tilted. There is no fixed and reliable viewpoint for the viewer. Ambiguity reigns, whether it concerns the boy hopelessly in love in *Feest* or the delirium of the main character in *De Vierde Man*. Within this genre of manipulative reality, the Hitchcockian theme of the double identity plays a role as early as *Eén Hagedis Teveel*. In that sense *RoboCop* and *Total Recall* should also be included in this category, because both Murphy/RoboCop and Quaid/Hauser struggle with an ambivalent personality. It is not for nothing that these films, together with *Basic Instinct*, have been called the 'psychosis trilogy' by the film-maker. The situations (such as the difficult love affair in *Eén Hagedis Teveel*) as well as the characters (Renée Soutendijk in *De Vierde Man*, Sharon Stone in *Basic Instinct*) have something satanic – Verhoeven gives his main characters an infernal look at life and death.

The fiercely realistic Verhoeven can be found in his documentary about Mussert and in his films *Turks Fruit, Keetje Tippel, Soldaat van Oranje, Spetters, Showgirls*, as well as the project *Christ, the Man* – in which myth has to be separated from man. In these films – which, with the omission of the adjective 'fiercely', include *Wat Zien Ik* (although the comedy genre to which this commissioned film belonged has its own laws) – the director has an unadorned vision of his main characters. They seem unable to find real earthly happiness, but they do not allow themselves to be overcome by events. When Olga in *Turks Fruit* dies, Eric throws her wig into a refuse-lorry; he is heading for a new future. In *Spetters* a snack-bar is opened on the rubble of a recently smashed-up pub – the property of the father whose son has just committed suicide. After her Las Vegas adventure, Nomi from *Showgirls* goes off in the direction of Los Angeles – Hollywood, to be precise. In addition to being coloured by Nietzschean nihilism, the main characters from Verhoeven's fiercely realistic films could also be termed 'nuanced': they have both good and bad traits. Erik in *Soldaat van Oranje*, for example, fights for queen and country, but this heroic idealism is considerably tempered by his egotistical behaviour.

It is interesting that the realistic films are those which most offended the film critics. When Verhoeven concerns himself with the here and now, as in *Spetters* or *Showgirls*, his equally explicit and uncompromising view of reality is considered extremely unpleasant, a slap in the face. The film-maker allows the viewer no means of escape – he neither tells a fairytale nor gives the impression that, as in *Basic Instinct*, the viewer is watching an extended metaphor. In that sense especially *Showgirls* defied all Hollywood laws. Nomi does not turn out to be a sympathetic main character who at the end of the film finds her hard-earned deliverance in a happy ending; she is an opportunistic bitch.

To understand his work, it is crucial to realize that Verhoeven does not put poetry above prose, does not consider artistic merit nobler than 'popular art' – as *Newsweek* once called his fiercely realistic dramas. Now that, after so much experience as a film-maker, he has reached a state of visual perfection, he can play almost carelessly with the various genres. In *Showgirls* the surreal horror-film spotlight under which Nomi comes into view as she watches her rival Cristal being taken to hospital suggests that she is possessed by demons. The next shot is no less magic realist: Nomi appears from the bottom of the image in extreme close-up – she is about to dance 'Goddess' – and Verhoeven gives her a halo. She is finally where she wants to be – after which *Showgirls* returns to its realistic starting point. That Verhoeven can also play out elements of his genres in reverse was already evident from the fiercely realistic way in which he opened his surreal thriller *Basic Instinct*. The blood bath with the ice pick was simply graphic.

Although Verhoeven also shows his dreams in the mythic films, he seems to be particularly fascinated by his nightmares. With a tarnishing clarity, reminiscent of Hieronymus Bosch or in our time Francis Bacon, he portrays the vulnerability of the human body in many of his films. 'In our deepest being we are no more than a piece of flesh,' Verhoeven explains. 'When you pull off the skin, the whole thing is exposed, as you can see in my films. The scene may be revolting, but what it proves to me is the transitoriness and total worthlessness of the human body: a collection of flesh, bones and muscles. An inferior entity.'

In its defencelessness, man's mortality makes him furious. Verhoeven says. 'Of course I want us to be indivisible and immortal *à la* RoboCop, but reality teaches the opposite. From this dialectic I shoot my films: it may look like pure provocation, but it is rage at the insignificance of our design. That feeling is in *Soldaat* when the president walks across the "freshers" as if they are dead bodies – you have the feeling that you are watching an image from Auschwitz. It is in *Total Recall* when Arnold uses the body of a dead man as a shield on the escalator, but also in *Turks Fruit* when the dog licks the bride's amniotic fluid.'

For Paul Verhoeven and for most of his anti-Utopian main characters, the anger at the banality of our existence is also fed by the belief that at the end of the already pointless journey through life there is no reward, no deliverance. When in November 1991 the *Vancouver Sun* interviewed Verhoeven about his participation in the Jesus Seminar, this theme clearly emerged. After explaining how the Christ figure has become a symbol for those who hope to survive death, he says, 'I have, in my own life, had the most terrible dreams about my death. The essence of the dream is the tangible feeling of being in hell. It is the complete isolation of the soul. Complete aloneness.'

These are thoughts that Paul Verhoeven formulates with some regularity. The following is a passage from his diary written at a time of crisis with producer Rob Houwer:

31 May 1978

I immediately get an anxiety dream that I am going to die, I will have to leave everything behind and enter the absolutely terrible; in front of my bed are three people who have come to collect me. A few times that night I think that Martine has gone and that my bedroom is in the hereafter. The hereafter is so horrible!

And yet Verhoeven insists that it is too easy to say that exorcism *alone* is the fuel for his work. He is simultaneously fascinated by the attraction of destruction and chaos, the universal need to portray a vision from hell. 'Dante's *Inferno*, is that exorcism or invocation? The work of Hieronymus Bosch, is that exorcism or invocation? I think you could defend either explanation quite easily. Just like me they must have had a perverse, decadent, negative pleasure in showing horrors. To the ultimate extreme and with an absolute, clinical feel for detail.' He calls it an unfathomable fascination. Verhoeven does know that when his head is filled with a new project or when he is on the set, he sleeps much better. 'Filming is a basic necessity of life. Something like eating.' Then he worries not about eternity, but at the most about a camera viewpoint, some dialogue or a special effect, after which he sometimes gets up with the idea, 'Right, today I am going to shoot something they will talk about for years.'

December 1994. A showroom at Columbia-TriStar, in Century City, Los Angeles. While the director is still busy in Las Vegas with *Showgirls*, producer Jon Davison starts the trailer of what is to become Verhoeven's next film, *Starship Troopers*. It shows army units of planet Earth fighting gigantic insects.

The trailer lasts five minutes. After the insects have caused mayhem, the bloody limbs of crushed soldiers come into view, as if to underline his statement about the insignificance of our design.

Verhoeven's signature is unmistakable. In daily life he has proved to be friendliness itself, a man who is totally against murder with ice picks, killing with swords, gang rape, apocalyptic explosions, ripped bodies, cleft eyes or *ad hoc* castration, but as an artist he never is, if it is necessary for the plot – and, as far as he is concerned, in a Verhoeven film it always is.

When the showing of *Starship Troopers* has finished, Jon Davison's guests come outside. Verhoeven's daughter Claudia is the first to give her reaction.

She says tenderly, 'Typical of Daddy.'

Filmography

1960 *One Lizard Too Many (Eén Hagedis Teveel)*

Director: Paul Verhoeven
Producer: The Netherlands Student Film Industry
Scriptwriter: Jan van Mastrigt
Cinematographer: Frits Boersma
Editor: Ernst Winar
Music: Aart Gisolf
Cast: Erik Bree, Marijke Jones, Hermine Menalda, Hans Schneider,
P. A. Harteveld
35 minutes: black and white
First prize at the 1960 Cinestud Student Film Festival

1961 *Nothing Special (Niets Bijzonders)*

Director: Paul Verhoeven
Producer: The Netherlands Student Film Industry
Scriptwriter: Jan van Mastrigt
Camera: Frits Boersma
Cast: Jan van Mastrigt, Marina Schapers
9 minutes: black and white

1962 *The Hitchhikers (De Lifters)*

Director: Paul Verhoeven
Producer: The Netherlands Student Film Industry
Scriptwriter: Jan van Mastrigt
Camera: Frits Boersma
Editor: Ernst Winar
Cast: Geerda Walma van der Molen, Jaap van Donselaar, Maarten
Schutte, Jan van Mastrigt
17 minutes: black and white

1963 *Let's Have a Party* (*Feest*)

Director: Paul Verhoeven
Producer: Paul Verhoeven
Production Supervisor: Frits Boersma
Scriptwriter: Jan van Mastrigt
Cinematographer: Ferenc Kálmán-Gáll
Editor: Ernst Winar
Sound: Max Berg
Music: Dick Broeckaerts
Cast includes: Yvonne Blei-Weissmann, Dick de Brauw, Pieter Jelle Bouman, Wim Noordhoek
28 minutes: black and white
First prize Cork Film Festival, Ireland – commended at the Oberhausen, Locarno, Melbourne and Paris film festivals

1965 *The Marine Corps* (*Het Korps Mariniers*)

Director: Paul Verhoeven
Producer: Multifilm
Camera: Peter Alsemgeest, Jan Kijser, Jos van Haarlem
Sound: Nick Meyer, Ron Haanschoten
Editor: Ernst Winar
Music: H. C. van Lijnschoten
23 minutes: colour
Winner of the Silver Sun for military films, France

1968 *Portrait of Anton Adriaan Mussert*
(*Portret van Anton Adriaan Mussert*)

Director: Paul Verhoeven
Producer: VPRO television
Compiled by: Paul Verhoeven, Leo Kool, Hans Keller
Commentary: Hans Keller
Cinematographer: Jaap Buis
50 minutes: black and white
Broadcast: 16 April 1970

1969 *Floris*

Director: Paul Verhoeven
Producer: Max Appelboom for Max Appelboom Production
Scriptwriter: Gerard Soeteman
Cinematographer: Ton Buné
Editor: Jan Bosdriesz
Music: Julius Steffaro

Cast includes: Rutger Hauer, Jos Bergman, Hans Culeman, Diana Mar-
let, Ida Bons, Tim Beekman, Ton Vos, Hans Kemna, Henk van Ulsen,
Hans Boskamp, Hammy de Beukelaer
30 minutes per episode: black and white
Broadcast in 12 episodes:
Part 1   *The Stolen Castle (Het Gestolen Kasteel)* 5.10.69
Part 2   *The Copper Dog (De Koperen Hond)* 12.10.69
Part 3   *The Black Bullets (De Zwarte Kogels)* 19.10.69
Part 4   *The Man from Ghent (De Man van Gent)* 26.10.69
Part 5   *The Three Jesters (De Drie Narren)* 2.11.69
Part 6   *The Hairy Devil (De Harige Duivel)* 9.11.69
Part 7   *The Permit (De Vrijbrief)* 16.11.69
Part 8   *The Mandrake (De Alruin)* 23.11.69
Part 9   *The Burning Water (Het Brandende Water)* 30.11.69
Part 10 *The Miracle Worker (De Wonderdoener)* 7.12.69
Part 11 *The Byzantine Cup (De Byzantijnse Beker)* 14.12.69
Part 12 *The Healing (De Genezing)* 21.12.69

1970 *The Wrestler (De Worstelaar)*

Director: Paul Verhoeven
Producer: Nico Crama
Production Supervisor: Dick Mandersloot
Scriptwriter: Paul Verhoeven and Kees Holierhoek
Cinematographer: Jan de Bont
Editor: Jan Bosdriesz
Sound: Ate de Vries
Music: J Stoeckart
Cast: Jon Bluming, Bernhard Droog, Wim Zomer, Mariëlle Fiolet
20 minutes: colour

1971 *Business is Business*
(also known as *Any Special Way*) (*Wat Zien Ik*)

Director: Paul Verhoeven
Producer: Rob Houwer
Production Supervisor: Kees Groenewegen & Ineke van Wezel
Scriptwriter: Gerard Soeteman, based on collection of short stories by
Albert Mol
Cinematographer: Jan de Bont
Editor: Jan Bosdriesz
Sound: Ad Roest
Music: Julius Steffaro
Set Design: Massimo Götz & Henk Koster

Cast includes: Ronny Bierman, Sylvia de Leur, Piet Römer, Bernhard Droog, Henk Molenberg, Albert Mol, Jules Hamel, Eric van Ingen, Trudy Labij
93 minutes: colour

1973 Turkish Delight (*Turks Fruit*)

Director: Paul Verhoeven
Producer: Rob Houwer Films
Production Supervisor: Mia van't Hof
Executive Producer: Rob Houwer
Scriptwriter: Gerard Soeteman, based on a novel of the same name by Jan Wolkers
Cinematographer: Jan de Bont
Editor: Jan Bosdriesz
Music: Rogier van Otterloo
Art Director: Ralf van de Elst
Cast includes: Rutger Hauer, Monique van de Ven, Tonny Huurdeman, Wim van den Brink, Dolf de Vries, Hans Boskamp, Manfred de Graaf, Marjol Flore, Maartje Seyferth, Olga Zuiderhoek, Hans Kemna
112 minutes: colour
Oscar nomination for Best Non-English-Language Film, 1973

1975 Cathy Tippel (also known as *A Girl called Keetje Tippel*) (*Keetje Tippel*)

Director: Paul Verhoeven
Producer: Rob Houwer Films
Production Supervisor: Kees Groenewegen
Executive Producer: Rob Houwer
Scriptwriter: Gerard Soeteman, based on the memoirs of Neel Doff
Cinematographer: Jan de Bont
Editor: Jane Sperr
Music: Rogier van Otterloo
Art Director: Roland de Groot
Costumes: Robert Bos
Cast includes: Monique van de Ven, Rutger Hauer, Eddy Brugman, Peter Faber, Hannah de Leeuwe, Andrea Domburg, Jan Blaaser, Fons Rademakers
109 minutes: colour

1977 Soldier of Orange (*Soldaat van Oranje*)

Director: Paul Verhoeven
Producer: Rob Houwer Films/Gijs Versluys

Production Manager: Mia van 't Hof
Scriptwriter: Gerard Soeteman, Kees Holierhoek, Paul Verhoeven, based on a novel of the same name by Erik Hazelhoff Roelfzema
Cinematographer: Jost Vacano
Art Direction: Roland de Groot
Costumes: Elly Claus
Editor: Jane Sperr
Music: Rogier van Otterloo
Sound: René van der Berg, Bill Wolfs
Special Effects: Robert Leerinck, Aat van Westen
Assistants to the Director: Jindra Markus and Hans Kemna
Cast: Rutger Hauer, Jeroen Krabbé, Edward Fox, Peter Faber, Derek de Lint, Eddy Habbema, Lex van Delden, Huib Rooymans, Belinda Meuldijk, Susan Penhaligon, Andrea Domburg, Guus Hermus
153 minutes: colour
The film received a Golden Globe in 1980

1979 *Gone, Gone (Voorbij, Voorbij)*

Director: Paul Verhoeven
Producer: Joop van den Ende for KRO Television
Scriptwriter: Gerard Soeteman
Cinematographer: Mat van Hensbergen
Editor: Ine Schenkkan
Music: Hans Vermeulen
Cast: André van den Heuvel, Andrea Domburg, Piet Römer, Hans Veerman, Guus Oster, Jan Retèl, Hidde Maas, Leontien Ceulemans, Riek Schagen, Maarten Spanjer
58 minutes: colour

1980 Spetters

Director: Paul Verhoeven
Producer: Joop van den Ende for VSE Productions
Production manager: Gijs Versluys
Director of Production: Jos van der Linden
Scriptwriter: Gerard Soeteman
Cinematographer: Jost Vacano
Editor: Ine Schenkkan
Music: Ton Scherpenzeel and Kayak
Assistant to the Director and Location Manager: Jindra Markus
Assistant to the Director and Casting Director: Hans Kemna
Art Direction: Dick Schillemans
Costumes: Yan Tax

Cast: Hans van Tongeren, Renée Soutendijk, Toon Agterberg, Maarten Spanjer, Marianne Boyer, Rutger Hauer, Jeroen Krabbé, Peter Tuinman, Hugo Metsers, Kitty Courbois, Rudi Falkenhagen, Hans Veerman, Gees Linnebank
115 minutes: colour

1983 *The Fourth Man* (*De Vierde Man*)

Director: Paul Verhoeven
Producer: Rob Houwer for United Film Company of the Netherlands
Production Supervisor: Remmelt Remmelts
Scriptwriter: Gerard Soeteman, based on a novel of the same name by Gerard Reve
Cinematographer: Jan de Bont
Editor: Ine Schenkkan
Sound: Ad Roest
Sound Effects: Floris van Manen
Music: Loek Dikker
Art Direction: Roland de Groot
Costumes: Elly Claus
Special Effects: Harrie Wiessenhaan, Chris Tucker
Assistant to the Director: Jindra Markus
Cast includes: Jeroen Krabbé, Renée Soutendijk, Thom Hoffman, Dolf de Vries, Geert de Jong, Hans Veerman, Hero Muller, Caroline de Beus, Ursul de Geer
90 minutes: colour
Winner of the Los Angeles Film Critics' Award, 1984; International Film Critics' Prize, Toronto, 1984; Special Jury Prize, Knokke Film Festival, 1984; Special Jury Prize, Avoriaz Film Festival, 1984; Winner, Houston Film Festival, 1984; Winner, Sao Paulo Festival, 1984; Critics' Prize, Madrid, 1984; 'Silver Music Stand' for composer Loek Dikker at Dutch Film Days Festival, 1983

1985 *Flesh + Blood*

Director: Paul Verhoeven
Producer: Gijs Versluys for Riverside Pictures, Orion
Production Supervisor: Remmelt Remmelts, Carlos Orengo
Scriptwriter: Gerard Soeteman
Cinematographer: Jan de Bont
Editor: Ine Schenkkan
Sound: Tom Tholen, Ad Roest
Music: Basil Poledouris
Art direction: Felix Murcia

Costumes: Yvonne Blake
Cast includes: Rutger Hauer, Jennifer Jason-Leigh, Tom Burlinson, Jack Thompson, Susan Tyrrell, Ron Lacey, Hans Veerman, Kitty Courbois
126 minutes: colour
Golden Calf for best film and best director, Dutch Film Days Festival, 1985

1987 *Robocop*

Director: Paul Verhoeven
Production company: Orion Pictures
Producer: Arne Schmidt
Executive Producer: Jon Davison
Scriptwriter: Edward Neumeier, Michael Miner
Cinematographer: Jost Vacano
Editor: Frank J. Urioste
Sound: Robert Wald
Art Direction: William Sandell
Costumes: Erica Edell Phillips
Special Effects: Peter Kukan, Robert Balack, Dale Martin
Music: Basil Poledouris
Robocop Design: Rob Bottin
Sequences Ed-209: Phil Tippett
Cast includes: Peter Weller, Nancy Allen, Daniel O'Herlily, Ronny Cox, Kurtwood Smith, Miguel Ferrer, Robert DoQui, Ray Wise, Felton Perry, Paul McCrane, Del Zamora
103 minutes: colour
Oscar nomination for film editing to Frank J. Urioste

1990 *Total Recall*

Director: Paul Verhoeven
Production Company: Carolco Pictures
Producer: Buzz Feitshans, Ronald Shusett
Executive Producer: Mario Kassar, Andrew Vajna
Scriptwriter: Ronald Shusett, Dan O'Bannon, Gary Goldman, based on the story 'We can remember it for you wholesale' by Philip K. Dick
Cinematographer: Jost Vacano
Art Direction: William Sandell
Editor: Frank J. Urioste
Sound: Nelson Stoll, Fred Runner
Music: Jerry Goldsmith
Costumes: Erica Edell Phillips
Visual Effects: Dream Quest Images

Special Effects: Scott Fisher
Assistant to the Director: Vic Armstrong
Make-up Design: Rob Bottin
Cast includes: Arnold Schwarzenegger, Rachel Ticotin, Sharon Stone, Ronny Cox, Michael Ironside, Marshall Bell, Mel Johnson Jr, Michael Champion, Roy Brocksmith, Ray Baker
Distribution: Columbia-TriStar Films
109 minutes: colour
Oscar for Special Achievements awarded to Rob Bottin, Eric Brevig and Alex Funke

1992 *Basic Instinct*

Director: Paul Verhoeven
Production Company: Carolco/Studio Channel +
Producer: Alan Marshall
Executive Producer: Mario Kassar
Scriptwriter: Joe Eszterhas
Cinematographer: Jan de Bont
Editor: Frank J. Urioste
Art Direction: Terence Marsh
Sound: Nelson Stoll
Music: Jerry Goldsmith
Costumes: Ellen Mirojnick
Special Effects: Rob Bottin
Cast includes: Michael Douglas, Sharon Stone, George Dzundza, Jeanne Tripplehorn, Denis Arndt, Leilani Sarelle, Bruce A. Young, Chelcie Ross, Dorothy Malone, Wayne Knight, Stephen Tobolowsky
130 minutes: colour
Oscar nomination for film editing to Frank J. Urioste

1995 *Showgirls*

Director: Paul Verhoeven
Production Company: Carolco/Chargeurs
Producer: Alan Marshall
Co-producer: Charles Evans, Ben Myron
Executive Producer: Mario Kassar
Scriptwriter: Joe Eszterhas
Cinematographer: Jost Vacano
Editor: Mark Goldblatt, Mark Helfrich
Production Designer: Allan Cameron
Sound: Joseph Geisinger
Music: David Stewart

Costumes: Ellen Mirojnick
Choreographer: Marguerite Pomerhn-Derricks
Distributor: MGM/United Artists
Cast includes: Elizabeth Berkley, Gina Gershon, Kyle MacLachlan, Glenn Plummer, Robert Davi, Alan Rachins, Gina Raverra, Lin Tucci, Greg Travis, Al Ruscio, Patrick Bristow, William Shockley
131 minutes: colour

1997 *Starship Troopers*

Director: Paul Verhoeven
Studio: Sony Pictures/Disney
Production: Big Big Pictures for TriStar/Buena Vista Int.
Producers: Alan Marshall and Jon Davidson
Co-producer: Ed Neumeier
Script: Ed Neumeier
Based on the book by: Robert Heinlein
Photography: Jost Vacano
Creaure Visual Effects Supervisor: Phil Tippett
Special Effects: John Richardson
Editor: Mark Goldblatt
Second Editor: Caroline Ross
Music: Basil Poledouris
Production Design: Allan Cameron
Costumes: Ellen Mirojnick
Prosthetic Make-up Supervisor: Kevin Yagher
Creature Animatronics: Tom Woodruff and Alec Gillis
Distributor: Columbia/TriStar (domestic-USA) Buena Vista (foreign)
Cast includes: Casper Van Dien, Dina Meyer, Denise Richards, Jake Busey, Neil Patrick Harris, Michael Ironside, Clancy Brown, Seth Gillian, Patrick Muldoon and Marshall Bell

Acknowledgements

This book, written and researched over the period 1992–1996, would never have been realized without the co-operation of Paul and Martine Verhoeven. In addition, I would like to thank all the others in Hollywood, the Netherlands and beyond who were willing to be interviewed, supplied me with invaluable information and generously gave their professional and personal views on the life and work of the director. The actress Sharon Stone, the Dutch producer Rob Houwer and the journalist/film-critic Jan Blokker were, for various reasons, not available for interview.

Furthermore, I would like to express my gratitude to Stacy Lumbrezer, Paul Verhoeven's indefatigable assistant, and to my Dutch friends who supplied their support, criticism and friendship duing this project.

I would especially like to thank Sandra Donker, whose patience, sense of humour and sound journalistic judgement proved, once again, beyond price.

Rob van Scheers
Utrecht
June 1997

The editors would like to express their gratitude to Sebastiaan Bommelje, from Bijleveld publishers, for his sympathetic support and assistance during the time it has taken to put this book into the English language. Thanks are also due to Saskia van Roomen for coming in at the eleventh hour with her translation skills; to Victoria Buxton for her editorial assistance; and to Ian Bahrami, Justine Willett and Clare Mellor for the care and attention they gave to the production of the book.

Index